THEY ALL PLAYED
RAGTIME

BY RUDI BLESH AND HARRIET JANIS

Oak Publications, New York
Music Sales Limited, London
1971

ML
3561
J3
B49
1971

67420

ILLUSTRATIONS

Ragtime Contest Poster
Cliff House (photograph courtesy the late Percy Wenrich)
Tom Turpin's Rosebud Cafe (photograph courtesy William
    Russell)
Frank Early's Cafe (photograph courtesy William Russell)
Faust Restaurant (photograph courtesy Robert Darch)

Tony Jackson about 1918 with the Panama Trio (photo-
    graph courtesy George W. Kay)
Jelly Roll Morton in Storyville about 1903 (photograph
    courtesy Mrs. Amede Colas)
Clarence Woods, Carthage, about 1911 (photograph
    courtesy Robert Darch)
James Scott, Carthage, about 1904 (photograph courtesy
    Howard Scott)
G. Tom Ireland in 1960 at age 94 (photograph courtesy
    Robert Darch)
John Stark (photograph courtesy Margaret Eleanor Stark)
Charles Warfield (photograph courtesy the late Charles
    Warfield)
Glover Compton (photograph courtesy Nettie Compton and
    John Steiner)
Joseph F. Lamb 1915 (photograph courtesy Amelia Lamb
    and Max Morath)
Joseph F. Lamb 1959 (photograph by Russell E. Cassidy)
Joseph F. Lamb 1959 (photograph courtesy Amelia Lamb)
Old Man Finney's Ragtime Band (photograph courtesy the
    late Harry P. Guy)
Eblon Theatre Orchestra (photograph courtesy Franklin
    S. Driggs)
May Irwin (photograph courtesy Mike Montgomery)
Willard "Bill" Bailey and the Mrs. (photograph courtesy
    Mike Montgomery)
Jimmy Durante's Jazz and Novelty Band (photograph
    courtesy Jimmy Durante)

Eubie Blake (photograph courtesy Eubie Blake)
Luckey Roberts
James P. Johnson (photograph by Skippy Adelman)
Fats Waller
Don Lambert (photograph by Charles Peterson)
Willie "The Lion" Smith (photograph courtesy George
    Hoefer)
Wally Rose (photograph by Bill Young)
Ralph Sutton (photograph by Ronnie Rojas)
Johnny Maddox
Don Ewell
"Ragtime Bob" Darch
Max Morath
Tom Shea
Charlie Rasch and Kate Ross
John Arpin
Peter Lundberg
St. Louis Ragtimers
Bob Wright
Ann Charters
John "Knocky" Parker
Max Morath
Maple Leaf for eight hands (photograph courtesy NBC)
Billy Taylor
Hank Jones
Jaki Byard
Ray Bryant

Blind Tom

Blind Boone

Ben Harney in 1917

William H. Krell in 1896

Williams and Walker

The Real Cakewalk (from the 1903 Edison film Uncle Tom's Cabin)
center: Tom Fletcher

Der Cake Walk bei den amerikanischen Negern.

Der Cake Walk in einem pariser Salon.

THE CAKEWALK INVASION OF EUROPE
(from a German Magazine, 1900)

Front Street, Dawson City, Yukon, 1898

Scott Joplin about 1900

Scott Joplin about 1904

Scott Joplin about 1911

Arthur Marshall's home in Sedalia

THE KING OF RAGTIME COMPOSERS

Arthur Marshall in 1899

Scott Hayden in 1899

John Stillwell Stark

Sarah Ann Stark

Queen City Concert Band about

FRONT ROW, l. to r. —
A. H. Hickman, R. O. Hender
Henry Martin, W. H. Carter,
Al Wheeler, Jimmy Stewart
2ND ROW, l. to r. —
William Travis, James Chisc
James Scott
3RD ROW, l. to r. —
G. Tom Ireland, Nathaniel Di
Ed Gravitt
REAR, l. to r. —
C. W. Gravitt, Emmett Cook

THE SEDALIA T

SEDALIA, MISSOURI Saturday, AUGUST 3: 1901

George R. Smith College,
Sedalia

The Maple Leaf Club (building) in Sedalia in 1949

EVERYTHING IN THE LINE OF HILARITY

Louis Chauvin about 1904

Louis Chauvin about 1906

The Hurrah Sporting Club

ST. LOUIS DAYS: CHAUVINIANA

Mississippi Rag, cover

Harlem Rag, cover

Original Rags, cover

SHEET MUSIC THAT STARTED AN ERA

Thomas Million Turpin

Artie Matthews

Joe Jordan

Charley Thompson

Brun Campbell, "The Ragtime Kid"

Charles L. Johnson, Dill Pickles
as good as ever

Percy Wenrich, "The Joplin Kid."

Charles H. Hunter, cotton bolls
and sassafras

Axel W. Christensen, "Play ragtime
and be popular"

J. Russel Robinson. He packed
the nickelodeon

RAG TIME PIANO CONTEST
==AND BALL==
GIVEN BY THE PIANO PLAYERS SOCIAL CLUB
For Championship of Middle West
AT ELKS REST, 4034 South State Street
Monday Evening October 9th, 1916, From 8 to 4 a. m.
There will be Three Prizes: First, Second and Third

SOME OF THE CONTESTANTS

Glover Compton, Louisville, Ky.	C. W. Wilborn, Boston	Fred Irvin, New York
Sparrow, West Baden, Ind.	Ike Smith, St. Louis	Robt. Lilly, Louisville
Harry Crosby, New York	Earl McKinney, New York	Maurice Warfield, Chicago
John Moore, St. Louis Mo.	Paul Gay, Chicago	Squire't Ulth St., Chicago
Wickersham Sanders, Chicago	Ed Hardin, New York	Paul Turner, West Side, Chicago
William Gillis, Louisville, Ky.	Bert King, alias, Black Diamond, Indianapolis	Fred Newman, Toledo
Tony Jackson, New Orleans	Walter Farrington, St. Louis	Clarence Peyton, Duluth, Minn.
Clarence Jones, New Monogram Chicago	Rich Palmer, Chicago	Lonnie Curtis, Chicago
	Chas. Warfield, New York	Wild Cat Joe, Kansas City

OFFICERS:

Chas. Warfield, Pres.   Arthur Dixon, V. Pres.   Medicine Man, Treas.   Harry Mallory, Sec'y.   Birt King, Floor Mana
- Ed Welch, Asst. Floor Manager   Buster Brown, Sargt-At-Arms   Julius Wright, Dancing Master

Tickets on Sale at Jones' Music Store, 3409 South State Street
Every one wishing to Enter Contest will leave names at Music Store

Come out and Root for your Choice   Good Music, Dancing and Refreshme
Music by Brown Skin Brothers Orchestra

Ragtime Contest Poster

Police Gazette Ragtime Medal

Off for a champagne breakfast at the Cliff House, San Francisco, 1903
(Percy Wenrich in the first electric automobile)

Tom Turpin's Rosebud Cafe,
St. Louis

Frank Early's Cafe, New Orleans

Faust Restaurant, St. Louis — Joe Jordan and James Scott played here in
1904 during the World's Fair

ny Jackson about 1918 with the Panama
Trio

Jelly Roll Morton in Storyville
about 1903

Clarence Woods, Carthage, about 1911

James Scott, Carthage, about 1904

John Stark, 1927 (last kno[w]
photograph)

Tom Ireland in 1960 at age 9[?]

Charles Warfield in St. Louis about 1904.
A Chestnut Valley sport

Glover Compton in Louisville, abo[ut]
1903

Joe Lamb, about 1915

Joe Lamb, at home, 1958

Joe Lamb, in Toronto, 1959
(last known photograph)

LAMB: A LION OF RAGTIME

Old Man Finney's Ragtime Band
(front row, far left, Ben Shook; center, Fred S. Stone; far right, Harry P. Guy)

Eblon Theatre Orchestra, Kansas City, about 1924 (second from right, James S. Sc

STRIKE UP THE BAND

rwin, mama of the red-hot mamas

Willard "Bill" Bailey and the Mrs.
"Remember that rainy evening"

Jimmy Durante's Jazz and Novelty Band, 1921

Eubie Blake, Shuffle Along for $700

Luckey Roberts, ragtime for the "4

James P. Johnson, symphonies can be hot

Fats Waller, laugh and the world I
with you

STRIDING THROUGH HARLEM

d Lambert,
eton "graduate"
ide

Willie "The Lion" Smith, "Don't you
hit that lady dressed in green"

Rose, he brought the Barbary
Coast back to 'Frisco

Ralph Sutton, let your left hand know
(Pops Foster in the rear)

BLACK AND WHITE RAGSTERS

Johnny Maddox, Crazy Otto sold a
million

Don Ewell, man here plays fine

"Ragtime Bob" Darch, ragtime dead?
hell it ain't even sick

Max Morath, they rezoned the Di
but not the music

SOME OF THE NEW PROFESSORS

Tom Shea,
prairie ragtime

Charlie Rasch and Kate Ross, "Ragtime Charlie" and
"Sister Kate"

Peter Lundberg, spreadin'
rhythm over Sweden

John Arpin, The Maple Leaf in Canada

THE PROFESSORS STRIKE AGAIN

St. Louis Ragtimers and guest (clockwise from left:
Al Stricker, banjo; Carrie Bruggeman Stark, guest;
Trebor Tichenor, piano; Don Franz, tuba; Bill
Mason, cornet)

Bob Wright, Chicag
barrelhouse and ra

Ann Charters, a lady professor!
Why not?

John "Knocky" Parker and ragtime

THE RETURN OF THE PROFESSORS

Max Morath in his television series, The Ragtime Era, 1960

Maple Leaf for eight hands: Those Ragtime Years, 1960
(left to right : Ralph Sutton, Dick Wellstood, Eubie Blake, Hoagy Carmichael)

TV RECEPTION: CLEAR BUT RAGGED

Billy Taylor, back from bop to ragtime

Hank Jones, this is ragtime no

Jaki Byard, let's stride again

Ray Bryant, soul, roots, ragti

RAGTIME: IT CAN GO HOME AGAIN

To the memory of **SCOTT JOPLIN**

> *Here is the genius whose spirit, though diluted,*
> *was filtered through thousands of cheap songs*
> *and vain imitations.*   JOHN STARK

Oh go 'way man, I can hypnotize dis nation,
I can shake de earth's foundation wid de Maple Leaf Rag!
Oh go 'way man, just hold yo' breath a minit,
For there's not a stunt that's in it, wid de Maple Leaf Rag!

MAPLE LEAF RAG SONG (1904)
Music by Scott Joplin
Words by Sydney Brown

CONTENTS

RAGTIME MUSIC
COMPLETE PIANO SCORES

Maple Leaf Rag, by Scott Joplin   follows p. 50
   (complete score of original Sedalia edition, 1899)

YESTERDAY

follows p. 209

Pan-Am Rag, by Tom Turpin, arranged by Arthur
    Marshall
Calliope Rag, by James Scott
The Alaskan Rag, by Joseph F. Lamb
Pear Blossoms, by Scott Hayden
Missouri Romp — Slowdrag Two-Step, by Arthur Marshall
Century Prize — March and Two-Step by Arthur Marshall
Silver Rocket, by Arthur Marshall

TODAY

The Golden Hours (To the memory of Harriet Janis)
    by Max Morath
One for Amelia, by Max Morath
Opera House Rag — A Sterling Selection, by Robert R.
    Darch
Business in Town, by Donald Ashwander
Friday Night, by Donald Ashwander
Gothenburg Rag, by Peter Lundberg
Brun Campbell Express, by Thomas W. Shea
Chestnut Valley Rag, by Trebor Jay Tichenor

It has been seventy years -- two full human generations as historians (and the electric computer) figure these things -- since a young Kentuckian named Ben Harney, playing and singing a ragtime song in a Gotham vaudeville theatre, inaugurated a remarkable era. Seventy years -- long enough for an American music to arise and bloom, to enthrall a nation (and Europe too), to fade and be forgotten. And then to be remembered again.

Ragtime is an American word, humorous and deprecatory or not. Its second syllable seems to have been its key syllable -- for one thing, how its metrical time started music to swinging. And for another thing, what passing time (seven decades of it) has done for, and to, a music so happy, so tuneful, and so American that in its youth it seemed as if it were our country singing to herself.

In 1950, when this book first appeared, it was mainly what had been done to ragtime following its brilliant international Gay-Nineties s u c c e s s; i t s commercial wringing dry and then its contemptuous rejection as old-hat by the selfsame public that had barely ceased embracing it. From that gross miscarriage of musical justice on, it has taken a lot of time to open our ears again to what was not only the first genuinely American music but was in reality a milestone in musical history. Fifty years and more ago, the London _Times_ called ragtime the seed of a national art. Yet not until 1963 did the New York _Times_ so much as nod its head to the music. Its initial gesture was, however, a grand one. On September 1, the following obituary was placed squarely at the top of the _Times_ vital statistics page:

TIMES, SUNDAY, SEPTEMBER 1, 1963.

) KING, 74, DIES

ant Served orld Wars

ork Times
, Aug. 31—
, a specialist
ine and a
the Harvard
ical Schools,
y at the age
red a stroke

lition to his
medicine in
rs, served in
d was a con-
nited States
ice.
, Ohio, Dr.
ted in 1912
e, where his
rchill King,
5 years. Dr.
ine at West-
rsity and at
ical School,
a degree in
cticing med-
n with the
onary Force
l he took up
and from
head of the
assachusetts

War II Dr.
nel as chief

George Thomas Ireland Dead; Ragtime Clarinetist Was 97

SEDALIA, Mo., Aug. 31 (AP)—George Thomas Ireland, an early ragtime clarinetist and long-time newspaperman, died yesterday at the age of 97.

Mr. Ireland was born in Louisville, Ky., shortly after his mother had been freed from slavery. She and his grandparents brought him to Sedalia in an oxcart when he was 2 years old.

Center of Ragtime

Tom Ireland grew up in the bustling railroad hub of Sedalia, which became in the eighteen-nineties a syncopating center of the new ragtime.

The prairie town attracted musically talented Negroes from all over the Mississippi and Missouri Valleys, and Negro bands and minstrel shows flourished. It was there that Scott Joplin composed his early "Maple Leaf Rag," regarded as a masterpiece of serious ragtime.

As solo clarinetist, Mr. Ireland played with Joplin in the Queen City Concert Band, which became a leading Negro band in the state. For a few years he followed the lure of the tent-show circuit, accompanying

such musicians as W. C. Handy, composer of the jazz classic "St. Louis Blues."

Soon, though, Mr. Ireland decided that the nomadic life on the road was not for him, and he settled down in Sedalia, spending most of his life in newspaper work.

For a few years he owned and edited The Western World, a weekly Negro newspaper. Then he worked for The Sedalia Democrat for almost 50 years.

He graduated from Central Tennessee College, now Walden University, in Nashville.

In "They All Played Ragtime: the True Story of an American Music," Rudi Blesh and Harriet Janis described Tom Ireland in 1950 as a well-known octogenarian in Sedalia who still rode around town on a bicycle. He was a widower and had two married sons.

The book reported that "the affection of white Sedalia for this erect, wiry, alert old gentleman is succinctly expressed in the current city directory, in which after the name G. Tom Ireland the obnoxious customary word 'colored,' with its implication of segregation, is conspicuously absent."

STEPHE. DERM.

CHICAG
Dr. Stephe
tologist an
of medicine
Chicago, di
versity ho
years old.
Dr. Roth
university's
partment
decades, w
Hungary.
He was
staff at the
pest from 1
in hospital
University
from 1921
at the Soc
of Hungary
He becam
the dermat
the Univer
1938 and w
head in 19
until 1960,
professor e

Last Dec
received a
American
tology for o
tions in the
president o
matological
ciety for I
tology, a f

AMERIGO VASSO, 69, | **Laurence L. Olvin, 57, Dies;**

Old Tom Ireland, colorful survivor though he was, was only a minor figure in ragtime. Forty-six years before Ireland's death, on April 1, 1917, a major ragtime figure, Scott Joplin, died in New York. But the New York <u>Times</u> did not even list his name in its obit-less column of Deaths. What has happened to the <u>Times</u> -- and to America -- during those forty-six years?

The <u>Times</u> in 1963, quite evidently, was echoing its patronym, time itself. For time, which destroys, also restores. It had been quietly, obscurely at work from 1917, when ragtime was a <u>demodé</u> outcast, to the 1960's when it was well along toward final recognition as the major creative movement it had been from the start.

Ragtime began in a simpler time, when entertainment was live performance. Even then technology was working to end all that, and in 1897. actually, an infant musical technology -- the player piano -- helped to spread the new music. And soon the phonograph record, first cylinder then disk, began supplying canned music in the amuse-ment arcades and at home. People gradually ceased play-ing and singing and let the phonograph do it. This hit ragtime below the belt, because the early phonograph could not reproduce the piano, ragtime's instrument, nor would it be able to do so until well into the 1920's. This barred the great early composer -- players like Scott Joplin, James Scott, Tony Jackson, and Louis Chauvin, from ever recording, while the early records adapted ragtime to the recordable banjo and xylophone -- a little like arranging Mozart for steam calliope.

Ragtime kept a place only in a diminishing number of public spots and in vaudeville. Then a still newer medium, the then-silent motion picture, began driving vaudeville out. True, piano players accompanied the films but ragtime was only part of a standardized repertory ranging from <u>Hearts and Flowers</u> to the <u>William Tell Overture</u>. With all of this added to rampant commerciali-zation, classic ragtime ceased to develop. Then, in 1917, jazz took over. By the time the sound pictures came, for all anyone knew, ragtime was gone.

But not forgotten: too many people had loved ragtime --
its gay and haunting melodies, its intoxicating rhythms.
Having faded during one world war it began coming back
during another -- with the old player pianos installed
in the USO canteens! Here a new generation first heard
ragtime. Its appeal proved undiminished. Only -- like
all music -- its minimum requirement was to be heard.
New players began to appear; older players found spots
again. Here and there a brave recording company made
a record or two.

It was very slow, but so was the concomitant return
of L'Art Nouveau and Tiffany glass. While perhaps too
much of ragtime has latterly been presented as a quaint
antique -- with a little more than necessary of the gas-
light atmosphere of straw hats and sleeve garters --
ragtime has the decided longterm advantage over the
other fin-de-siècle artifacts that it does not need to be,
as antique dealers say: of the period. In the last fifteen
years -- as shown by the lists at the end of this book -- an
impressive amount of new ragtime has been written. It
is impressive because it is far more than in any com-
parable period since 1915. It is even more impressive
because it is coming from new writers, with its serious
workmanship and modern conception clearly showing that,
apart from a too-frequent honkytonk presentation, ragtime
is finding a new nexus with creativity. The time, in fact,
seems to have come when the music itself -- the old and
the new, classically played -- will be enough to satisfy
the nostalgia of an older generation without foreclosing
the respect of a younger one. In fact, many other developments since 1950 seem, similarly, to point to the
coming permanent restoration of a charming and valuable
music (it should not be forgotten that Bach, forgotten,
had to be restored a century ago).

Among recent developments, for example, has been the
recording and issue of nearly two hundred longplay
albums since 1952. They must have sold: their issue is
now accelerating. Ragtime had not sold a million of
anything since Scott Joplin's Maple Leaf Rag of 1899
passed that mark in sheet music sales. Then in 1955

along came pianist Johnny Maddox with his Crazy Otto rag medley record. It is a true parallel a half century apart: Maple Leaf established a music publishing house; Crazy Otto established a prosperous recording company.

Less sensational but even more singularly symptomatic is the surprising return of the foot-pumped player piano to this electronic age, with individual artisans patiently cutting ragtime rolls by hand to supply eager collectors unable to find old rolls.

The new, spreading interest has produced organizations and periodicals. The flourishing Ragtime Society of Canada, founded in 1962 by John Fisher and presently headed by James Kinnear, claims aficionado membership all over the world. The Society sponsors concerts (it aided ragtime pianist Bob Darch to bring the patriarchs Eubie Blake and Joseph F. Lamb to Toronto), issues longplay records of contemporary ragtime playing and compositions both classic and new, and mails out an excellent bi-monthly publication. The Canadian organization also -- teaming with the widely-read Ragtime Review, edited by Russ Cassidy and Trebor Tichenor in St. Louis -- reprints ragtime classics long out-of-print.

If all this indicates a ferment going on, consider the number of young pianists consecrated to ragtime continuously coming on the scene since the early 1940's. Wally Rose in his early fifties, John "Knocky" Parker and Ralph Sutton in their forties, are already patriarchs of a growing clan of ragtime "professors" including Robert "Ragtime Bob" Darch, Max Morath, Johnny Maddox, with a still younger host coming on (to mention only a few): Trebor Jay Tichenor, Tom Shea, Bob Wright, Charlie Rasch, Bob Durst, John Arpin, and Donald Ashwander -- to whom should be added Peter Lundberg, a young Swede in Goteborg, and a lady "professor," charming Ann Charters.

It is significant that many of these are already accomplished and original ragtime composers. The work of several appears in the music section of this book. And even more significant may be the return of the Negro to the music he made and which was, in effect, stolen from him. This return has begun, both in playing and composing, with brilliant young Negroes like Billy Taylor, Hank Jones, Jaki Byard, and Ray Bryant.

A new entertainment circuit is developing to showcase the new ragtime of this new talent. Replacing the long-vanished honkytonk and redlight chain of the turn of the century, there now are colorfully named but thoroughly respectable cocktail lounges and supper rooms that offer live ragtime. Just as in the old days, the chain runs from Gotham to 'Frisco and from Florida to the Klondike.

This ground network is growing; making room for more players; expanding the ragtime public. Overhead in the air, the all-important television networks have begun to recognize ragtime. Max Morath, reincarnation of the old-time all-round ragtime entertainer, has written and produced two complete series, The Ragtime Era (twelve programs, 1959-60) and Turn of the Century (fifteen programs, 1961-62), for the National Educational Television Network, which reached millions of viewers. In 1962, NBC produced an hour-long program, Those Ragtime Years. Shown twice, this "documentary spectacular" starred Hoagy Carmichael and presented a trio of brilliant players, pioneer Eubie Blake and the younger men Ralph Sutton and Dick Wellstood. More recently the Bell Telephone Hour has separately featured the ragtime of Max Morath and Bob Darch.

No matter how or where ragtime gets presented it needs no huckstering. It needs only to be heard to be loved. But now in the 1970's the time is different in important ways from that heedless heyday of the 1890's: ragtime's story has been chronicled; now it has its honorable history and its proper heroes; it is returning to the people; its true value and basic esthetic integrity, so long obscured, are now apparent; ragtime is now, at last, being accepted as the fine musical art it is and has always been.

The hostile musical establishment is at last being turned around. Its younger post-Van Cliburn keyboard heroes refuse to abide by the old bigoted cliches. These

newer concert stars are programming classic ragtime
-- where it has always belonged -- alongside Mozart,
Schubert, Chopin. It is being released on classical --
not pop -- record labels, played by the trained fingers
of a Joshua Rifkin or an Alan Mandel. Young composers
are writing contemporary rags, playing and recording
them. For example, there is William Albright of Michigan, and there is William Bolcom, already noted for
his contemporary operas, who programs his own rags
with the germane masters, Joplin, Turpin, Chauvin,
Scott and Lamb. And there is Donald Ashwander, in-
ternationally known musical director of the children's
theater, The Paper Bag Players. Ashwander, virtuoso of the electronic harpsichord, has an LP of his own
distinctive rags.

In 1971, too, the works of Scott Joplin are at last
receiving a multi-volume memorial publication. Piano
rags, songs, and the historic opera Treemonisha, all
edited by Vera Bodsky Lawrence, are being issued
under the New York Public Library imprimatur. Meanwhile Treemonisha, orchestrated by the prominent black
musicologist T.J. Anderson of Atlanta University, is
headed for all-star public performance.

It will have taken seventy years. Its early creators,
its first champions, and the millions who once sang in
American parlors and cakewalked in the streets of
Paris -- all are gone. But for all of us here today it
will have been worth waiting for.

Finally, though They All Played Ragtime was -- and
still is -- dedicated to the memory of Scott Joplin, I
wish personally to dedicate this, the fourth edition, to
the memory of Harriet Janis. Of all our books this was
her first and best love. She, not I, conceived it, and in
the fullest sense she was its co-creator. I wish she
were here to see it -- as she would have wished it --
along with the music it celebrates, new and young again.

New York City, March 31, 1971   RUDI BLESH

ACKNOWLEDGMENTS

WRITING the first book on ragtime presented special problems. In the virtual absence of written source material, it was necessary, and in any event would have been desirable, to rely almost exclusively on personal interviews or correspondence with the actual personalities who made ragtime one of the greatest musical crazes in history. The majority of these personalities were not easy to find. Many, of course, were dead. Most of those who had survived, thirty years since the ragtime craze ended and over half a century since it began, had lapsed into obscurity. We were fortunate, however, in locating all the important surviving key figures and the relatives and friends of those who are dead.

Too profuse thanks cannot be given to the scores of people who talked with and played for us, for without the help they gave so enthusiastically this book would have been impossible to write.

The story of Sedalia, the cradle of ragtime, and much of that of St. Louis, its quondam capital, are from the words of Arthur Marshall, G. Tom Ireland, the Reverend Alonzo Hayden, C. W. Gravitt, and William G. Flynn. The Sedalia picture was filled out by correspondence with Charles R.

Hanna, music critic of the Sedalia *Democrat*, and Mrs. Julia Cross, sister of Scott Hayden. S. Brunson Campbell (The Ragtime Kid), an early friend of Scott Joplin, generously furnished us with a part of the early stories of Joplin and Sedalia and permitted us to quote from his short history, *When Ragtime Was Young*, which appeared in installments in the *Jazz Journal*, London.

St. Louis history was unfolded by Sam Patterson, Artie Matthews, Charley Thompson, George Reynolds, Webb Owsley, Lester A. Walton, Mrs. Edward Mellinger, Charles Warfield (who also contributed to the Chicago picture), Sylvestre Chauvin, nephew of Louis Chauvin, and the St. Louis ragtime enthusiast Dr. Hubert S. Pruett.

The New Orleans chapter was filled out by George (Pops) Foster, Miss Ida Jackson and Mrs. Mariah Sutton (sisters of the late Tony Jackson), Sammy Davis, Tony Parenti, and Dr. Edmond Souchon, and by Jelly Roll Morton posthumously through his interviews with Alan Lomax and the 1938 documentary records he made for the Library of Congress archives. The rights to use this material were granted to Circle Records by the Morton Estate and its Executor, Hugh E. MacBeth, thus making it available to the authors. Invaluable, too, in the New Orleans connection were the reminiscences of the perennial prophet of ragtime, Roy J. Carew. To him also go our thanks for permission to quote from one of his published articles, for access to his sheet-music collection, and for his patient hours of playing the old ragtime masterpieces for us.

The life story of the late James Scott of Neosho and Kansas City was reconstructed from interviews and correspondence with his sister, Mrs. Lena King, with his brothers, Howard and Oliver, and with his cousins, Mrs. Patsy L. Thomas, Mrs. Ruth Callahan, and the late Ada Brown, and with a fellow musician of Scott's, Lawrence Denton.

Chicago's large part in ragtime was related by Nettie Compton, Glover Compton (who also contributed much about Louisville), Charlie Elgar, Hugh Swift, Hurley and Horace Diemer, and George Filhe. The story of the first and most successful of the chains of ragtime schools was told by

Carle Christensen for his father, Axel Christensen. Shepard N. Edmonds furnished sidelights on the Chicago World's Fair. Both he and Wendell P. Dabney furnished valuable comments on early phases of Negro music.

The course of white ragtime in Kansas City was outlined in interviews with Charles L. Johnson, and that in Indianapolis by conversations with Emil Seidel, J. Russel Robinson, and Noble Sissle, the last also contributing much of value about Eastern ragtime. The Detroit scene at the end of the century was brought alive through the descriptions of Ben Shook and Harry P. Guy.

Nearly everyone interviewed contributed to the picture of the towering figure of Scott Joplin. Invaluable, of course, were the memories of his widow, Lottie, but Joplin left a deep impress on the memories of all who knew him. The history of John Stark, who pioneered classic ragtime with Joplin, comes from interviews and correspondence with his surviving relatives: his daughter-in-law, Mrs. William P. Stark, his eldest son, Etilmon J. Stark and his wife, his son-in-law, James Stanley, his grandson, John Stark, and the intimate picture of Stark's last years from his favorite granddaughter, Margaret Eleanor Stark.

The separate saga of Eastern ragtime was amplified through a long series of personal interviews enlivened by much playing and singing For these we thank Eubie Blake, Luckey Roberts, James P. Johnson, Willie (The Lion) Smith, Will Vodery, Walter Gould (One-Leg Shadow), Donald Lambert, Bobby Lee, Louis N. Brown, Wesley (Kid Sox) Wilson and his wife, Coot Grant, and Mrs. Anita Waller and W. T. (Ed) Kirkeby for special information regarding the late Fats Waller.

White ragtime in the East and the checkered story of Tin Pan Alley came from talks with Jimmy (The Schnozzle) Durante, Pete Wendling, Jean Schwartz, Max Kortlander, and Fred Burton (The Human Pianola). Percy Wenrich (The Joplin Kid) furnished wide information not only on Tin Pan Alley, but on Chicago ragtime and the folk ragtime of Missouri. Arthur Pryor, Jr., helped us to draw the brass-band picture with information about his father, the late Arthur Pryor.

The story of Joseph Lamb, one of the greatest of ragtime composers, came from the best of all possible sources, Lamb himself, whom we located after a strenuous search. The fullness of our story of the late Ben R. Harney's ragtime pioneering is due to Ludwig Pfundmayr, and in particular to Roscoe Peacock, who put at our disposal his correspondence with Harney's widow, the late Jessie Boyce Harney. Especially valuable Harney information came, too, from Bruner Greenup.

The story of the blind ragtimer of Nashville, Charles Hunter, was almost unknown until various people of his native city came to our assistance, supplementing information from Roy Carew. These were Kenneth Rose, of Ward-Belmont Conservatory of Music, Mrs. Elmer Schoettle, Claude P. Street, and a friend of Hunter's piano-tuning days, Guy Francis.

Thanks of a special nature go to Rupert Hughes, who at seventy-eight graciously responded to our written request by reaffirming the critical appraisal of ragtime that he had written in 1899, and to W. N. H. Harding, of Chicago, who made available to us his superb collection of ragtime and minstrel music. Jerry Heermans assisted with lists of ragtime compositions; William Russell furnished similar information and also recalled for us a visit with the St. Louis ragtimer Robert Hampton; John Ludas made available certain rare recordings; E. F. McTighe furnished special data on Scott Joplin's first years in New York; Conrad Janis helped with the reproduction of illustrations, and his wife, Vicki Janis, was our indefatigable interviewer on the Pacific Coast. We are obliged to Eddie (Sheet Iron) Barnes for information on early ragtime contests, and to Willis Laurence James, of Spelman College, for notes on the early songs of Stephen Foster. The distinction of finding long-lost Sammy Davis goes to John Heinz, who communicated the news to us immediately. Listings of ragtime players were furnished us by Elliott Shapiro. Permission to reproduce the second cover of *Maple Leaf Rag* (that with the silhouetted maple leaf) was granted by Lloyd Keepers.

Ralph Sutton, brilliant ragtime pianist, earned our gratitude by devoting many a Sunday to playing by sight scores of difficult rags. His skill and sympathy brought to life for us over a hundred numbers unheard for a generation or more.

We thank Leslie H. Bradshaw for his meticulous copy-editing of the script and supplying additional data, as well as lists of early cylinder phonograph records and sheet music.

We express appreciation to the many who loaned us rare and irreplaceable photographs to use for illustrations. Thanks go to the *New Orleans Item* and to Thomas Sancton for permission to reprint parts of an article by Mr. Sancton entitled "The Old Days—Gone Forever"; to Melrose Music Corporation for granting us the privilege to print in full the musical score of *Maple Leaf Rag;* and to Harry Von Tilzer Music Publishing Company for allowing us to quote from the lyrics of *Moving Day*, written by Andrew B. Sterling and composed by Harry Von Tilzer.

In any special research such as ours, libraries and institutions are a present help. The Library of Congress was both rich in information and enthusiastic in its co-operation. Of the many staff members who assisted us we wish especially to mention Richard S. MacCarteney, Chief of the Reference Division, and his assistant, E. Genevieve Norvell, and William Lichtenwanger, of the Music Division. Similarly we are grateful for fine factual material and personal help from the staffs of the Theatrical Section and Music Room of the Central Public Library in New York and the Schaumberg Collection at the 136th Street (Harlem) branch. Comparably helpful were the public libraries at St. Louis, Chicago, and Cincinnati. Valuable, too, were the music collection of the Grosvenor Library in Buffalo, and the assistance of its curator, Miss Margaret Mott.

From these rich and varied sources has come our true story of an American music, which has waited fifty years for the telling.

ACKNOWLEDGMENTS
FOR THE THIRD EDITION

The revisions, new data, new illustrations, and musical scores in this new edition are in great measure due to the friendly help of many people. From the pioneer ragtime generation there was ready help, as always, from Arthur Marshall and from Amelia Lamb. For the rest, a whole new generation of ragtime lovers and performers in this country, Canada, and abroad, sprang to my assistance when the ragtime journals announced that a new edition was coming of the book that for fifteen years they have called "The Bible." So many-sided has been the help of all that I can find no practical way to render thanks to so many except, for the most part, to list the names: John Arpin, Idamay MacInnes, James Kinnear, John Fisher, and The Ragtime Society of Canada; Russell Cassidy, Trebor Jay Tichenor, Don Franz, and The Ragtime Review of St. Louis; Nettie Compton, John Steiner, George Hoefer, Wally Rose, Professor John W. "Knocky" Parker, Johnny Maddox, Samuel Charters and Ann Charters; Billy Taylor, Hank Jones, and Jaki Byard; J.D. Nunn and Audiophile Records; Pauline Rivelli and <u>Jazz</u> Magazine, New York; Henri Parisot and <u>Le Jazz Hot</u> of Paris.

Peter Lundberg, Bob Wright, Charlie Rasch, Tom Shea, and Dave Lorentz; Bob Durst, John Gleason, Frank Powers, and Percy Franks; the Detroit Public Library; and Hollis Music, Inc., Ragtime Music Publishing Co., and Cornish Music Publishing Co.

Of the hundred people we interviewed in 1949-50 only a bare handful are still alive today. The help of this newer generation, therefore, was crucial. In this light it can be understood that the above names -- no matter how cursory may seem their mere mention -- are to me an honor roll. I feel impelled, however, to single out several people whose help, springing from friendship, has especially deep personal meaning to me. I must first mention that last survivor of the Sedalia and St. Louis days, Arthur Marshall, who is eighty-four years old as I write this. And Eubie Blake, active surviving patriarch of Harlem stride ragtime, now eighty-two. And Amelia Lamb, widow of Joe Lamb of ragtime's original Big Three. Melie gave me unpublished scores by Lamb and by Lamb with Joplin, as well as unpublished photographs of Joe. And beyond all that, the same warm friendship I have long treasured.

Donald Ashwander, one of ragtime's newest composers did the fine handmade music scores by many composers that appear in the middle of this book. Even more, he gave me two of his own beautiful and unusual rags to print, Business in Town and Friday Night.

Max Morath played scores for me as Ralph Sutton did fifteen years ago for Harriet Janis and me. More -- Max wrote The Golden Hours, the haunting, bitter-sweet little rag, half waltz and all feeling, to be published herein in Mrs. Janis's memory.

Bob Darch, in the middle of professional travel, sent reams of data, fine old photographs, his own Opera House Rag for inclusion, and (forgoing their first publication by himself) two priceless pieces he had retrieved from oblivion, James Scott's Calliope Rag and Scott Hayden's Pear Blossoms. Lamb's Alaskan Rag is here, too, by Darch's permission as he owns the copyright,

Mike Montgomery converted boundless energy and enthusiasm (not to mention understanding) into real right-hand help of amazing scope and amount. A one-man bureau of investigation, Mike contacted people everywhere, soliciting needed materials, wheedling and/or commanding information, then sifting, sorting, collating, and classifying it all for me. Ten computers plus ten Military Police could not have accomplished what Ragtime Field Marshall Montgomery did.

David Jasen researched and contributed the updated list of ragtime on longplay microgroove records, page 343.

And this I save for the last: special thanks to three wives of the most miraculous patience, who let their husbands give so freely of time and help. I mean Peggy Darch, Norma Morath, and Sue Montgomery. Theirs was a sacrifice above and beyond the call of wifely duty.

RUDI BLESH

ERRATA

Note: first number refers to the number in margin opposite each error; second number (in parentheses) is the text page number where each error occurs.

1 (105) Fred Stone died about 1912.
2 (116) Recent research indicates that James Scott recorded no piano rolls.
3 (159) Correct titles are "Silver Rocket," "Century Prize," and "Missouri Romp." They were copyrighted in 1966. Included in the musical section of this book, they constitute an invaluable addition to the classic ragtime repertory.
4 (181) "King Porter Stomp" was composed in 1906, and published in 1923 by Melrose.
5 (224) Correct name is Phil Ohman.
6 (232) Recent research indicates that the only rolls handplayed by Joplin came later, in late 1915 or early 1916. Made in the culminating period of his illness, they are more evidence of his fading powers than of his playing style at its earlier best.

THEY ALL PLAYED RAGTIME

The True Story of an American Music

Iᴛ ʜᴀs been two generations since ragtime piano came along to give to its own first decade in the public eye the name of the "Gay Nineties." It was unmistakably a new idea in music. America took it straightway to its heart—it was love at first sight. And, following America by a matter almost of months, Europe too fell under the syncopated spell. Soon the French were cakewalking in the streets of Paris to *le temps du chiffon*. In 1897 the electric light and the telephone were new and the horseless carriage a crackpot contraption. America boasted none of today's methods of rapid musical communication—radio, movie, television—yet ragtime spread like wildfire. Itinerant pianists sprang by the thousands from nowhere; minstrel shows, brass bands, and vaudeville teams—from the jerkwater acts to specialists like Ben Harney and top-flight entertainers like May Irwin and Williams and Walker—spread the happy gospel of the new syncopated music. Songs went by word of mouth, and barber-shop patrons gave tongue to the accompaniment of the shine boy's raggy guitar or banjo. There were the wax Graphophone cylinders, too, and the slotted paper rolls of the ubiquitous Pianola or player piano.

Beyond all these forces was one even stronger, one that

scarcely exists in America today. This was the sheet music on the square piano or the cabinet reed organ that was to be found in every parlor from Fifth Avenue in New York to Market Street in San Francisco and from Florida's tip and the Rio Grande to the mining camps of the Klondike. There were not so many fancy cans for America to take its music from in those days; Mother, Dad, sister, and little brother made it themselves.

Perhaps this country is a little jaded with entertainment nowadays—or perhaps it is entertainment that is jaded—but those were fresh and eager days near the turn of the century. People were hungry for amusement; they found it at home or went miles for it on foot, by horse and buggy, trolley, and excursion train. For a decade one costly exposition succeeded another: the World's Columbian Exposition at Chicago in 1893, the Trans-Mississippi at Omaha in 1899, the Pan-American at Buffalo in 1901, and the Louisiana Purchase at St. Louis in 1904. The general public first heard ragtime on the Chicago Midway, but its catchy name had yet to be found.

When the first instrumental ragtime sheet music appeared in 1897, no costly, high-powered promotion was needed to put the music across. Ragtime was far and away the gayest, most exciting, most infectiously lilting music ever heard, and its very name was a "natural." America's own music had come, as native as pumpkin pie and baseball, and within a year it seemed as if it had always been here. No introversion here of Brahms and the late romantics—ragtime was as healthily extrovert, as brimful of energy, as the barefoot American boy.

Ragtime's advent was timely to the essence. The long depression of 1893–8 made a burning issue of Free Silver, and a street-corner slogan of William Jennings Bryan's "You shall not crucify mankind upon a cross of gold." The land was galled and restless with riots, hunger marches, and threats of revolution; the people overready to smile again and to dance the cakewalk. It was all like a fresh start; no past associations, good or bad, clung to the new music; there was not a tear in ragtime, and no irony, malice, bitterness, or regret hid in its laughter.

4

There is irony to be found, however, in the very fact of ragtime's vast success. The commercial tunesmiths of Tin Pan Alley did their level best to ruin the music, to wring every last dollar from cheap and trumped-up imitations of a folk music, and to glut the market to the last extreme of surfeit. They succeeded only too well. The popular nature of ragtime's acceptance, too, stamped it in the minds of serious music-lovers as mere ephemeral trash, and this *a priori* judgment still prevails. Yet at the core of the whole thing, separate from the cheap fakery and unknown to the high and mighty, was—and is—a music of enduring worth, revolutionary in concept and development.

There is much in a name. Without even hearing the music, "sonata" is so much grander than "ragtime" that to prejudge is only human. What, however, if ragtime's greatest composer, Scott Joplin, the Negro, had found refuge under Dvořák's wing when the Czech was championing Negro music against the embattled prejudice of the American long-hair conservatives? What indeed! Joplin's masterpiece, the *Maple Leaf Rag*, would have been entitled something like *Étude in Syncopation*, Opus 1, and would, at the very least, have escaped frivolous and captious judgment.

The real story of ragtime is not that of Tin Pan Alley and its million-dollar hits, of hacks and copyists, of song hucksters. That story, with its glamorous allure in the glare of Broadway lights, has been told often enough. The real story of ragtime is that of a song that came from the people and then got lost. It is the story of a music that millions of Americans remember still, with affection and regret. It is a story that has never been told. One thing may certainly be said: this book, as the first about ragtime, is at least a third of a century overdue. Perhaps this first ragtime book will help to set the record straight, to rescue an irreplaceable part of the American tradition, the ragtime masterpieces that are hidden behind their charming, colorful old covers in vast, musty piles of sheet music.

The sheet music of yesterday! Faded, dog-eared, and torn, it is an astonishing heap of mementos that seem as lost in the recesses of time and as fruitless to scan as someone else's old valentines. Schottisches and quadrilles, coon songs and Irish

5

ballads and Mother songs, military and descriptive marches and overtures, quicksteps and two-steps, grand galops de concert—and ragtime. One can fairly see the Tin Pan Alley presses running day and night; one feels like pushing it all aside as well-forgotten junk.

But let us go carefully through the piles that we once rejected. The time has come to listen, to sort out and to weigh. One can find the work of serious men, of forgotten geniuses: Scott Joplin, Tom Turpin, James Scott, and Joseph Lamb. It is time for us to discover the work of these men, to piece out the lost stories of their lives.

It is not too late; it is even, perhaps, the right time. For today we can catch the perspective that our grandfathers missed. We can know what they could not foresee: that ragtime would not really die when the hucksters were finally through with it that year the doughboys went sailing off to France. We can know that ragtime has lived on in jazz and even in swing music; that our last fifty years of popular music have had a lilt and a syncopated lift that they never knew before ragtime came; that, unacknowledged, the classics of the European masters are played today with an unwontedly sharp and accurate rhythm, and that the new "serious" compositions are full of ragtime's echoes. We can see young players, the country over, awakening to ragtime, and like them we can rejudge its real masterpieces with the acuity of hindsight. And we can discover, too, that when pure ragtime seemed to disappear, it went back, instead, into that underground stratum of our society from which it had first emerged.

Mid-century is a time for harvest, for looking back as well as forward; and, as far as ragtime is concerned, it is a time of many terminations and many culminations. Although ragtime's special brilliant period ended when we sent our legions to France in 1917, its spirit is perennially young. Its greatest pages have never faded, for good ragtime, like all good music, is essentially timeless. While we mistakenly link it with a vanished period, it is no less American now than then, no less expressive of our tempo and the unique bent of the American spirit.

Our first requirement is to know something about the sort of music ragtime really is and about the differences between the real and the imitation, between the first-rate and the second-, third-, and fourth-rate.

The first distinction that needs to be made is that the merit of a piece of music and the success in musical commerce that it did or did not achieve have nothing in common. Sheet-music sales cannot be used to judge the value of a ragtime composition. Although a real masterpiece like Scott Joplin's *Maple Leaf Rag* was a national hit, so was many an inferior piece of the period. By the same token, many great ragtime compositions virtually remained to be discovered by our generation.

Ragtime is mainly distinguished from most other music by its use of the rhythm loosely called syncopation. The really unique thing about ragtime when it appeared was the way the pianist opposed syncopations (or accents on the weak and normally unaccented second and third beats of the measure) in his right hand against a precise and regularly accented bass. Syncopation in its simple form—that is, uncombined with regular rhythm—is a familiar device used a few measures at a time with fair frequency in European music. It is disturbing in a context of regular meter; its upsetting of the normal pace led to the Italian term for syncopation, *alla zoppa*, meaning lame or limping. Continued syncopation, however, far from limping, builds up greater and greater momentum, hence the old English term for syncopated notes: "driving notes." Continued syncopation is deeply stimulating and exciting, and European masters seem always to have been wary of it. So the thorough use of these delayed and misplaced accents (misplaced, that is, in the sense of our regular meters) and their employment with regular meters to set up complex multiple rhythms, or polyrhythms, were never seriously explored in our music. The use of this driving, exciting propulsiveness in the most complexly developed ways is, on the other hand, a commonplace in the Negro music of Africa and the Americas. Retained for over three centuries in this country, it is used by the Afro-American to transform all of our music.

Piano ragtime was developed by the Negro from folk melodies and from the syncopations of the plantation banjos.

7

As it grew, it carried its basic principle of displaced accents played against a regular meter to a very high degree of elaboration. *Opera Magazine* in 1916 observed: "Ragtime has carried the complexity of the rhythmic subdivision of the measure to a point never before reached in the history of music." The treatment of folk music, both white and Negro, according to African rhythmic principles (for in the African drum corps one or more drums play in off-beat rhythms over the regular meter of another drum), produced a completely new sort of music. It also produced a music truly American.

Although ragtime originated on the folk level, several outstandingly gifted composers of both races carried the music to a creative level that can only be termed classical. The term, while a just one, admittedly has the fault that it may be confused with our ordinary use of "classical" to denote the work of the great European composers. It is necessary to use it, nevertheless, to describe the work of men like Scott Joplin, James Scott, Joseph Lamb, and others. The reader should therefore understand that where ragtime is termed classical, it is meant that the syncopated music thus described is highly articulated and developed along ragtime's own proper lines, and not that it is in any way necessarily similar to or in imitation of the classics of European music. The term "classic" as applied to piano ragtime has, in fact, the sanction of long usage. It was first employed early in this century by the pioneer ragtime publisher John Stark. By 1912 or 1913 it was a commonly accepted term and was not confused by reference to European music.

While ragtime rhythms characterize all Negro singing and pervade the topical songs, like the coon songs of the 1890's and early 1900's, classical ragtime is instrumental music for the piano. In general, when one refers to ragtime, one refers to music composed for this instrument.

Negro life in America, both in and out of slavery, has of necessity been to a considerable degree hermetic. Prejudice has forced this gifted minority to develop its own musical culture behind a sort of iron curtain, and natural musical tendencies have proved stronger than imitativeness. Many top-layer Negro intellectuals may be dismissed from this consideration because, although they reject Negro culture *in toto* in order to embrace white culture, their influence is scarcely felt in the layers of Negro society where real musical creation goes on. It should be noted, though, that in the intellectual group there are strong and influential dissidents from the group point of view.

Although segregation, as it determines environment, is the anthropologist's explanation for the preservation of the racial character of Negro music, a far stronger factor exists in a basic motivation that springs from the Negro's musical needs and operates regardless of the environment in the vast majority of the people. The Negro needs a music that is complex in its rhythmic structure and exceedingly powerful in its emotional effect, a music that is capable of inducing a state of ecstasy, as African music, American Negro church singing, and jazz are. The scientific acceptance of the fact of this need as a racial attribute would be a far more satisfactory explanation of many things than the far overextended theories of environment. It would explain why racial characteristics like those of the Negro persist in new surroundings despite a natural imitativeness and why and how imitative borrowings are transformed into more native shapes.

The position of the Negro in American society predetermined the fact that ragtime music for a considerable part of its early history would be developed and heard in the surroundings of the white underworld. This fact caused ragtime to be rejected by many elements of society that, had they been able to consider the music apart from its unfavorable environment, would have been highly likely to accept it. This might seem sufficient excuse to understress the circumstances that led to the rejection. On the other hand, the character of ragtime reflects in certain ways the environment of its youth. The Negro too, with the adaptability that has been the saving of his race, utilized this environment to forward the development of his music, while at the same time its remarkably non-erotic quality is proof of how he himself was able to dissociate his musical creation from the surroundings in which he was forced to work.

The extraordinary gaiety that is one of the greatest charms

of ragtime remains to recall the vanished honkytonk and sporting house. And yet even this gaiety, which is so innocent, is not a direct expression of the haunted, hectic merriment of the bordello. Of the two main phases of his own music, it is the one that Negro found suitable to sporting-house audiences. In the inner world of Negro life there have always been the two kinds of music, the melancholy or pathetic on one hand, and the gay and even jubilant on the other. There are, in short, the blues and ragtime; and there are the spirituals of lament and the jubilee hymns that apostrophize ultimate victory. Rupert Hughes, writing of ragtime in the *Musical Record* in 1899, said: "The Negro music of slavery days was largely pathetic; and no wonder. But . . . if Negro music has its 'Go Down Moses,' so it had also its hilarious banjo-plucking and its characteristic dances. It is the latter mood that is having a strange renascence and is sweeping the country."

The music of the Negro has always continued strongly in this country because he needs it, and he will continue to make it for himself until, in a relatively undiluted form, it can become a part of our general culture. It should be observed here that although ragtime was widely accepted by white Americans, it was a music that had primarily been made not for white honkytonk audiences, but by Negroes for Negroes.

One might assume that Negro music in its purest form is too strong for white acceptance, and it is true that many profess to find it too challenging. And yet instrumental jazz, far more powerful in its emotional effect than ragtime, has had a lasting acceptance in France and other countries. One must conclude that the attitude of white Americans as a whole toward Negro music in this country is subtly and powerfully conditioned by our attitude toward its creators as human beings. The fact, generally recognized abroad if not at home, is that ragtime, with the jazz that stemmed in part from it, is the only distinctively American music and, in addition, our most original artistic creation.

Negro music, to be sure, has never been without white champions, although these have been isolated figures. Some have been conscious, in every generation since the Negro first came to America, that the race was producing a unique music here. It is interesting to note that, outside of these supporters, white listeners allowed this music to speak more directly to their hearts when the Negro was enslaved than in the years of Negro progress since Emancipation. Yet from Thomas Jefferson to Louis Moreau Gottschalk, Lucy McKim Garrison, Charles Pickard Ware, and William Francis Allen, and from John Mason Brown (a writer of the Civil War period, not the present-day author) to George W. Cable, Lafcadio Hearn, H E. Krehbiel, Rupert Hughes, and right down to the present, some in each generation have rediscovered as a vital new experience the age-old fascination and profound feeling of Negro music.

There have been, in addition, certain times when specific happenings in the social scene have precipitated a general public acceptance of a current phase in the continuous stream of Negro musical creation. These acceptances occurred after Emancipation, and the way for them was paved by the white imitation of Negro music and dancing in the blackface minstrels. The burnt-cork entertainment originated in New York in the 1840's and was the first original American theatrical form. The minstrels were a highly diverting novelty, and their popularity both here and abroad was very great. Some real Negro songs, like *Jump Jim Crow* and *Lucy Long*, found their way into the repertory, but most of the banjo-playing, singing, and dancing were casual and stereotyped imitations.

The picture of the Negro as viewed by the white audiences of the minstrels, mildly contemptuous and derogatory of Negro character, was so thoroughly etched into the general consciousness that it still persists. Still worse, it has been too often used as an instrument to incite hate and facilitate vicious repression. Nevertheless, it should be recognized that the minstrels prepared the way for ragtime and all subsequent syncopation, and through the later admission into their ranks of Negroes themselves, for the entry of colored performers in their own right on the American stage.

Currents flow strongly but are insulated in the societies on either side of the American racial iron curtain. It is easy to see that whenever direct cultural contact on a wide scale takes place between the two, like electric wires suddenly joined,

11

something vital and electric in the arts must happen. There have been several notable instances of this.

The first occurred soon after Emancipation in the sudden public awareness of the Negro spiritual. The Reconstruction wave of pro-Negro sentiment in the North set the stage for all of this, and for a time all of the factors favored it. Not only did the spiritual become the symbol of a noble people just freed from slavery, and not only was it a religious form acceptable both to moralistic and to unmusical people, but it was also intrinsically of high musical value. The newly founded Negro colleges sent their singers out to capture Europe and America, and the gates seemed open.

But a pattern was set during the course of the epoch of the spiritual that has been followed since. As the Negro seemed about to win a permanent cultural contact with the white world and through this presumably a more general social one, contrary forces began to rouse into action. In the case of the spirituals, unlike the later emergences of Negro music, the reactionary aims were not realized blindly through a white commercial corruption of the music working hand in hand, although unknowingly, with overt prejudice and the actions of many Negroes themselves. It was simply that the original spirituals, completely unsingable by white artists, were gradually transformed by the falsely sophisticated college Negroes into a white art song with only faint traces of racial coloration. The "spiritual" as sung now by Marian Anderson and Paul Robeson represents the end product, a song that any trained singer can perform well.

With this essentially meek subsidence into mere conformity to white standards of what was to have been the triumph of the Negro, another thing happened that is also a part of the continuing pattern. The mass of Negroes, whence the spiritual had emerged, took it back to themselves, and there, in that submerged and estranged world, it has been sung ever since, developing generation by generation from new form to new form, but always as a Negroid music.

The second great emergence of Negro music came in the 1890's, two decades after that of the spirituals. This was ragtime. The way for it was prepared by the genuine Negro minstrels, who became possible after Emancipation and who began to carry the syncopation and phrasing of the Negroes to white audiences everywhere. By dint of conforming to a degree with the stereotype—a case, in Biblical language, of agreeing with thine adversary whiles thou art in the way with him—the Negroes projected ragtime rhythms into the public consciousness through the medium of the coon songs. The vogue for these swept the country. They were sung by colored and white performers and combined with the banjo-ragtime rhythms of dances like the buck and wing, the Virginia Essence, the stick and the sand dances, and the soft-shoe routines. At this time, too, the cakewalk, which had been a part of minstrel entertainment, was on the verge of becoming a fad.

In the meantime the Negroes were developing a radically new musical form, that of piano ragtime. Its combination of regular and syncopated rhythms on an instrument of great technical and musical resources was the best form yet found for the instrumental expression of the complex and forceful multiple rhythms of the race. On the piano the almost overpowering impact of Negroid music became a thing of infinite charm, with a seductive melodic lilt. Here was a music that white America was able to embrace, to respond to, to understand without reservation. If the minstrels fifty years before had been a hit, this was nothing to compare with the veritable ragtime rage that swept America. Riding in on the cakewalk, ragtime was an overnight national obsession.

With this music the wires of dark and white America crossed and the vital currents were flowing back and forth. The way for the Negro seemed finally open, the iron curtain rising, if ever so slightly. But this was only the first act of the ragtime drama. What followed, what came of it, what it all led to, is the story that the following chapters will tell.

Chapter 1

THE SEDALIA STORY

Nocturnal Main Street of Sedalia, Missouri, in 1896 was the town "sporting belt." Its seed stores, harness shops, and hardware stores, which held forth during the day, were closed. Their neighbors, the sporting houses and honkytonks like the Maple Leaf Club and the "400," were wide open and ready for business at sundown. By nightfall the wooden sidewalks were thronged with jostling gamblers, sports, pimps, hip-swaying girls, and the ordinarily conventional male citizenry out for a high time. On every street corner, bets were placed or assignations made with equal casualness, and from the open doors of the clubs and the discreetly closed ones of the bordellos came the sounds of laughter that mixed like a cocktail with the rippling, infectious, syncopated strains of ragtime. Ragtime was everywhere.

The visitor of that day who looked in at the Williams brothers' Maple Leaf Club saw a large room dominated by a Victorian bar of carved walnut and filled with pool and gaming tables, around which the customers, both Negro and white, stood or sat in old-fashioned tavern chairs. The lighting could scarcely be called adequate. The hanging gas chandeliers were like beacons in a fog, seeming to swing in the swirling tobacco smoke and noise. As the visitor's eyes became accustomed to the half-light, he would perceive that the music he had heard came from an upright piano in the far corner. There on the old plush-covered stool sat a Negro pianist. From under his agile fingers came the "new" ragtime syncopations that long ago had journeyed from Africa to the plantation banjos and the corn fiddles of the American South.

As the visitor lingered, a quartet was almost sure to gather round the pianist, and the rich Negro voices would give a syncopated, barber-shop treatment to the newest song hit of the day. Without looking up from dice games, from the poker hands, or from a delicate shot for the corner pocket, the men throughout the room would join in the refrain:

> *Oh! Mr. Johnson turn me loose,*
> *Got no money, but a good excuse,*
> *Oh! Mr. Johnson I'll be good.*

> *Oh! Mr. Johnson turn me loose,*
> *Don't take me to de calaboose,*
> *Oh! Mr. Johnson I'll be good.*

On the mornings after, however, with the sun beating down on it, East Main was a far different street from the one that bloomed at night lit by rosy lamps and veiled with a tawdry glamour. By daylight Main Street revealed an ordinary face touched with the wrinkles of the mundane, grayed with a look of disillusion. Negro boys were sweeping out the honkytonks, from which, only a few hours before, the late-playing pianists had departed. The earliest pool-playing sports were not yet due. The shuttered bordellos were tired and quiet, the madams and their girls fast asleep.

Just an ordinary dirt road, flanked by plain one- and two-story buildings of brick or wood, some with corrugated-iron awnings over the sidewalk—this was the prototype of any small Midwestern Main Street. But this did not mean the Midwestern town of today, ruled by its Chamber of Commerce, its local Baptist and Methodist churches, and dreaming of Prohibition. The central Midwest of those days half a century ago was still part frontier.

The frontier was more a fading idea, to be sure, than an actual state of affairs, but it was still potent in the mind. Growing business and conservatism and a new reaching for a thing called "being respectable" lived at this transitional stage with a hard-dying respect for the rights of the individual to a good time and a considerable latitude of behavior.

Around Sedalia's Main Street clustered a prosperous town of some fifteen thousand people, set in the midst of the rolling, fertile fields of central Missouri. Settled in 1860, Sedalia had been a Union military post and at the war's end had resumed its period of pioneer growing up. By 1896 the Pettis County seat was host to the annual Missouri State Fair, had somewhat narrowly missed becoming the state capital, and, as terminus of four divisions of the Missouri Pacific and three of the "Katy"—the Missouri, Kansas, and Texas—was a considerable railroad center. The "Katy" general car and repair shops were located there on a plot of thirty-seven acres, as they are to this day.

The wealth of labor openings brought large numbers of Negroes to Sedalia. Besides working on the railroads, these new arrivals found jobs in the commercial houses, in hotels, restaurants, barber shops, and saloons, as well as on the farms out of town. Some ran their own restaurants, barber shops, stores, and bars, and several Negro-owned newspapers thrived. It is to Sedalia's credit that it treated its Negro population with somewhat more enlightened fairness than was typical of the times. Good Negro schools, the use of park facilities, and less than the usual quota of racial prejudice were features of this compact little city.

That Sedalia was at this time a center of piano ragtime was due only slightly, if at all, to these conditions. It was not the respectable Sedalia that supported the beginnings of what was to become the classic ragtime. East Main Street, with its honkytonks, clubs, and bawdy houses, was the patron of syncopated music. Such was the Negro's position in our society that it was inevitable that this rich new vein of music should be previewed for white America in whorehouses. In the tenderloins—and nowhere else—there was entree for these musical originators; but in the tenderloins at least were the free and easy conditions, the ready money, and the freedom for a pianist to play pretty much as he pleased.

So there existed in Sedalia and throughout the country, a large class of Negro—and some white—pianists, many of them highly gifted and all of them close to the sources of folk music. Drifting from one open town to the next, following the fairs, the races, and the excursions, these men formed a real folk academy. After the tonks and houses closed, they would meet in some hospitable back-room rendezvous to play on into the morning. Ideas were freely exchanged, and rags, true to one meaning of the name, were patched together from the bits of melody and scraps of harmony that all contributed. Among the tribe were men of great potentialities who created complete and beautiful rags and songs, yet the feeling of proprietorship scarcely existed; commercial rivalry had not entered this Eden. It cost little to live, and money was got as easily as fruit from a tropical tree. Occasionally in a strange town a pianist needing a few quick dollars would sell a tune for publication. Despite the fact that many might have contributed to the number, the general feeling was that by the mere acts of sale and copyright one became the rightful owner. This was all to be changed in time, but during the formative years each player had but two aims: the making of music and the achievement of a personal playing style. Under such circumstances ragtime developed naturally and rapidly.

Everywhere the tight-knit clan was meeting—at Tom Turpin's Rosebud Cafe in St. Louis, at the Frenchman's in New Orleans, at Johnny Seymour's Bar in Chicago, at the Maple Leaf Club in Sedalia, in Louisville, Nashville, Little Rock, Indianapolis, and El Reno in the old Oklahoma Territory—and only the sporting world and husbands secretly out for a fling were there to hear the music.

In 1896, the year of which we have been speaking, two of these wandering ragtime troubadours returned to Sedalia on the train from Joplin. They had been away two years. They were Otis Saunders, about twenty-four, of Springfield, Missouri, and his friend Scott Joplin, of Texarkana, Texas, just twenty-six years of age. Both men were Negroes of medium

17

height, Saunders light in color, handsome and snappily dressed, Joplin dark, plain and neat in dress, and markedly serious in expression. There was nothing unusual to mark these two as they threaded their way along the crowded station platform. And yet Joplin was within a very few years to be known as the greatest composer of a new music and the man who, more than any other, shaped its entire course. Scott Joplin, despite his reserve, was a magnetic person with a dynamism doubly effective because of its quietness. These qualities, coupled with an already evident musical genius, had drawn to him the technically trained musician Saunders. They had met three years before at the Chicago Exposition, where hundreds of the itinerant piano clan had gathered, and there had become friends. In the intervening years Otis Saunders had been of considerable help to Joplin, particularly, perhaps, by merely listening to the composer in his most serious moments. This helped the writer to clarify his own musical ideas.

Able pianists were no rarity in this segregated nether world of music, but Joplin was more. Instrumental ragtime of the most classic type, permanent in published scores rather than as evanescent as its mere playing, was already forming in his consciousness, always superactive with creative ideas. Sedalia itself was to become for a short time a focal point in the introduction of serious ragtime through Joplin's activity there, and particularly, three years later, by virtue of the fact that his *Maple Leaf Rag*, acknowledged and perennial masterpiece of the new musical genre, was to be published in this prairie town.

The two itinerants, Joplin and Saunders, were no strangers to the Pettis County center or, for that matter, to the whole area of the Mississippi, Missouri, and Ohio Rivers, where folk ragtime was being born. They were familiar figures in most of the open towns of the huge Mississippi Valley, in vast sprawling Texas, and in the still raw frontier of the Indian and Oklahoma Territories. The musical life of Sedalia; of which Scott Joplin was now to become a part, was active and full in both the white and the Negro segments as well as on either side of the railroad tracks of respectability. Joplin was able to operate in the respectable Negro world even while finding his chief opportunity in the "District." Two years earlier he had played second cornet with the star Sedalia aggregation called the Queen City Concert Band, and he also sang with quartets and played solo piano for many of the colored social gatherings. Now, as he went to live for a few months in the family home of young Arthur Marshall, he became Arthur's classmate at the George Smith College for Negroes, which was operated by the Methodist Church. At college Joplin took advanced courses in harmony and composition to supplement the childhood training he had in Texarkana and the knowledge picked up in his travels.

Much of the musical activity of that day centered in the brass band. This was the era of the great Frederick Neil Innes and John Philip Sousa, with the smallest country hamlet boasting its own bandstand in the square, where each Sunday afternoon the "Silver Cornet" band held forth. Sedalia, as befitted a young city, supported not one but several organizations. There were two good white groups, the twelve-piece Independent Band and the Sedalia Military Band, a reed and brass aggregation of eighteen members, which had a subsidiary fourteen-piece dance orchestra.

The Negroes, with several bands, were far from lagging behind. The paramount group was the twelve-piece Queen City Concert Band, also called the Queen City Cornet Band, led by cornetist Ed Gravitt. This sterling organization had repeatedly proved its leadership by the handy way in which it defeated all comers in band contests from Sedalia as far as Kansas City. Two front-page articles in a contemporary issue of the colored *Sedalia Times* tell a short, short story of one of these occasions:

OFF AND GONE

The Queen City Concert Band and the Sedalia Browns will leave this morning for Lexington where a band contest will be held. The band will do its best to bring back the honors, and if justice is given them from the hands of the judges they will surely win the blue ribbon, while the

19

baseball boys will do their best to hold up Sedalia as a crack baseball center.

BAND CONTEST IS CALLED OFF

The band contest that was to be held in Lexington today between Sedalia and Kansas City colored bands has been called off on account of the latter backing out.

The personnel of the Queen City Concert Band at the time of Joplin's return to Sedalia was as follows: Ed Gravitt, solo cornet; W. H. Carter, slide trombone; G. Tom Ireland, solo clarinet; Nathaniel Diggs, clarinet; Al Wheeler, tenor horn; James Scott, solo alto horn; James Chisholm, alto horn; R. O. Henderson, baritone horn; A. H. Hickman, tuba; C. W. Gravitt, bass drum; Emmett Cook, snares; and Henry Martin, drum major. To the roster should no doubt be added the mascot, little Jimmy Stewart. Today, fifty years later, only drummer Gravitt and clarinetist Ireland are left; even little Jimmy is dead.

Tom Ireland today is a well-known Sedalia figure as, at eighty-five, he still rambles around town on his bicycle. Louisville born, Tom was educated at Central Tennessee College, now Walden University, in Nashville, before settling in Sedalia. Up to his retirement several years ago, he spent most of his life in newspaper work. For three years around 1894 he owned and edited a Negro paper, the *Western World*, "published in the interest of the Colored Race every Sunday Morning." Like all the Southern Negro newspapers of that day, the *Western World* breathed a spirit of racial optimism and reflected an active interest in politics that now languishes in many sections where the poll tax has taken the vote from the poor of both races. After nearly half a century with Sedalia's leading white paper, the *Democrat*, Tom was pensioned. Although he has two married sons, he lives a widower independently alone, in his tiny cottage in north Sedalia. The affection of white Sedalia for this erect, wiry, alert old gentleman is succinctly expressed in the current city directory, in which after the name G. Tom Ireland the obnoxious customary word "colored," with its implication of segregation, is conspicuously absent.

Ireland loves to talk about the old music. He describes the wealth of talent that was once in Sedalia. More than most towns of its size, Sedalia attracted the gifted because ample employment made possible the cultivation of music as an avocation. This railroad center of a rich agricultural and cattle empire was thus a lodestone for musical Negroes from the Mississippi and Missouri valley area. There many of them lived while their class was creating the ragtime style that is both most classic and nearest to the folk roots. The traveling minstrel and tent shows came regularly to Sedalia, as much to recruit talent as to give performances. The Queen City Concert Band signed on for a season with the De Kreko Bros. Carnival Show. The *Sedalia Times* refers to its winning the honors against "several good white bands" in Iowa and to its members meeting while in Iowa several members of Professor Barnhouse's famous band and being highly complimented on their playing. The Barnhouse publications at that time were the nucleus of the standard march repertory. "They planned to go," the *Times* adds, "with the same show for several months through the Southern states."

Many Sedalia Negroes fell for the lure of life on the road. A few months with W. A. and Jack Mahara's Minstrels were enough, however, to prove to Tom Ireland that nomadic show life was not for him. Some of the youths went never to return or, like Arthur Marshall, who joined McCabe's Minstrels and got as far from home as New York, stayed long enough to make a nest egg and then quit. Arthur was with McCabe intermittently from 1900 to 1902, playing piano during the shows and beating cymbals in the parades, both under the direction of Bunk Johnson, the famous pioneer jazz cornetist of New Orleans, who died in 1949. "A really great player," Arthur recalls.

At home in Sedalia the members of the Queen City Concert Band were workmen or little businessmen who were musicians in their spare time and on holidays and were prominent in Negro social life. Henderson and James Scott (not the great ragtime composer of whom we shall hear later) were champion local hunters. A newspaper account tells of one of their exploits:

MADE THEM SUFFER

James Scott and R. O. Henderson spent Wednesday hunting rabbits. When they returned Scott had 17 hanging around him and Henderson had 8. From all appearances it is dangerous for a rabbit to jump up within 200 feet from these marksmen. Scott will enjoy rabbit hams for the next few weeks.

A few days later, however, the editor asks querulously: "Why didn't Scott bring those rabbits he promised? One man in this office doubts about his killing any at all."

The Queen City Concert Band had its orchestra offshoot, a seven-piece outfit organized and led by W. H. Carter, who, besides being the band trombonist, was editor and publisher of the *Times*. The orchestra, with trombonist Carter now bowing the double brass, rehearsed weekly in the *Times* offices, at 120 East Main Street, directly across from the Williams brothers' Maple Leaf Club.

The band and orchestra occupied the respectable musical niche known as legitimate, and though the honkytonk music later to be called ragtime was not referred to as illegitimate, the inference was clear. At this time Carter, when the evening noise from the Maple Leaf interfered with his editorial reflections or disrupted the orchestra rehearsals, could write smugly: "We are informed that orders have been issued to shut down the piano 'thumping' on Main Street." Failure to enforce the orders brought forth the editorial complaint: "Why is it not stopped? Someone answer the question." In the same issue he wrote enthusiastically of a "grand musical being given at Quinn Chapel . . . composed of high class musicians." It was not long before Carter, an adaptable and politic man, was to change his tune both editorially and actually. Only a few years later he was to write in glowing terms of his visit with Scott Joplin, the Ragtime King, in St. Louis. The syncopated idea was growing anyway, and when it began to be generally accepted by whites, and the erstwhile despised honkytonkers to become kings, the Negro bands and orchestras decided to do what came naturally.

The Queen City Concert Band continued to play marches, as, of course, any self-respecting brass band would do, but the other music was seeping in. The boys were working out on coon songs like *My Coal Black Lady, Ambolena Snow, Dora Dean,* and *Sweet Kentucky Babe,* and the overtures became medleys of plantation and "down South" melodies. The first published rags, like Tom Turpin's *Harlem Rag* of 1897, went immediately into the repertory. The sedate faces above the natty uniforms belied the new, sparkling accent the bandsmen put into their music. The orchestra followed suit, and the dancers began stepping the cakewalk and doing the two-step as the time-hallowed quadrilles and schottisches quickly began to be forgotten. Even the waltzes began to have a syncopation never dreamed of by Waldteufel and Strauss. Scott Joplin's small dance orchestra formed from members of the Q.C.C.B., became more popular than ever.

Ragtime was ragtime, in fact, in everything but name, and in 1897 it got the name too. Tom Ireland recalls that up to that time ragtime piano was called "jig piano," and the syncopating bands, like Joplin's, were called "jig bands." This term, taken from jig dances, even came a little later to be a designation for the Negro himself. Ireland remembers events like the Colored Elks Street Fair in 1898, when the "jig bands played from booth to booth. They would play for the trapeze act and then to each event in turn. For the circus they played 'quick time,' which were marches played double time."

More than any other man Scott Joplin was responsible for the drastic change in attitude of Sedalia's respectable colored society. Quiet and retiring, he was in the center of things musical. He moved freely between the respectable world and the underworld, able to do this because he gave himself to neither world, but only to his music.

With all his varied activity—and all his life Joplin was nothing if not superactive—he continued to develop his playing skill and to work seriously at composition. He was becoming

23

more and more facile at scoring the syncopations that for years had eluded the white arrangers of Negro music. He could thank Otis Saunders and Will Williams, who with his brother Walker owned the Maple Leaf Club, for this new facility, for it was on their recommendation that he had entered Smith College. His lessons in the fine four-story building northeast of Sedalia (burned down in 1925), had materially eased the exacting mechanics of composition. His orchestra of cornet, clarinet, baritone, tuba, and his own piano began to play his new works. Long before their publication they were favorites of the local Negro society. It is not likely that Joplin's group was the first ragtime band in America, although it was unquestionably the first instrumental group to feature Joplin tunes. After all, at this very time Buddy Bolden's horn was shaking New Orleans and Fred S. Stone's band was enlivening Detroit. And there were, of course, many others long since forgotten. Ragtime was in the air.

"Rags were played in Sedalia before Scott Joplin settled there," says Arthur Marshall, "but he got to making them really go." This is a tribute to the musicianship that Joplin brought to the whole matter. He was the first to shape folk inspiration into the clear picture of a finished musical form with an indisputable right to be accepted in all quarters as serious music.

One can search the files of the white newspapers of 1897–8 almost in vain for a mention of ragtime. Word of it had not penetrated to the city desks. But news got around without help of the press. Meandering players ceaselessly on the move were an underworld grapevine that functioned as a Ragtime Associated Press. The ink was hardly dry on *Harlem Rag*, the first full-fledged Negro rag to reach publication, before the fact was known in Sedalia. Scott Joplin was ready with a number of finished rags including the first collaborative piece written with Marshall.

Joplin's first contact early in 1898 with the Sedalia music house of A. W. Perry & Son, at 306 Broadway, was fruitless. Either they were not ready for ragtime or they may have requested the composer to change the name of his *Maple Leaf Rag*. Their reason probably would have been their slightly earlier publication of a *Maple Leaf Waltz*—a most mediocre piece by one Florence Johnson—and Joplin's answer would have been a refusal. For one thing, his number was already widely popular in Sedalia under its original name; for another, Joplin felt deeply grateful to the brothers Williams for the support and the haven they had given him.

Joplin seems to have dropped plans for publication for a time and to have returned to composing. There is no evidence that he saw John Stark at this time. Stark ran Sedalia's other music store, at 514 Ohio Street, and had himself already taken a flier at music publishing with a song and the purchase of the seven-number catalogue of a small publisher. But this is certain: in December 1898, with his compositions under his arm, Joplin boarded a train for Kansas City. Carl Hoffman, the publisher, encouraged by his arranger, bought a number called *Original Rags*, but passed up the *Maple Leaf Rag*. *Original Rags* was published in March 1899. The cover shows an old plantation Negro picking up rags in front of a cabin; under the title are the words: "Picked by Scott Joplin—Arranged by Chas. N. Daniels." This acknowledges Daniels's help in encouraging the purchase of the rag. The music itself seems to bear no trace of any but Joplin's hand.

Back in Sedalia, Joplin had a new stature. He may have enjoyed—and doubtless did enjoy—the new local fame, but over the course of the years acclaim never altered his reserve or diminished his generous affection for his friends. Scott had many musical friends in Sedalia. There were Ida and Jim Hastings, Chandles, and A. Chestine, who later moved to Omaha. There were Melford Alexander and Tony Williams, owner of the "400" Dance Club, where, because, unlike the Maple Leaf, it had no bar, the guests brought their own liquor. Tony played a fair ragtime piano himself, and of course there was his old friend and supporter "Crackerjack" or Otis Saunders, outstandingly talented and so light-colored and smooth-haired that Tom Ireland remembers him as a white man.

And here in Sedalia, as in every town where he settled for any length of time, were the gifted youngsters whom Joplin, with his sense of the importance of syncopated music, would

25

teach and encourage. Two of them from Sedalia went on, after the start that he gave them, to publish compositions and win a high place in ragtime history. Both were youths of about fifteen when Joplin took them in hand in 1896.

Scott Hayden was a sensitive and handsome light-skinned boy, slender and of delicate health, with a talent that was markedly melodic. He was born on March 30, 1882 at 133 West Cooper Street. The house, still standing, is now number 109. His parents were Marion and Julia Hayden. When Joplin met young Hayden, he was attending Lincoln High School, from which he was graduated in 1900. Under Joplin he quickly became an adept ragtimer and was soon playing at dances in and around Sedalia. His melodic talent was expressed in singing, too. C. W. Gravitt, one-time drummer of the old Queen City Concert Band, says: "He sang very well, too."

Through Joplin's marriage a year or so later to one of Scott Hayden's relatives, they came into even closer relationship. In the Sedalia days before Joplin removed to St. Louis and his protégés followed, the older man was assisting young Hayden with a piece published in 1901 as a collaboration. This is *Sunflower Slow Drag*, one of the most captivatingly melodious of all ragtime pieces.

The other Joplin protégé was, of course, Arthur Marshall. Joplin stayed for five or six months at the Marshall house at 117 West Henry Street while he was looking for permanent quarters. This was long enough for the boy to come under the Joplin influence and to be incurably bitten by the ragtime bug. Arthur, like Scott Hayden, had had the best legitimate training that colored Sedalia afforded, and he too became a first-rate ragtime player. Many a night at the Marshall home the older man helped the youth with his first ragtime compositions, which, published later as collaborations, are among the masterpieces of classic ragtime. It is no wonder that Marshall, sixty-nine years old today, has the same veneration for the Ragtime King as he had when those sessions burned themselves into his youthful memory. Before Joplin moved into a room at John Wesley's home at the northeast corner of Lamine and Cooper, Joplin had added a fine characteristic trio to

26

three beautiful themes by Arthur. The result was the collaboration, *Swipesy Cake Walk*, published in 1900.

Arthur Marshall was only a few months older than Scott Hayden. He was born on November 20, 1881 on a farm in Saline County, Missouri, near the birthplace of the Negro musical genius Blind Boone. Arthur was only three or four years of age when his family returned to Sedalia, where they had lived before he was born, and bought the little cottage on West Henry Street. Arthur and Scott Hayden went through the Sedalia schools together.

Both Hayden and Marshall kept badgering Joplin to get them into the Maple Leaf, where they could hear their special idol and the "battles of music" between the many players. After some occasional forays they soon began to play professionally at the clubs and what Marshall still delicately calls "parlors," and the boys were really in the thick of things and committed to a life in ragtime. Arthur had to "stand the taddlin' " for staying out late, and a big scene came when his mother finally discovered where he spent his time. But when she found out that he was gainfully employed and that the better tips came between ten and the early morning hours, it was a different matter. After all, money was none too plentiful. Before this compromise between scruples and necessity had been effected, Arthur's brother Lee would slip him into the house when he returned.

At the Maple Leaf and at Nellie Hall's and Mrs. L. Wright's "parlors" the salary was a nominal dollar and a half a night, but from seven to ten dollars were to be made in tips. Particularly generous were the cattlemen and wholesale grocers completing a successful trip. Moneyed crowds would come in, too, especially at fair time, on the railroad excursions that were a big feature of those entertainment-hungry days. No special occasion seemed to be needed to schedule an excursion all spring, summer, and fall. If a railroad division needed to make some money, that was occasion enough. When a colored excursion came in on the M.P. or the Katy, there would be a big barbecue picnic, a dance, and a ragtime contest at Liberty Park, rented for the occasion from the white officials.

Arthur Marshall recalls the old times: "Joplin and I and

many of the others played for numerous dances at the parks, all piano only. We played all the rags of note and they did dances to the ragtime. They would do a buck and wing, a regular routine, and then make up six or seven different steps just like the eccentric dancing that came later and the jitter-bugging today—no difference.

"There was a fellow they called High Henry—he was nearly seven feet tall. He would suddenly do a flat fall forward while doing the buck and wing just as if he had suddenly fainted. When he hit, his elbows would throw him right back up as stiff as a board—he looked like a telephone pole coming down and then going up again."

Little if any was the discrimination in the honkytonk and sporting-house circuit with regard to entertainers. Negroes predominated in this period because white pianists were just beginning to learn the syncopated intricacies of the rag. But white players came in early. One, typically colorful, was S. Brunson Campbell, known before he was fifteen as "The Ragtime Kid." And this was before 1900, because the Kid was born in Washington, Kansas, in 1884. He tells his own story:

"When I entered school in Arkansas City I also commenced to take music lessons. By fourteen I was playing all the popular songs. One day a doctor's son and I ran away from home to Oklahoma City to a celebration that was in progress there. We became separated and I wandered into the Armstrong-Byrd music store and commenced to play over some of the tunes of the day. A crowd soon gathered; they began to encourage me with applause and asked for more.

"After a time there emerged from the crowd a young mulatto with a light complexion, dressed to perfection and smiling pleasantly. He came over to the piano and placed a pen-and-ink manuscript of a piece of music in front of me and asked if I would play it. The manuscript was entitled '*Maple Leaf Rag* by Scott Joplin.' I went through the piece and he seemed to be struck by the way I played it. He afterwards told me that I had made only two mistakes.

"It turned out that the mulatto's name was Otis Saunders, a fine pianist, a pal of Scott Joplin and one of ragtime's great

28

pioneers. I learned from Saunders that Joplin was located at that time in Sedalia.

"After returning home for a while a roaming propensity and a newly awakened interest in ragtime prompted me to run away again—this time to Sedalia, where I lost no time in locating Otis Saunders and Scott Joplin. They were both playing piano in a tavern there. At Saunders' suggestion I played the piano for Joplin, and after hearing me he agreed to be my teacher.

"He taught me to play his first two rags, *Original Rags* and the *Maple Leaf*. Joplin and Saunders nicknamed me 'The Ragtime Kid,' and that name was to stick with me all through my early ragtime career.

"When I bade Scott Joplin good-by as I left for my home in Kansas in 1899, he gave me a bright new silver half-dollar dated 1897 and calling my attention to the date said: 'Carry this for good luck and remember that it is dated the year that I finished my first rag.' As he handed it to me he had a very strange and sad expression in his eyes. I have never forgotten that look."

Brun Campbell continues his adventures, telling of the family's moving to El Reno, Oklahoma. "I hated to leave Arkansas City and my friends," he says, "and especially my sweetheart, 'Taffy.' I was sixteen years old at the time and playing a pretty hot ragtime piano. El Reno was overflowing, the opening up of that land having attracted people from all over the nation. The town was a beehive of gamblers. Every game known to science was operated right out in the open, in the streets and on the corners. There were roulette wheels, drop case, spindle wheels, dice tables, three-card monte dealers, besides many gambling houses operating with stacks of silver and gold coins on the tables. There never was nor ever will be a city wherein so much gambling was done out in the open.

"Many interesting and funny sights were to be seen. I saw the original 'Arkansas Kid' break the Attic Gambling House there. I saw Frenchy La Britton, a high-powered gambler, win ten thousand dollars on a cut of the cards. But my biggest

29

thrill was playing Scott Joplin's *Maple Leaf Rag* in the parlor of the Kerfoot Hotel for Pawnee Bill (Gordon Lillie). Twenty years later I met him in Tulsa and he asked me to play it again.

"Being a boy who could play the piano and who had been raised on excitement, I shortly struck out on my own again. I played wherever I could find a job; in honkytonk saloons, pool halls, restaurants, confectionery stores, theaters, with minstrels and medicine shows, ten- twenty- thirty-cent weekly dramatic shows, steamboats, etc.

"I had kept up a correspondence with my kid sweetheart, Taffy. . . . She was still living in Arkansas City, where my mother and younger brother were then located, so I decided to pay them all a visit. I arrived decked out in a loud checkered suit. Cloth-top, colored patent-leather shoes with pearl buttons, a light-colored hat with a loud hatband, and that ever-lovin' brilliant silk shirt, together with a loud-patterned necktie, about made my ragtime dress complete. . . . I thought Taffy would faint when she saw me, and my mother stood dead in her tracks.

"While home I met another pianist named Ted Hill. One day we decided to take our .22 rifles and go frog-hunting at the river near by. We got into a friendly argument as to who was the better shot, and I took a silver half-dollar out of my pocket. It was the one that my Negro piano teacher, Scott Joplin, had given me for a lucky piece in Sedalia. I put it in a crack on top of a fence post as a target. We measured off fifty feet. My friend shot first and missed. I shot and hit it dead center, the slug's impact stretching the piece into the shape of a thimble. . . . I went into a blacksmith shop, and flattened it back out. Afterward I carried it for a pocket piece until one day I somehow spent it."

For ten years the Ragtime Kid played his music and carried the gospel of Negro syncopation and Scott Joplin and the *Maple Leaf Rag* throughout the Southwest, before retiring to less glamorous fields. Today, at sixty-six, he is a barber in California, with a large clientele of ragtime enthusiasts who love to reminisce with him. One of the tales he tells them is the sequel to the tale of the lost half-dollar:

"I had forgotten all about ragtime and the old days when on May 1st, 1930, a customer came into my place of business, made a purchase, and paid for it with the half-dollar that Scott Joplin had given me back in 1899 and which was used as a target when I went frog hunting in 1903. My half-dollar lucky piece had returned to me! I could hardly believe my eyes, but there it was. As I kept looking at it and turning it over in my hand the panorama of my life as a ragtime pianist unfolded before me. . . . That half-dollar seemed to say: Don't you think it would be nice to make a recording of Scott Joplin's *Maple Leaf Rag* just as he taught you to play it back there in Sedalia in 1899, and use the revenue from these sources to erect a memorial over his grave for what he did in the field of American music?"

Brun Campbell did just that. But instead of erecting a monument on Joplin's grave, he sent the money to Joplin's widow and turned over his entire collection of Scott Joplin's musical works to Fisk University, in Nashville, "who have set up the Scott Joplin Memorial in their library alongside the other great composers. So at last the 'Original Ragtime Kid' has been able to memorialize his old piano teacher, Scott Joplin, the greatest of all the ragtime pioneers."

The stories of Arthur Marshall and the Ragtime Kid give some small indication of what a strong germinating force in the new music Scott Joplin was. His activity and his constructive help to younger men were more extensive than could be imagined. Greater still, however, was the force that Joplin was soon to exert on thousands of people he never saw. His compositions, typifying the essence of ragtime in its most perfect composed form, were to spread throughout the country. They were to shape the whole trend of piano ragtime on its serious or classic side as opposed to the haphazard improvisations of the many second- and third-rate players and the Tin Pan Alley "rag" concoctions that were soon to begin pouring forth.

Of Joplin's more than fifty published ragtime compositions, his second, *Maple Leaf Rag*, exerted the widest, deepest, and most lasting effect. When Joplin returned from Kansas City and the sale of *Original Rags* in 1899, he began to make efforts to secure the publication of *Maple Leaf*. Chance at this point played into his hands. The legend of how this happened may also be the fact.

Will and Walker Williams were excessively proud of the lovely rag that bears the name of their club and were fond of asking Joplin to play it for their special customers, so the story

Advertisement in Tom Ireland's Western World (1896)

goes. One summer afternoon John Stark dropped in for a cool beer and heard the rag. Something was in his mind, for he asked Joplin to bring the music into his store. Early next morning the composer walked down Lamine Avenue and turned in at 114 East Fifth Street, where Stark & Son had recently moved. At the proprietor's request, he sat down at a Jesse French upright and ran through the rag. Under his supple and legato but crisply accented right hand and the bass that, Arthur Marshall says, "swung exceedingly well," the four beautiful themes really sang. So John Stark bought the *Maple Leaf Rag*, and there is no reason to believe that he had any sort of premonition that this piece would lead him into a new city and a new life and, for as long as he lived, would be the central fact of that life. Nor is there reason to doubt that, as Joplin walked back down Lamine, he knew these things and more. For Arthur Marshall has told us that when the number was first completed and written down, Joplin said to him: "Arthur, the *Maple Leaf* will make me King of Ragtime Composers." But neither Stark nor Joplin could have known that their meeting meant the end of their part in the ragtime story of Sedalia, Missouri.

Sedalia, like many other towns, was changing. A new era was coming in with the new century. Reform, which had been slowly gathering momentum, particularly at this period in the smaller towns, was wiping out the old frontier. The following items from the *Sedalia Times* typify the change that was taking place. There was a sudden shame of the free lawlessness of the old days. A certain prudishness began to replace the devil-may-care attitude of the hardy frontiersmen. Such things as the young ladies' methods of locomotion began to be matters of great concern:

WALKING GIRLS

When the girls walk out evenings with the sole purpose of picking up a young man and continuing the walk, it is time to have a curfew law that will include children over 16. The restlessness that comes upon girls upon summer evenings results in lasting trouble unless it is speedily controlled. The right kind of man does not look for a wife on the streets, and the right kind of a girl waits till the man comes to her home for her.

When the girls took to "wheels," the *Times* reprimanded two "proud young ladies" for bicycling in public on Main Street: "These ladies do not seem to care for the wind blowing on the lightness of their costume. . . . Men gathered in large crowds on the corners and in front of pool rooms for sight seeing." It would seem that later the snooping *Times* reporter peepèd through sundry keyholes to great advantage, for the shameful fact was heralded that the same young ladies "spent Thursday evening at the Brewery drinking common beer."

Prissily Victorian as these editorializings are, they were the trivia of a new age that reached out for respectability, part and parcel of the chautauquas and the ladies' Browning clubs and of the fearsome saloon-wrecking of the ax-wielding, iron-jawed Carry Nation.

The old free and easy strongholds were falling one by one. The faithful *Times* reports in 1901: "Hustler's Hall has closed its doors. The mixed assemblages of toughs of both sexes have ceased to congregate there and the 'can' is no longer a familiar sight flitting in and out of the door. It is a clear case of 'good riddance to bad rubbish.' "

By 1909 the old District was entirely gone. Although the joints and the houses operated for a while surreptitiously at the north and east edges of the town, music and musicians were departing. The gaiety of sporting life had become mere furtive sin. Silence had fallen on the ragtime pianos of Sedalia.

Chapter **2**

PIONEERS UNDER THE SKIN

FROM the meeting of Scott Joplin and John Stark in Sedalia in 1899 on to the very end of the ragtime period, the history of classic ragtime revolves around these two men. Without them little of it would be preserved for us today in the permanence of the printed score. Negro ragtime was essentially an instance of racial improvisation. With all its brilliance, with all its deep ties to the profound sources of Negro energy and inspiration, it was nevertheless the music of ten thousand wandering troubadours living as they could and compulsively pouring out the song of a race. No matter how beautiful, no matter how ravishing, even, this song might be, its duration at the end could well have been only that of its last dying echoes.

The genius of Joplin was twofold: the tyrannical creative urge and the vision. With the first alone, even had he been, perhaps, the greatest of all the ragtime players, his most perfectly constructed pieces, unscored, would today be one with all the others, lost with a lost time. But his vision was the sculptor's, molding transitory vision into stone's indestructibility. He was at once the one who makes and the one who saves. Through the labor of this one "homeless itinerant" the vast outcry of a whole dark generation can go on sounding as long as any music will sound.

John Stark was the man indispensable to the actualization of Scott Joplin's vision. A white man, able to operate in the white man's world, he could and did effectuate the black man's dreams. Here was the communal and fruitful labor of the dark-skinned and the white American, the practical brotherhood of which enlightened white Americans and most Negroes have been dreaming for all these long generations. Stark caught Joplin's vision, and from that summer's day in Sedalia the life of a small-town merchant became that of prophet, champion, and zealot. Across the imagined barriers of race he moved to become the alter ego of a Negro genius, as close as the mirrorlike correspondence of their initials: S. J.—J. S. And this partnership of effort was to work effectually all their lives: powered by the vision, it was to triumph past estrangement, even after final alienation.

To believe that a partnership so rare, not only in the annals of the two races in America, but in the story of human beings anywhere, is a thing that just happened is to overstrain credibility. In the lives of Scott Joplin and John Stark was something that at the right time brought them inevitably together; or if it was an accident, then there is unperceived inevitability in the very laws of chance. Perhaps this inevitability, this logic, may become clear as we see what sort of men they were, what they had done, and what had happened to them in the years before they met.

The story of Scott Joplin begins on Tuesday, November 24, 1868 in the little city of Texarkana, which is situated in the extreme northeast corner of Texas, just across the line from the Arkansas town of the same name and not far above the prehistoric Caddo Lake of Louisiana. On this date Giles Joplin, of North Carolina origin, and Florence Givens Joplin, who had come from Kentucky, welcomed a new baby into their modest dwelling.

Scott grew up there with two brothers, Will and Robert, and two sisters in a household that, though poor, could afford music. His father played the violin, and his mother sang with the natural flexibility and richness of the unschooled Negro voice, and she played the banjo as well. Will played the guitar at first, and under his father's instruction the violin later, while Robert's boyish voice gradually deepened into a notably rich baritone.

By the time he was seven, Scott was already fascinated by a neighbor's piano. Whenever he was allowed to touch it he showed clear signs of musical promise. Giles Joplin, despite a desire, natural in near poverty, for his son to learn a trade or like himself to work for the Iron Mountain and Southern Railroad, nevertheless scraped the money together to buy a somewhat decrepit square grand. Scott was at this out-of-tune instrument every hour he could manage, and before he was eleven he played and improvised smoothly and with a rhythm and harmonic sense remarkable even in a Negro.

Much as the famous Blind Boone of Missouri only a half-dozen years before had first attracted local attention, Scott's self-taught ability began to make him the talk of the Negro community and the surrounding countryside. Such news seeped eventually into the white houses through servants' talk, perhaps even through the stories of a mother about the exploits of her child, for Scott's mother was a laundress. An old German music teacher heard of young Joplin, and what he heard interested him.

The opportunity came for the boy to play for the old teacher. As a result he received not only free lessons in technique and sight reading but also an initial grounding in harmony. The professor conceived a real affection for the little black boy and would play for him and talk of the great European masters, and particularly of the famous operas. In later years Joplin never forgot his first teacher and sent him occasional gifts of money up to the time the older man died.

As he entered adolescence, the quiet, gentle boy began more and more to dream of the day when his musical ability would banish his family's poverty forever. At the same time his father became increasingly insistent that he find work in a trade. It finally came to an issue and, fortified in his decision by the death of his mother, Scott, like so many Negro boys of his age and of his time, set out on his own. He was then in his early teens.

His natural ability found him ready employment in a period when itinerant musicians could land in any strange town, seek out the honkytonk district, and go right to work. Age made little difference; players from twelve to eighty were hired. There were no child-labor restrictions or welfare investigators in those uncensored days. Young Joplin wandered all over Texas, Louisiana, and the Mississippi Valley, a boy moving about in the midst of a teeming adult life. He gained experience, but, more than that, in an area that was the cradle of ragtime he heard hundreds of self-taught musicians and singers and a wealth of folk music. Later this was to be the basis of an unfailing melodic inspiration. His whole orbit of saloons, honkytonks, pool halls, poor restaurants, and the Forty-niner Camps—the traveling tent shows depicting the California gold-rush life and featuring the cancan dancer and the roulette wheel—was a world near the soil. Civil War songs, plantation melodies, jigs and reels, country dances, ballads, hollers, and work songs were still current coin for Scott to hoard.

At this impressionable, formative stage of his life these experiences were far more valuable than the *Gradus ad Parnassum* of any conservatory. For it was the American musical heritage in which Joplin, like the other early ragtime writers, was nurtured that made possible an American music. Moreover, that these pioneers were Negroes ensured—through the rhythms treasured and kept alive from far-away Africa—that this American music would be the music to be called ragtime.

Joplin was just seventeen when, in 1885, he landed for the first time in St. Louis, then a wide-open town in the full frontier sense. The old eighteenth-century French trading post had grown into a sprawling levee city that fronted a broad Mississippi swarming with rafts, keelboats, and mackinaws and dominated by the tall-stacked, majestic packets. At this apex of the river-boat age the levee apron rang with the chant of work songs, the first moaning measures of the levee blues, and the shouts of roustabouts coonjining to the plink-plank of banjos.

A first-hand description of the river workers is given in the memoirs of another great ragtimer, Ferdinand (Jelly Roll) Morton of New Orleans:

"I trucked cotton in a New Orleans levee camp. The fellows who trucked it were called longshoremen. The fellows who put bales in place were screwmen. These were permanent people. Made tremendous salaries. Around $18 a day, and that is way back.

"Another class on the levee are on river boats. Handled all kinds of things. They were called roustabouts. Weren't treated like other fellows. Had a captain over them with a whip or lash in their hands. I have never seen them whipped, but I have often heard they whipped them to keep them going. They would carry on their backs all kinds of things, big boxes of lard. Carried this stuff up the gang-planks. Looked like a man couldn't carry so much. Singing and moving to rhythm of songs as much as they could. People who works on a levee called levee camp people. There is nothing to do on a levee except when the city is in danger.

"Roustabouts would never dream of striking on river boats. They were just like in slavery. And on the other boats they were getting big money. Longshoremen didn't get as much as screwmen. I never heard of those guys quitting."

Industry thrived and money flowed up over the levee bank down into St. Louis, to gather like a golden pool in the Chestnut Valley sporting district around the bawdy houses and saloons of two notorious streets. It was on Chestnut and Market Streets that the professional gamblers waxed prosperous; that the madams piled up the gold their girls earned from rich cattlemen, traveling businessmen, and the idle, moneyed local sports. The money got around: the dapper, foppish "macks" or "sweet-back men" in their Stetsons, boxback coats, and St. Louis "flat" shoes got their gambling stakes from the girls.

These glittering thoroughfares were the heaven of the wandering musician. The joints rang with the archaic, jangling jig-piano syncopations that in only a few years would be a developed music to be dubbed ragtime. By 1899 it would be pleasantly tinkling in these two bawdy highways while on near-by Targee Street, as the legend goes, Allen (Johnny) Britt said to Frankie Baker: "Bye-Bye Babe, I was your man but I'm just gone," and Frankie pulled the trigger and then turned away, the smoking pearl-handled forty-four in her hand. Within a week the ragtime pianists would make a song of it and the pretty octoroons and the pimps would think up a hundred verses—many unprintable—for the district to sing:

> *Frankie and Johnny were lovers,*
> *Oh, lawdy how they could love;*
> *Swore to be true to each other,*
> *True as the stars above.*
> *He wos her man, but he done her wrong.*

> .   .   .

> *Eleven macks a-ridin' to the graveyard,*
> *All in a rubber-tired hack.*
> *Eleven macks a-ridin' to the graveyard,*
> *But only ten a-coming back.*
> *He was her man, but he done her wrong.*

In the center of all this, behind his bar at the Rosebud Cafe or seated at his upright piano, would be the one stable, unmovable figure in the whole licentious melee, Thomas Million Turpin, the tall, heavy, imperturbable Negro of the rough manner and the gentle heart. He was the man who in 1899 would count in the District, whether one meant music, liquor, or gambling. In his way he would be both patron and practitioner of the arts. His piano would seldom be silent. When not shaking under the force of his huge hands rolling out the rhythms of his rags, its strings would be yielding up the honkytonk chordings and rippling runs of every ragtime pianist worth his salt who was to be found in St. Louis. It would be then, too, that Scott Joplin would find his way to the Rosebud and Tom Turpin, and between them the two men would make a long friendship based on the quiet, rich generosity and the inward dignity that each possessed.

But in 1885, when Scott Joplin first came to St. Louis, Tom and his older brother Charlie were off in Nevada, trying their luck at mining. It would not be until 1894 that they would both be back home permanently and Tom would have set himself up at the Rosebud. In the meantime his father, "Honest John" Turpin, who ran the Silver Dollar, was the central figure in this world. It was to this place that Scott Joplin found his way.

For the next eight years St. Louis was a base of operations for Joplin. When he was not playing along Chestnut or Market Streets, he was somewhere near, at Hannibal, Columbia, Jefferson City, or Sedalia, across the river in East St. Louis, or perhaps as far north as Springfield or as far east as Cincinnati or Louisville. In 1892 the talk of the sporting element as well as the musicians turned constantly to the forthcoming World's Columbian Exposition at Chicago. When the fair opened, in 1893, pianists from all over the central United States converged on the amusement thoroughfare called the Midway, as well as the huge Chicago red-light district that extended from Eighteenth Street to Twenty-second and from Dearborn all the way to the Illinois Central tracks. Few were the players who went unemployed as the thousands of visitors poured into the Windy City, and all amusements, both licit and illicit, flourished.

Joplin formed a small band and went to work straight off in the District. During the exposition year he met the pioneer ragmen in Chicago, among them "Plunk" Henry, named for the banjo he had played earlier and from which he had derived his piano ragtime rhythms, and Johnny Seymour, a sensation in those days, who ten years or so later gave up playing to open a saloon that became the unofficial club of local and visiting piano-players.

It was in Chicago, also, that Scott made a new friend, Otis Saunders. Otis, deeply impressed by Joplin's original musical ideas, foresaw a great future for the Texas Negro. Otis became not only his close friend, but also for several years his unofficial adviser and quasi-manager. The exposition over, Saunders accompanied Joplin back to St. Louis, where both got playing jobs in the Tenderloin. Sometime in 1894 the two went to

41

Sedalia, and it was there that Joplin played with the Queen City Concert Band and also began to commit his musical ideas to paper. The latter marks an all-important transition. The young Texas pianist now became a composer.

The first written numbers to come from Joplin's pen are two waltz songs, *A Picture of Her Face* and *Please Say You Will*. Although there are no intimations here of the coming ragtime composer, it is not surprising that Scott should have begun with songs. For one thing, Joplin, like most other ragtime players of his day, was an entertainer too. They all sang and played, and with piano and voice as well as the harmonizing barber-shop groups from among their listeners they kept the dancers happy and furnished all the casual entertainment required by that generation.

At the end of the Victorian era sentimental songs were frequently requested, and this type of composition would appeal to Joplin as the most likely to achieve immediate publication. At the same time only a few isolated bars of syncopation in the real ragtime sense had as yet appeared in instrumental sheet music, and the unimaginative, average publisher could be expected to shy away from the novelty. As one old-timer says, "White or colored folk didn't even know how to write ragtime syncopation. A system had to be worked out before ragtime got to be published." Three years later in Chicago the ice was to be broken with the publication of *Mississippi Rag* by band-leader W. H. Krell, but 1894 was still too early for ragtime piano sheet music to appear.

The first Joplin songs are rather long—*A Picture of Her Face* runs for 120 measures—and, taken for what they are, have attractive melodies well harmonized. Joplin's lyrics cleave to the typical sentimental Victorian pattern. The chorus of *A Picture* belongs in the Americana collections of old obituary poems and the mourning pictures with weeping willows that were once constructed from locks of the dear departed's hair. The words quoted below evoke the maudlin sentimentality of a day that had not yet experienced the shock treatment of ragtime syncopation:

> *I've yet a treasure in this world*
> *A picture of her face,*

It brings joy to me when oftimes sad at heart.
Her picture I can see and sad thoughts then depart.
Although my love is dead, my only darling Grace,
My eyes are oftime looking on
A picture of—her—face.

The plunge into song-writing gave a new bent to the composer's efforts. It was in this period that Joplin organized a vocal harmonizing group, the Texas Medley Quartette, a double quartet or octet, with brother Will singing the tenor lead and Robert the baritone. Other members were John Williams, baritone; Leonard Williams, tenor; Emmett Cook (of the Queen City Concert Band), tenor; Richard Smith, bass; Frank Bledsoe, bass. Joplin himself sang solos with the group under his direction. The Medley Quartette sang in and around Sedalia, and by 1895 was booked on the early vaudeville circuits of Oscar Dame, of St. Louis, and the Majestic Booking Agency. They rendered plantation and popular medleys and plugged Joplin's new songs. Their first travels carried them as far east as Syracuse, New York, where Joplin sold the songs mentioned above. Both appeared in the same year (1895) in that city, *Please Say You Will* bearing the publisher's imprint of M. L. Mantell, and *A Picture* that of Leiter Bros.

Another tour in the same year carried the singers into Missouri, Kansas, Oklahoma, and Texas, where in mid-November, at the town of Temple, Joplin effected his next publications. These numbers, first essays at piano instrumentals, included *The Great Crush Collision March*, *Combination March*, and *Harmony Waltz*. The first bears the imprint of John R. Fuller, and the others that of Robert Smith, whose business connections are indicated by an international copyright and the name of "Chas. Sheard & Co. London" below his own.

The *Crush Collision March*, a period piece, is more of a descriptive overture than a march. A bombastic opening of descending octaves leads to three separate sixteen-measure themes, the last a trio, and each repeated. These are followed by a long section of thirty-two bars, consisting of two separate themes. The description of a railroad wreck is in the first part

43

of this last section. As heavy treble chords are played over a rapid running chromatic bass, the printed, between-the-lines description reads: "The noise of the trains while running at the rate of sixty miles per hour." Then: "Whistling for the crossing," with four-note treble discords, two long and two short; then "The train noise," followed once more by "Whistle before the collision," conveyed by four short, frantic discords higher up. Then comes "The collision," a heavy low double forte chord on the diminished seventh.

The closing theme is quietly pastoral. Cosmic peace is settling over the scene of carnage. The naïve description was suited to a public that only a few years later in sophisticated New York was thrilled beyond measure by Edison's film *The Great Train Robbery*. Nor is *Crush Collision* unduly remarkable for showing Joplin's acquaintance with light classics of the *Light Cavalry* and *William Tell* order, for the ragtime pianists were already "wowing" their audiences with syncopated renderings of the classics.

The notable feature of Joplin's *Collision March* is not even that it indicates in advance his later interest in opera. *Crush Collision* is to be remembered because the second and third themes, printed unsyncopated, cry out for syncopation when one plays them—almost "sound" syncopated in their regular meter. Unquestionably Joplin played this number in ragtime. Undoubtedly, also, the publisher shied at issuing it in that form. American publishers of popular music consistently stood in the way of good ragtime composers, their objections, somewhat later, centering on the difficulty of playing the really good numbers. Many a fine composition was discarded in its original form for a more salable, simpler version. Years later Joplin, recognizing this, was to write in his *School of Ragtime:* "That real ragtime of the higher class is rather difficult to play is a painful truth which most pianists have discovered."

The Texas Medley Quartette finished its tour in Joplin, Missouri—a tour that had been successful, at least in the fact that Joplin was now a published composer. The group disbanded and its members found various employments. Going into the local district, Scott found Otis Saunders working there, and the two decided to go to Sedalia together. Robert and Will followed later. This brings us to the point where, at the beginning of the previous chapter, we saw them alighting from the train at the Sedalia depot.

We can now turn to the pre-Sedalia story of John Stark, pioneer of the rough country roads and trails. Sooner told, perhaps, than Joplin's nomadic tale, it is in its own way fully as adventurous.

John Stillwell Stark was the son of Adin Stark and Eleanor Stillwell Stark. The Starks were both of early American stock, Irish in extraction. Adin had been born in 1795 in Shelby County, Kentucky, of Virginia-born parents; Eleanor Stillwell had been born in the same county four years later. Adin and Eleanor were married in 1818 and set up a home in Shelby County. Their children, as recorded in the Stark family Bible, were as follows:

Norborn Perry, son	*born February 5, 1819*
Etilmon Justus, son	" *May 5, 1820*
Mary Ann, daughter	" *May 5, 1822*
Dorothy Colin, daughter	" *May 14, 1824*
Arbelia Tyrene, "	" *July 4, 1826*
Effie Arcada, "	" *April 11, 1828*
Canadasa Ellen, "	" *April 25, 1830*
Atlantas America Livada, daughter	" *November 21, 1833*
Nancy Sardinia "	" *July 10, 1835*
Thomas P. Dudley, son,	" *August 15, 1838*
John Stillwell, "	" *April 11, 1841*
Lucinda C. J., daughter	" *January 2, 1844*

After the last entry is the notation in florid script: "Mother and child died at birth." Taylorville, where Eleanor and Lucinda are buried, is now the seat of Spencer County, which was split off from Shelby.

Effie Arcada was sixteen and already married when her mother died. She gave three-year-old John a home until he was six and then Etilmon rode on horseback to Kentucky down from Gosport, Indiana. The boy rode behind his older brother on the horse's blanketed rump all the way back. John lived on the farm and did rough farm work, and he got his log-cabin schooling during the days when the country politician

Abraham Lincoln was rising and the conscience of the North was becoming more and more troubled by slavery.

John Stark was not quite twenty-three years of age when on New Year's Day 1864 he joined the 1st Regiment of the Indiana Heavy Artillery Volunteers and was assigned as bugler to Captain William H. Blankenship's Company B. He was a fair, strongly muscled, blue-eyed youth, five and a half feet in height, as he went into his country's service. The Indiana Volunteers, moving right into New Orleans, which Federal General Butler had occupied early in the war, did garrison rather than combat duty for the duration of the war.

A widow by the name of Mrs. Casey was an almost daily visitor to the Volunteers' barracks, where she sold her home-made molasses cookies to the soldiers. Her children followed her as she went around with her wooden tray. It was thus that John Stark first saw Sarah Ann Casey, a beautiful, slender colleen, nearer thirteen years of age than fourteen. He fell in love with her, and married her in a parish church.

Sensibly enough, John Stark sent his child bride up through the Federal lines to Etilmon in Gosport, where she could complete her schooling in the log cabin where her husband had studied. As soon as John was honorably discharged, on January 10, 1866, he went north by river boat to join her.

Etilmon had prospered in Indiana. By this time his land holdings were more than 2,200 rich acres. John and Sarah Ann went to live on one of their brothers' farms. It was there in 1868 that the first son was born and christened with an old Anglo-Saxon family name, Etilmon, originally Ethelmonde, in honor of John's brother. The middle name of Justus is Biblical. One year later the three Starks set out for Missouri and virgin land in a brand-new Conestoga covered wagon. During weeks of hard travel John fished teeming streams and shot plentiful game for the food that Sarah Ann cooked over the campfires. At night, after the oxen were tethered off the rough trails, they slept with the baby in the wagon bed, John's Civil War rifle alongside.

Near Maysville, in northwestern Missouri, John Stark got his homestead, chopped trees, and built a log cabin. He then cleared his land and, behind his oxen, plowed the first furrows that had ever scarred the rich, dark soil. In 1870 a second son arrived, who was named William Paris, and John came in from the fields and added a little log and clay ell to the house. Nellie, named Eleanor for the mother whom John had lost in childhood, followed in 1872.

There were evenings, with the cattle lowing outside and the prairie wind rustling in the locust trees around the house, that the three children never forgot; evenings when the now bearded John Stark strummed the guitar and sang *Jump Jim Crow* and *Old Dan Tucker* from his memories of the white and Negro folk music he had heard in Shelby County as a child—and the hour before bed when Sarah Ann, still slenderly lovely with her blue eyes and raven-black hair, told them the fantastic Irish fairy stories of her own imagining that all her life she could make up on the spur of the moment.

Years of sun and snow had grayed the old house, and young Etilmon was just entering adolescence when John Stark's feet at length wearied of following the rough furrows behind his oxen, and he sold his farm. Moving to Cameron in northwest Missouri, he entered the then new business of ice-cream making. To supplement the trade the small town offered, Stark took to peddling his product around the countryside in his old wagon with the canvas top removed. He did so well that in a couple of years he moved about twenty miles east to the larger town of Chillicothe.

Stark soon built up a flourishing business in the new location. When he was pressing the saturation point in ice-cream sales, he cast about for a supplementary source of income to take better care of the growing needs of his family. He hit on an idea that fitted his role of country peddler. Whether he bought the first Jesse French cabinet organ that, covered like veiled sculpture with a tarpaulin, he loaded on the roomy Conestoga wagon bed is uncertain. One story has it that an enterprising traveling Jesse French drummer, cannily appraising Stark's salesmanship and the long route his wagon covered, got his factory to consign the first instrument to the country peddler.

In any event, John Stark carried the instrument around, browbeating and cajoling one customer after another until he sold it, and then he promptly got another, next a piano, then an organ, until in every other house on his route unwilling children were being driven to practice on the carved-walnut instrument in the best parlor, with, of course, Stark ice cream awaiting them when they finished their stint.

This sort of thing could not go on indefinitely. Stark had been in Chillicothe about two years when he realized one day that he had his foot in the back door of the music business and needed only to push the door. Chillicothe and its environs, however, had organs and pianos up to the neck. Stark needed a bigger field, and he looked over his adopted state. The town that caught his eye—not too big and not too small—was the railroad center of Sedalia, eighty miles south. There was, he found out, only one music store in Sedalia, Perry's, with plenty of people and money in this good payroll town left over to support another.

With Stark, thought and action were one. The old Conestoga made another trip as the five Starks moved again. It was around 1885 when the new company, called John Stark & Son to include fifteen-year-old William, moved into temporary quarters. In a few years there was a fine store in the spanking new Richardson-type Romanesque red-brick building at 514 Ohio Street. This bit of nepotism characteristically ensured that Will would go to work forthwith and would not strike out on his own. Etilmon was already studying violin and planning a career in music. In the years that followed, John Stark & Son planted its collective self firmly on the Sedalia map.

In 1895 his daughter Eleanor, who had shown unusual musical talent, left for Germany for study with Moskowski, not to return for two years. In the meantime Etilmon had become musical instructor at the Marmaduke Military Academy. Regular musical soirees, including piano quartets, were being held at the Stark store.

John Stark, ex-farmer, reveled in the new life. Discovering in himself a desire for learning and the arts, he read history and philosophy and embraced the classics of music. Particularly and always music was the thing he loved. At this period he was two men in one: the pioneer and the man of the

48

new cities, the farmer with folk music in his veins and the new man of culture with opera in his head. In five years more, in 1899, he was to meet a stranger whose music would unite these two men into one with a single purpose and give him, at fifty-eight, still another frontier to pioneer.

By 1894, the year that Scott Joplin first came to Sedalia, the Starks were in the middle of the picture, as a yellowed local newspaper clipping attests:

SERENADERS

Waking the Echoes
Of the Stilly Night
And Quiet Sleepers

In the night time, when nature is at rest, to be roused from pleasant dreams by a beautiful duet, between strong, well trained voices, is something which leaves a flavor of delight to the senses. A writer of the Gazette was thus pleasantly roused about 12 o'clock Friday night. A duet between Miss Nellie Stark and Mr. Ernest Clark, which was followed by one of Liszt's rhapsodies. A piano in a furniture van, brought from Stark's piano rooms, added immensely to the effect of the serenade.

By 1899 John Stark had become a grizzled man with the rounded beard and heavy mustache typical of the day. The beard, however, went unnoticed by those who met him because his face was so completely dominated by his intense blue eyes, piercing and intelligent, under the large, full brow. John Stark seemed to others a huge man; only after his death did most people realize that he was comparatively short. His inner stature made him seem tall and commanding. For all his good humor and his Irish imagination, there was no nonsense about him. He was forthright, honest, and forceful, with no compromise in his nature. For all his farm beginnings, no one would have called him a "rube" or thought of calling him a "city slicker." All in all, not only was John Stark a respected figure of the community; he was very much a man.

And this brings us to the turn of events.

It was, as we have seen, late in the summer of 1899 that

Stark met Scott Joplin at the Maple Leaf Club and heard the rag named after it. It was in their conference next day at the music store that Stark bought the number for fifty dollars and royalties to the composer—good terms for that time. The number was printed by Westover in St. Louis and in late September went on sale, without benefit of advertising, over the Stark counters. The only promotion was by Joplin himself, who played it for customers, his smooth fingers making its intricacies sound like child's play. The tuneful, irresistible number, with the new syncopation, which in those first days was like an intoxicant, took hold immediately.

In its first dozen or so years the *Maple Leaf Rag* sold hundreds of thousands of copies—a phenomenal sale for the early years of this century, before music publishing had organized itself into a big business. But the first six months' sale was enough to decide John Stark's next move: to the big time, to metropolitan St. Louis. The Starks went by train on that particular day. Left behind was the ancient Conestoga. "It had been a good old wagon but it done broke down."

The complete score of MAPLE LEAF RAG *follows. The cover here reproduced is that of the original Sedalia edition (1899).*

Maple Leaf Rag

COMPOSED BY

SCOTT JOPLIN.

PRICE 50¢

SEDALIA, Mo.
PUBLISHED BY
JOHN STARK & SON.

PERMISSION TO USE THE ABOVE PICTURE KINDLY GRANTED BY THE AMERICAN TOBACCO CO. MANUFACTURERS OF OLD VIRGINIA CHEROOTS BY WHOM IT IS COPYRIGHTED.

MAPLE LEAF RAG.

BY SCOTT JOPLIN.

Tempo di marcia.

TRIO.

Chapter 3

RAGTIME AT THE ROSEBUD

Wᴴᴇɴ John Stark and his family moved to St. Louis, the ragtime craze was already sweeping the whole country. The big publishers, East, North, and West, were leaping on the ragtime bandwagon, with a flood of rags and pseudo-rags and old unsyncopated schottisches, quadrilles, and marches republished with the word "ragtime" hastily overprinted on cover or title page. Obscure little publishers and small-town music stores all through the Middle West were getting out rags written by local talent or by itinerant players who chanced to be around. John Stark in Sedalia had been only one of these.

This localized activity, part of the small-business "rugged individualism" of that day, was similar to the beginnings of the motion-picture and the phonograph industries and to the first days of the automobile, when any small-town buggy-maker could scrape a few hundred dollars together and forthwith place a new brand of horseless carriage on the market. Today, of course, all of these businesses are centralized in a few hands, and with their heavy capital have a stranglehold on distribution outlets. The newcomer, the little man with ambition, an idea, and little else, can scarcely break in. The big boys of today—in music business as in the other industries—are themselves mainly the few early operators who survived the bitter battle of attrition and are now in the saddle.

Ragtime carried the folk music of frontier days over into the newly developing urban life and the beginnings of sophistication. It is our folk music made the basis of a national music. It began inevitably, at a time when the picture of dancing plantation Negroes and the westbound pioneers plunking banjos and singing around the campfire was fading, and the new one of the bustling town, the clanging trolley, and the gaslit variety or continuation house was brightening in its place.

Joplin's *Maple Leaf Rag* is only one of scores of richly folksy rags that got published only because this little-man regional enterprise was still possible in that day. But *Maple Leaf* was the one incomparable fusion of folk music and learned music, of prairie and town, and it remains so fifty years after its first copies, damp from the presses, appeared on the Stark sales counters in Sedalia.

As John Stark in 1900 settled his family at 3848 Washington Boulevard, *Maple Leaf* already had made him potentially the leading ragtime publisher of the country. *Maple Leaf* bought for him a printing plant at 3615 Laclede Avenue. During the first year, as the copies rolled off the small hand press that John and William operated, the money rolled in and new rags were bought and published. It was an auspicious start for a man beginning a new business in a new city at what was then considered an advanced age. Some years later, in his seventies, John Stark wrote with wry humor in a letter to the *Rag Time Review:* "There is an impression that old men should be chloroformed at sixty."

The next rag to go on the Stark presses was Arthur Marshall's cakewalk, with its trio by Joplin. This trio is conceived with taste and sympathy to set off perfectly Arthur's songlike cakewalk themes, with their real Missouri feeling. *Swipesy Cakewalk* appeared in 1900 bearing the two composers' names. The cover design and the name came about in the casual way in which many rags got their titles. The publisher's shoes were frequently shined by a little Negro boy of the neighborhood, and Stark had him brought in and photographed. His likeness appears in the center of the cover. The bashful head hanging down suggested to Stark the look of someone who had just filched some cookies, so he said: "Let's call it Swipesy."

Joplin's last step before leaving Sedalia was to marry Belle Hayden, a widow and Scott Hayden's sister-in-law. Immediately after the ceremony they went on to St. Louis and took quarters at 2658-A Morgan Street, where they remained until 1903. There Joplin's life took a new pattern, one more to his liking than that of traveling the honkytonk circuit and more in accord with the seriousness of his nature. He withdrew from active participation in the sporting world, though he maintained his friendships and his contacts. Partly supported by the *Maple Leaf* royalties, as he was henceforth to be by his various compositions, he was able to set up as a teacher. He supplemented the earnings from these two activities by making his residence into a boarding and rooming house, though to what degree this was profitable is unknown because the musician tenants "at liberty" were never pressed to pay. Scott Hayden came from Sedalia in 1901 with his wife, who had been Nora Wright, and joined the Joplin menage.

One of the finest of all ragtime compositions was completed in Sedalia before Joplin's marriage to Belle Hayden and their moving to St. Louis. This is the *Sunflower Slow Drag*, a collaboration with Scott Hayden. John Stark wrote: "This piece came to light during the high temperature of Scott Joplin's courtship, and while he was touching the ground only in the highest places, his geese were all swans, and Mississippi water tasted like honey-dew. . . . If ever there was a song without words, this is that article; hold your ear to the ground while someone plays it, and you can hear Scott Joplin's heart beat."

Joplin helped Hayden complete the composition, supplying at least one theme and the introduction, as he had done with Marshall. The trio, striking the ear with a singular freshness in a different key from the preceding strains, is unquestionably Joplin's work. It is incomparably and infectiously melodious and has the light-footed lilt that is the hallmark of the Joplin trio. Like the folksong that it really is, it haunts the memory for days after it is heard. Hayden's themes, rhythmic and full of melody, fit to perfection with this section.

The year 1901, with five numbers published, demonstrated the success of *Maple Leaf* and signified Joplin's new position as the composer to be reckoned with in ragtime. *Sunflower Slow Drag* appeared; and *Peacherine Rag*, *The Easy Winners*, *Augustan Club Waltzes*, and a song, *I'm Thinking of My Pickanniny Days*, to words by Henry Jackson, appeared under Joplin's name. The instrumentals were Stark publications, but the song was issued by the small St. Louis house of Thiebes-Stierlin. This release by another house incidentally makes doubtful the story—not corroborated by Stark's descendants—that Joplin signed a five-year contract with John before leaving Sedalia. The song, which received little distribution and less notice is a beautifully harmonized folk melody somewhat in the Stephen Foster vein.

Easy Winners is a lovely and typical Joplin rag, its first three themes full of cakewalk feeling, the second with an effective upward run of sixths on the diminished seventh. The fourth theme, in heavy chords, shows what Joplin absorbed from the honkytonk "fakers." It rocks with the rhythms called "barrel house," and its chord groups are like the inventions of the self-taught itinerants. An unusual feature is the use of the same ending for both the trio and the final theme.

Although Joplin could now withdraw from active participation, the tempo of sporting life in the St. Louis District was speeding toward the crescendo it would reach during the 1904 World's Fair. Tom Turpin still ruled the red-light roost, his activities including gambling at his Rosebud Cafe at 2220 Market Street, and a "hotel" upstairs. The Rosebud had a bar in the front, and this, as well as the wine room in the back, dispensed liquor. The wine room, accessible from the bar or through the side "family entrance," was where the sports and the girls gathered around the piano to hear Turpin's strong playing as well as the ragtime of many others. This room was the established rendezvous for every St. Louis or visiting pianist. The hottest sessions, however, witnessed only by the musicians themselves, generally took place in the parlor of Mother Johnson's' house, across the street from the Rosebud. Sam Patterson, one of the younger players at that time, recalls that "Turpin would give her a half-dollar for the use of her piano to hear some new fellow that had just come to town play, and this would last for three or four hours. There was sure to be a 'cutting' contest between him and some St. Louis boy. Maybe it would be New York and St. Louis get together and play it out. *There* were two different ragtime styles!" All of this centered in Turpin, who had pioneered syncopated piano in the Missouri metropolis and was ragtime patriarch there, as Joplin had been at Sedalia.

The Hunting and Shooting Club, within the Rosebud, was the sanctum of a select group who liked the outdoor life as well as the indoor variety. This room smelled of leather and tobacco. Its walls were covered with hunting trophies, fishing pictures, and well-filled gun racks. In the corner a huge Morris chair, with a spittoon near by, was Turpin's throne. There was not even a piano in this cubicle of monkish withdrawal.

About a block from the Rosebud, in an alley between Chestnut and Market Streets, the Turpins had a small shack called the Hurrah Sporting Club. This, a more private rendezvous for members of the Hunting and Shooting Club and their guests, had a piano, but for drinks the boys had to repair to the Rosebud. The old photograph of the Hurrah Club that we print was taken in those years. The brilliant and ill-fated young pianist Louis Chauvin sits in the center in the place of honor, with Tom's brother Charlie, president of the club, at his left, and Sam Patterson standing just behind Charlie. The boy of eight or nine in the snapshot is "Little Goat," already a talented player and because of this a junior member of the club. Seated at the far right, holding a dog between his knees, is Charlie Warfield. Hangers-on, a Pullman porter, the excellent guitarist Clarence Holden (standing to the right of Warfield), and an assortment of gamblers complete the group.

"Those fellows had money," says Sam Patterson. "We used to go hunting four and five times a winter, even way up in Michigan. We sent a man in advance, like a show, to arrange where we would sleep and eat. I never saw such food in my life: chicken, turkey, stews, ham, and venison, everything on the table."

A great new generation of St. Louis pianists had arisen since

Scott Joplin had last stayed there six years before. They were all about of an age. Joe Jordan, born in Cincinnati, was eighteen in 1900; Sam Patterson, St. Louis born, but whose father was from Cincinnati, was nineteen. There were the Moore brothers, Bob and John, and "Klondike," a fine player just back empty-handed from the gold fields. There was Charlie Warfield, from Tennessee, who had come to St. Louis in 1897 at fourteen; last, but most gifted of them all, was young Louis Chauvin, sometimes called "Bird Face," who was then only seventeen, and who had been born next door to the Patterson house on Lucas Avenue of a Spanish-Indian father from Mexico and a Missouri-born Negro mother. The slight, light-skinned Chauvin, whose features were only faintly Negro and as Indian as they were Spanish, left only three published musical compositions and not a single phonograph record when he died in 1908, and yet those still alive who knew Louis Chauvin remember his playing as if they had heard it yesterday. Scores of players prominent in those first two decades of ragtime are recalled but dimly if at all, but the playing of this genius who died a mere boy was of such startling beauty and originality, so rich in feeling, that it has never been forgotten by players whose byword was technical brilliance. Although impractical Louis Chauvin failed to get his many beautiful compositions published, the impress of his style, personality, and fertile musical ideas was left on every player and composer in St. Louis in those days when the Missouri metropolis was the fountainhead of classical ragtime.

Sam Patterson, Chauvin's boyhood friend, who knew him best of all, has among his mementos only Louis's picture from all the St. Louis ragtime players whom he knew. It hangs in the midst of the pictures of Sam's own family. "He had lots of original tunes of his own—never had names for them," says Sam. "He would sit right down and compose a number with three or four strains. By tomorrow it's gone and he's composing another. You can talk about harmony—no one could mistake those chords. Chauv was so far ahead with his modern stuff, he would be up to date now.

"As a boy I thought I was some peanuts, but I knew then I

would not be the artist Chauv was. I had lessons, and he taught himself. When he was thirteen you never heard anything like him. When he would first sit down he always played the same Sousa march to limber up his fingers, but it was his own arrangement with double-time contrary motion in octaves, like trombones and trumpets all up and down the keyboard. . . . And Chauv had so many tricks, my God, that boy!"

Sam and Louis both went to Alexander Dumas Grade School and then to Sumner High. When Patterson left school at fifteen, Chauvin, who did not like school, quit. This was in his freshman year, when he was thirteen. In the summer of that same year Sam and Louis were already on the road with a company called the Alabama Jubilee Singers. Together with spirituals—*Go Down, Moses* was a favorite with their audiences —the company featured variety, and the two boys did a straight-comedy act. Sam had a song in between while Chauvin quick-changed into a dress, and then the two did a cakewalk as a finish. "Chauvin looked good in that dress and wig," Patterson remembers. The Jubilee Singers traveled from St. Louis through three months of one-nighters to western New York State, where they appeared at the Buffalo Roof Garden, upstairs over a brewery.

Both boys rapidly became expert entertainers. Chauvin had a fine tenor voice and sang and danced superbly, buck and wing, regular and eccentric tap. Only a little later, back in St. Louis, they helped to form a vocal quartet. Known as the Mozart Comedy Four, of which Chauvin was first tenor and Patterson second, this group, which alternated straight arrangements from light opera with comedy routines, made a great success around St. Louis. It had many different tenors because Chauvin and Patterson would leave for other dates, but their places were open for them whenever they returned.

Louis and Sam, like Joe Jordan, were already in the District in their teens, and it was in these surroundings, where he could play as he wished, that Louis Chauvin developed. All of the boys had come under the early guidance of Tom Turpin. Tom's playing was the standard by which all other playing was judged. He would play the first strain of his *Harlem Rag* in C, the next in G, and then the trio in F, with lightning two- and three-chord modulations from key to key. Again Sam is talking: "I only played the style of rags that Tom Turpin wrote. Chauvin didn't play that style—he would change them. He could play anything he heard, but he put things in harder keys than they came in. If it was in C, Chauvin put it in B. Turpin was great, but Chauvin could do things that Turpin couldn't touch. He had speed fingering and he tossed off octaves overhand. But when I think of him, it's the music I remember, and not the skill."

In the four years before the Louisiana Purchase Exposition opened in St. Louis, Chauvin and Patterson shuttled back and forth between show business and playing the tonks. Each was finding in one or the other of these worlds the one in which he wished henceforth to move.

The two formed the team of Chauvin and Patterson, with Sam in blackface and Chauvin playing straight. When Louis tried the burnt cork make-up, he proved such a natural comedian that the roles were switched. Then Williams and Walker came to town and repaired one night after hours to Turpin's Rosebud, where the boys put on their act for the two great comedians. Word of the praise these leaders of the Negro show world had given them got around, and local bookings opened up like magic. Charlie Turpin had his tent show at that time in the vacant lot on which his Booker T. Washington Theater was later built. There the new act, with its rapid-fire routine of two-piano work, original duet songs, comedy, and dancing was a grand success. They played the parks, and chautauquas in and around town. There is every reason to believe Sam's opinion that the two friends could have gone a long way together in the legitimate entertainment world.

Joe Jordan tells of a semiprofessional musical group that formed at this time the piano and vocal quartet that included Tom Turpin, Chauvin, Patterson, and himself. To imagine this gifted group at four pianos working out on *Maple Leaf*, Turpin's new *Rag Time Nightmare*, one of Chauvin's originals, or doing a richly accompanied "coon shout" is to regret that it never reached the phonograph record. This quartet and the Chauvin-Patterson piano-vocal duo made occasional appearances at the clubs and even at a number of church socials.

On the instrumental side, neither individual ragtime players nor groups such as these restricted themselves to ragtime. Light classical overtures were played straight with precise spacing and beautiful counterpoint, and marches were either rendered "legitimately" or syncopated in the way that Buddy Bolden's ragtime band was concurrently playing them at tough old Masonic Hall in New Orleans. And there were the concert waltzes, dreamy and slow in the age-old fashion of these pieces, and the ragtime waltzes, tantalizing in their syncopation of three-quarter time, later merging into the hesitation waltz, but a lost art today. The ragtimers' repertory, finally, included descriptive overtures. These prefigured the early photoplay interpretation of the nickelodeon pianos, which grew, in the picture palaces of the 1920's, into their great console organs rising from the floor.

Sam Patterson was a champion at the cakewalk, and the opponent he was always coming up against was huge two-hundred-pound, six-foot-two Dan Washington, now living in Harlem. "He was an artist," Sam says, "but I used to beat him because I was little." Whenever Sam entered a cakewalk tournament he could count on the support of Chauvin. Louis would tear himself away from his fair friends in the District and would be at the back windows "even at the Coliseum, which was big as Madison Square Garden." There he would slip Sam a white carnation for his buttonhole, always neglecting to bring flowers for Patterson's lady partner. Sam was puzzled why he never came into the dressing-room until Chauvin explained that his first attempt had been rebuffed by the stage doorman. Little Louis had said: "I'm Sam Patterson's partner," and the reply was: "Sure, and I'm William Jennings Bryan."

In 1903, when Sam was twenty-two, and Chauvin barely twenty, they published their first and only joint composition, one of the three examples of Chauvin's handiwork that survive. The publication was a purely incidental thing in a way that was typical of the show business of that day. The two inseparable friends joined forces in writing the score and sketchy story for a musical show. *Dandy Coon* was a frank imitation of the early type of Williams and Walker show. Joe Jordan acted as musical and stage director of the project, and the three went into the District for several hectic weeks with the avowed purpose of earning enough in tips to produce it. They then assembled and rehearsed a cast of thirty-odd that included a beautiful octoroon chorus, and hopefully set out. It was in Des Moines that they finally stranded. "We nearly walked back to St. Louis," says Sam, "but then Chauv and I took a song of ours into a music store and sold it. We jumped a train before the others found out. Of course," he adds, "the song wasn't one from the show, but another one of ours."

Bearing the names of Chauvin and Patterson, *The Moon Is Shining in the Skies* came out the same year with the imprint of the Des Moines store of S. Z. Marks. The piece died quickly with this local appearance. As it survives in the filed copies in the Copyright Division in Washington, it is a pretty little song with ragtime verse and chorus in waltz tempo, revealing Chauvin's haunting chord sequences and his individual flair for melody.

Despite all these varied activities, Chauvin kept returning to the sporting district. There was the life that appealed to him. This was the only world open to a Negro that approximated the true bohemian life his nature needed, which was open only to white artists. That life, typical of Paris, could exist in fact, even in the American white society of that period, only in centers like New York and Chicago and a few cosmopolitan cities like New Orleans and San Francisco.

The lurid little inner sphere of bawdy houses and wine rooms was the doomed Bohemia of the gifted boy Chauvin and scores of his dark-skinned fellow artists. The madams were practical patrons of the growing ragtime art even though their interest in music might be nonexistent. While Dvořák and a few American intellectuals carried on their unworldly debates on American Negro music, the madams, their girls, and their patrons gave these men a home that, however shoddy, was lively, warm, and sympathetic.

When Lulu White, mulatto proprietress of a famed house on Basin Street in New Orleans, came to visit her friend Madam Betty Rae in St. Louis, she heard Chauvin and Patterson play.

"Lulu wanted us both to come down to play Mahogany Hall," says Sam, "but we were making enough money in St. Louis. In those days a good meal cost a quarter and a fine tailor-made suit twenty-five dollars. With ten to twenty a night in tips, a piano-player had more than he could spend so long as he didn't gamble or play the ponies. Lots of players didn't even bother to work except when they felt in the mood or needed a few dollars, and the pimps were so well taken care of by their girls they practically stopped working at all."

Madam Mame de Ware, with her two houses, one with colored girls and one with white, Countess Willie V. Piazza, "Ready Money," "The Suicide Queen," and their sisters all over the country did something for ragtime, in any event, while all the conservatories and composers in the whole civilized world did nothing then. Ex-peddler John Stark, too, with his hand press on Laclede, did more to save a true American music than was ever done by the whole music industry, which was later to be such a powerful enemy of the true musical values Stark stood for.

But the underworld *was* a doomed Bohemia for those who remained in it. If the whorehouse and saloon provided a haven for unrecognized genius, they provided the lotus, too. It was easy—too easy—just to drift. This was no Bohemia the artists themselves had made; it offered refuge more than incentive, and only the most hardy and clear-sighted ambition could survive in it or summon the strength to break from it as Joplin had eagerly done the moment that opportunity offered. In this world where all was transient, the reality of music was pretty likely to fade even for a man whose whole life it had been. And so it was with Louis Chauvin, whose gift was the brightest of all.

When the World's Fair opened in 1904, Sam Patterson lured Chauvin momentarily from his women and from the District. They worked on the Pike at a beer-hall and restaurant concession called Old St. Louis, owned by a Chicago brewery. They played their two-piano rags and made up a vocal trio with the baritone of the old Mozart Quartet days. But at the fair's end Chauvin slipped back into Easy Street. It is likely, indeed, that he was unable to cope with any other world.

61

Two years later Chauvin moved to the Chicago District. Earlier in 1906 Sam Patterson had left St. Louis for good with a new act, the Five Musical Spillers. Outwardly Chauvin seemed still the boy whom Sam described earlier, "about five feet five and never over 145 pounds. He looked delicate with his fine features and his long, tapering fingers, but he was wild and strong. He never gambled, but he stayed up, drank, and made lots of love. He loved women, but he treated them like dirt. He always had two or three. He loved whisky, too, but he only seemed to be living when he was at the piano. It's authentic, I guess, that he smoked opium at the last."

Chauvin was still a boy when a life that was meant only for hardened men caught up with him at last. The Tenderloin was a deadly mistress. On March 26, 1908, at St. Luke's Hospital, Louis Chauvin, like a Thomas Chatterton of ragtime, came to the blank end of his Easy Street. He had been in Chicago for five months, had even played for a short while at Pony Moore's club at Twenty-second and Dearborn. But the blight had struck deep. He was at the hospital for twenty-three days, but shortly after his arrival there he sank into a coma from which he never awakened.

The old friendship and the memory of a music that only Chauvin ever made are still strong with Sam Patterson as he loyally says: "Chauvin died of 'complications.' Joplin wired me that Chauvin was dead while I was at Keith's Jersey City. It was the week of April 20th. We could have gone places together—farther than I've ever gone alone. But Chauvin wouldn't bother to read music—he had a couple of women, always had money, never wanted for anything. I told him I was going to branch out and I would be glad to help him. But he liked the tonks, never really wanted to leave it. When I tell you that, I wonder why he ever moved to Chicago."

The red lights cast dark shadows. But the time was coming when they were to be snuffed out like evil candles and when the districts one by one were to close. When New Orleans' Storyville was shuttered in 1917, it was one of the last to go. For years after, however, Lulu White's Mahogany Hall stood, a lonely Basin Street survivor at the edge of a modern housing development that had replaced the old bagnios, saloons, and cribs. Mahogany Hall was suffered to stay on to be used as a department-store warehouse. In 1950 it became altogether useless and was torn down.

The *New Orleans Item* wrote the Basin Street obit with some nostalgia, but with the clear eye of mid-century made the indictment that must stand against the warehouses of love where the Negro pianists had come to play their ragtime and improvise masterpieces a thousandfold that echoed, all of them, away into oblivion with the popping corks and the forgotten laughter:

"Basin Street—a product of Victorian hypocrisies, of the double standard of morality—gave employment to some marvelous and unique musicians like Jelly Roll Morton, Buddy Bolden, King Oliver and Louis Armstrong. There were houses like Lulu's Mahogany Hall where string trios and small jazz combinations produced one of the most vital and creative periods of the art. And perhaps, in sustaining . . . a powerful and colorful musical language it contributed more to the world than it took away.

"But the misery-breeding side of life was there, and perhaps it is best that it not be forgotten in the re-telling of old legends. This was in the days before '606'—'Salvarsan'—'the silver bullet'—a great German doctor's discovery of a way to administer silver solution to human body to kill the syphilis germ. It was long before the 'one-shot' penicillin treatments and government V.D. stations.

"It was a day when victims of the shadow-plague walked the streets of New Orleans and other great cities, living corpses, eyelids dropping in early paralysis, hands and body shaking with a palsy not caused by old age. It was a day when young sports decayed and died of the 'rales.' The younger generation hardly knows the word today. But old-timers remember it well."

Truly, as the *Item* writer, Thomas Sancton, concluded, "That's the debit side of the old legend that one has to balance against the color, the humor, and the power and glory of the music that came out of it all."

Chapter 4

A GUEST OF HONOR

THE quick success of the *Maple Leaf Rag* enabled
Scott Joplin to leave the hectic life of honkytonk player for the
quieter labors of teaching and composition. Although *Original
Rags* had brought him an agreeable local fame in Sedalia, its
sale to Hoffman in Kansas City had been outright. The opportunity to enter a new life both congenial and in line with
Scott's ambition was due to the generous royalty arrangement
that he had consummated with John Stark. It should be
observed that such an arrangement, a matter of course today,
was one highly unusual for 1899, as a contract between a
white businessman and a Negro. For many years, in fact, the
gifted Negroes who created ragtime were considered the legitimate prey of every unscrupulous tune-thief, and the publisher who bought a fine composition free and clear for a
ten-dollar bill was apt to consider himself more philanthropist
than opportunist. Theirs was the old Spanish proverb: "Take
what you want and pay for it, says God." This practice is at
least rarer and more covert today.

Scott Joplin, however, was fortunate to be dealing with a
John Stark. By 1903 he was able to buy a thirteen-room house
in a good neighborhood at 2117 Lucas Avenue, only eight

blocks from the birthplace of Chauvin and the boyhood home of Sam Patterson. In the St. Louis city directories of that period Joplin is listed as a music teacher.

He came to St. Louis in 1900, not as just another itinerant, however gifted, but as the man who wrote the *Maple Leaf Rag*. A new generation of pianists who had never even seen Joplin had gathered around Tom Turpin in the preceding six years. Theirs were the standards of the player; their heroes the "dispensers" who won the cutting contests. Although Tom, the leader, by 1900 had himself published the notably successful *Harlem Rag* as well as the *Bowery Buck* and *Ragtime Nightmare*, the piano kings of Market Street ruled by virtue of their keyboard proficiency. So when word got around of the arrival of this new paragon, every eye turned to him with curiosity and the natural Missouri "show me" challenge.

But Joplin disappointed them all by going into the seclusion of writing and teaching. Rare were his visits to the haunts "down the line." It seems not to have occurred to him that the disappointment of some and the envy of others would come out as a rumor that he was dodging competition. Joplin could derive satisfaction from fame, but not from inspiring envy. His natural drive was to work for the music he loved, not only through his own efforts but by assisting other talents. Nor did he ever intentionally make an enemy. An old friend says: "Scott never hurt anybody. A kitten could knock him down. He wasn't much socially, but most everyone had a lot of respect for Scott because he never threw himself away."

Lesser men, of course, started the whispers. Tom Turpin understood Joplin, and the two became colleagues, not rivals. Chauvin too was inherently generous, and secure, besides, in his own large creative powers. Natural bonds of affection and respect grew among these three men. But some of the insecure smaller men, even those of great playing ability who were nevertheless short on creative ideas, were consumed by an envy that had to be concealed.

The point of attack was Joplin's playing—a supple, legato, singing style of moderate tempo, thoroughly musical and suited to his rags. In St. Louis a new cosmopolitan style had arisen that featured a staccato speed technique and brilliant

65

display. Among the new St. Louis men Chauvin was almost unique in retaining the legato cantilena with virtuoso tempos. So it came about that many seized every opportunity to cajole Joplin into playing and then took delight in publicly topping him. Their favorite stunt was to get him to play his own *Maple Leaf*, and then display their own "variations" taken at a ruinously breakneck speed. It is strange that all of this should have disturbed Joplin so deeply, but he came from the playing school himself, and he took it harder than anyone knew; how hard, indeed, is shown by the line his new compositions took.

The drive for a ragtime classicism that could compare with the seriousness of the best of European music becomes evident in this period. The classicism that in *Original Rags* and *Maple Leaf* had already lifted folk melody to a serious, syncopated level was stimulated vastly by these public humiliations. Joplin's answer was an "I'll show you." The net result, however, was that of an acceleration of his own natural tendencies.

The year 1902, signalized by Stark's publication of four delightful rags—*A Breeze from Alabama*, the *Elite Syncopations*, *The Strenuous Life*, and *The Entertainer*, as well as *Cleopha Two Step* and the 6/8 *March Majestic*—is the notable year in which Scott Joplin revived an earlier first essay in a longer ragtime form. This is *The Rag Time Dance*. Joplin had completed the revision of *Rag Time Dance* in April, when W. H. Carter, editor of the *Sedalia Times*, who some years before had deplored the "piano-thumping" on Main Street, visited St. Louis. Carter published the following article upon his return:

OUR TRIP TO THE WORLD'S FAIR CITY

The editor and publisher of the TIMES spent Monday and Tuesday in St. Louis and while there called on . . . Mr. Scott Joplin, who is gaining a world's reputation as the Rag Time King. Mr. Joplin is only writing, composing and collecting his money from the different music houses in St. Louis, Chicago, New York and a number of other cities. Among his numbers that are largely in demand in the above cities are the *Maple Leaf Club* [note the editorial slip], *Easy Winners*, *Rag Time Dance* and *Peach-*

erine, all of which are used by the leading players and orchestras.

A little later Carter wrote:

"The TIMES was the first Sedalia paper to begin giving Mr. Joplin a public boom as a Negro composer of the catchy music known as 'Rag Time.' Among the first was the *Maple Leaf Rag* which was named after a social club in our city. . . . The next was the *Sunflower Slow Drag* which was and is now a great favorite among Sedalians. . . ."

Nothing succeeds, it is said, like success, and anyway Carter's change of heart may in no small measure have been caused by an article that had appeared in the *St. Louis Globe-Democrat*, of Sunday, June 7, 1903. Written by Monroe H. Rosenfeld, a prominent Tin Pan Alley tunesmith of New York, it had this to say:

"St. Louis boasts of a composer of music, who despite the ebony hue of his features and a retiring disposition, has written possibly more instrumental successes than any other local composer. His name is Scott Joplin, and he is better known as 'The King of Rag Time Writers' because of the many famous works in syncopated melodies which he has written. He has, however, also penned other classes of music and various local numbers of note.

"Scott Joplin was reared and educated in St. Louis. His first notable success in instrumental music was the *Maple Leaf Rag* of which thousands and thousands of copies have been sold. A year or two ago Mr. John Stark, a publisher of this city and father of Miss Eleanor Stark, the well known piano virtuoso, bought the manuscript of *Maple Leaf* from Joplin. Almost within a month from the date of its issue this quaint creation became a byword with musicians and within another half a twelfthmonth, circulated itself throughout the nation in vast numbers. This composition was speedily followed by others of a like character. Until now the Stark list embraces nearly a score of the Joplin effusions. Following is a list of some of

67

the more pronounced pieces by this writer, embodying these oddly titled works:

> *Elite Syncopations*
> *A Strenuous Life*
> *The Rag Time Dance*
> *Sunflower Slow Drag*
> *Swipesy Cake Walk*
> *Peacherine Rag*
> *Maple Leaf Rag*

"Probably the best and most euphonious of his latter day compositions is *The Entertainer*. It is a jingling work of a very original character, embracing various strains of a retentive character which set the foot in spontaneous action and leave an indelible imprint on the tympanum.

"Joplin's ambition is to shine in other spheres. He affirms that it is only a pastime for him to compose syncopated music and he longs for more arduous work. To this end he is assiduously toiling upon an opera, nearly a score of the numbers of which he has already composed and which he hopes to give an early production [in] this city."

Such a discerning account by a writer of ordinary "pops" may be read with interest. There are just two errors in the article. Joplin, of course, was not from St. Louis any more than, as Editor Carter now claimed, he was from Sedalia. The other error, as we shall see, refers to the opera on which Joplin was working. In it he did not eschew syncopation; on the contrary, the entire work was based on this rhythmic idea.

But to return to Joplin's completion of the *Rag Time Dance*, it was not easy to get John Stark to undertake the expensive publication. The number was conceived as a sort of folk ballet with narrative soloist and choreography based on the popular dances of the day. The entire piece, filling nine printed pages, requires more than twenty minutes to perform. Some of Joplin's most beautiful work is embedded in this score. The words describe the dance routines, as the narrator incites the dancing couples to more and more inspired efforts:

Let me see you do the "rag time dance,"
Turn left and do the "cake walk prance,"
Turn the other way and do the "slow drag"—

Now take your lady to the World's Fair
And do the "rag time dance."

Let me see you do the "clean up dance,"
Now you do the "Jennie Cooler dance,"
Turn the other way and do the "slow drag"—

Now take your lady to the World's Fair
And do the "rag time dance."

While Stark held back, the composer set energetically about the task of converting him. Three years earlier, in Sedalia, after selling *Maple Leaf*, Joplin had financed a public performance of the *Rag Time Dance* at Wood's Opera House. A number of girls executed the dances, and his brother Will sang the vocal part, which is derived from the old-time "caller of the figgers," while Joplin conducted the small orchestra in a country Mozartean style from the piano. It was then too early to sell such an ambitious project to Stark, though it is possible that, had Nell Stark been in Sedalia at the time, she would have got him to accept it. For it was Nell, brilliant, rising young concert pianist, who convinced Stark in St. Louis. Joplin re-presented it for the Starks privately, played by an orchestra made up of Lije (Elijah) Cross and the Vassar Boys. The handwritten orchestral parts represented weeks of unremitting labor by Joplin and painstaking copy work by Arthur Marshall. Nell responded immediately and with enthusiasm to the beautiful and rhythmic music so pungent of their common native soil.

Somewhat against his will—and sales justified his pessimism —John Stark published the *Rag Time Dance*. Three years later he recouped a part of this loss by issuing a condensed instrumental version of the number. But sales or not, the original *Rag Time Dance* score remains to this day as a proof of Joplin's ability to think in terms other than that of the short instrumental rag piece.

69

In the year 1903 the St. Louis Fair was scheduled to open, a fact celebrated prematurely by Tom Turpin with a fine *St. Louis Rag* that shows a new melodiousness gained from knowing Joplin. The latter was more fortunate in his timing with the publication in 1904 of *The Cascades*, a rag descriptive of the fair's sensational water course. The fair's postponement was a blow to St. Louis civic pride. Various things were blamed for the failure to open on schedule. One newspaper, following the lead of trust-buster Theodore Roosevelt, came up with the most satisfying excuse of all: "Place the responsibility on the steel trust." Before this fiasco Scott Joplin was hard at work in his new Lucas Avenue quarters. Here he was coming to grips with the large musical form that fitted the shape of his ambition. The oak roll-top desk began to pile up with manuscript pages that bore at the top in Joplin's florid Spencerian script the title:

A GUEST OF HONOR

A Rag Time Opera

Words and Composition

by

SCOTT JOPLIN

In the files of the copyright offices in Washington, Roy Carew discovered a card, dated February 18, 1903, that bears this title and in addition reads: "Published by John Stark & Son, copyright 1903 by Scott Joplin." Despite this official data, *A Guest of Honor* was never published. A written later notation on the card reads: "Copies never received." All trace of the original manuscript has vanished, although many remember the opera and recall its beautiful raggy music. The Stark descendants relate that *Guest of Honor* was a family topic for years; it seems to have been a project planned and postponed and planned again, but never accomplished. Apparently all hinged on the writing of a stronger book for the opera, and this seems never to have materialized.

Dependable as ever, the *Sedalia Times* gave a clue in an item of April 11, 1903: "Scott Hayden has been in the city all week visiting parents and friends. He has signed a contract with the

Scott Joplin Drama Company at St. Louis in which Latisha Howell and Arthur Marshall are performers."

A letter from the authors of this book to Arthur Marshall brought forth the following information:

"I had to concentrate to be as correct as I could remember about the facts. The Drama Company was formed and rehearsed very strenuously. Mr. Will Joplin was a lead Character in the featuring of Joplin's Rag Time Dance. Latisha Howell, Ludie Umbles, another girl, Murrte Whittley, Henry Jackson, Frank Bledsoe, Henry Burres, Lourenda Brown and myself. Latisha's stage name was Zaorada Tosschatie used when prima donna of McCabe's Minstrels.

"I did ragtime specialties on the piano and some numbers with other members of the company. Scott Hayden did some of the same. Joplin played piano when we were performing other than quartette and specialties. There were new joiners but some of us left for other jobs and it finally disbanded.

"As for the Rag Time Opera, *A Guest of Honor* was performed once in St. Louis. In a large hall where they often gave dances. It was a test-out or dress rehearsal to get the idea of the public sentiment. It was taken quite well and I think he was about to get Haviland or Majestic Producers to handle or finance the play, also book it. I can't say just how far it got—as I was very eager for greater money, I left St. Louis for Chicago."

We can only conjecture today whether some of its individual parts ever were published as separate, renamed rags. The opera was Scott Joplin's first project of this size and his first major disappointment.

The fate of *A Guest of Honor* is the story of what might have been, for the time was right for syncopated opera. It was certainly time for the romantic-costume idea of light opera as epitomized by the sentimentalities of Victor Herbert to be superseded by something more American, and there is no doubt that America itself was ready for it and that Joplin was the man equipped to write it. It was still timely over a decade later in 1914, when ironically Irving Berlin, who then led the Tin Pan Alley pseudo-rag men, was quoted in the New York *Dramatic Mirror*:

> "Berlin has one dream, other than to always continue writing hits—'If I live long enough . . . I shall write an opera completely in ragtime. I have not yet fully developed my story but it will of course be laid in the South. . . . The opera will be following out my idea that beautiful thoughts can best be expressed by syncopation. It alone can catch the sorrow—the pathos of humanity. That note in ragtime is almost unexplainable. I call it the wail of the syncopated melody.' "

Berlin's ragtime opera has not yet materialized.

George Gershwin did write *Porgy and Bess*. Remote as was this folk opera from first-hand sources and classic ragtime, its success showed that, more than thirty years after *A Guest of Honor*, the ragtime-opera idea was still timely. And so it is today. But the lost opera by ragtime's master hand evidently will never be produced.

Although *A Guest of Honor* appeared, only to disappear, in 1903, the same year saw five other Joplin numbers published. Four of these were bought by publishers other than Stark. *Weeping Willow* and the new Joplin-Hayden collaboration, *Something Doing*, were copyrighted by Val. A. Reis of St. Louis, who had published the early Turpin rags. *Palm Leaf Rag* was mailed to and accepted by Victor Kremer in Chicago; and another Joplin song, *Little Black Baby*, was issued by a small Chicago firm, Success Music Co.

Much variety exists among Joplin rags, and there are no inferior ones. *Weeping Willow* is more songlike throughout than many of the others, the trio, often with Joplin a highly rhythmic section, here continues the flowing cantilena. The whole piece leaves a nostalgic feeling as of old remembered plantation songs.

In the early summer of 1904 the gates of the Louisiana Purchase Exposition were finally opened. The St. Louis Fair, as it was generally known, was perhaps the largest and gaudiest American exposition yet conceived. Its architecture was more grandiose and, if possible, in even worse taste than that of its predecessors; the emphasis remained on the mundane and the commercial and, where it touched art at all, ran the gamut from calendar art to the stodgiest academism of the day. A European visitor might have walked through the huge exhibition halls and up and down the Pike among the sensational side shows and tented curiosities without ever discovering that a native Afro-American music existed or even that there were millions of Negro American citizens.

Accept or dismiss, as you please, these basic shortcomings, the St. Louis Fair was quite a show. Down the great avenue flanked by florid domed buildings flowed the Cascades, tumbling at night over the glow of colored lights. A lavish use of electric light was, in fact, a fair-wide feature. That and brass bands, for this period marked the peak of American enthusiasm for brass march music. Scores of bands played in the big pavilion; the Garde Républicaine from Paris, the Philippine Constabulary, and regimental bands from England and Scotland were among those imported. First among the Americans were the famed aggregation of John Philip Sousa and that led by handsome Frederick Neil Innes, "a fine, chesty fellow who got there blowing his own horn." Both Sousa and Innes were soloist graduates from the band of Patrick Gilmore, "the Columbus of the modern American Brass Band." William Weil's St. Louis organization was the official exposition band. Weil gained fame during the opening days by a highly publicized quarrel with his union over extra dues. After he had been forced to pay a thousand-dollar fine, he played *The Union Forever* every pay day.

Sousa's original brass band had swollen into a highly trained concert group of sixty-four musicians, with a full reed section that included English horns, oboes, bassoons, flutes, piccolos, and saxophones, as well as the usual clarinets. The brasses included exotica like flügelhorn, euphonium, French horn, and Sousaphone, and trumpets also were added to complement the customary cornets, trombones, alto horns, and tubas.

The repertory, like the band, had grown. To the thrilling, brassy marches were now added overtures and an increasing

73

number of arrangements from the classics. This tendency finally has made the large military band a gauche sort of symphony orchestra, no longer a proper brass band at all.

Sousa himself, though his marches, like *The Stars and Stripes Forever*, *El Capitan*, *Washington Post*, and the others, are straight military compositions, was among the first of the band-leaders to feature cakewalk syncopation. He made a huge success with the cakewalks of two New York composers, Abe Holzmann and Kerry Mills, particularly the former's *Smoky Mokes* and *Hunky Dory*, and the latter's *At a Georgia Camp Meeting*. J. Bodewalt Lampe's *Creole Belles* was another cakewalk that received a big response. The Kerry Mills number owed its vogue, following its publication in 1897, in no small measure to Sousa, and its popularity has lasted through the years. The bearded, bespectacled bandmaster was responsible, through his sensationally successful tours, for the spread of cakewalk syncopation to Europe.

Echoes from the Paris streets even filtered faintly into the ivory towers as evidenced by the *Minstrels* (*Ménestrels*) and *Golliwog's Cake-Walk* of Claude Debussy. But these were merely nods from the tower balcony down to the people in the crowded street—there were no ivory towers with "to let" signs for young Negro geniuses—and scarcely ever again did ragtime disturb the piano's song of moonlight in the whole-tone scale, though it did subtly and permanently affect the nature of European composition.

Sousa beyond any question had a superb brass-band organization. The *Metronome* in 1901 had observed that the European press "without a single exception praised the admirable sonority of the brass, the . . . purity and refinement of the wood-wind, and the artistic perfection of the entire ensemble." With all this, the huge band still lacked truly Negroid phrasing and use of syncopation and suspended beats. Arthur Pryor, the great Missouri-born trombone soloist who had formed his own band and left Sousa only a year before, had made the latter's cakewalk arrangements, scoring them with a full use of syncopation. The failure of Sousa's band to achieve the complete swing of the music was later explained by Pryor himself. "The regulation bands," he said, "never got over being a little embarrassed at syncopating. The stiff-backed old fellows felt it was beneath their dignity and they couldn't or wouldn't give in to it."

Sousa's cakewalk playing nevertheless scored another sensation at St. Louis in 1904. Meanwhile the visitor searching the fair for a truly native American music could find it only as unobtrusive background music in small, obscure concessions. He might have happened on it, purer than the Cascades water and innocent of ballyhoo, in the Old St. Louis beer hall. If he did, all unknowingly he heard an authentic musical prodigy, twenty-one-year-old Louis Chauvin. Or he may have chanced on Arthur Marshall at the Spanish Café, where, for less than a month, he played for twelve dollars a week until the noisy band at Hagenbeck's Animal Show across the Pike drove him out and an Iberian orchestra took his place.

The exposition, with its fine regard for the imported, the sensational, and the ordinary, had contests galore, ranging from brass-band music down to pie-eating, but the cutting contests that were developing Negro ragtime into an American music had no place on the agenda. Nevertheless, one such contest, nation-wide in scope, was held during the fair. Word went out over the sporting-house grapevine long before, and a large field of contestants assembled for the preliminaries of the tournament, which was run by the Turpin brothers.

Jelly Roll Morton told of hearing about the contest. "The girls were willing to finance me. I was a half-hand big shot, what you call. But then I heard Tony Jackson was supposed to be in it, so I didn't go." Tony, the entertaining sensation of Storyville, however, was not there after all. "Imagine my disgust," Jelly continued, "when I heard that Alfred Wilson of New Orleans won it. I could have taken him with one hand tied!" Charlie Warfield of Tennessee took second place.

The searcher in St. Louis in 1904 hunting for American Negro music would really have needed to go the the District, into which the respectable World's Fair visitor never dreamed of penetrating. Certainly the exposition, in its ostensible role of dispensing culture, contented itself with the second-rate and the imported. The average visitor came away with the false impression that the brass band's ponderous echoes of the

Negroes' light-footed syncopation were the real and original thing.

There is no record that Stark approached Sousa to play any of his publications at this or any other time, and there is cause for wonder in this, for the band-leader was advertising for new cakewalks, and *Swipesy* or *Sunflower Slow Drag* would have been ideal for his purpose.

Meanwhile, very much out of the World's Fair bustle, Scott Joplin produced three more rags in addition to *The Cascades*. John Stark issued *Chrysanthemum, an Afro-American Intermezzo*, and, by a sort of poetic justice, A. W. Perry & Son finally published a Joplin rag, *The Favorite*, in Sedalia. Will Rossiter of Chicago brought out *The Sycamore—A Concert Rag*, which the composer had mailed to him. The subtitle of *Chrysanthemum* is probably due to John Stark, as this rag is more markedly classical and less African—except for the rhythmic cast—than many other Joplin rags.

The 1904 rags are heavy scores that, skillfully played, become a light syncopation unlike anything heard before ragtime. All of them—especially *Chrysanthemum*—ring with triumph.

1906 saw a fruitful harvest of six published numbers. *Eugenia*, a rag with the Rossiter imprint, is in classic vein. *Leola Two Step*, published by the American Music Syndicate of St. Louis, is structured like *Maple Leaf* but different in melody. Bahnsen Music Co. of St. Louis issued two waltzes, *Binks* and the wonderfully syncopated *Bethena Concert Waltz*, as well as a song, *Sarah Dear*, with words by Henry Jackson. The year's list is completed by Stark's issue of the 6/8 march *Rosebud*, "Dedicated to my friend, Tom Turpin."

Bethena is a composition superb by any standards. Neglected for nearly half a century, the waltz is a first-rank piece that is evidence that serious composition could grow from ragtime. If the music did not remain as its own proof, it might seem rash to say that this waltz, together with the Joplin rags and marches and the lost opera, should have been the keystone of our serious American music of today. It is indeed almost amazing that until now most of these compositions have been consigned to oblivion, while only a few survive in the low role of perennial popular-entertainment pieces.

The basic syncopative device of *Bethena* places unaccented eighth notes alternating with accented quarter notes in the treble over the conventionally accented three-quarter notes of the bass. With its cakewalk feeling, the device is virtually the same as a four-over-three polyrhythm. *Bethena* abounds in the most subtle variations of this and other syncopated ideas. In its seven pages are set forth no less than five themes in as many keys, and the instruction *"cantabile"* does not belie the sheer beauty of each melody in its richly scored harmony.

Binks Waltz is no masterpiece like *Bethena*. It is unsyncopated and in a light salon vein, though it has some of Joplin's characteristic melodic invention. One is tempted to say—and it might not be wide of the mark—that Afro-American rhythms are so completely of the composer's nature that his finest work could be done only in such a form.

An interesting feature sets *Sarah Dear* apart from other popular songs of the day. The chorus, a variation of the old ribald levee song sung by the roustabouts up and down the Mississippi and elsewhere, will serve as an excellent example of the way the folksong wandered through its own level of society. The same tune is incorporated in Barney and Seymore's 1904 rag *The St. Louis Tickle*, and was later immortalized as of 1895–1900 New Orleans origin by Jelly Roll Morton. He recorded it as *Buddy Bolden's Blues*, with its introductory words: "I thought I heard Buddy Bolden say," and its second chorus:

> *I thought I heard Judge Fogarty say*
> *Thirty days in the market, take him away*
> *Give him a good broom to sweep with, take him away*
> *I thought I heard him say.*[1]

The composer Virgil Thomson remembers it as a river song heard in his boyhood in Kansas City, and Dr. Newman Ivey White reports it in his book *American Negro Folk-Songs* in the following form, sung as a work song by Negro laborers in Augusta, Georgia:

[1] From *Buddy Bolden's Blues*, by Jelly Roll Morton. Reprinted by permission of copyright-owner, Tempo Music Publishing Co.

Thought I heard—huh!
Judge Pequette say—huh!
Forty-five dol-lars—huh!
Take him away—huh!

Dr. White adds his own memory of the tune as a street song in 1903 in Statesville, North Carolina. A very early published appearance of this folk melody is Ben Harney's *The Cakewalk in the Sky*, issued by M. Witmark & Sons in 1899, in which the theme is given several types of syncopated treatment. It was one of the hit songs of this early pioneer of ragtime playing. While the preceding examples use the entire tune, still another instance shows up in Louis Chauvin's ballad *Babe, It's Too Long Off* (Witmark, 1906), which reveals the very characteristic chord sequence of this folk tune in the verse.

Och Himmel! the carpets wave up und wave down
Und der light she go 'round mit a schwing
Dot hot razzle dazzle--I can't find der notes
Und der time he gone crazy by Jing
    'Raus mit der new fangled stuff of to day
    I blays der same biece dot my grand'vatter blays.

It was in 1905 that a nineteen-year-old Negro came into St. Louis from the town of Joplin. The short, slender, light-skinned youth went straight to the Rosebud to find the way to Scott Joplin. It was the composer of *Maple Leaf* he was looking for, not a man already known to him. When James Scott rang the bell at 2117 Lucas Avenue, Joplin himself received the young pilgrim with his usual warmth. In a few minutes James was playing his rags for the master, who found little to correct in them and little to add. In the fact of the pieces being firmly based on the *Maple Leaf* model, Joplin felt a tribute to himself, while with generous vision he saw the originality that showed through as well.

He commented on the name and initials that he and the youth bore in common as a good omen, and lost no time in introducing the young piano wizard to John Stark. One rag was bought immediately and was published in 1906. *Frog Legs* gave clear indication that another top-rank ragtime composer was rising. After this successful foray James Scott returned to his southwestern Missouri home.

In the meantime the home life of the Joplins was developing tension. A baby girl had been born, but she was ill from birth and lived only a few months. The occupants of the thirteen-room boarding house knew little of the domestic trouble that was brewing "but," says Arthur Marshall, "his composing and teaching of ragtime music was greatly disturbed." So tactful and delicate is Marshall in detailing this phase of Joplin's life that we quote his own words:

> "Mrs. Joplin wasn't so interested in music and her taking violin lessons from Scott was a perfect failure. Mr. Joplin was seriously humiliated. Of course unpleasant attitudes and lack of home interests occurred between them.
>
> "They finally separated. He told me his wife had no interest in his music career. Otherwise Mrs. Joplin was very pleasant to his friends and especially to we home boys. But the other side was strictly theirs. To other acquaintances of the family other than I and Hayden and also my brother Lee who knew the facts, Scott was towards her in their presence very pleasing.

"A shield of honor toward her existed and for the child. As my brother, Lee Marshall, Hayden and I were like his brothers, Joplin often asked us to console Mrs. Joplin—perhaps she would reconsider. But she remained neutral. She never was harsh with us, but we just couldn't get her to see the point. So a separation finally resulted."

Mrs. Joplin was, for all that, seriously affected by the course of events. Marshall reports that she "went in poor health, and passed." This was perhaps two years after the death of the child.

After the separation Marshall bought the rooming house and continued to operate it for a time. During the fair he had married, but this proved an ill-advised and short-lived relationship, so he left for Chicago. Joplin, in the meantime, deeply saddened by the collapse of his household, dismissed his pupils and went through the motions of composing. But for long months no melody would flow.

St. Louis and Missouri were finished for him. It was necessary, apart from any practical considerations, for him to look elsewhere. He thought of the young Scott Hayden, whose wife, Nora, had died in childbirth. Hayden now lived in Chicago at the rooming house of Mrs. Katie Ellis Green, "one of our Sedalia women." Joplin thought of Arthur Marshall, who had gone there to remarry; he thought of these two boys whom he had befriended, and some of the warmth he had given them came back to warm his chilled heart.

Chapter 5

PEREGRINATION FOR THE PASTRY

Ｗ HEN Scott Joplin arrived in Chicago in 1906, he was revisiting the Great Lakes city for the first time in thirteen years. During those years a series of rapid-fire developments had wrought changes in the American musical and entertainment world. The eighties and nineties that were the composer's background were the time in which America had begun to discover the secular music of the Negro. Such was its creators' position in this country—first as slave and then as underprivileged minority—that the music had been a long time indeed on its way to discovery. To understand the changes and the developments that led to them we must look back to the middle of the last century.

Long before ragtime rose like a musical flood over the riparian lands of the great Mississippi system, its rhythms had come to America from another land of vast rivers: equatorial Africa. Inland and upstream on the plantations of our old South the tide of drumbeats became the sound of tools in the fields and the singing and clapping of hands in the "meetin'" house; its syncopations lived on in the swing of work song and spiritual. But down on the Delta in New Orleans a phase of African music remained strongly pure in La Place Congo, where until the 1880's the slaves were allowed their Sunday diversion. And it was a youthful New Orleans composer who first wrote in musical notes the beat of the drums, the hollow fanfare of the wooden horns, and the authentic rhythms of what was later to be developed into ragtime.

It was in 1847, a half century before the first ragtime composition was published, that eighteen-year-old Louis Moreau Gottschalk, son of an English cotton broker and a highborn French Creole lady, wrote the long, vastly difficult piano fantaisie *La Bamboula—Danse des Nègres*. A prodigy at fifteen, Gottschalk had already established himself in concert at the Salle Pleyel in Paris with huge public success and the praise of the great Chopin. *La Bamboula* is the composer's Opus 2; *La Morte* (Gottschalk was playing this "Ode to Death" with a fantastically huge nine-hundred-piece orchestra at Rio de Janeiro when fatally stricken in 1869) is his Opus 60, but the earlier work with its strong Negroid inspiration is considered his masterpiece.

Henry Didimus (Henry Edward Durell) wrote a biography of Louis Gottschalk in 1853 in which the Bamboula dance is described as the composer himself had often seen and heard it in New Orleans. This is the earliest known description of the African dancing in Congo Square:

"In order to appreciate the full merit of this popular composition, one should have seen something of the dance upon which it is founded. Let a stranger to New Orleans visit of an afternoon of one of its holydays, the public squares in the lower portion of the city, and he will find them filled with its African population, tricked out with every variety of a showy costume, joyous, wild, and in the full exercise of a real saturnalia. As he approaches the scene of an infinite mirth, his ear first catches a quick, low, continuous, dead sound, which dominates over the laughter, hallo, and roar of a thousand voices, while the listener marvels at what it can be doing there. This is the music of the Bamboula, of the dance Bamboula; a dance which takes possession of the Negro's whole life, transforms him with all the instincts, the sentiments, the feelings which nature gave to his race, to sleep for awhile, to be partially obliterated by the touch of civilisation, but to remain forever its especial mark.

"Upon entering the square the visitor finds the multitude packed in groups of close, narrow circles, of a central area of only a few feet; and there in the center of each circle, sits the musician, astride a barrel, strong-headed, which he beats with two sticks, to a strange measure incessantly, like mad, for hours together, while the perspiration literally rolls in streams and wets the ground; and there, too, labor the dancers male and female, under an inspiration or possession, which takes from their limbs all sense of weariness, and gives to them a rapidity and a durability of motion that will hardly be found elsewhere outside of mere machinery. The head rests upon the breast, or is thrown back upon the shoulders, the eyes closed, or glaring, while the arms, amid cries, and shouts, and sharp ejaculations, float upon the air, or keep time, with the hands patting upon the thighs, to a music which is seemingly eternal.

"The feet scarce tread wider space than their own length; but rise and fall, turn in and out, touch first the heel and then the toe, rapidly and more rapidly, till they twinkle to the eye, which finds its sight too slow a follower of their movements."

Drumbeats open Gottschalk's *La Bamboula*, and the principal motive that follows—later sung by the Creoles as "*Quand patate la cuite na va mangé li*" ("when that 'tater's cooked don't you eat it up")—is the Place Congo chant with its hollow background chords of wooden trumpets. Nearly forty years later, in the *Century Magazine* for February 1886, the New Orleans novelist George W. Cable wrote of this fierce dance: "The bamboula still roars, and rattles, twangs, contorts and tumbles"—and then "the music changes. The rhythm stretches out heathenish and *ragged*.[1] The quick contagion is caught by . . . the crowd, who take it up with spirited smitings of the bare sole upon the ground, and of open hands upon the

[1] Italics the authors'.

thighs." This new dance is the Counjaille, with its "rhythm long and smooth like a river escaped from its rapids, and in new spirit, with more jocund rattle"—the same "coonjine rag dance" of the levee men and boatmen all up and down the Mississippi, the Missouri, and the Ohio.

In the fifty years that followed Gottschalk's *La Bamboula*, until ragtime burst out into the open, this fierce dance and its milder African cousins, the Calinda, the Chacta, the Babouille, and the Counjaille, as well as that fiercest of all, the Congo, traveled along the big rivers and through the valleys. Blending with the gentle Anglo-American folksongs, the hypnotic almost feral rhythms that had struck Cable as heathenish slowly became the irresistible syncopated momentum of the "shout" song and ragtime.

In the vast ferment of this music there sprang into existence, as we have already noted, a large group of itinerant Negro players and singers that came, by the 1890's, to include a considerable number of white members. All were composers in a true folk sense, men who took the melodies and the words all around them, added their own, and strung them together in march and quadrille style to make the composite pieces called rags.

The music of the white man's blackface minstrels, though much of it was mere travesty, was still a sort of tribute to the charm and power of the real thing. From the 1840's on, it prepared the way for the acceptance of Negro music, though it defined in advance much of the nature and extent of the acceptance, very much as the obnoxious poll tax at the end of the last century began to define the political boundaries of poor Southern citizens of both races.

The whole minstrel episode is schizoid, like America's attitude toward its Negro minority. The comic portraits of the Negro that were drawn in burnt cork were at once sympathetic and belittling. They left in the public mind two enduring after images. One was the good-hearted simpleton, loose-jointed, shuffling, and awkward, who could paradoxically break into an intricate buck and wing or make the banjo talk. The other was the Negro dandy, who wore the habiliments and the customs of his white "superiors" so absurdly, and whose dignity, though preposterous, was highly diverting. White America loved these myths of chicken-stealing and fibs, and in its laughter was able to forget its immemorial mistreatment of the dark-skinned human being so remote from the legend and so superior to it. The blind motivation of these portraits of the Negro as he was wished to be, not as he is, could scarcely mystify the freshman psychology student.

And yet there is evidence that the worst sin of *early* minstrelsy was little more than a certain obtuseness or lack of understanding rather than hostility. In witness of this is the dedication of an 1849 publication, *The Ethiopian Glee Book* of the famed Christy's Minstrels. The *Glee Book* series, published by Elias Howe of Boston, are song books of the company repertory; they include a large proportion of fairly authentically transcribed folk material. The "author," Gumbo Chaff,[1] was banjo-player to an imaginary African chieftain. Gumbo writes: "To all de Bobolashun and Antislabery 'Cieties truout de World, dis Book am most 'spectfully 'scribed by de orther." In his preface, furthermore, Gumbo writes: "De 'Scriber am pressed wid de vast 'sponsibility ob presentin' to de whole . . . Popalashun ob dis world de genus ob de colored pofessors ob de 'vine art."

The minstrels from start to finish were compact with irony. The good-natured imitation by whites became, in time, cruel ridicule that fostered vicious prejudice. The canny Negro, on the other hand, turned *his* version of the burnt-cork divertissement into a subtle but devastating caricature of the white *Übermensch*, employing the blackface like an African ceremonial mask, and through the whole thing insinuated his way onto the white stage.

Although the coon song of the minstrels was a tool of strategy in Negro hands, as well as racial libel in white hands, most of these songs are with much justice considered today as relics of barbarism. The coon song begins very early. A typical Negro-dandy number is included in the *Ethiopian Glee Books* of 1848–9. This is *The Dandy Broadway Swell:*

[1] Pseudonym for Elias Howe.

> *Dey may talk ob dandy niggers*
> *But dey neber see dis coon,*
> *A prombernarding Broadway*
> *On a Sunday afternoon.*
> *I'se de sole de-light ob yellow gals,*
> *De envy ob de men;*
> *Ob-serve dis child when he turn out*
> *And talk ob dan-dies den.*
>
> CHORUS:
>
> > *For I'se de grit, de go, de cheese,*
> > *As every one may tell;*
> > *De dark fair sex*
> > *I sure to please,*
> > *I'se de dandy Broadway swell.*

From this it is evident that the coon song was featured in the minstrels from the very first, and probably predated even the minstrel. Other coon songs in the Christy series are *Stop Dat Knocking, Oh! Mr. Coon*, and *Zip Coon*. The last tune—latterly under the title *Turkey in the Straw*—has been a perennial favorite since its publication by Atwill's Music Saloon of Baltimore in 1834. While it is cited in Sigmund Spaeth's book *A History of Popular Music in America* as being possibly of Irish melodic origin, it appears as a coon song in the earliest known versions.

The term "coon" is scarcely less opprobrious today than "nigger." Yet the word "coon" in 1848 was merely one of a whole variety of designations for the Negro. Besides the dignified "Ethiopian," which appears on the covers of the *Glee Books*, other song titles in the series were: *The Jolly Darkey, Virginny's Black Daughter, Yaller Gals, De Nigger's Banjo Hum, De Cullered Cokett, Dinah Doe and Mr. Crow*. Virtually all are stereotypes today, and this will progressively be the fate of each term applied to the Negro with every new generation until prejudice itself is removed.

While there was a lapse during the Civil War, the coon song picked right up again in the seventies, when many of the earlier minstrel numbers, such as *The Dandy Broadway Swell*, were revived. By the eighties new songs of this type were published with fair regularity. In 1881 *Coonville Guards* was published, in 1882 *The Coon Dinner*—both by Jacob J. Sawyer —and J. S. Putnam's *New Coon in Town* appeared in 1883, and so on through the decade. By the nineties the coon song was in full vogue, having milled around as minstrel and topical song for at least fifty years before it attained national popularity.

Although coon songs, written by Negroes as well as whites, are now in strong disfavor, some of them are almost documentary in their revelation of the Negro's social predicament. Sterling and Von Tilzer's *Moving Day* is one such. Another, D. A. Lewis's *Missus Johnson's Rent Rag Ball*, of 1897 in its first printed version, has this to tell:

> *Ol' Missus Johnson . . .*
> *Had an awful time*
> *Fo' to keep her home*
> *And take care of them pickaninnies sweet;*
> *And so last month when things was awful bad,*
> *Missus Johnson said,*
> *"Now I must give a rag*
> *For to raise my rent,*
> *Or out I'll have to go."*

There is much more than humor in the situation depicted here.

Many coon songs, too, are filled with folklore and with descriptions of dances then in vogue. A. Shaw's 1897 number *Rag-Ma-La* combines the characteristic Negro dance called the Pas Ma La and ragtime into a new dance and "calls the figures":

> *S'lute your babies all;*
> *Hotfoot it down the hall;*
> *Give your honey the inside track;*
> *Now do the Palmer House coming back,*
> *And then the Wenches Chain;*
> *Swing around again,*
> *Back to place, with due grace—*
> That's *the Rag-a-ma-la!*

Dar's a New Coon Wedding, by A. S. MacKenzie (1892), tells of the sort of band used at social functions and also describes the almost forgotten "sand dance," a shuffle on sand thinly spread on the floor:

> *Dar's a new coon weddin' in de town;*
> *Spread de news for miles around,*
> *For old Professor Johnson and his banjo will be dar.*
> *Tell all de yaller gals to fix and curl their hair;*
> *Tell Bill Jones to fetch along de sand;*
> *And we'll dance to the music of Johnson's Colored Band.*
> *Don't forget Ole Rastus and be sure and bring him round,*
> *Cause dar's a new coon weddin' in de town.*

And then there are the 1897 song by Hillman and Perrin, *Mammy's Little Pumpkin Colored Coons*, published by Witmark, which is a charming lullaby, and others of this type, nostalgic or idyllic rather than derisive. A top writing team of this period consisted of the Negro poet Paul Laurence Dunbar and the noted Negro composer and conductor Will Marion Cook, whose early works are signed Will Marion. Among their coon songs were *Who Dat Say Chicken in Dis Crowd?* and the highly successful coon marching song *On Emancipation Day*. The versatile George M. Cohan wrote a number of songs in the coon vein, and another exceptional composer in this medium was Hughie Cannon, who with John Queen formed the successful song-and-dance team of Queen and Cannon. Jazz bands still play his 1902 hit *Bill Bailey, Won't You Please Come Home?* a song that initiated a series of Bill Bailey songs by various composers. Other outstanding writing-composing teams were the three Negro combinations Cole and Johnson (two different Johnsons, J. Rosamund and Billy, make up the latter half of this team), Creamer and Layton, and Chris Smith and Cecil Mack (R. C. McPherson). The first two combinations wrote exceptional musical comedies, and Bob Cole is remembered for an all-time hit, *Under the Bamboo Tree*, published in 1902.

The Negro often used the coon song as an apparently innocent way to get something said. The famous little stuttering comedian Irving Jones wrote several such songs. One was the aftermath of a certain St. Patrick's Day when he left his home in East Orange, New Jersey, to go to Manhattan. Getting on the train, he found it packed with Irish merrymakers. "Where you from?" asked one of them, looking at the Negro. For one horrible moment little Irving thought of the fatal name of his home town before his wit saved him. "From East Tangerine," he said. His true feelings came out a little later in the hit song entitled *St. Patrick's Day Is a Bad Day for Coons.*

A coon number of the famous Negro comedian Ernest Hogan was the unwitting means of bringing down on him the universal condemnation of the whole present Negro generation. *All Coons Look Alike to Me* was one of the great hits of the nineties. It came to be used with derision by the whites for its apparent inference that all Negroes are a lot of look-alike nobodies. Quite different was the song's intention, as the words reveal. A Negro girl jilts her lover because she has fallen in love with another. The key line of the song is her declaration that all Negroes *except the new one* look alike to her, sentiments obviously shared by all women in a similar situation.

A single coon song can illustrate the schizoid character to which we have referred. In the 1897 song *Syncopated Sandy*, by Ned Wayburn and Stanley Whiting, which has a regular as well as a ragtime accompaniment, the Negro is freely credited with the origination of ragtime:

> "The authors and publishers in presenting *Syncopated Sandy* to the public have succeeded in illustrating the absolute theory of the now famous Rag Time music which originated with the Negroes and is characteristic of their people. . . . Careful attention to the accent marks will enable the performer to obtain perfect rag time and give the basic principles whereby any music ever written can be arranged and played in Rag Time, The Musical Rage of the Century."

But on the page with the tribute appears a "Coon Parody" intended as humor, yet with the most vicious inference. Nevertheless it becomes apparent, a half century after the height of the coon songs' vogue, that in both their literary and their musical aspects they deserve to be, not totally rejected, but objectively considered.

In any event, there is little justice in the open contempt that today's leaders of Negro thought feel for their fellow artists of that day who accepted the coon role. It has been forgotten that the Negro in all periods moves forward as he can, adapting his methods to the conditions that prevail. Forgotten, too, is the fact that these early compromises advanced the Negro immeasurably and were essential to the advances being made today.

Bert Williams, apparently shuffling and loose-jointed, and with the gift of perfect timing and incredibly understated satire, and George W. Walker, the uppity dandy, immaculately dressed in high style, but, as was expected of him in his first days on the stage, groaning and rubbing his tightly shod feet, characterized to perfection the dual Negro portrait of minstrelsy. It might be well to remember a cold and bitter fact of the 1890's: namely, that no Negro, however divinely gifted, could then walk well-dressed onto a white American stage. Walker's insignificant, minimum gesture was a masterpiece of efficacy. Williams and Walker must be credited, too, first with reducing the whole minstrel show to a two-man vaudeville act that got them on the leading stages of America; then with proceeding to full-fledged shows of the most phenomenal success. Simple logic can perceive that the very possibility of subsequent triumphs hinged on these first steps.

Bert Williams in demonstrating his own genius demonstrated the unique genius of his race. His shows with Walker were such that the leading white critics wrote in this tenor: "This 'colored show' stands with the foremost of musical entertainments . . . the piece comes very close to opera comique"; or, in unqualified words, of Bert himself: "Bert Williams is a genius." There is not even the prejudice of faint condescension in these encomiums. It was a man of his own race, Booker T. Washington, a fighter in his day though he would not be militant enough for today's developments, who said of Bert: "He has done more for our race than I have. He has smiled his way into people's hearts; I have been obliged to fight my way."

We by no means wish to imply that "gradualism" is any longer a method to be used in the campaign for equal rights for the Negro. Today the South has been put on notice by the white North and by the Negroes themselves. It can no longer plead that its "Negro" problem is its own concern, tied up in some mystical fashion with states' rights. Despite the seeming aggressiveness of the Solid South, it is not so solid and is now on the defensive.

The trend of the times is clearly shown in the stand being taken by many Southern judges and other people of prominence. For example, Federal Judge J. Waties Waring, referring to his ruling allowing Negroes to vote in the South Carolina primaries, recently stated: "In my city they said blood would flow in the streets if Negroes were allowed to vote. No blood flowed. I ruled that any violators would be sent to jail, and they believed me."

Today, too, the National Association for the Advancement of Colored People can carry the issue of Negro admission to Southern institutions of learning all the way to the Supreme Court and can win the victories granted, in name only, two full generations ago. But it is well for all concerned to remember that the Supreme Court, in whose hands the final decision rests, was only yesterday a far differently constituted and less liberal body in racial matters.

So yesterday was another matter. It was a time for compromise while positions were being prepared. To such a compromise is owed the very survival of ragtime. Many a devoutly religious Negro, and many as serious-minded as Scott Joplin, worked among the red lights in order to work in their own new music at all. To concessions like theirs is owed not only *Maple Leaf* and scores of other masterpieces, but all subsequent Negro hot music, even the very eminence today of society bands like that of Duke Ellington. As we write the word "hot" we realize that this, too, is a thing of disrepute, and yet the true spiritual is as hot as jazz. A musical term that refers specifically to off-beat, syncopated rhythm and to the fervor of creative improvisation cannot be one of derogation or of shame. It is muddled thinking that confuses the word with the tenderloin milieu.

91

From such baseless ideas as these arose the furore that met the 1896 publication of Bert Williams's *Dora Dean*, a song that was nothing more or less than a direct tribute to the rhythmic dancing of one of the outstanding Negro cakewalkers of the day.

> *While down at sister Holley,*
> *We all did feel so jolly,*
> *Each one tried to cut a pigeon wing;*
> *When up jumped Dora Dean,*
> *Who said, "I am the Queen,*
> *I can beat you in a dance for anything."*

> *That just suited ol' Aunt Dinah,*
> *Who sang a tune in minor,*
> *Thinking that she could the music make;*
> *So we started in to test*
> *To see who was the best,*
> *And Dora walked off with the cake.*

> CHORUS:
> *Oh have you ever seen*
> *My Dora Dean?*
> *She's the hottest thing you ever seen;*
> *I'm gwine to make this gal my Dora Queen,*
> *Next Sunday morn I'm gwine to marry Dora Dean.*

The subtitle, "The Hottest Thing You Ever Seen," started a tempest among teapots, and certain women's clubs in New York complained to the Post Office Department, which ruled it obscene and unmailable. A hasty reprinting substituted the word "sweetest" for the objectionable adjective.

One not unfavorable aspect of the coon songs was crystallized in the general feeling of fun shared by all colors and creeds, though it is difficult to appreciate this today, when every shoulder has a chip and each minority has become self-conscious. Nevertheless, in the literary and entertainment worlds of that day there was a general spoofing of the Irish and the "Dutch," of pig-tailed "Chinee," of Negro and of Jew that, though crude perhaps, was productive of a certain intentional camaraderie. More than a reasoned tolerance, it was a recognition of the natural differences that exist between peoples. These differences are one source of racial strength rather than weakness. To deny their use in humor seems, unfortunately, to mean today the unrealistic denial of them all. Much merriment was abroad where today all is deadly seriousness. Gone with the easily spared crudities of much of the dialect comedy is the superb, mordant satire of Negro funmaking. We have all—scientist and sociologist, together with each well-intentioned layman—compulsively discarded much that is good along with the bad.

Syncopation began to invade American printed music with the rise in popularity of the coon songs in the nineties, though there were many songs dating back at least to the beginnings of minstrelsy that had a measure of syncopation here and there, or a general feel of off-beat accenting. In many of these songs the syncopating comes from the vocal part rather than the piano treble, so that if the right hand plays the vocal part over the bass as printed, a fair sort of ragtime comes out of it. Here and there, as in Irving Jones's 1894 *Possumala*—with its quaint twist to the name of the Pas Ma La dance—there can be found a few measures of real ragtime scoring. There is one exception, however: a song by Ben Harney, published in 1895, which will be discussed later.

The sister team of May and Flo Irwin were instrumental in bringing Negroid ragtime singing into the white music halls. In 1896, before the name "ragtime" was in general use, May's singing of her big hit *I'm Lookin' for de Bully* was called "coon-shouting." W. C. Handy points out in his book *Father of the Blues* that *The Bully* was an old roustabout song from St. Louis, "later adopted and nationally popularized by May Irwin." The song was written out for her by the New York sports writer Charles Trevathan, and published as *May Irwin's Bully Song* in 1896.

1896 was the year when a twenty-five-year-old white player, Ben Harney, from Middleboro, Kentucky, made the first public New York hit with piano ragtime. The February 17, 1896 issue of the old theatrical weekly the *New York Clipper* commented: "Ben R. Harney, another stranger at this house [Keith's Union Square Theater], jumped into immediate favor through the medium of his genuinely clever plantation Negro imitations and excellent piano playing."

Harney's hit song, *Mister Johnson* (*Turn Me Loose*), was published in early April of the same year by Frank Harding of New York. The tune, however, like Harney, who had been barnstorming since the turn of the decade, had a past history. It had already been copyrighted and published about two months earlier, in January 1896, by G. W. Warren, of Evansville, Indiana, with the authorship credited to Haering and Green. The Evansville song is dedicated to Harney, and a cover note states: "Sung with Immense Success by Ben R. Harney & Tom Mack." The cover has a photo of a performer dressed like a Keystone cop, one hand holding his night stick and the other firmly grasping the coat collar of his diminutive Negro vaudeville partner. The almost identically scored melody of the two versions is printed over differently scored accompaniments, the Harding-Harney publication having nine or ten measures of rudimentary ragtime, the early one none. With Harney's New York success, Witmark bought the number from Harding and the third and final version came out late in the year, its stiff, unsyncopated measures betraying the staff arranger's hand. The story of the Evansville version is this: the tune had been heard by a pianist, Harry Green, who knew Harney in Louisville. Green took it to Evansville and sold it there without Harney's knowledge.

There is a remarkable feature in *Mister Johnson*. The first fourteen-measure portion of the verse deserves careful scanning, for this section is nothing less than a Negro spiritual already half-transformed into the blues, with its double statement and single answer. Here, sixteen years before the earliest previously known blues publication, is the familiar four-bar statement, repeat of equal length, and answer. The answer in *Mister Johnson* is of six measures. Although the blues have now settled into a 4–4–4 form of twelve measures, many folk singers, like the late Lead Belly (Huddie Ledbetter), customarily allow the answer to vary from four to seven bars, the musical criterion for this as a rule being the number of words to be fitted in. Many have opposed the belief that the blues came out of the spiritual, yet the musical form has always supported the idea, and among the rank and file of Negroes, even many religious ones, it is regarded not as a theory but as a fact.

How remarkable a pioneer Ben Harney was is forcefully pointed up by the authors' discovery that his famous 1896 Witmark hit, *You've Been a Good Old Wagon but You've Done Broke Down*, was actually bought by Witmark from Bruner Greenup, who had published it in Louisville in January 1895. Besides the patent fact that the words of this song are in definite blues imagery, the piano accompaniment and the concluding instrumental "dance" section are bona fide, if elementary, ragtime. It must be borne in mind that in the early 1890's the best of the coon songs had only a measure or two of ragtime and that the scoring of this syncopation was an art not mastered by arrangers until 1897. These facts establish Harney's unassailable priority as a pioneer of printed ragtime—if one disregards a mere matter of nomenclature or titling—and amply explain his own staunch conviction that he "originated ragtime." The words of *Good Old Wagon* follow:

> *Standin' on the corner, didn't mean no harm*
>   *This mawnin';*
> *The copper grabbed me by the arm, without warnin',*
>   *Took me down to the jail house door.*
>
> *Place I had never been before*
>   *This mawnin',*
> *Put me on board a Frankfort train,*
>   *Loaded me down with a ball and chain.*
>
> *Every station that I passed by*
>   *I could imagine my baby cry:*
>
> CHORUS:
> *'Bye-bye my honey, if you call it gone, O Babe,*
> *'Bye-bye my honey, if you call it gone, O Babe,*
> *'Bye-bye my honey, if you call it gone,*
>   *You been a good old wagon but you done broke down*
>   *This mawnin'.*

To any student of the blues, the traditional imagery is apparent and the refrain words are typical blues "answers": the "O

95

Babe" and the "This mawnin'" (as in the traditional folk blues *So Soon This Mornin'*) appear in countless examples of the old rural blues.

It was after the mid-nineties that "peregrinating for the pastry," as the minstrel interlocutor would grandiloquently present the cakewalk, became a national obsession. Its copper-hued belles in velvet ballet skirts or long gowns and great ostrich-plumed hats, and its silk-hatted dusky gentlemen in tails, were leaders of the Darktown four hundred, materialized in the flesh from the pages of the songs.

The cakewalk itself was no minstrels trumpery, but a dance of ancient origin within the Negro race. Shephard N. Edmonds speaks of the plantation form of this flamboyant "walk-around." Edmonds, now almost eighty, was prominent in the Negro entertainment and music world before he deserted it to become the first Negro private detective in the United States. Born in Tennessee, the son of freed slaves, he recalls that "the cakewalk was originally a plantation dance, just a happy movement they did to the banjo music because they couldn't stand still. It was generally on Sundays, when there was little work," his description continues, "that the slaves both young and old would dress up in hand-me-down finery to do a high-kicking, prancing walk-around. They did a take-off on the high manners of the white folks in the 'big house,' but their masters, who gathered around to watch the fun, missed the point. It's supposed to be that the custom of a prize started with the master giving a cake to the couple that did the proudest movement."

From the plantations the cakewalk went on into the minstrels, and for many years its steps were used by colored waiters in the fashionable resort hotels at Saratoga, Greenbrier, and elsewhere. Very early, too, the promenade for the cake went into the variety show as one of the acts in this predecessor of vaudeville. By 1877, in the middle of their show the famous team of Harrigan and Hart presented a feature called "Walking for Dat Cake," publicized fulsomely in their playbill as an "Exquisite Picture of Negro Life and Customs, professed by all to be the most masterly production ever placed upon the stage." The song that the cakewalkers sang appeared in the same year, published by Wm. A. Pond & Co. in New York. The music for *Walking for Dat Cake* was by Dave Braham, who for many years wrote the Harrigan and Hart music, and the words were by Harrigan.

The cakewalk circulated around the show world for nearly a quarter century before it leaped into the national spotlight. Will Vodery, prominent Negro composer and arranger, who for years was Flo Ziegfeld's musical director, credits the team of Smart and Williams with having had considerable influence in this direction in the early 1890's.

One of the first large cakewalk extravaganzas ever held took place in New York. James Weldon Johnson writes in his *Black Manhattan* about this gala affair and the triumph of a Negro singer:

"Sissieretta Jones had studied and been singing in concert for several years, but first gained wide publicity by her singing at a Jubilee Spectacle and Cake-Walk which was staged at Madison Square Garden April 26–8, 1892, for which she had been specially engaged. She sang three nights and carried off the honours of the affair. The next day the New York papers gave her space and head-lines, and by one critic she was dubbed 'Black Patti.' "

The *New York Clipper Annual* of 1896 contained a courtesy ad from the production *South before the War*, a successful road show that was originally a Ben Harney production. The ad characterizes the show as:

A BRIGADE OF BEWILDERING BUCK & WING DANCERS
A HOST OF CAMP MEETING SHOUTERS & SHOOTERS
THE GREATEST CAKE WALK EVER PRODUCED
AND THE ORIGINAL PICKANINNY BAND

and about the same time the *Police Gazette* noted: "Harry and Sadie Fields have made a hit with their original Hebrew cake-walk."

In 1896 Bert A. Williams and George W. Walker appeared in *The Gold Bug* at the Casino Theater. "*The Gold Bug* did not quite catch Broadway's fancy," Weldon Johnson writes, "but

Williams and Walker did." Immediately thereafter at Koster and Bial's on the Fourteenth Street Rialto, where they spent forty weeks, the two comedians made the cakewalk fashionable. "They were assisted by two girls," Johnson continues; "one of them, Stella Wiley, was the cleverest coloured soubrette of the day. Cake-walk pictures posed for by the quartet were reproduced in colours and widely distributed as advertisements by one of the big cigarette concerns. And the execution of cake-walk steps was taken up by society."

As a publicity stunt, Williams and Walker called at the Vanderbilt mansion on January 16, 1898 and left the following letter:

TO *Mr. William K. Vanderbilt*
Corner of Fifty-second Street and Fifth Avenue
New York

DEAR SIR:
   In view of the fact that you have made a success as a cake-walker, having appeared in a semi-public exhibition and having posed as an expert in that capacity, we, the undersigned world-renowned cake-walkers, believing that the attention of the public has been distracted from us on account of the tremendous hit which you have made, hereby challenge you to compete with us in a cake-walking match, which will decide which of us shall deserve the title of champion cake-walker of the world. . . .
                    Yours very truly,
                    WILLIAMS AND WALKER

Apparently either the Vanderbilt humor or the Vanderbilt skill were not equal to the occasion, for no chronicle records the holding of the contest.

Roy Carew, who has been a ragtime enthusiast since the first rags were published, tells about the spread of the fad: "People would see the cakewalk performed and come home and learn how to do it. Road shows and minstrels carried it to small places everywhere. It was often featured in the olio, which was the central variety part of the traveling burlesques. Just before 1897 there was a huge cakewalk craze and every hamlet in the country had contests. White people that did it would often make up in black face."

Cakewalking developed into a real art, but it never froze into a set form, as it depended on each couple's gifts for improvising steps, struts, and kicks to fit the ragtime syncopations. The larger contests featured sizable prizes and drew contestants from far and near. The winners received as much as two hundred and fifty dollars—a substantial amount in those uninflated fiscal days—and the first three couples to place got a vaudeville booking. Even stage actors entered the tournaments to get more work.

The *Chicago Inter-Ocean* of January 2, 1898 describes the dancing at a nonprofessional contest, in the words of character actor Joe Belgium, who acted as judge:

"The band started a march with a tremendous crash. Mr. Dave White led off with Miss Patty Willow, a very stout colored woman in a ballet dancer's costume made from yellow calico, and behind them seventy-five more couples. From the judge's stand it was a whirling ring of kaleidoscopic colors accompanied by shuffling feet in time to the music. Long men mated with short women and had they been automatons moved by wires their movements would not have been more perfectly in time with the music.

"The friends of the walkers stood around the outside and yelled encouragement to the candidates and as the music got into full swing and quickened its time a bit, they began to shuffle and to sway in rhythm. Every walker strained his or her muscles to put in extra steps and as the procession swung around the corners, each one had his or her own way of making the turn. Some of them did it with a nice precision. Others executed a few steps from a wing dance, then, as they were around, settling down into the steady shuffle that would bring them to the next turn."

The dance was everywhere—in fashionable salon and small-town cottage and even in the streets, and prominently, of course, in the leading shows and top variety houses. Comedian

Joe Howard was by common consent the foremost white cakewalker in his mastery of Negro rhythm and style. "Joe Howard sure did walk your brains out," is Shep Edmonds's comment on the veteran comic performing at Billy Rose's Diamond Horseshoe as these lines are written. The old plantation walk-around reached the immortality of literature in 1905 when a play by José Jackson Veyan, *El Cake Walk*, was published in Madrid. By that time the fad had moved on into the twentieth century and had already been introduced at the Paris Exposition of 1900 by Sousa's famous band.

Ragtime ascended with the cakewalk rocket and by 1897 was a hit in its own right. The two were twin attractions at the contests and jubilees in metropolis and village. A dozen or more pianists played their allotted ten minutes each or less for the ragtime prize, and then the cakewalkers strutted for theirs. Awards were made sometimes by judges and sometimes by audience acclamation. Ragtime was in society, too. As the liveliest, most infectious music ever, it too was taking the cake.

Early in 1897 the first instrumental number completely in ragtime and so titled rolled off the printing presses. A newspaper writer of Chicago whose identity has been forgotten is credited as the first to use the name "ragtime" in print; the apt designation took instantly and touched off a race between several local publishers to get the first "rag" in print.

What specific event or appearance of a well-known performer—if either—spurred the article that rechristened the oldtime "jig" piano remains a mystery. But there was a publishers' race, and the entrants and winner can all be found in the copyright entries. The following chart shows the neck-to-neck closeness of those who finished "win," "place," and "show." The last two columns, "Starting Time" and "Finish Time," indicate, first, the date of the mailing of the copyright application and, second, date of its official receipt in the Copyright Division in Washington.

As the starting gates opened in Chicago, there were immediate entries in other towns. Philip Kussel of Cincinnati brought out *A Bundle of Rags*, a good archaic rag by Robert S. Roberts; George Elliott of St. Paul published his own *Happy Little Nigs, Ragtime Two-Step* (reissued in 1898 by W. J. Dyer

RESULTS OF THE 1897 CHICAGO RAGTIME SWEEPSTAKES

Place at Finish	Horse	Jockey	Owner	Starting Time	Finish Time
1.	*Mississippi Rag*	W. H. Krell	S. Brainard	Jan. 25	Jan. 27
2.	*Ragtime March*	Warren Beebe	Will Rossiter	Jan. 27	Jan. 30
3.	*Ragtime Patrol*	R. J. Hamilton	National Music	Feb. 20	Feb. 22
4.	*A Night on the Levee*	Theo Northrup	Sol Bloom	Mar. 18	Mar. 20
Also ran	*Missus Johnson's Rent Rag Ball*	D. A. Lewis	National Music		May
	The Rag Time Instructor	Harney	Sol Bloom		Sept.
	Louisiana Rag	Theo Northrup	Thompson Music		Oct.

& Bros.); a New Orleans entry was Paul Sarebresole's *Roustabout Rag*, published by L. Grunewald Co.; Witmark of New York leaped in with a synthetic *Rag Medley* arranged by Max Hoffman; and there were others.

It was on December 17, as previously noted, that the first rag by a Negro composer was copyrighted. De Yong of St. Louis brought out Tom Turpin's *Harlem Rag* and afterwards sold it to Stern of New York, who printed two editions, one of them with a special arrangement by the noted West Indian Negro composer William H. Tyers.

Although strict justice would have demanded that a Negro rag be the first published, *Mississippi Rag* is far from an unworthy piece. Its finished workmanship, its melodies, and their scoring all show how long folk ragtime had been current in the Mississippi area before its appearance. During his tours as successful band leader through the Mississippi River country, composer William Krell had ample opportunity to hear the music. An 1895 feature number of his band was his *Cake Walk Patrol*, a Brainard publication. *Mississippi Rag* was already a "click" number of the Krell aggregation when it was rushed into print. The legend on the cover reads: "The First Rag-Time Two-Step Ever Written and First Played by Krell's Orchestra, Chicago." Krell was equipped to make a first-rate composition out of the material. The arrangement of the four themes: cakewalk, plantation song, trio, and buck-and-wing dance, together with the introduction (also used as coda) and the interludes, follows the general form of a band

101

fantasia. This, of course, is not the usual quadrille-like thematic scheme of the Negro rag classicists. The latter scheme in its usual form can be diagrammed thus: A-A, B-B, A, C-C, D-D.

The remaining three of the first-published rags are in this record only because of their early date. Not one of them is really a rag or has even the syncopation of a third-rate cakewalk. Northrup's *Night on the Levee* is typical of the lot: all but one of its themes are inappropriately based on the Tin Pan Alley idea of American Indian music; the other is lifted from a section of Liszt's *Second Hungarian Rhapsody*.

Except for the lack of Negro contributions, this initial output fairly sets the pattern for the flood of rags that was to follow: for each composition of value a half-dozen or more pieces of trash turned out to capture the pieces of eight.

Ben R. Harney claimed from first to last to be the originator 9f ragtime. On the cover of his *Rag Time Instructor*, the first book of studies for this music, the claim is already being made for Harney: "Original Instructor to the Stage of the Now Popular Rag Time in Ethiopian Song"; and at the beginning of 1897 in the *Clipper Annual* covering events of the previous year there appears his own "courtesy" advertisement, reading as follows:

BEN R. HARNEY, author, musician and comedian.
Originator of the only Absolute Novelty in this
Season's Vaudevilles. Piano Playing in
cyncopated [*sic*] or "rag time," singing his own
"Coon" melodies and doing his original dancing.
AN ABSOLUTE HIT EVERYWHERE

Despite his belief, Harney was only a step in the popularization of an art of folk origins. Still, he was beyond doubt an important one. His 1896 success at Keith's and Tony Pastor's in New York skyrocketed him into the public eye, though he had no inconsiderable success around Chicago and on the road in the Midwest. If one was to choose the likeliest and best-equipped figure in show business to have catalyzed the ragtime situation in Chicago in December 1896 or January 1897, Ben Harney would be a good choice. But the event and the member of the Fourth Estate who reputedly named the music are both forgotten. A reference is to be found in the *Stage* monthly of September, 1904:

> "The slave song then is the folk song of a nation that had no music before the coming of the slaves. The comical side of Negro life, singing, and buck dancing, created a syncopated movement which they played on the banjo, guitar and piano without being taught. This branch of music was later named 'rag time' by a white newspaper critic who was not aware that he had discovered a name for it even after other writers and the public had taken the name up and used it."

The obvious reason that this writer did not know that he had coined a name was simply that he did not coin it, but was the first to print a name already in common use.

There is yet one more tiny item that bears on the ragtime race. It appears in the "Amusements" column of the January 24 *Chicago Inter-Ocean*, one day before the Krell application was mailed to Washington. It reads: "Howard & Bland will give rag-time selections on the piano." Minor artists these, and never heard from again, but there *was* something happening there in Chicago that in their own small way they were trying to cash in on.

The Mississippi River and its coonjining roustabouts figure most significantly in many of the first rags. There was a consciousness then of whence and from what the music had originally come. Pictures of Negroes dancing on the levee to banjo-picking and the clapping and stomping of onlookers grace the covers of *Mississippi Rag*, *A Night on the Levee*, and *Roustabout Rag* among others. Northrup's number stresses the subtitle "Rag Dance."

Rupert Hughes, in an important article that we shall have occasion to discuss more fully, wrote on April 1, 1899:

> "Negroes call their clog dancing 'ragging' and the dance a 'rag,' a dance largely shuffling. The dance is a sort of frenzy with frequent yelps of delight from the dancer and spectators and accompanied by the latter with hand clapping and stomping of feet. Banjo figuration is

103

very noticeable in ragtime music and division of one of
the beats into two short notes is traceable to the hand
clapping."

A description like this evokes not only a picture of the levees
and the decks of flat-bottom scows, but also of the Sunday
festivals in Congo Square. When Shep Edmonds spoke of the
roustabouts, he was speaking of the descendants of those who
danced the Bamboula, the Congo, and the Counjaille in the
old square and on many a bayou and Gulf Coast plantation.
"There were fifty or so of these roustabouts on each boat," he
said, "and they would load and unload the freight at each
stop. Traveling between stops, they would be on the cotton
bales playing their banjos while the best dancers did the
coonjine."

Publication of Turpin's *Harlem Rag* meant that the Negro
and St. Louis ragtime were in the race. Another Negro rag
followed shortly in 1898, *Ma Ragtime Baby*. Whitney-Warren
of Detroit published this and an 1899 successor called *Bos'n
Rag*, both authored by Fred S. Stone of that city. The remarkable Stone inherited the musical leadership of Detroit
from the equally remarkable "Old Man" Theo Finney. The
latter had started a music business in the Michigan city during
the Civil War, and from that beginning had built up a formidable musical dynasty. Finney's—and then Stone's—orchestras monopolized the Detroit entertainment and social world
to the almost complete exclusion of white performers. This
almost unbelievable state of affairs continued well up into the
1920's, when the plugging of the obnoxiously standardized
"name" bands by radio and the music business finally began
to crumble the Finney-Stone empire.

Before this happened, however, Fred S. Stone and his
stalwart colleagues—men like Cleveland-born Ben Shook,
composer of *Dat Gal of Mine* (1902) and Harry P. Guy, from
Zanesville, who once sang with the Fisk Jubilee Singers—
unionized the Detroit musicians and built the fine head-
quarters and club that are still in use. It was the white players
who had to petition for admission to the union, apparently
the only local in the country where this was the case.

Fred S. Stone died in the middle 1930's, but amiable 1
seventy-six-year-old Shook and scholarly Harry Guy, now
eighty, are still living as this book is written. Both look back
with pride on the brilliant old days that are now gone. Ben
Shook, who once studied in Leipzig, says: "The colored have
more wealth in Detroit than any other city in the U. S. We
own five hotels outright, like the Garson. But there is prejudice
now in some of the eating places. When war came and they
had to send for labor to come to Detroit, prejudice came, too.
In my lifetime the colored population here has grown from
1,500 to 350,000." But neither Ben in his beautiful home nor
old Harry in his modest widower's quarters has any pride in
music as it is today. "We are not developing the great musicians any more," says Shook. "You can only get to a certain
point by study alone. Music here—and everywhere else—got
to be a schoolboy's game and I did not want any more of it."

Chapter 6

AN ALBUM OF OLD PORTRAITS

IN THE little more than ten years between the publication of the first rag and 1908, a baker's dozen of men from both races came forward in the ragtime country to become serious composers of the new music, the adjective "serious" referring specifically to the enduring excellence of their work in relation to the vast current production of nondescript "rags." Another dozen writers produced work only a little less enduring, or else too limited in quantity to give them top ranking. Were the masterpieces of a Joplin not enough to establish the permanent value of ragtime, the large number of first-rate composers and top-rank rags produced before commercialism got in its work, or in spite of it, would assuredly secure that value.

Let us look at the roster of the men who created a music that many with good reason believe to be the first *original* American secular music to transcend the barriers of race for all to share. To be sure, there had been the ballads of Stephen Foster and James Bland (the Negro composer of *Carry Me Back to Old Virginny* and *In the Evening by the Moonlight*), but the continuing syncopation poised over regular rhythm ensures the complete originality of ragtime, a music that, in addition, is both vocal and instrumental. And it is a discovery so basic, too, that the Foster songs themselves are stripped of their occasional sentimentality and given a new form and spirit when they are "ragged."

Stephen Foster, like Louis Gottschalk, was an early innovator in the use of American Negro melodies and rhythms in white composition. Where Gottschalk based compositions of the European classical sort on this source material, Foster consciously tried to make faithful renderings of Negro river songs and the like. According to Willis Laurence James, of Spelman College, Foster as a child was carried to a Negro church by the family maid. In the four years (1846–50) that Foster spent as river-boat agency employee in Cincinnati, he had the opportunity of absorbing the coonjine dancing and singing of the boatmen. Foster's best and most Negroid songs —although not necessarily his most familiar ones—derive from this experience. Among these are *My Brudder Gum* (1849), *De Camptown Races* (1850), *Nellie Bly* (1850), and *The Glendy Burk* (1860). Foster, being himself musical, was unable to avoid alterations of the melodic line and distortions of the rhythm in the direction of our non-Negroid music.

Willis Laurence James calls *The Glendy Burk* a true ragtime song, adding that one, has to pat the hands and feet while singing it to feel the "ragged rhythm" in full tilt. The regular meter of hands and feet is, of course, the regular bass of ragtime, missing in the Foster songs. It was ragtime piano's combination of regular-metered bass and off-beat treble, as we have seen, that was its original contribution to scored music.

The great Negro ragtime pioneers, Scott Joplin and Tom Turpin, were followed by James Scott, Louis Chauvin, Arthur Marshall, Scott Hayden, Tony Jackson, and Ferdinand Joseph (Jelly Roll) Morton. Their ranking white ragtime brothers were Charles H. Hunter, Charles L. Johnson, Percy Wenrich, George Botsford, and Joseph F. Lamb. Joe Lamb, the white ragtime composer nearest to the Joplin classicism, is the exception that proves the rule. This New Jersey phenomenon is the only one not born or brought up in the folk-rag area.

107

As we follow the list, we follow the rivers: Scott Joplin, Texarkana, Texas; James Scott, Neosho, Missouri; Louis Chauvin born and Tom Turpin raised in St. Louis, Missouri; Arthur Marshall and Scott Hayden, Sedalia, Missouri; Tony Jackson and Jelly Roll Morton, New Orleans, Louisiana; Charles Hunter, Nashville, Tennessee; Charlie Johnson, Kansas City, Kansas; Percy Wenrich, Joplin, Missouri; and George Botsford, born in Sioux Falls, South Dakota, but raised in Iowa.

Following 1907–8 there comes a second generation of ragmen who, despite the accelerating distortion of the Negroid syncopated concept in Tin Pan Alley, maintained a pure output up to the very end of the ragtime era. By their entry on the scene in 1909, three white composers, J. Russel Robinson, Paul Pratt, and Henry Lodge, gain temporal precedence. They are followed in 1913 by three great Negroes, the third and last of the St. Louis ragtime generations: Artie Matthews of Minonk, Illinois; Charley Thompson of St. Louis; and Robert Hampton from the Arkansas Ozarks. The stories of the second generation will be told later.

Parenthetically we must observe at this point that concurrently with the birth and growth of the "classical" or folk ragtime in this area, another sort of ragtime was rising along the Atlantic seaboard. The account of this distinctive music—different both melodically and harmonically from classic ragtime—and of its leading figures, men like Luckey Roberts, James P. Johnson, Eubie Blake, Willie (The Lion) Smith, Fats Waller, and a number of others will be told in later chapters.

The first generation of classical Negro ragmen was led by Joplin and Turpin, the one born shortly after the Civil War and the other in the early seventies. The others were born in the early 1880's with the exception of James Scott, whose birth was in 1886. Once more, at the risk of being repetitive, it must be emphasized that there were large numbers of first-rank ragtime players and composers who never got a number published. Once ragtime publication began, it was always easier for the white writer to sell his numbers. It is doubtful, however, if any circumstances could have kept Scott Joplin, who was fired with the drive of genius, from publication and the top-rank position that he merits.

It is interesting to note that the classical European tradition rather than lack of opportunity kept one other talented Negro from perhaps making up a pioneer trio of rag composers with Joplin and Turpin. This was the child prodigy Blind Boone, born in 1864 at Miami, Missouri. Boone was musical successor to the dichotic phenomenon Blind Tom, who, though said to be semi-idiotic, repeated the most complex piano compositions after one hearing, including the mistakes often planted to trap him.

Boone, however, was in possession of all his faculties, and his musical powers were part of a well-rounded endowment. His heritage was the folk tradition of the ragmen. The childhood band he led, consisting of two tin whistles, jew's-harp ("juice-harp"), and triangle, was a country rag band. In 1874, when in the midst of classical training he quit his St. Louis school, it was into the alley dives of the Franklin Avenue and Morgan Street tenant belt, ringing with archaic piano and banjo ragtime, that he disappeared. When he was recaptured by his conventional sponsors, the "evil" spirit of ragtime was exorcised by a renewed application of the sonata treatment. Other safety-valve episodes, regarded at the time as "going on the bum," periodically interrupted his signally successful concert career. During the 1890's, however, Boone published a coon song or two, and in his later years, from his prosperous semiretirement at Columbia, Missouri, two "illegitimate" piano compositions came from his pen. These were *Boone's Rag Medleys*, No. 1 and No. 2, published by the local house of Allen Music. In No. 1 the "Strains from the Alley" include the folk tune *Make Me a Pallet on the Floor*. No. 2 is entitled "Strains from Flat Branch." The strains in this medley are *Carrie's Gone to Kansas City, I'm Alabama Bound, So They Say*, and *Oh, Honey, Ain't You Sorry?*

It is not with Boone, however, but with the first generation of ragmen, uninhibited by conservatory-bred frowns, that we are concerned at this moment. We already know Chauvin's short life and the slim trio of published tunes that remains from the wealth of music he created, as well as the tales of

Marshall and Hayden up to 1905. The rest of their histories we shall learn later. Tony Jackson's achievements and Jelly Roll Morton's highly colorful saga and an account of his prodigious output of one hundred and twenty copyrighted compositions, almost all of equal brilliance, belong with later chapters. Ragtime patriarch Tom Turpin's story and that of James Scott are the ones to tell now.

Thomas Million Turpin's father, John L. Turpin, and his mother, Lulu Waters Turpin, were from Savannah, Georgia, where the father was active in the rugged Reconstruction days. Indeed, there remains in Savannah a street, Turpin Hill, named after the family, and it was in this city that the older son, Charles, and his younger brother, Tom, were born, Charles about 1867 and Tom about 1873 or a few years earlier. The family, augmented by the birth of two daughters, moved to Mississippi and on to St. Louis, arriving there in the early 1880's.

Tom inherited his rugged physique and his independence from his father, "Honest John," a man who took lifelong pride in two facts: one that he had never done a day's work for another man after Emancipation, and the other that he had never fought with his fists. He did well as his own master, with his Silver Dollar Saloon (torn down with the rest of that district in 1903 to make room for the Union Station and the Plaza) and his livery stable. He made enough money, in fact, to afford the loss of large amounts on his own race horses. And he never lost a fight. "Old Man Jack" was Missouri state champion at the strong man's sport of butting heads. An elderly survivor of those days describes what it felt like. "John never fought a man—he would just grab your wrist and butt you in the head—just kiss your wrist good-by—you'd be blind for a week."

By the time Tom was fifteen he was a good six feet in height; later he was to weigh around three hundred pounds, with large hands and head and strong features. Tom and particularly Charlie, with their wavy hair and pale skin, could easily have "passed" if they had chosen to do so. By this time the former was a fine self-taught pianist, but to him music was always an avocation.

Tom was about eighteen when Charlie and he acquired an interest in the Big Onion Mine near Searchlight, Nevada. They spent a year or so there, but, getting only a pittance of gold, gave it up. Charlie went to Mexico as a jewelry salesman, and Tom wandered around the West for a time. Eventually both brothers returned to St. Louis, where Tom, in his early twenties, opened his own saloon, the Rosebud, at 2220 Market Street, in the sporting district. It was in this meeting-place of the St. Louis pianists, where he taught Sam Patterson and Louis Chauvin the rudiments of ragtime, that Tom Turpin was first introduced in an earlier chapter.

It was at the Rosebud also that he wrote his rags. The list of those published is short, but each one is a prototype of early folk ragtime at its purest and is strongly stamped with the Turpin personality. *Harlem Rag*, which we know as the first published Negro rag, was followed by the *Bowery Buck* (1899), with its buck-and-wing figures. Both of these rags refer to New York trips, and the latter may have been written there. *A Ragtime Nightmare* (1900) comes next. There is a legend that this is a Chauvin rag. Certainly the music, which has neither the typical Chauvin harmony nor his melodic handling, supports no such story, and Patterson, lifelong friend of Chauvin, says that it is definitely not so.

St. Louis Rag (1903) is Turpin's next, and the list of publications closes with *The Buffalo Rag* (1904). *Buffalo*, like *St. Louis*, compared with his earlier numbers, shows an added melodiousness, doubtless deriving, as we have observed, from Turpin's association with Joplin. *Buffalo* in particular has the characteristic tunefulness and dancelike rhythmic figures of plantation music. This aspect comes out strikingly in a banjo rendition like that of the late Vess L. Ossman, which may be heard on an early Victor record. The natural process by which piano ragtime developed from the plantation and levee camp banjos is here reversed with the most revealing results.

Three Turpin numbers were copyrighted but never published. Tom sent in the application for *Siwash—Indian Rag* from Butte, Montana, in 1909. This is followed by *Pan-Am Rag*, arranged by Arthur Marshall and registered in 1914. The last appearance of Turpin's name in the Copyright Division is on the application covering his instrumental number of 1917, *When Sambo Goes to France*, arranged by J. H. Harris.

In Tom's busy life as saloon-owner, gambling boss, "hotel"-keeper, and deputy constable, he found time to write eight copyrighted rags and to foster and guide the greatest generation of ragtimers any one city ever produced. Much more music came from his pen in the early 1900's for the weekly programs at his brother's tent show and later, in frequent collaboration with Artie Matthews, for the Booker T. Washington Theater on the same site. All of these rags, waltzes, and song skits have long since disappeared. On August 13, 1922 big, bluff, beloved Tom Turpin died. His widow survived him, and although he left no children, he had fairly earned his title of Father of St. Louis Ragtime.

Charlie Turpin got into politics as constable, the first Negro ever elected, it is said, to public office in Missouri. He later became justice of the peace and was active in St. Louis politics until his death, on Christmas Day 1935. When he died he left a trust fund of $105,000 to his family. Charlie had survived his younger brother by thirteen years.

In the tiny town of Neosho, Missouri, in 1886, when James Sylvester Scott was born into the humble Negro household of North Carolina bred James and Mollie Scott, prolific Missouri had added a name that, though it appears in no news items or directories of the day, was later to designate ragtime's second greatest composer. Today, twelve years after his death, James Scott's early years are recalled by his cousins Ruth Callahan and Ada Brown, the blues singer, and particularly by his sister Lena and his younger brothers Howard and Oliver.

James was about thirteen or fourteen when the family moved to Ottawa, Kansas, where his cousins lived. Before this he had become an accomplished pianist. Partly he owed this to an older Negro in Neosho, John Coleman, himself a fine player, who gave the boy about thirty lessons, including sight reading after Jimmy had already made considerable progress by ear. He had been born with that rarity, a sense of absolute pitch, which as a child he loved to exercise as a guessing game. Instead of guessing single notes, however, he insisted on chords. His training was all a catch-as-catch-can process because the Scotts owned no piano. James played his first composition on the cabinet organ in the Ottawa home of his cousin Ruth. It is amusing to speculate that the old, handed-down reed instrument may originally have been one of those sold from the ice-cream wagon of peddler John Stark.

The two families moved together down to Carthage, just above the town of Joplin in Missouri's southwest corner, where Kansas, the old Indian Territory, and Arkansas bordered the "show me" state. In Carthage, James continued to practice on the ancient reed organ until Ruth Callahan's family moved away. At this point Scott's father bought a piano for his talented son. James was next to the oldest in the family of six children housed in a wooden frame cottage at Fifth and Valley Streets. Lena was older than he, and he was followed by Douglas, Oliver, Bessie, and Howard. Their mother played the piano, and the other children became fair players by ear.

James never exceeded the five-foot-four height that he had then reached, though he later became more stocky. He was a quiet youth of a quick, knowing alertness. He went to work to help support the family, his first job being that of shoeshine boy in a Carthage barber shop. He was only sixteen when he got a job at the Dumars music store washing windows and learning a Dumars sideline, the art of framing pictures. One day the owner, hearing the muffled sound of syncopated strains coming through the stockroom door, surprised James playing on one of the pianos. He asked: "Can you read?"

"Read and play," said Scott, and from that day he waited on customers and plugged the sheet-music stock of the firm. He was spurred to composition, too, and one of his march tunes, capturing Dumars's ear, put the music dealer into the publishing business much as Joplin's *Maple Leaf* had started John Stark. The Dumars career as publisher was short in years and sparse in issue, for he hit no jackpot such as Stark had hit.

The first Dumars publication was Scott's *A Summer Breeze—March and Two Step*, brought out in March 1903, when its composer was seventeen years of age. His *Fascinator March* appeared in the early fall of the same year simultaneously with

113

a work called *Meteor March* by a fellow Carthage artist, Clarence Woods. The following year Dumars published Scott's *On the Pike March* in celebration of the St. Louis Exposition, and with this number the efforts of Scott's employer lapsed until 1909, when the firm, then called Dumars-Gammon, issued two Scott songs with words by Dumars himself. These are entitled *She's My Girl from Anaconda* and *Sweetheart Time*. Six compositions make up the known publications of this firm.

James Scott's first three instrumental numbers are finished products that, though reflecting the influence of *Maple Leaf*, show marked independence and originality. They are characterized by a flowing melodic content of strong Missouri country feeling.

Scott was a fixture with Dumars until around 1914, when at twenty-eight he ended his twelve-year connection with the music house and left Carthage. In the meantime he had visited St. Louis and met Joplin. His contact with John Stark gave him a publishing outlet that he felt he could depend upon for a long time to come. It was this year, which marked the outbreak of the First World War, that the St. Louis house brought out with considerable success one of Scott's masterpieces, the *Climax Rag*, as well as a waltz, *Suffragette*, which commemorates a war then raging on the home front.

The year 1914 also saw a James Scott song, *Take Me Out to Lakeside*, with words by Ida Miller, published by Ball Music Company of Carthage. Lakeside Amusement Park was located midway between Carthage and Joplin, about thirty miles away. Between the time of the three 1914 publications and the last of those by Dumars, no less than eleven James Scott numbers had appeared, beginning with *Frog Legs* in 1906 and ending with an orchestral arrangement of *The Fascinator* brought out in 1912 by Berry Music Company of Kansas City. Allen Music of Columbia (publishers of *Boone's Rag Medleys*) issued *Great Scott Rag* in 1909. The remaining nine numbers, bearing the new, punning Stark trademark, which shows a stork, included the top-rank rags *Hilarity*, *Grace and Beauty*, and *Quality Rag*—"*A High Class Rag*."

James Scott moved to Kansas City, Missouri, in 1914. Little is known about his first years there except that he married and began teaching music. In those first years he went from house to house giving lessons. By 1919 he owned his own house, with studio, and taught his pupils on a new grand piano that was his dearest possession. In 1916 he became organist and musical arranger for the Panama Theater, and for the next thirteen or fourteen years theater work was a large part of his activity.

His cousin Patsy Thomas describes James Scott as he was at this period:

"He was a small man, only my height, weighing about 140 pounds. He was a light brown color with a thin face and a lower jaw that protruded a little. Everybody called him 'Little Professor.'

"He always walked rapidly, looking at the ground—would pass you on the street and never see you—seemed always deep in thought. If anyone spoke to him on the street, he would jump, look surprised and pleased. For us, his cousins, he always wanted to kiss, no matter where. I was walking one day with my boy friend and we met Jimmy. He started to kiss me, but I only shook hands. From that day on, he disliked my boy friend, whom I later married. His parting words would always be 'Will you be home tomorrow? O.K. I'll come over and play my new piece for you.' With us this was always a delightful treat. We loved his music, although people who didn't understand it thought it was too fancy.

"Jimmy never talked about his music, just wrote, wrote, wrote, and played it for anyone who would listen. He wrote music as fluently as writing a letter, humming and writing all at the same time. He liked playing as many notes as possible under one beat with the right hand. I remember his hands so well: short fingers square at the ends, very thin fingernails cut very short—fingers that fairly danced as they covered the keyboard. He sat at the piano with the left leg wrapped around the stool, and his body kept very still, no bouncing with the rhythm as one sees today. His music thrilled me. Often today I hear his pieces on the radio, and if I close my eyes, I can still see his fingers flying over the keys."

During these years Scott stayed in touch with Stark, and nine more of his rags appeared in Stark's catalogue. *Evergreen Rag* (1915) and *Honeymoon Rag* and *Prosperity Rag* (both 1916) are outstanding among these, and the first is the only exception to an ever increasing complexity. His compositions reflect more and more his magnificently accomplished playing, though it must be said that no scores can completely convey the rhythmic subtleties of a great ragtime performance.

2   Scott made several piano rolls by the early direct-recording method. Other players describe these as sounding "like two people playing." Two of these rolls are listed at the end of this book.

The pages of the later Scott rags, abounding in four- and five-note treble chords and varied bass constructions, are what pianists call "black" scores. We owe the preservation of these compositions, so representative of serious ragtime, to John Stark, for no other publisher would have printed scores so impossible for the average player. At best they might have appeared in the simplified versions concealing many numbers that originally, under the composer's hands, were masterpieces.

Two other Scott numbers from 1919 were uncovered recently during an interview with Emil Seidel, who himself came as a ragtime player from the northwest Arkansas Ozarks, a hillbilly stone's throw from Joplin, Neosho, and Carthage. Midway on the path to his present high position in the musical-entertainment world, Emil engaged in music publishing with his brother Isadore. Emil exhibited two Scott originals bearing the date 1919 and the trademark of I. Seidel, Indianapolis. One, *Dixie Dimples*, is a rag; the other, *Springtime of Love*, a waltz.

In Emil's collection of sheet music appeared three further numbers by Scott's Carthage contemporary Clarence Woods. These were *Sleepy Hollow Rag* and *Graveyard Blues*, published in 1918 by Seidel, and a fine earlier number, *Slippery Elm Rag*, 1912, published in Dallas, Texas. Woods had evidently been around the Southwest for a number of years after leaving Carthage, for an item in the January 1917 *Rag Time Review* still dates him in this area: "An Austin, Texas paper has the following to say of a former Carthage, Missouri boy: Clarence Woods, the new pianist at the Majestic, is called the 'Ragtime

Wonder of the South' and well deserves that title; because he just makes that piano talk."

When Scott and his wife settled in 1919 at 402 Nebraska Street in Kansas City, he was working on *Pegasus—A Classic Rag* for Stark publication the following year. The titling of this rag to utilize the cover design of a 1908 publication of the same name by Robert B. Stirling expresses better than words the final waning of the ragtime vogue in those years. So, too, does the dwindling of the once copious Stark output to a mere dribble. But John Stark was sticking with classic ragtime to the end. That year he brought out two more Scott tunes: *Modesty Rag* and the song *Shimmie Shake*, with words by Cleota Wilson.

Only three subsequent James Scott numbers remain to posterity, all published by indomitable John Stark. *Victory Rag*, a "heavy" number of great difficulty, went on the market in 1921. Its companion in that year was *Don't Jazz Me—Rag* (*I'm Music*). Scott's swan song was *Broadway Rag*, issued in 1922. Stark's title, *Don't Jazz Me* (Scott's rags were sent in untitled), reveals the ragtime pioneer's opinion of jazz, which was eclipsing the already "old-fashioned" ragtime. Ironically, of course, jazz carries on much of the ragtime tradition in band form, but the public that once had been swept away by the new name "ragtime" was now being entranced by a name newer still.

In 1936, Paul Whiteman, guest-writing the Winchell "On Broadway" syndicated column, wrote: "In St. Louis, Missouri, we once met John Stark, the original 'rag' man. He was well over eighty then, and though his house issued the original 'Maple Leaf Rag,' he despised all forms of jazz. . . . Refused to attend our concert for any inducement."

In 1906, when John Stark had brought out his first publication by Scott, the scene had been different and the mood one of triumphant optimism. A far cry from the angry title on the 1921 opus was the blurb he had written then for *Frog Legs*: "Now we need adjectives in fifteen degrees with a rising inflection. We need letters a foot high and a few exclamation points about the size of Cleopatra's needle—but we won't tell you of this piece, we want to surprise you."

117

These early Stark words were right, as the publisher's blurb too often is not. The error in the general ragtime situation that John Stark did not share was that of its presentation as a mere novelty dependent on the fickle public fancy, an inescapable corollary of the Negro's position and the scenes in which ragtime was born. The dead inertia of society was against John Stark and Scott Joplin in their role of dedicated pioneers of "classic" ragtime as a serious music.

John Stark, once he had been converted to ragtime, formed a clear concept of its rightful place in musical history. Optimistically underestimating the hostile weight of prejudice and artistic snobbery and ignorance, he once wrote: "Since we forced the conviction on this country that what is called a rag may possibly contain more genius and psychic advance thought than a Chopin nocturne or a Bach fugue, writers of diluted and attenuated imitations have sprung up from Maine's frozen hills to the boiling bogs of Louisiana." Today the publisher's passionate convictions seem ready for vindication.

In those last years James Scott busied himself with teaching and in addition formed an eight-piece band that played dances and beer parks until well into the 1930's. He played solo and as orchestra leader and arranger in various movie theaters—the Panama on East Twelfth Street, the Lincoln at Eighteenth and Lydia, and the Eblon on bustling Vine Street in the Negro district—until sound pictures came in. He stayed on at the Eblon as organist until around 1929 or 1930, when, in company with thousands of fellow musicians throughout the country, the film-track music drove him out of the theaters for good. And during all this time James Scott, second only to the great Joplin as ragtime master, sat at his grand piano and composed syncopated pieces of an ever increasing complexity and seriousness, pieces that are lost forever.

When his wife, Nora, died, James, childless but accompanied by his piano and his pet dog, moved in with his cousin Ruth Callahan at 1926 Springfield across the Missouri River, in Kansas City, Kansas. His health was poor and began to decline rapidly in a condition of chronic dropsy. "Even then," Ruth recalls, "he kept on composing and playing, although his fingers were swollen and very painful." On August 30, 1938 James Sylvester Scott, aged fifty-two, died at Douglas Hospital. Two days later his body was laid beside that of his wife in Westlawn Cemetery.

From 1914 to 1938, the years that James Scott lived in Kansas City, he was a fellow citizen of genial, alert Charles L. Johnson, one of the white pioneers of folk ragtime; but for many reasons the two men never met. Johnson was born in that city December 3, 1877, and has lived in the twin Kansas towns all his life, a full musical life of many accomplishments. His syncopated publications begin in 1899, the year of the *Maple Leaf Rag*, and his total printed compositions, including pop songs, ballads, waltzes, teaching pieces, and so on, run into the hundreds, having appeared under three different pseudonyms besides his own name. He is a respected member of ASCAP, and today, at seventy-four, maintains an office at 806 Grand Avenue in the Missouri city, where he is busy with composing and arranging. His biggest money-making hit was the sentimental ballad *Sweet and Low*. On this one song alone Charles Johnson made thirty thousand dollars. When it appeared, in 1919, the folk composer had already become a part of the Tin Pan Alley set-up.

The two men, James Scott and Charles L. Johnson, nevertheless were fellow folk artists in their beginnings. Whatever the differences of opportunity in their two worlds, both showed early aptitude. Charlie Johnson had what is commonly considered the better training, although the conservatories hardly countenanced ragtime and therefore were not likely to improve it. His classical teacher, Professor Kreiser, and he parted company over this very issue after three years—a beautiful friendship broken on the rocky reefs of ragtime.

In 1899, while James Scott was shining shoes in Carthage, Johnson's *Doc Brown's Cake Walk* was being published by the local J. W. Jenkins music store, and when Sousa came to Kansas City, Jenkins arranged for the March King to play it. "The number," says Johnson, "was named after an old, eccentric colored fellow who wore a swallowtail coat, carried a cane, and wore a plug hat. He would cakewalk on the street for a nickel or dime. Jenkins photographed him for the cover."

119

Charles Johnson needed no John Stark to fight battles for his music. His succession of bucolic rags, *Dill Pickles, Apple Jack (Some Rag), Fine and Dandy, Beedle-Um-Bolo—Slow Drag,* and so on by the dozens, up through *Hen Cackle Rag* and *Teasing the Cat* to the *Snookums Rag* of 1918, achieved ready publication and ample, nation-wide plugging. For many years Johnson was able to issue his own numbers and take the publisher's profit too. Then finally he sold the whole catalogue for a fine price to Rossiter in Chicago. *Dill Pickles* today stands out, not only as Johnson's own favorite among them, but also as the piece worthiest of all of his to stand among the top-rank rags.

Charlie Johnson was but one of a successful group of white Kansas City musicians. Another was Charles N. Daniels, who is credited with arranging Scott Joplin's *Original Rags* in 1899. Daniels wrote the fabulously successful *Hiawatha—A Summer Idyl* in 1901 under the pseudonym of Neil Moret. This number made him independently wealthy and set the style for a flood of Indian intermezzos, including Johnson's *Iola* and the Helf-Hager *Laughing Water.* Daniels moved to Detroit as arranger for the Whitney-Warren '(later Remick) music-publishing house and wrote a number of hits, which include *You Tell Me Your Dream, I'll Tell You Mine; Poppies;* and *Chloe.* He later established the Villa Moret publishing house in San Francisco, where he died on January 23, 1943.

Then there was E. H. (Harry) Kelly, who wrote the hit instrumental slow drag, *Peaceful Henry,* the same year that *Hiawatha* appeared. Johnson tells the by now typical, stereotyped story of the christening of this number. "It was named after an old colored janitor in the basement and we all called him Peaceful Henry."

In this coterie, too, were Ernie Burnett, remembered for the perennial favorite *My Melancholy Baby,* and Lucien Denni, whose *Oceana Roll* was a hit of the 1911 season. Denni, whose foreign origin makes him unique in a Midwestern group, was born in Nancy, France, in 1886. But of all these men, Charles L. Johnson wrote the rags that are remembered most.

Charles H. Hunter, of Nashville, Tennessee, is a white pioneer of ragtime whose life, by contrast with the lives of

Charles Johnson and his worldly and successful group, reads like that of a Negro composer. The short span of his years in some ways parallels the brief story of Louis Chauvin. One cannot say that in 1878 at Columbia, Tennessee, Charles H. Hunter first saw the light of day, for he was born almost totally blind. Hunter was a red-haired, freckled youth, muscular, and of medium height, when he left the School for the Blind and went to work for the Jesse French Piano Company in Nashville at the piano tuner's trade which he had learned in school. Among the pianos he was free to learn an art, too, that of the self-taught pianist. There was no classical training, no technique of roulades and trills or intricate fingering to stand between the blind, good-natured, but keenly sensitive boy and the folk music that filled the streets of Nashville and the small hill farms that surrounded it.

The pure strains of the people are in Charles Hunter's music, and the evocations too of scenes his blind eyes never saw, of possum and sweet-potato feast on the rough table of the log cabin, of hunting among the hackberry trees, the sumacs and the aromatic sassafras on the slopes, of cotton bolls gleaming white on the bushes among the laborers' black hands and faces.

F. G. Fite, of Nashville, published Hunter's first rag in 1899. *Tickled to Death* bespeaks in its archaic and very raggy measures a genuine talent, one much akin melodically to that of Tom Turpin. This first Hunter number became very popular throughout the country and is to be found on a number of early piano rolls as well as early phonograph cylinders and disks. The fine rag, *A Tennessee Tantalizer*, appeared the following year under the Nashville imprint of H. A. French. The same firm brought out two Hunter works in 1901, *'Possum and 'Taters* and *Queen of Love—Two Step*. The latter number, it is true, is arranged without syncopation in the score, but it rags very easily and there is no reason to doubt that as played by Hunter it was a ragtime number. The same year Fite copyrighted *Cotton Bolls*, published by O. K. Houck Piano Co., of Nashville.

In 1902 Charles Hunter was transferred to Jesse French's St. Louis store. The same year saw Fite's publication of his

Just Ask Me. Why We Smile appeared under the same publisher's trademark in 1903. Although it may have been composed in St. Louis, it is a fine folk rag full of Tennessee memories.

Two years elapsed before another Hunter rag appeared, this one published by Charles K. Harris of New York. Its title, *Back to Life*, signalizing its composer's return to the lists, was one of bad omen otherwise, for in less than two years the gifted blind man was dead. One further tune remains from Hunter's pen. This is *Seraphine Waltzes*, a 1905 Stark publication.

Before all this, however, the free life of the St. Louis District had opened up its doors for Hunter as it had for Louis Chauvin. He forsook his job to spend his time there. Led from wine room to wine room, he played for the underworld and received in return the gift of thoughtless living. Liquor and women hastened his steps down the road that Chauvin was following. Some time in 1906 Hunter straightened himself out and married, but it was too late. Tuberculosis possessed his body and late that year or early in 1907, only six weeks after his marriage, he died.

Before Charles Hunter's work began to appear, H. A. French brought out in 1898 a composition by another Nashville writer, Thomas E. Broady. This is *Mandy's Broadway Stroll*, a simply arranged but first-class and truly Negroid piano rag. French also published *A Tennessee Jubilee* in 1899 by Broady, and one year later his *Whittling Remus* rag.

George Botsford, who belongs in the group of white pioneers, was born in Sioux Falls, South Dakota, in 1874, but was brought up from childhood in Iowa. His first copyrighted number, the *Katy Flyer—Cake Walk, Two Step*, appeared in Centerville in 1899. His first and biggest syncopated hit was *Black and White Rag*, published in 1908, a number widely recorded for phonograph and pianola and—like *Dill Pickles, Maple Leaf, Grace and Beauty*, and the ubiquitous *Twelfth Street Rag* of Euday Bowman—still widely played today. Good Botsford rags that followed this tune include, up to 1916, *Grizzly Bear, Pianophiends, Texas Steer, Universal*, and *Boomerang*.

Botsford, like Charles L. Johnson, went into Tin Pan Alley,

but he moved to its center in Manhattan. Around 1914–15, when he had his own publishing company, he made a series of experiments in "miniature operas," written to be sung by three or four people. This interesting idea never received acceptance. The best of Botsford's early rags, like *Black and White*, have much of the folk-melodic tradition. They are excellent numbers, lacking only a little the direct melodic statement and differentiation between themes of Johnson's *Dill Pickles*. After a long career, productive of many sorts of music Botsford died in New York in January 1949.

The last picture in the album is that of modest, gifted, lovable Percy Wenrich, born on January 23, 1880, in Joplin, Missouri. We speak to the portrait: "Mr. Wenrich, you are one of the pioneers of ragtime." The features come alive, and he replies: "Maybe, and a few coons like Ernest Hogan and Scott Joplin." Percy Wenrich, who sits by the window in his room in Manhattan's Park Sheraton Hotel in 1950 at seventy years of age, is still "The Joplin Kid" of the 1890's.

"I was raised in Joplin and was twenty-one when I left. I was just a typical hick-town pianist. It seems like I always played and always syncopated. Mother taught me—she called herself 'the Berry Country pianist.' My father was a fine tenor. He was a staunch Republican and wrote campaign songs for the various candidates. He was postmaster from 1896 right on through Teddy Roosevelt's time.

"Speaking of Teddy reminds me of a time that he came to Missouri for an old-fashioned possum and coon hunt. It seems that the best hounds in the county were owned by an old Negro who said he wouldn't loan them even to Teddy Roosevelt unless he could come along and watch after them. So he came along all right. When it came time for the barbecue dinner, Teddy looked around at everybody before they could raise any objections and said: 'Now, Uncle eats with us white folks, because we're all Americans here.'

"Well, anyway, my older brother, my little sister, we all played piano. When the minstrels came through we heard the tunes and sang them in our own minstrel shows. I had rhythm in me. Oh, I thought I was a hot shot playing Sousa's *Liberty Bell*!"

Shifting in his wheel chair, Percy Wenrich talks on: "Joplin, Missouri, was a Western gambling and mining town in those days. The north end of Main Street was as wide open as a barn door. When you left the hotel, there was just a barber shop and then you were right in there at the House of Lords Saloon—bar on the first floor, gambling on the second, and sporting house on the third.

"I heard colored fellows play all the time, and there were piano players you never heard of and no one ever will—a piano and all its keys was just a toy to them. Lionel (Babe) La Tour, a gambler from Sedalia, knew all the colored players. He used to take me around when I could have been hung for even being there.

"I was only twelve and playing *The Darkey Tickle*. Rube Stones worked for the J. Frank Walker music store; they were farther south on Main Street. We would get on two pianos near the front door and play it together. Walker never objected to the crowds.

"I saw all this sheet music and figured I could compose too. I made up a 6/8 two-step with a fancy title: *L'Inconnu*, and paid Sol Bloom, the Chicago publisher, to print it. I was seventeen at the time. I got one thousand copies and sold them from door to door in Joplin and Galena, Kansas, but I guess I sold most of them up on North Main Street.

"Well, I was twenty-one when my brother and my folks turned my nose away from the House of Lords and pointed me towards Chicago. So I went to the Chicago Musical College run by Flo Ziegfeld's father. I studied for a little while, but I wasn't used to handling my own money. I got around the saloons down on Twenty-second Street in the District and one day I was broke. My teacher, Louis Falk, loaned me some money. I used it to go back to Joplin. But Chicago had done something to me. I couldn't stand Joplin after a month, so my brothers financed me back north.

"I got a job at Joe Suits, played back in the wine room, one dollar a night, but I was too good for the place—I could read music. In a couple of weeks I went on to Charlie Smith's Utopia Cafe and Bar, two dollars to two and a half a night, and then Jack Crawford's swell joint on Wabash, ten dollars on a good night. I was still such a rube I passed the basket for tips. The White Seal Wine man, Simmy Weinman, wised me up. He said: 'Kid, you don't have to pass the kitty. Let 'em walk over to it.'

"In 1902 I was making real money, never less than one hundred dollars a week. I was at Freddie Train's then, a famous place at 2008 Wabash, never a dirty word there. The best people in Chicago came there, the Potter Palmers, Sidney Love, Ashton Stevens, and the rest. It was a decent place with the atmosphere of a dump.

"I wrote my first song there—kept deviling Jim O'Dea, who wrote the words for Daniels's *Hiawatha* song, to write some lyrics for me. One night he gave me a set of words called *Wabash Avenue after Dark*. I fitted music to it and we started singing it with close harmony at the end. It was never published, but it got to be a famous song all over Chicago:

> *New York has its famous tenderloin*
> *And a good old place it is;*
> *Frisco is blessed with its Barbary Coast,*
> *Where life is one dream of bliss;*
> *Boston and Philly have thoroughfares gay,*
> *New Orleans, too, is in line;*
> *But Chicago, you see,*
> *Possesses for me*
> *A spot that is truly divine.*

CHORUS:

> *Its Wabash Avenue after dark!*
> *Fancy, well I should so remark,*
> *If you'd know where gaiety reigns,*
> *Stop in a while at Freddy Train's.*
> *There's Dotties and Toddies,*
> *And Gussies and Freds,*
> *Girls that ought to be*
> *Home in their beds—*
> *They're all good fellows when out on a lark,*
> *On Wabash Avenue after dark,*
> *On Wabash Avenue after dark.*

125

> *While stepping about on the Avenue*
> *And imbibing Lemp's good beer,*
> *There is Fleming's and the Bohemia,*
> *Where one will find good cheer;*
> *But if 57 Varieties of popular songs you'd hear,*
> *Bobbie Adams and Sid,*
> *And The Joplin Kid*
> *At Train's will delight your ear.*

"That started me off writing. I wrote hundreds of little numbers for the McKinley Music Company at five dollars apiece. Don't ask me about them—they were junk for the ten-cent-store counters. But they got me out of the District—just in time, maybe. Anyway, I never went back.

"There was a Walker Company in Chicago that advertised 'We Write Music to Your Words' and made big promises about getting the stuff published. They charged ten dollars a song and nothing ever got published, of course. Uncle Sam finally put them out of business. When I was working for them," Wenrich continues, "I got a dollar and a half for each song and did fifteen a day. I got it down to a system. If the words were too long I wrote 'To be recited' over part of them and put in some patter chords for the piano underneath.

"One of my first published numbers was *Ashy Africa*, issued by Buck & Carney in 1903. This was a good many years before Frank Buck was to be known as the 'Bring 'Em Back Alive' African explorer.

"*Noodles* was my first real rag. Arnett-Delonais published it in 1906. It's 'Missouri' all through, I think. *The Smiler* came out the next year. When Forster bought it from Arnett, they put 'A Joplin Rag' under the name. They meant it for the town, but if they had meant Scott Joplin it would have suited me. I made it real 'Negro' the way I felt it.

"A year after that I went to New York."

Percy Wenrich looked out the window. After a pause he added: "I never went back to the District. It wasn't my kind of life. I did it for a while for a reason. It gave me my start."

With that start Percy Wenrich, "The Joplin Kid," became one of the best-known and most successful figures in a Tin

Pan Alley that was waxing opulent in the first three decades of this century. He is first to admit that he has written a lot of stuff just to sell. This is not remarkable, but it is a matter to excite surprise to find, every few years, a real Missouri folk tune coming from his pen. "My biggest hits," he says, "were ones that I had to fight the publishers to take. They said: 'They are too homey, the public wants glamour.' When they published *Put On Your Old Grey Bonnet*, it opened their eyes."

And it is those "homey" tunes like *Grey Bonnet*, *When You Wore a Tulip*, and *Kentucky Days* and the racily idiomatic early rags, *Noodles*, *The Smiler*, and *Crabapples*, that will keep Percy Wenrich's name green.

Chapter 7

RAGTIME IN ~~TEN~~ TWENTY EASY LESSONS

THE appearance of Ben Harney's *Rag Time Instructor* in the fall of 1897 signalized that ragtime, figuratively speaking, had cast off its rags and was now being received in polite society. A quick revolution had taken place, effected by May Irwin's fashionable coon-shouting and Williams and Walker's dapper cakewalking, and topped off by Harney's theater appearances as the first white ragtime performer. Ragtime was no longer a thing exclusively of the Negro world and of the tenderloin, whispered about but never heard. It belonged now to the people, and everyone wanted to learn to play it just as they wanted to cakewalk.

The Negroes had originated something that overnight developed a commercial value, and presto! as suddenly as a ten-dollar bill vanishes from a magician's hand, it became the white man's property. The main course of a folk music that already, in Scott Joplin's work, had moved over the border-line that separates folk art from fine art was channelized in a new direction. As an article of commerce it must be so simple as not to tax the hands of schoolgirls; it must be banal because money has always professed to know "what the people want";

it must be producible by Tin Pan Alley hacks. Ragtime, in short, was a hit.

Although Scott Joplin and John Stark could not know it at the time, they were already checkmated. Realization of the Negro composer's dream—which the white publisher had come to share—of fine ragtime accepted as classic was a thing that neither man would live to see. But they kept on fighting. A hundred ragtime masterpieces by James Scott, Joseph Lamb, and the Texarkana master are ours today because Joplin and Stark did not know that they were licked.

This rapid-fire development of events had taken place in a bare twelvemonth's time. After the slow build-up into the earlier 1890's, the cakewalk leaped into the national spotlight in 1896, and from the stage spotlight it moved on into fashionable homes and throughout the whole white social structure. The music went along with the cakewalk, and suddenly late that year the roustabout's name for it, ragtime, clicked and was taken up by everyone. Simultaneously the music arrangers, who had pecked away at syncopation for ten or more years, learned suddenly how to score the tricky rhythms. Music business, with the precocious know-how that was soon to build a huge industry, initiated systematic plugging and organized distribution. Music dealers and later even the ten-cent stores began a sales drive with sheet music and Pianola rolls. Sentimental ballad, Irish ditty and dialect song, and the coon song were overshadowed by the new arrival.

But the sheet music that had seemed so easy to play as the plugger ran through it at the store fairly bristled with difficulties at home. The notes did not seem to fit as they had in the waltzes, the polkas, and the galops. The syncopations and the accents falling strangely on the weak beats would not come right. So the teachers came in, as they will always come in when there are people to be taught, and with them the instruction books. Harney's *Rag Time Instructor* was only a start, a hastily assembled collection of scattered exercises padded out by some of Theo Northrup's "ragtime" arrangements of numbers like *Come, Thou Fount* and *The Man That Broke the Bank at Monte Carlo*. The book fell far short of its claim to be "full instructions how to play rag time." The Harney obituary forty-one years later in *Variety* made the comment: "He was . . . the author of *The Rag Time Instructor*, but he could not endow his readers with the nimble fingers which were the basis of his artistry."

For the next few years the demand for instruction grew as the rags continued to pour on the market. After *Maple Leaf Rag* scored its big success in 1900 and its technical difficulties became the frustration of the amateur, ragtime teachers began opening studios and hanging out the new shingles: "Learn to play ragtime and be popular." Here was a golden opportunity for the right man, and the right man was in Chicago, ready. He was twenty-two-year-old Axel Christensen, born in Chicago in 1881 of Danish parents. In 1903 many readers of the *Chicago Daily News* paused at an ad that bore the bold heading: "RAGTIME TAUGHT IN TEN LESSONS."

In the twelve years after this initial ad appeared, the small studio hired by the hour had expanded into a nation-wide empire of thirty-five well-staffed schools ruled by Axel W. Christensen, "Czar of Ragtime." Earlier than this, however, young Axel as a ten-year-old piano student had been the typical American boy, to whom piano practice is drudgery while the kicks and bruises of football are fun. By fifteen, nevertheless, he had been suborned into learning pieces like the *Battle of Waterloo* and *Silvery Waves*. Then, attending a party, he was shocked to find himself crowded from the piano by a callow, pimply youth who immediately captivated all the girls with the syncopated strains of *My Coal Black Lady*. Axel immediately took his musical education into his own hands, and his progress thereafter with numbers like *Dora Dean* and *Mister Johnson, Turn Me Loose* amazed parents who had heard him struggling for years with his *Waterloo*.

In seven more years Axel Christensen, by then considered a highly adept player, took the studio mentioned above. Entering the building the day after he had advertised, he found it crowded with people waiting to learn ragtime at fifty cents a lesson. Next day his wife registered new pupils while he frantically taught. In a few weeks they moved to larger studios in the Fine Arts Building, on Michigan Boulevard. After a busy week of lessons running into hours of overtime, Christensen was summoned to the office of the managing director of the building. He found himself on the carpet, arraigned by his long-haired neighbors. The complaints were: one, misdemeanor—advertising, considered as unethical for music teachers in those days; two, felony—teaching ragtime. Sentence: that he leave the premises for good.

Stout-hearted Dane that he was, Axel refused to budge. But he shortly changed his mind after the Bach-Beethoven-Brahmins began picketing in the hall outside and disrupting his lessons with their derisive chant: "Any rags, any bones, any bottles today?"

"I secured quarters in the Athenaeum Building," Christensen recalls. "They were not so fussy there—as a matter of fact, the janitor asked me if I intended to sleep in the studio."

Although thousands were clamoring to learn the music, it can be seen that the ragtime road was far from easy. A bitter minority was dead against it, and the attacks were articulate and loud. A real controversy arose. While the vast American majority went right on liking ragtime, its enemies established one ostensible fact and burned it into the popular mind: "Ragtime is an inferior music and a mere passing fad." So successful was this propaganda that many white people played ragtime with a faint sense of guilt as if they were being unfaithful to Bach and their own better natures.

The controversy continued at a lively pace for over twenty years, as long as the ragtime vogue itself lasted. The embattled and bloody combatants were able then to turn on one another once more over the new "jass" music.

The earliest notable defender of ragtime was Rupert Hughes, who wrote "A Eulogy of Ragtime" for the Boston *Musical Record* of April 1, 1899. "It is young and unhackneyed and throbbing with life," he wrote. "And it is racial." A part of his eulogy follows:

"Ragtime music meets little encouragement from the scholarly musician. It has two classes of enemies: the green-eyed, blue-goggled fogy who sees in all popular music a diminution of the attention due to Bach's works; and the more modern scholar who thinks he has dismissed

the whole musical activity of the Negro by a single contemptuous word.

"It is only a reminiscence of Scotch lyrics; behold the
Scotch snap, or regarding ragtime, 'It is only a distorted
reminiscence of Spanish and Mexican dances; behold the
syncopation.'

"But neither the reproach of 'reminiscence' nor the
equal odium of 'innovation' has ever succeeded against a
vital musical idea, and I feel safe in predicting that ragtime has come to stay, that it will be taken up and developed into a great dance-form to be handled with respect, not only by a learning body of Negro creators, but
by the scholarly musicians of the whole world.

"To attempt to prove what the future is going to do
would be idle; and I must rest content with trying to
describe rag-time music as it is, after pausing to remind
the sceptic that all oaks were once acorns; that the
venerate sonata was once a bundle of popular dances."

On the other side, one line of prosecution was the "low
origins" of ragtime. *Musical America*, in its issue of March 29,
1913, condemned ragtime as a city music rather than a folk
music, which latter is a "product of the idyllic village atmosphere, mirroring the joys and sorrows, hopes and passions of
the country people." The article "discovers" that ragtime was
born and developed in the city. "It exalts noise, rush and
street vulgarity. It suggests repulsive dance-halls and restaurants." (Strange how romantic a restaurant became if
situated in Vienna or Budapest!) *Musical America* concludes
its denunciation with a sparkling bit of fact-finding: "There
is no trace of any racial idiom in ragtime." This choice
datum was apparently based on a belief that cities are not
inhabited by people.

"Ragtime is music meant for the tired and materially
bored mind," reads one typical criticism. "It is essentially
obvious, vulgar, yet strong. Like a criminal novel, it is full of
bangs and explosions, devised in order to shake up the over-
worked mind." One Professor Liebling, in the *Musician*,
March 1900, had a reply for this: "There is no such thing as

good music or bad music in a moral sense. You may set good music to bad or vicious wordings and the music becomes bad by implication. So with ragtime. It is now lending itself to low vaudeville, in the main, and because of that association the music is denounced."

Only the bold employed such frontal attacks as that quoted from *Musical America*. The favorite approach was: "There's nothing new in syncopation, the old masters all used it." These critics ignored the absence from European music of that day of the African polyrhythms in which Negro ragtime is rich, as well as the basic invention of ragtime's syncopated treble against regularly accented bass. They find ragtime everywhere, in the snap of the Scotch reel, in Hungarian gypsy music, and in the classics from Frescobaldi to Brahms. On the snide level of this sort of depreciation is the squib of one A. J. Goodrich in the *Musician* of November 1901: "Unusual rhythmic combinations and syncopations have been used so extensively by high-class composers that it is not possible for coon song composers to invent anything along these lines."

The real highbrow elaborated this thesis along more erudite lines. The tactics, however, were likely to backfire, and this happened to a writer in the February 1913 issue of *Musical Opinion* (London). He started out bravely to bolster his statement that ragtime syncopation exists in all music *by first citing the Negro spirituals*. He then quotes a short passage from Beethoven, and brings up rather lamely with: "I should say that this figure from *Leonora No. 3* is better described as syncopation than ragtime, though I should be sorry to be suddenly asked why. I can only say that I feel in my bones it is so." Feeling around for a clincher to bolster his collapsing argument, this deponent comes up with a gem: the *Golliwog's Cake-Walk* of Debussy.

An unknown writer quoted in *Opera Magazine* in 1916, tired of this sort of sniping from the "me too" camp, unburdened himself as follows: "If any musician does not feel in his heart the rhythmic complexities of the *Robert E. Lee*, I should not trust him to feel in his heart [those] of Brahms." He enthusiastically expanded his point: "Ragtime has carried the com-

133

plexity of the rhythmic subdivision of the measure to a point never before reached in the history of music. It has established subtle, conflicting rhythms [and] has gone far beyond most other popular music in the freedom of inner voices (yes, I mean polyphony) and of harmonic modulation."

The staid old London *Times* was saying: "Ragtime is absolutely characteristic of its inventors—from nowhere but the United States could such music have sprung. . . . Nor can there be any doubt about its vigour, brimming over with life. . . . Here for those who have ears to hear are the seeds from which a national art may ultimately spring."

America's *Metronome* magazine (May 20, 1901) was gloating, "Rag time's days are numbered. We are sorry to think that anyone should imagine that ragtime was of the least musical importance. It was a popular wave in the wrong direction."

On the other hand, the conservative, respected composer Charles Wakefield Cadman said in the *Musical Courier* of August 12, 1914: "Underneath all the asininity of most of the Broadway output . . . is found the germ of a national expression. . . . The restless energy and indomitable will of America [are] somehow symbolized in terms of an intelligent syncopation. A few American composers have consciously or unconsciously cast certain large orchestral and chamber works in this pattern . . . why not experiment still further?"

Myron A. Bickford, in the *Cadenza* (Boston) of September 1913, divided the warring musical fraternity into five classes: (1) those who can play ragtime and play it properly; (2) those who cannot play it and know it, but would like to; (3) those who cannot play it and don't know it; (4) those who can play it and will not; (5) those who cannot play it and will not try. As to the fourth class, he observes: "To hear them tell it they are the majority but they are careful not to put their alleged ability to the test."

A Harvard junior, John N. Burk, wrote discerningly in the *Harvard Musical Review* of January 1914: "Unfortunate surroundings constitute probably the main reason why ragtime fails to gain recognition in the musical world. There are few of those above the ragtime sphere who will admit having caught its fascination. Most people seem to have a peculiar, highly sensitized faculty of closing their ears to what they are unwilling to recognize as music." He adds with a wisdom in advance of his time and beyond that of most of his elders: "When ragtime was entirely in the hands of the Negroes to whom its origin is due, it had little of its modern taints . . . its happy, carefree nature . . . was created with an irrepressible love of music and an extraordinary sense of rhythm."

In 1901, in the midst of the battle, the American Federation of Musicians declared a state of emergency and commanded its members to cease playing ragtime. The august president said: "The musicians know what is good, and if the people don't, we will have to teach them." The *Cincinnati Post* commented on this official disaster: "If you hear music and like it, be sure that somebody will explain to you that it is popular and therefore immoral; that it lacks soul and technique and verve. Leave us our *Coal Black Lady*!"

Amid the tempest students flocked to the Axel Christensen schools, union musicians went right on ragging, and Tin Pan Alley turned out rags that, frankly examined, justify all but the worst criticism and a handful that justify none, while Scott Joplin and a few authentic composers continued to write music that was then, as it is now, above all the senseless wrangling of the day. Paul Laurence Dunbar, poet laureate of the Negro, summed up the matter—and a real but concealed issue—in a verse from his *When Malindy Sings:*

> Oh, de white ban' play hits music, an' hit's mighty good to hyeah,
> An' it sometimes leaves a ticklin' in yo' feet;
> But de hea't goes into bus'ness fu' to he'p erlong de eah,
> W'en de colo'ed ban' goes marchin' down de street. . . .
>
> But hit's Sousa played in rag-time, an' hit's Rastus on Parade,
> W'en de colo'ed ban' comes ma'chin' down de street.[1]

The "colo'ed" bandsmen marched along at their usual dollar-a-day, but there was gold in ragtime, and the white bandsmen were finding it. Christensen was one of these. By the end of 1903 he had given courses to well over a hundred

[1] Reprinted by permission of Dodd, Mead & Company from *The Complete Poems of Paul Laurence Dunbar.* Copyright, 1896–1913, by Dodd, Mead & Company.

pupils. A year later his roster had quadrupled. By his second year *Christensen's Instruction Book No. 1 for Rag-Time Piano Playing* was copyrighted, printed, and in use. Revised and enlarged editions followed in 1906, 1907, 1908 and 1909. In 1909 the manual was a large-size thirty-six-page publication that sold for one dollar. In 1912, with the Christensen School system rolling along, a supplementary series of five books, *Christensen's Instruction Books for Vaudeville Piano Playing*, went into use. These, which sold at fifty cents each, were as follows:

BOOK 1. *Lessons in Sight Reading*
BOOK 2. *Lessons in Elementary Harmony*
BOOK 3. *Playing from Violin Parts, or Vaudeville "Leader Sheets"*
BOOK 4. *Playing from Bass Parts—Transposing, Modulating, etc.*
BOOK 5. *Vaudeville Cue Music—What to play and how and when to play it. Contains a collection of all necessary incidental music required for vaudeville or moving picture shows, such as cue music, bucks, reels, clogs, entrances, introductions, etc.*

The *Christensen Instruction Book for Ragtime* in 1927 became one for jazz piano, and in the early 1930's, as chameleon-like as ragtime rhythm itself, it conformed to the still changing popular names. The book "for Modern Swing Music" is still in use, a ninety-two-page opus that sells for two dollars and is prepared to initiate the novice into the following mysteries: "Jazz Piano Playing; Keyboard Harmony; Breaks and Bass Figures; Harmonizing Melodies; Boogie-woogie, Blues, etc." It is interesting to note that the rhythmic figurations of the basic études are identical. The foundation of each course is to be found in three "movements." For example, the "First Ragtime Movement" of 1904:

remains as a "Swing Movement" in 1937, as follows:

The "Second Ragtime Movement" of 1904:

in 1937 is "another way of breaking up whole note chords":

and so on. The ragtime motor and chassis are still running under the new streamlined bodies as the public crowds in to see the "new" models.

The method came from the completely formed philosophy that Christensen brought to his teaching. He realized that the endless inventiveness of the Negro player, with whom each playing of a tune creates a distinct variation or even a new composition, would only confuse the white student. In a recent interview Christensen put the matter with more diplomatic indirection:

"In 1902 and 1903 there was no accepted method or system of playing ragtime, or syncopated music if you prefer, by people as a whole, either for piano or orchestra. The public got its knowledge of ragtime, for the most part, by listening to trick pianists in vaudeville, or at music halls, and the information they obtained was unsound because at that time no two pianists ever played syncopated numbers alike. They couldn't because . . . there was no set system in vogue—and that also applied to the ivory ticklers in New York's famous Tin Pan Alley, where most of the 'rags' emanated.

"There was still another vital angle to analyze. If such pieces were published with the music written as it was played by . . . ragtime composers and musicians, not one pianist in a thousand could play them. Don't get the wrong slant on syncopation. It takes a skillful musician to play ragtime flawlessly; no 'dub' can master it with any degree of perfection . . . eminent authorities have never denied that many so-called popular pianists can play the most intricate classics satisfactorily, but adversely a comparative few of the outstanding classical pianists are able to satisfy audiences with the way they render syncopated numbers.

"I'm not attempting to suggest that such scholarly musicians lack the mental capacity. The deficiency is due to the fact that their training is so widely divergent, and so profoundly steeped in the deep canons of old-school tradition and training that they are temperamentally unsuited and academically unfitted.

"It seemed to me that the time was ripe for a method which would overcome the difficulties encountered in individual improvisation . . . a system which would standardize the fundamentals of syncopation for the piano, and enable all pianists, amateur or professional, to grasp the idea quickly, easily, and inexpensively."

Teaching experience led Christensen to lengthen his curriculum. It became "a course so thorough and yet so simple that it would incorporate all the necessary fundamentals of music and still be elastic enough to teach the rawest beginner how to play ragtime in twenty lessons."

The degree of simplification Christensen arrived at is displayed in his essential reduction of ragtime playing to three basic syncopated movements. Professional ragtime, of course, employed many more, and the master Negro pianists went far toward exhausting the development of delayed and anticipated timing, of odd-numbered over even-numbered meters, and of shifted accent. From the ultra-simple syncopation of the early cakewalk grew a complex rhythmic system that offered a wholly new pathway for composition and that even today eclipses the rhythmic work of any "serious" composer, just as the Dahomeans on the Chicago Midway had shown "the most remarkable rhythmical sense and skill" that had ever come to H. E. Krehbiel's attention. His observation that "Berlioz in his supremest effort . . . produced nothing to compare in artistic interest with the harmonious drumming of these savages" was even more applicable to the American Negro and ragtime. But Krehbiel, sad to relate, followed the pattern of his day. Logic succumbed to prejudice when he was faced with ragtime as it rose from the honkytonks. Ragtime, a superb welding of African drum rhythms to our own harmony and melody, became a threat to decency, "a survival of African savagery."

To return to Christensen, his three little movements "with a meaning all their own" made a whole American generation of ragtimers, who, using them, could even get through *Maple Leaf* and *The Cascades* after a fashion. What counted was that his pupils were satisfied. San Francisco was the location of the first Christensen branch school. Cincinnati came closely after in the same year, 1909. St. Louis followed in 1910, the school there being run by Ed Mellinger, whose *Corrugated Rag* and *Contagious Rag* were published by John Stark & Son in that same period. Christensen, incidentally, wrote and published a number of rags, beginning with *Ragtime Wedding March* (apologies to Mendelssohn) in 1902 and *Irmena* in 1908 and followed by *The Cauldron Rag* a year later. Up to his *Ragtime Rings the Bell* of 1918 he published eight or more.

By 1913, ten years after "Ten Easy Lessons" had opened the door of the first studio, there were four Christensen Schools in Chicago, and one or more branches in New York, Philadelphia, Boston, St. Louis, Cincinnati, Buffalo, Des Moines, San Francisco, Oakland, Los Angeles, Seattle, and Kansas City, as well as a Honolulu branch that presumably taught a ragtime hula. By 1918 the network had spread to twelve more cities and operated in twenty-five metropolitan centers and

139

small cities all together. Christensen branched into vaudeville as a sort of ragtime Will Rogers. Today, nearing seventy, he is still a sought-after pianist, monologist, and homespun philosopher at conventions and banquets.

Coincidentally with his entry into vaudeville in 1913, the Czar completed a home-study course for would-be ragtimers in the sticks, launched a mail-order campaign, and became a national advertiser. The fate of Russia's Czar Nicholas II in 1917 very shortly gave his title an antiquarian sound, and the word "ragtime" was simultaneously becoming old-fashioned. Presently Axel W. Christensen was being billed as "King of Jazz Pianists."

There was no dropping off, however, in the popularity of the Christensen system for winning friends and influencing people with a few hot piano licks. The 200,000 students registered from 1903 to 1923 grew to the 1930 cumulative total of 350,000 graduates, and by 1935 or thereabouts it was to reach the mildly astronomical figure of a half-million graduates of the Christensen system.

And that is the success story of Axel W. Christensen. As mass-production ragtime teacher he had no serious competitors. He simplified ragtime but never debased it. With a school-chain like his, Tin Pan Alley's job of spreading its ragtime music was greatly aided. Christensen's schools, staffed with white teachers, were mainly for white pupils. Nor did he allow his successful business methods to affect his choice of music. His quasi-house-organ, the *Rag Time Review*, published for several years from 1914 on, featured the compositions of men like James Scott together with simpler scores suitable for students. In addition to the news and small talk one would expect from the Christensen schools, its pages contained international news and comment about ragtime, as well as articles by John Stark and others. And if classical ragtime could have been established, Axel Christensen would have been ready with the conservatory to turn out its long-haired concert pianists.

Scott Joplin and John Stark made their teaching effort, of course. In 1908 *The School of Ragtime—Six Exercises for Piano* by Scott Joplin appeared, a thin, unpretentious book with no system of schools behind it. There is no sugar-coated simplification here, nor was there a simplified *Maple Leaf* any more than there is a simplified *Sonata Appassionata* in the conservatories. Joplin bluntly prefaces his études:

"What is scurrilously called ragtime is an invention that is here to stay. That is now conceded by all classes of musicians. That all publications masquerading under the name of ragtime are not the genuine article will be better known when these exercises are studied. That real ragtime of the higher class is rather difficult to play is a painful truth which most pianists have discovered. Syncopations are no indication of light or trashy music, and to shy bricks at 'hateful ragtime' no longer passes for musical culture. To assist amateur players in giving the 'Joplin Rags' that weird and intoxicating effect intended by the composer is the object of this work."

Studying the six Joplin *Études*, one is immediately struck by the subtle time divisions and the way in which the syncopation and the "three over four" are built in, so to speak, in the music itself. The *Études* virtually need only to be played to swing by themselves: the very arrangement of the notes tends to throw the accent from the main beats to where it belongs.

When the Christensen and Joplin exercises are compared, the former seem a little contrived, the latter to have a natural flow. This is what one would expect when comparing the analytical method of the pedagogue and that of the creative originator himself. One can begin to understand, too, the wooden, mechanical effect produced by most white ragtime playing and its tendency to deteriorate into mere tricks or technical display. Syncopation appeared to the average white performer merely a way of tricking up a melody, while to the Negro it is the basic way of creating melodies. The white syncopates a melody, the Negro conceives one syncopated in its very form.

The Christensen method was a thing of value, of course, in its total effectiveness. Its condensed instruction in the various keys and in modulating back and forth between them, as well as in basic harmony, makes it the most complete ragtime

141

course ever attempted. Joplin offers no such general instruction. His exercises are intended for the advanced student. The interesting speculation remains as to how much more effective the Christensen system might have been had it been taught by Negro instructors equipped to convey the subtleties and spirit that pedagogical systems, by their very nature, must omit.

It seems important to reproduce the Joplin *Études* here, together with the composer's comments:

EXERCISE NO. 1

"It is evident that, by giving each note its proper time and by scrupulously observing the ties, you will get the effect. So many are careless in these respects that we will specify each feature. In this number, strike the first note and hold it through the time belonging to the second note. The upper staff is not syncopated, and is not to be played. The perpendicular dotted lines running from the syncopated note below to the two notes above will show exactly its duration. Play slowly until you catch the swing, and never play ragtime fast at any time.

EXERCISE NO. 2

"This style is rather more difficult, especially for those who are careless with the left hand, and prone to vamp. The first note should be given the full length of three sixteenths, and no more. The second note is struck in its proper place and the third note is not struck but is joined with the second as though they were one note. This treatment is continued to the end of the exercise."

142

Slow march tempo *(Count Two)*

EXERCISE NO. 3

"This style is very effective when neatly played. If you have observed the object of the dotted lines they will lead you to a proper rendering of this number and you will find it interesting."

Slow march tempo *(Count Two)*

EXERCISE NO. 4

"The fourth and fifth notes here form one tone, and also in the middle of the second measure and so to the end. You will observe that it is a syncopation only when the tied notes are on the same degree of the staff. Slurs indicate a legato movement."

Slow march tempo *(Count Two)*

EXERCISE NO. 5

"The first ragtime effect here is the second note, right hand, but instead of a tie, it is an eighth note rather than

143

two sixteenths with tie. In the last part of this measure, the tie is used because the tone is carried across the bar. This is a pretty style and not as difficult as it seems on first trial.''

EXERCISE NO. 6

"The instructions given, together with the dotted lines, will enable you to interpret this variety which has very pleasing effects. We wish to say here, that the 'Joplin ragtime' is destroyed by careless or imperfect rendering, and very often good players lose the effect entirely, by playing too fast. They are harmonized with the supposition that each note will be played as it is written, as it takes this and also the proper time divisions to complete the sense intended.''

144

Scott Joplin, the short, black-skinned quondam itinerant from Texarkana, was a stubborn as well as a dedicated man. Until he died he persisted in believing that his syncopated music belonged with the European classics.

Chapter 8

PRETTY BABY

THE year 1906 is generally remembered in America for the April holocaust of earthquake and fire that wiped out the heart of San Francisco. When this disaster filled the newspapers and monopolized public attention, ragtime's first brilliant public decade was drawing to a close. During those ten years the group of greatly talented Negroes who ushered in the art of piano syncopation had made St. Louis the ragtime capital of the world. But new forces had already separated the two patriarchs Turpin and Joplin, and their respective St. Louis and Sedalia groups, united only six years before. These forces led to a regrouping of ragtime's creative talents elsewhere.

First to desert the Chestnut Valley fold, Scott Hayden went to Chicago in 1902. Although he returned briefly to the Missouri metropolis, in 1903 he moved to Chicago to stay. Later in 1903 Joe Jordan, bidding the stranded *Dandy Coon* company farewell in Des Moines, likewise headed for Chicago.

At the end of the decade the final dispersal took place. In 1906 Sam Patterson joined the Five Musical Spillers, a vaudeville group, and set out on tour. He left his boyhood friend Louis Chauvin to his self-elected obscurity, playing in the Gilt

Edge Bar, a dive upstairs over Pickett's drug store. Then Chauvin left for his last few months of life in the Chicago District.

Gone, too, was Arthur Marshall, leaving only Scott Joplin from the Sedalia group, since Joplin and Otis Saunders had come some years before to the parting of the ways. Saunders nursed a bitterness about the parting and when "The Ragtime Kid," Brun Campbell, encountered him in 1904 in Guthrie, capital of the Oklahoma Territory, Saunders was claiming that he had composed both the *Maple Leaf* and *The Favorite*, and that he had sold several of his rags to Turpin, at least one of which, the *St. Louis Rag*, he said had been published.

The ragtime world, still so close to the folk ways of making music, was full of this sort of tale. There was a constant exchange of ideas among players in the clubs while they waited for calls to play at the houses, and this had had much to do with the actual development of the music. It was a pleasurable practice, shared in with much generosity by most of the players and by younger men just coming up. There were, of course, unquestionable instances of tunes being appropriated in their entirety. But with known composers the music itself is the best evidence of the truth or falsehood of the claims. As for the rags that Saunders claimed to have authored, no other evidence is needed, for *St. Louis Rag* is clearly in the style of Tom Turpin, and only Joplin could have fashioned the other two.

Campbell has furnished all that is known of the rest of Otis Saunders's wanderings. The handsome mulatto left Guthrie for Oklahoma City about 1907, shortly before Oklahoma City became the state capital by the simple device of removing from Guthrie all the state papers and documents as well as the official seal. He went back to the "house" on West Third Street where he had played for a short while in 1898. This palace was run by a white madam whose forbidding expression was characterized by her nickname, Scar Face Mary. In a few years Saunders drifted on to Kansas City, Missouri, and was last heard of in Chicago shortly before America's entry into World War I.

But to return to the St. Louis scene of 1906, Tom Turpin stayed on after Joplin went to the Marshalls in Chicago. New faces were appearing at the Rosebud and the Hurrah Sporting Club, and the cast was gathering for the last act of the ragtime drama in St. Louis. Joplin's gaze actually was set on New York rather than on Chicago. John Stark had established his office in Manhattan almost a year before, though the printing plant remained on Laclede Avenue in St. Louis. Stark's presence in New York was a factor in Joplin's decision, but one perhaps stronger still was the composer's increasing drive toward greater classicism and complexity in his music, and the feeling that its seriousness would attain recognition in the East.

Simpler but equally cogent were the reasons that drew the others to Chicago. One of these is well expressed in the words of Jelly Roll Morton of New Orleans:

"There were not so many colored people at that time in Chicago," he said. "Both colored and white went to the theater and there was no ill feelings. In Chicago at that time you could go anywhere you wanted regardless of creed or color. This is why most famous musicians went to Chicago. That was not true of Kansas City. I came to Kansas City in the year 1911. I had been to Chicago much earlier. Kansas City did not have one decent pianist. The people were prejudiced also in St. Louis. But they had a lot of good musicians in St. Louis because there was a publishing company by the name of Stark & Company that published Negro music special. They were also publishers of Scott Joplin, known throughout the world as the greatest ragtime writer that ever lived."

The main reason for Chicago's attractiveness to the Negro musician resulted directly from this comparative lack of prejudice; for there the Negro and white worlds met and dark-skinned talent could move in entertainment circles that offered far greater remuneration and chances for fame. Consequently much of the talent was drained from St. Louis and from Kansas City as well, from New Orleans, Louisville, Memphis, Little Rock, Oklahoma City, and a score of other places, as well as from the hinterlands of the deep South and the old "Wild-Goose Nation" of Texas. From the deep rural and marginal areas like those of Texas came pianists who played a primitive blues-piano style. These men isolated themselves in Chicago's South Side. The white public was not ready for them or their music. The backwoods pianists "laid down the beat" and "stacked the blues." They played their unique and very African music with its sound of far-away train whistles and the wail of the blues where the ragtimers had gaily and dexterously played theirs, in the cheapest and most obscure saloons. Part of their world, too, were the Negro rent-raising parties known as Skiffles in Chicago, Buffet Flats in St. Louis, House Shouts in New York, and House Hops in Washington, D. C. Called boogie-woogie, their music, so remote from ragtime, first reached popularity some thirty years later, in 1938, at New York's downtown Café Society through the formidable eight-to-the-bar pianistics of Meade Lux Lewis, Albert Ammons of Chicago, and Pete Johnson of Kansas City.

White Chicago, however, if not ready for the boogie-woogie blues in 1907, was more than ready for ragtime. When Joe Jordan arrived in 1903, the early period of Chicago syncopation was drawing to a close. Its earliest Negro players, who had already been performing in the District while the Dahomeans were startling World's Fair visitors in 1893 with the original African form of the same rhythms, had prepared the scene for the newcomers. Negro ragtime was ready to reach the general public in the city where in 1897, in secondary white versions, it had first achieved publication.

The World's Columbian Exposition had, in fact, prepared the way for ragtime, even though a few years elapsed before its publication started. While the sensational dancing of Little Egypt is likely to be remembered by old-timers, the Dahomean Village was an equally sensational attraction. Between the two of them a spate of exotic dances became the talk, from the hoochie-coochie to the bombashay.

The Village was uniquely authentic amid the spurious curiosities of the Midway. Its native occupants entertained all day with drumming and chants. They came from the African West Coast, where America's slaves had once been captured, and the rhythms of the drum batteries and the

149

haunting chord-chains of their chorales held in their essence the transforming contribution that the Negro has made to American music.

H. E. Krehbiel, commonly considered dean of American music critics of that day, as we have already seen was greatly impressed by the Dahomeans. In his book *Afro American Folk Songs* he describes the typical West African orchestra with its hand-beaten leader-drum, a three-foot hollowed log with single head that sounds the fundamental tone, the variety of smaller drums of different pitches that fill out the five-tone or six-tone scale, the four clear-toned iron bells held mouth-up and struck with sticks, and the eight-stringed harp less than a yard long. This harp, Krehbiel states, was "tuned in the diatonic major system omitting the fourth tone," but in reality this is a six-tone-scale tuning not related to our diatonic system. He continues: "All day long the Dahomean minstrel sat in front of his hut and sang little descending melodies. To this gentle singing he strummed an unvarying accompaniment on a tiny harp. His right hand played over and over a descending passage of dotted crochets and quavers [quarter notes and eighth notes] in thirds; with his left hand he syncopated ingeniously on the highest two strings." [1] All unknowingly, a description of the ragtime combination of syncopation over regular meter could scarcely have been clearer.

At least one newspaper notice attests the impact of Dahomean rhythm on popular music. The *Chicago Chronicle* in 1897 reviewed a new song, *There's No Coon That's One Half So Warm*, as follows: "M. B. Garrett, during the World's Fair, long before the 'coon' song epidemic became prevalent, was impressed one day during a visit to the Dahomey Village with a melody in strict 'rag-time' played by the natives. He jotted down the notes, filed them away and forgot about them. When the rage for Negro songs commenced . . . he at once set about arranging it into a song. *No Coon Is One Half So Warm* is now one of the most sought-after songs of the popular order before the public."

The Dahomeans were not quickly forgotten. In 1902 Bert

[1] H. E. Krehbiel: *Afro American Folk Songs*. New York: G. Schirmer; 1914.

Williams and George Walker followed the Negro intellectuals of the day in an interest in things African and produced their smash hit *In Dahomey*. In the general confusion as to where the real values lay, they professed to desert ragtime, a music of genuine African rhythm, in the attempt, commendable in itself, to throw off the coon stereotype. Walker is quoted in the *Theatre* of August 1906 as saying: "At that stage we saw that the colored performer would have to get away from the ragtime limitations of the 'darky.'"

The Chicago Fair was also enlivened in typical fashion by brass-band music. The Sousa aggregation enjoyed a success due in no small part to two of his soloists, cornetist Herbert L. Clarke and virtuoso trombonist Arthur Pryor. The former was a "legitimate" musician whose specialty was solo arrangements of numbers like the *Carnival of Venice* and display pieces that exploited operatic arias with high range *fioriture* and double and triple tonguing in imitation of the coloratura soprano.

Arthur Pryor, born in St. Joseph, Missouri, in 1870, exploited the possibilities of the slide mechanism in the production of smears, as upward and downward trombone glissandi are called. Where Clarke's cornet was a serious-minded and romantic instrument, Pryor's trombone spoke in a humorous folk dialect. From this tendency came a whole line of band pieces called trombone smears, like *Trombonium*, *'Lasses Trombone*, and many others. These are authentic Americana preserving the flavor of the bands that once paraded the streets to advertise minstrel shows and circuses as well as electoral candidates. Arthur Pryor later formed a band that was a fixture on the American scene for many years, a group that played with far more syncopation than any other brass band. As a composer, Pryor is an important figure in the general folk picture that was the background of ragtime. *A Coon Band Contest*, *Mr. Black Man*, *Razzazza Mazzazza*—"*a Trombone Extravaganza*"—and *Southern Hospitality* (a ragtime cakewalk published in 1899) are typical numbers expressing in band arrangement some of the flavor of the ragtime piano.

The real old-timer of Negro ragtime in Chicago was Plunk

Henry, who was already well along in years at the time of the fair. He had been born in the 1850's and, as his name indicates, was one of the very early group in the Mississippi Valley area who developed the rudiments of piano ragtime from banjo syncopation. He died before 1906.

Johnny Seymour was a dozen years younger than Plunk. Shepard Edmonds remembers Seymour well, having been only seventeen when in charge of the Cairo Street concession on the Midway, which put on Egyptian, Sudanese, and African shows. Seymour's playing, which reflected the gaiety and excitement of the fair, created such a sensation among listeners and impressed Edmonds himself so deeply that he believed Seymour to be the inventor of ragtime. Edmonds remembers Eddie James as another fine syncopator in Chicago at that time. Seymour was about forty years old when he gave up active playing, around 1905. He did not, however, give up his connection with the District. With Pony Moore he opened a saloon at 2442 South State Street. This cozy but disreputable-looking spot had a wine room that became the ragtimers' hangout. Seymour was nearing eighty when he died, about 1942.

Another well-known figure on the early Chicago scene is introduced to us by an 1898 song, *This Coon Is Just the Card*, bearing the dedication: "To our friend Harry Crosby, better known as 'Squirrel,' Champion Ragtime Player." Squirrel was an intinerant, a "faker" or player by ear, who, like the rest of the Chicago group, had no aspirations toward composing for publication. The District was his home, and when the "parlors" and "circus houses" were closed, he stayed on. In the contestants' list of a ragtime piano contest at the Elks Rest, Chicago, in 1916, reproduced in this book, there appears the entry: "Squirrel, 18th St. Chicago."

Still another old-timer in the red-light zone was the "keen-dressed" light brownskin Needham Wright; and one who could challenge Johnny Seymour was short, stubby Fred Burke, who, like Seymour, was born at about the outbreak of the Civil War. Burke played at Pony Moore's saloon at Twenty-first and Dearborn. This was not the drinkery just mentioned that he owned with Johnny Seymour, but a very high-class place with private dining-rooms upstairs, each with a piano and each named after a different state, the name of which was engraved on a golden plate on the door. This nomenclature caused much fun and an occasional fight when Southern guests would reject a "damn Yankee" room or vice versa. Pony Moore catered to the élite, which meant not merely money but social prominence as well. His guests had to be someone. No girls stayed there—another mark of distinction—but the pick of the Everleigh Club, run by the famous sisters Minna and Ada, and the other really fancy manses were on call. Pony's ran around the clock. About four in the morning, when Fred Burke would be preparing to leave, a couple of open Victorias might drive up and unload a large party coming to finish the night. They would order wine upstairs and call for music. The players were always ready to please.

A familiar figure along Dearborn Street in the early years of this century was Charlie Warfield, still living in Chicago at this writing in the famous Mecca Flat at Thirty-fourth and State. Showing favoritism to Kentucky as a state, he says: "I was born in 1883 in Guthrie, Kentucky, on the Tennessee side of the line. I was raised in Nashville." He was only fourteen in 1897 when he went to St. Louis, where he learned the ragtime style that was later to win for him a whole string of ragtime contests. He left for Chicago in 1900, but went back to St. Louis for the fair in 1904 to play the contest in which, as we have already seen, he took second prize. It was during this period that he is to be seen in the photo of the Hurrah Sporting Club that we reproduce.

After 1904 Warfield returned to Chicago to play in the sporting-house belt. A number of his compositions have been published. The best-known are *I Ain't Got Nobody*, which came out in 1916 and was featured by Sophie Tucker and also by Bert Williams, and *Baby, Won't You Please Come Home?* a hit of 1919. Both numbers are still great band favorites. The first now bears only the name of Spencer Williams, while the second lists that of Clarence Williams as co-composer. Warfield says they are both his own tunes and that to get them published he had to allow the other names to appear as those of

153

co-composers. The first editions of both of these numbers, framed and hung with other souvenirs and mementos in his home, reveal the name of Warfield given precedence over that of the other men.

In his book *Black Manhattan*, James Weldon Johnson relates an earlier occurrence of this sort involving a colored barber of Philadelphia, Richard Milburn, who in the 1850's was famous for his guitar-playing and his whistling, particularly of one of his own tunes with bird-song effects. In 1855 one Septimus Winner published the tune as a song: "Sentimental Ethiopian Ballad—*Listen to the Mocking Bird*—Melody by Richard Milburn—written and arranged by Alice Hawthorne." In 1856 the credit was given *only* to Alice Hawthorne, and except for the excessively rare first edition, Milburn's name has never appeared on the song.

The roster of ragtimers in Chicago at century's end is too long to give complete, but several more should be mentioned. There were native-born George Kimbrough, called "Sparrow," and James White of New Orleans, called "Slap Rags," whose freak stunt was to stand up with his back to the piano while playing. It was Ed Hardin from Cincinnati who around 1900 ruled the Chicago ragtime roost. Hardin, now dead, is praised by all who knew him, and Glover Compton, himself a fine player, characterizes him as "King of all the piano-players. He had speed and ideas—he had everything." Ed Hardin was one of the not infrequent Negro pianists who "could hear a thing once and then play it right back." Habitual winner of ragtime contests, Hardin also held the unique honor of being the only player unable to read music ever to play in an orchestra led by perfectionist Will Marion Cook. Hardin reached his peak when he played at the old Pekin at Twenty-seventh and State Streets, around 1903–4, when it was a popular beer garden frequented by parties of white pleasure-seekers as well as by Negroes. The Pekin had been converted by its owner, Robert T. Motts, from the earlier saloon and gambling joint that had occupied the site.

By 1905 the Pekin became a full-fledged variety house, often referred to as the Pekin Temple of Music. The still popular cakewalk and coon songs, taken intact from the burlesque and minstrel olios, were featured there, along with comedy skits, close-harmony ballads, waltzes, and of course lots of ragtime. The following year Bob Motts built the new Pekin Theater on the same site. Joe Jordan, who had been intermittently connected with the old Temple of Music, assumed the duties of musical director and orchestra leader. The original contract between Motts and Jordan stipulates a salary of twenty-five dollars a week for his services, to begin with the grand opening on March 31, 1906. A tangible result of the earlier connection remains in Jordan's *Pekin Rag*, published in 1904.

Jordan brought varied experience to the palatial new Pekin as the South Side showplace prepared the Negro district to become the jazz center of 1915–25. Joe was versatile; though a fine ragtime pianist, as early as 1900 he also played violin and drums in the ten-piece Taborian Band of St. Louis. He could write an orchestration directly on the lined staves and have it ready in fifteen minutes. In 1902, at twenty years of age, he had been in New York, where he and comedian Ernest Hogan, "The Unbleached American," wrote the score of *Rufus Rastus*. Jordan toured with this company nearly through 1903. It was at the end of this connection that we found him, a few chapters back, starting on the ill-fated tour of Chauvin and Patterson's *Dandy Coon*.

In addition Jordan found time to organize the Memphis Students, a group of seventeen Negro men and women that made its debut at Proctor's Twenty-third Street Theater in the early spring of 1905. James Weldon Johnson credits this "playing-singing-dancing orchestra" with being "the first modern jazz band ever heard on a New York stage." He adds that in this group, which combined brasses and saxophones with banjos, mandolins and guitars, drums and piano, the performers were not students and were not from Memphis. In the latter part of the same year the Memphis Students opened in Paris; subsequently they played London and all the important cities of Europe. The lead voices of the Memphis Students for the first year were Tom Fletcher and Abbie Mitchell, the finely trained vocalist who was Will Marion Cook's wife. Joe Jordan wrote the Students' hit songs, *Rise and Shine; Oh, Liza Lady; Goin' to Exit;* and *Dixie Land*.

155

While in New York, Joe wrote Ada Overton Walker's *Salome Dance*, used by Williams and Walker. Speaking of this today, Jordan says: "We used an augmented orchestra of fifty men for this feature. The men arrived at the designated time just to do it. I composed, orchestrated, and conducted the number although I was at the same time doing the Hammerstein Roof Garden with my Memphis Students, the two engagements timed not to conflict."

Jordan also wrote *That Teasin' Rag* for Ada in 1909, a ragtime song that figured in a later controversy. Its principal strain was lifted by the white Original Dixieland Jass Band for the trio of their *Original Dixieland One-Step*. This number was published in 1917 when the band at Reisenweber's in New York launched the jazz craze. Hearing the Victor record by the O. D. J. B., Jordan brought action. The records were withdrawn and relabeled with the added credit line: "Introducing *That Teasin' Rag*," plus Jordan's name. As to the sheet music of *Dixieland One-Step*, Jordan wryly comments today: "Marks Music Company lost my identity with the second publication."

Jordan remained with Motts and the Pekin for one year. "While there," he says, "I wrote all the music of the shows, but only a few things were published. In those days a colored writer only peddled his song for a few dollars and there it ended, so, when as busy as I was, you just skipped the matter."

In 1909 Jordan worked with Bob Cole and Rosamond Johnson on *Red Moon*, a play that had a successful Broadway run the following year and that James Weldon Johnson calls "a true operetta with a well-constructed book and a tuneful, well-written score." Seventy-year-old Sam Lucas, of Ohio, who had been active on the stage from early minstrelsy and through the coon-song and cakewalk period, took a leading role in this show. *Red Moon* had other distinctions. In this connection Weldon Johnson writes a revealing comment:

"The Negro performer in New York . . . found himself freed from a great many restraints and taboos that had cramped him for forty years. In all those years he had been constrained to do a good many things that were distasteful because managers felt they were things that would please white folks. Likewise he was forbidden to do some other things because managers feared they would displease white folks. One of the well-known taboos was that there should never by any romantic love-making in a Negro play. If anything approaching a love duet was introduced in a musical comedy, it had to be broadly burlesqued. The reason behind this taboo lay in the belief that a love scene between two Negroes could not strike a white audience except as ridiculous. The taboo existed in deference to the superiority stereotype that Negroes cannot be supposed to mate romantically, but do so in some sort of minstrel fashion or in some more primeval manner than white people. . . . In the middle theatrical period Cole and Johnson had come nearest to breaking it in their *Shoofly Regiment* and *Red Moon*."

Still hyperactive, Joe Jordan wrote *Lovie Joe*, with Will Marion Cook's words, for Fannie Brice's feature number in the 1910 *Ziegfeld Follies*, and in the same year visited Germany with King and Bailey's Chocolate Drops and toured the English music halls. For the two following years he was again the Pekin musical director and wrote *Dat's Ma Honey Sho's Yo' Born*. Jordan was, in fact, more song-writer than rag-composer, although his *J. J. J. Rag* of 1905, among others, is a fine instrumental number. But his songs are highly individual melodically, with a really original and catchy tunefulness. An outstanding one, besides *Lovie Joe*, is *Oh Say, Wouldn't It Be a Dream*, featured by Hogan in 1907. Another is the wine-room favorite *Brother-in-Law Dan*.

Joe Jordan's subsequent career has included four prosperous years in Chicago real estate, one tangible result of which, the Jordan Building at Thirty-sixth and State Streets, is still standing. In 1919 he took a financial and assistant directing part in the New York Syncopated Orchestra of Will Marion Cook. This group played at the Forty-fourth Street Theatre in Manhattan. During the depression years in New York, Jordan conducted the Negro Unit Orchestra of the Federal Theatre Project, and those who saw the Orson Welles production of *Macbeth* heard Jordan conduct. The 110-piece orchestra included his old St. Louis friend Sam Patterson who took over part of the conducting duties when the orchestra toured the country.

Although Arthur Marshall and Scott Hayden were in Chicago during those Pekin days, they remained obscurely in the backwash of the rapid tide of events. Separated from Missouri and Scott Joplin they seemed lost. Hayden played away from the District in the roadhouses west of Chicago, sometimes solo piano and occasionally in orchestras. He remarried, but his second wife, Jeannette Wilkins, bore him no children. Always a boy of delicate health, he was only thirty-three when he died on September 24, 1915, of tuberculosis. Hayden had dropped out of music altogether a year or so before the end and was working in civil service as an elevator operator at the Cook County Hospital. Two last rags bearing Hayden's name appeared before his death. Like the earlier *Sunflower Slow Drag* and *Something Doing*, these were collaborations with Joplin. *Felicity Rag* came out in 1911, *Kismet Rag* early in 1913, both published by John Stark. The four collaborative efforts give an idea of Hayden's delightful melodic gifts, but are all that is known to remain of his music.

During his first summer in Chicago, Arthur Marshall played for Lewis's Saloon, a wine room and summer garden near the Choteau Amusement Park. The following winter he went to Charlie Baskett's Eureka Saloon and Winter Garden, at 3047 South State Street, where he remained for a year and a half as solo pianist and accompanist for the ragtime songs and ballads that the girls sang. Six months at the Mirror Restaurant followed. Marshall says: "There were so many mirrors I got lost looking at myself."

Marshall's last Chicago job was at the La Salle Hotel, on Clark Street. The manager, Batiste Pizza, paid only a dollar a night, but tips were good. The white girl entertainers were "on call." The men behind the La Salle were then reputed to be the most notorious white-slave smugglers in the country.

Marshall wandered back to Sedalia in 1909. A year later he was in St. Louis, where he stayed to work six years for Tom Turpin at his Eureka on Chestnut Street. His second wife, Julia Jackson, whom he had married in 1907 in Boonville, died just before World War I. Arthur was deeply affected by her death. He lost weight and developed a left-hand twitch that forced him out of music. He settled in Kansas City in 1917, regained his health, and eventually married a third time, but never went back to playing professionally. He lives there now, retired, in a house that is neat but virtually as modest as the one in which he was born. He spends his days between a trimly tended garden and a tiny chicken farm in the rear of his home.

Besides his two collaborations with Joplin, *Swipesy* and *Lily Queen*, four rags completely Marshall's own were published by Stark between 1906 and 1908. These are the fine *Kinklets*, *Ham And*, *The Peach*, and *The Pippin*. In addition Marshall still had in manuscript three excellent rags of the 1907-8 period that are in the Sedalia folk tradition, *Silver Arrow*, *National Prize Rag*, and *Missouri Romp—a Slow Drag*. These were copyrighted in 1950, and his playing of them and other numbers was recorded the same year on Circle Records. These are the first phonograph records that Marshall ever made.

Only one of the migrant St. Louis group, then, succeeded in affecting the musical picture in Chicago. This was Joe Jordan, and his impress was left on the theatrical rather than on the ragtime world. Louis Chauvin spent his last months there, but immolated, as was his choice, in the bawdy area. That one superb rag partly of his composition is preserved from this period is owing solely to Scott Joplin's visit with Arthur Marshall in 1906. This is *Heliotrope Bouquet*, by Joplin and Chauvin, published by the Stark firm in 1907. John Stark described *Heliotrope* as "the audible poetry of motion," but the Joplin title that the rag bears is even more accurately descriptive. The first two themes, those by Chauvin, show his extraordinary chord constructions most fully. Like certain chords of Chopin, these haunt one with the almost overpowering fragrance of hothouse flowers. The second theme, incidentally, lives a borrowed life today almost intact as the chorus of a perennial jazz favorite that was a hit of 1926. This is Boyd Atkins's *Heebie Jeebies*, but the original strain in *Heliotrope* is far more beautiful than the slightly altered jazz piracy.

New Orleans, not St. Louis, made the real impact on Chicago music, first with Tony Jackson's ragtime piano, then with

159

that of Jelly Roll Morton as it developed into stomping jazz with much ragtime retained. Finally came the first of the river-boat contingents, playing the brassy, contrapuntal jazz that had developed from ragtime in the streets of the Crescent City.

When Tony Jackson went to Chicago in 1905 with Bob Caldwell, an ordinary pianist, also from New Orleans, Tony was already known as "the World's Greatest Single-Handed Entertainer." The title gives Tony credit for his supremacy in piano-vocal entertainment and implies his great singing voice, his infectious gaiety of spirit, his incredible timing, and, above all, his phenomenal two-handed piano ragtime. He was nearly thirty when he began to play the South Side cafés. He was dark-skinned and of slender build, about five feet ten in height. A distinctive mark was a tuft of white hair in the middle of his head. His eyes were protruding and heavy-lidded; a receding chin made a prominent feature of his mouth. The mouth could open, though, in a most expressive grin, and the long-fingered hands that swung loosely with his arms were made for the piano.

Jelly Roll Morton, nine years younger than Tony, learned a great deal from him. He spoke of haunting Tony to learn piano tricks until "guys used to say to me: 'Get off that piano stool, you hurting the piano's feelings.' " Morton's characterization of Tony as an artist may be taken literally, for this fine rag-timer and greatest of jazz pianists was as accurate in judgment as he was sparing in praise. He said that Tony Jackson was "maybe the best entertainer the world has ever seen. He enjoyed playing all classes of music in the style they was supposed to be played in, from blues to opera."

We mentioned earlier how Morton refrained from entering the 1904 ragtime contest in St. Louis because of the unfounded report that Tony was an entrant. On the documentary series of recordings that Jelly Roll made for the Folk Archives of the Library of Congress (issued by Circle Records in the twelve-volume set *The Saga of Mr. Jelly Lord*), he tells of winning a later contest from Tony in Chicago, but says: "I never believed that the contest was given to the right party even though I was the winner."

On the same documentary series Jelly Roll played from memory "one of Tony Jackson's fast, speed tunes like he used to play years ago." The number is a very pretty unpublished rag that Tony used to play for the strip dances or "come-ons" in such Storyville "houses" as that of Antonia Gonzalez and Gypsy Schaeffer's Conti Street mansion. When Morton finished playing, the microphone caught his comment: "Tony used to play these things in the sporting houses for what they called the Naked Dances. Of course they *were* naked dances all right, for they absolutely were stripped."

Tony's piano style had the utmost variety of ragtime, and included the "single walking bass" and "double walking bass" of broken octaves that have since come to be associated with the boogie-woogie style. His fast fingering was spellbinding, but the slower tempos of his slow drags and blues rocked with rhythm too. His ballad accompaniments were famous, and his harmonic sense was as highly developed and as personal as that of Chauvin. Tony's singing voice featured extraordinary range and was topped off by a controlled falsetto that he used for comedy. He sang ragtime, coon songs, ballads, opera, and the blues equally well, with personal style and completely winning charm. His accomplishments attracted such a following that his services were sought after by the café-owners. Many a party of prominent rounders would conclude a night by going to "hear Tony sing before we break it up." As like as not, when they came in, Tony would be in the middle of the Andrew B. Sterling and Harry Von Tilzer song *Moving Day* ("Respectfully dedicated to Landlords"):

> *Moving day, moving day,*
> *Rip that carpet up from off the floor,*
> *Take your oil stove coon,*[1] *and there's the door.*
> *It's moving day:*
> *Pack your folding bed and get away*
> *If you've spent ev'ry cent,*
> *You can live out in a tent,*
> *It's moo—oo, oo, oo, oo, oving day.*

Or perhaps Percy Wenrich's coon lament, *What's the Matter with the Mail:*

[1] "Coon" changed to "man" when copyright was renewed in 1933.

I wonder what's the matter with the mail?
It never was so late before.
I've been up since seven bells
But nothin' slipped under my door.
Liza must have surely got her pay,
And promised me she wouldn't fail
To send me just a little—ev'ry sal-a-ry day—
DOGGONE! *What's the matter with the Mail!*

Tony had dozens of his own specialties too, instrumentals and songs that were great favorites, but until late in his life he refused to sell any for publication. Roy Carew, who knew him well before he left New Orleans and who was the first to revive Tony Jackson's name in recent years, asked him once why none of his ragtime was published. Tony's reply was that he would burn them before he would give them away for five dollars apiece. We may share Carew's regret for the many fine rags composed and played by Tony that were lost with his death.

During his sixteen years in Chicago, Tony worked at many places, always the choice spots. Around 1909 he was at Dago & Russell's Café, and during this period he was also heard at the Little Savoy and featured at the Monogram. One hangout where Tony entertained was the famous old Elite No. 1, at 3445 South State Street. Teenan Jones was the first owner of this spot, which Jelly Roll Morton characterized as "the most beautiful place on the South Side and the most famous place throughout the history of America of cabaret land. The trade was the finest class of trade, millionaires and good livers."

The Elite No. 2, at Thirty-first and State, followed, operated by Art Codozier, former partner of Teenan. "Mr. Codozier," Jelly Roll relates, "ran this place right into the deep blue sea, an A-No.1 failure with space enough to get Barnum & Bailey's circus in every night, using the type of entertainment he thought was best, such as operatic and symphonic musicians, old man Toomey being the leader of the orchestra and 'cello player, which was considered obsolete since the invasion of Tony Jackson and Jelly Roll Morton in the city of Chicago."

Codozier's successor was Lovie Joe, "a title that was supposed to be a great lover for the ladies," says Morton with doubt implied. "He wore plenty of diamonds, but he ran the place straight to hell." Teenan finally took over, with his brother "Give-a-Damn" Jones presiding as "cashier at the bar in the saloon department. "'Give-a-Damn' got his name through an argument," Jelly adds admiringly, "stating that he would go to Paris just to buy a drink there, which he then did just because he didn't give a damn."

When Tony Jackson finally decided to sell a song for publication it scored an instant hit. To secure publication Tony shared composer credit with Egbert Van Alstyne when Remick published *Pretty Baby* in 1916. The song was given revised lyrics by Gus Kahn to fit the baby characterization by Fannie Brice, who introduced it with smash success in the Shubert *Passing Show* of that year. Tony had played it in a slow tempo, almost a blues style, with his own words. His version is preserved in Morton's singing on one of the Library of Congress Circle recordings. Tony sang the chorus ending:

> *You can talk about your jelly rolls,*
> *But none of them compare*
> *With my baby, pretty baby of mine,*
> *Pretty baby of mine.*

Pretty Baby was, as Jelly Roll says, "a million-dollar hit within a year." Tony could unquestionably have capitalized on this to a far greater degree than he did. As it was, he sold a few more songs for publication, but he preferred to work on in the entertainer's informal, happy-go-lucky world.

A number of Tony's songs appeared in 1916 and the next year. These include several beautiful melodies like *Don't Leave Me in the Ice and Snow, Miss Samantha Johnson's Wedding Day,* and *Why Keep Me Waiting So Long?* An instrumental, *Pick It—Boy,* and a song *When Your Troubles Will Be Just like Mine,* reviewed in 1917 issues of Christensen's *Rag Time Review,* have never been found, and there are several other unverified Jackson tunes. Five other published numbers by Tony are known, as well as two unpublished ones that Glover Compton recalls. The first of these, *You're Such a Pretty Thing,* was written as a floor-show number for the soubrette Nettie Lewis, Glover's wife. The other, a beautifully harmonized drinking song called *The Clock of Time*, was a joint effort by Compton and Jackson. The latter dates from 1904, when the two were doing a piano and singing act at the Cosmopolitan Club on Walnut Street in Louisville.

Tony Jackson never married. For many years he lived in the bottom flat at 4111 South Wabash with his sisters Ida Jackson and Mrs. Mariah Sutton. His health was always good, the sisters tell, and his death was a freak medical occurrence. He had been drinking black coffee and lemon when he was seized by the hiccups, and nothing could relieve them. Despite the efforts of doctors and nurses for eight weeks, he died on April 21, 1921, at the age of forty-five.

Tony's big upright mahogany piano still stands today where it always stood, in the overcrowded little front room of the Wabash Street flat. A candle burns at a small shrine to the Virgin Mary on the mantelpiece, and Ida Jackson stands by the piano fingering her rosary as she says: "Tony never had any lessons. He taught his own self with the help of God."

When Tony died in Chicago, the old ragtime days were dead, too. Jazz had come up from his native city, and the pianists were just part of the rhythm sections in the bands. The clear, high, commanding trumpets of King Oliver and Freddie Keppard were sounding throughout the South Side, flowing over and wiping out all but the echoes of the striding piano bass and the rippling right-hand runs of the ragtime piano Scott Joplin, Tom Turpin, and Louis Chauvin had played. Only Jelly Roll Morton remained to write the keyboard part of jazz, the music that marched out of ragtime.

Chapter 9

EVERYTHING IN THE LINE OF HILARITY

NEW ORLEANS "in the land of dreams" and the hot music called jazz that began there; Basin Street and Buddy Bolden's horn; the bands that marched in parade and in funeral; Lulu White and Storyville; Congo Square and the French Opera House; dancing at the Lake, at the old Free and Easy, and at Lincoln Park—it is all a thrice-told tale. The history of jazz has been well chronicled. But not that of New Orleans ragtime.

As early as elsewhere there was a school of piano ragtimers in New Orleans, back so far indeed that the black, itinerant John the Baptist of that city, who roamed the mid-American red-light districts from the late seventies into the nineties, is almost a legend today. There, too, were the ragtime generations: Tony Jackson, Albert Carroll, and Alfred Wilson; Sammy Davis, Buddy Carter, and Ferdinand Morton. But the piano world kept to itself even more in the Crescent City than elsewhere. The popular emphasis was on various combinations of brasses, strings, and reeds, and the keyboard instrument scarcely entered the bands until after 1910.

Piano and band developed separately in New Orleans, but grew side by side into the same sort of music. New Orleans piano ragtime was from its very beginnings a somewhat different music from that of the great valleys that lie northward. Even at the start it contained the rudiments of jazz piano style. The reason for this is to be found in certain qualities that make New Orleans unique among the cities of the world.

The Delta City is the extraordinary place where for over a century the Romance cultures of France and Spain mingled with the pure African tradition kept perennially fresh and strong by the boatloads of slaves constantly unloading on the levee. And, as we know, native ceremonies were permitted in Congo Square, ceremonies forbidden on most plantations. There, too, because of the inborn laissez-faire of the Latin Catholic, was to be found a degree of nonsegregation unique in the Slave South, as well as the partly legalized intermarriage that quickly set up a free class of "Creoles of Color." These, the offspring of the extramarital unions of white gentlemen and beautiful quadroons or octoroons, were allowed to bear the paternal surname.

The first seventy-five years of American rule after the Louisiana Purchase of 1803 produced only a fractional alteration of the New Orleans Latin character, and even then the African revels went on in Congo Square. What Louis Moreau Gottschalk heard as a boy in 1840 was still to be heard by the casual bystander of 1880.

So the syncopated music of New Orleans developed both from African sources that were stronger and nearer, and from a far different folk music than that which fed the beginnings of ragtime elsewhere. This is why we find New Orleans ragtime different from other ragtime in musical form as well as in spirit. The melodic line and the harmony have a romantic quality derived from both the classic and the folk music of France, Italy, and Spain. The rhythm is even more African, more strongly accentuated, and, in a sense, wilder and more unrestrained than that of the classic ragtime of the Joplin school. The term "stomp," used to designate a hot number of dynamic rhythm, was derived in New Orleans from the stomping of bare feet in the Bamboula and the Congo.

There is in New Orleans music, finally, the tendency toward the use of two or more intertwined melodies, instead of classic ragtime's single treble melody over an accompanying bass. This use of multiple, concurrent melodies is designated musically by either of the two equally formidable terms "counterpoint" or "polyphony." The first means in simple English, *note against note*, the latter means *many voices*—both mean *two or more melodies played at the same time*.

The interesting thing about the counterpoint that characterizes New Orleans ragtime in part and New Orleans jazz wholly is that it is derived culturally from two sources. It comes from the French classics and the Gallic folk rounds like *Frère Jacques* and from the African chorales as well. These chants, sung by the leader and chorus, are antiphonal. To simplify once more, this means *voice following voice* or the *answer of the chorus to the leader*. In Africa, however, the parts or voices tend to overlap and to become continuous, and at that point the antiphony of the call and answer becomes a polyphony, but a polyphony far different from the regular-metered classic counterpoint of Europe. African counterpoint is sung in all manner of off-beat syncopations. The counterpoint that entered into New Orleans piano style is also that which entered into jazz. Its effect on the emotions of the listener is profoundly disturbing and exciting; where ragtime entices, jazz or Jelly Roll Morton's piano solos command.

We find the Romantic quality of harmony very evident in the surviving work of Tony Jackson, as well as in the distinctive tangos of Jelly Roll Morton. Rhythmic force appears in the early tendency of Tony Jackson, in common with other early New Orleans ragtimers, to use the rolling or walking basses of barrel-house music in hi, ragtime. These basses are like overpowering tympani, while the bass of classic ragtime is akin to the more conventional European bass accompaniment. We have seen how the regular-metered ragtime bass reacts with the off-beat treble to set up syncopations that can attain to a high degree of complexity. The rolling bass, however, played with the right-hand syncopations, sets up multiple rhythms, or polyrhythms, of even more complex structure. Finally, these running basses introduce a countermelody to the treble, so that in typical New Orleans ragtime passages of

167

this sort we have not melody and accompaniment but two concurrent melodies in counterpoint.

These various qualities develop still further in the ragtime-jazz piano of Jelly Roll Morton, to attain the highest development ever reached in band jazz, particularly in the 1926 jazz band, the Red Hot Peppers, of Jelly Roll Morton himself. The jazz band is founded on two groups: the melody section or "front line" of wind instruments, and the rhythm section, which includes some or all of the following instruments: banjo, guitar, string bass, tuba, piano, and drums. The two groups correspond respectively to the right hand and the left of the piano. But solo piano is played by one man, while the jazz band consists of from five to eight players. Ragtime bass, comparatively simple and never more complex than one hand can make it, becomes in jazz a combination of rhythms as formidable as the battery of African drums and bells. The one or two trumpets, one or two clarinets, and trombone, corresponding as a group to the ragtime player's single right hand, produce a three- to five-voice polyphony improvised around a melody. Any musician knows how complex a four-voice fugue can be, based as it is on regular meter This can give some idea of the musical complexity of jazz polyphony, based on syncopated rhythms.

These developments in the orchestra mark the distinctiveness of jazz, both as a development of the ragtime principle and as a direct-line continuation of the Africanisms of Congo Square. If we consider the trend of European music since about 1915–20, jazz, with its dissonances, its "blues" quarter tones and eighth tones, and its complex contrapuntal web of melodies and rhythms, is both pure in the African sense and far advanced in the light of the new paths of "serious" composers.

A question is bound to arise at this point: are jazz piano and band music superior to ragtime? First we should take into account certain misconceptions that tend to sway our judgments, as, for example: the complex or the large is *ipso facto* superior to the simple or the small, and the new is *ipso facto* superior to the old. Then the question may be answered Socratically: "Is Beethoven better than Mozart?"

The first generation of Crescent City keyboard men who would correspond to Joplin, Tom Turpin, and Plunk Henry elsewhere have left neither music nor any name, except that of the shadowy John the Baptist. Tony Jackson, Alfred Wilson, and Albert Carroll, approximate contemporaries, followed.

Antony Jackson was born in 1876 on First Street between Annunciation and Rousseau. He was one of twin boys, but the other, Prince Albert Jackson, died as a baby. The mother, who worked, put the infants in the care of two of her daughters. His sister Ida, whom Tony so much resembled, brought him up. By the time he finished his schooling in New Orleans College, at St. Charles and Soniat, he was already a natural singer and pianist and disinclined to follow a profession or a trade or to take holy orders, a step in which his devout family would have concurred. Instead, by his early teens he was playing in the honkytonks along with Carroll and Wilson, his ragtime style already formed along New Orleans lines. When the first Turpin and Joplin rags came out, Tony, like Chauvin in St. Louis, played his own personal versions of them.

By the time he was eighteen, Tony was the acknowledged leader of New Orleans entertainers. He was first out with the new tunes, which he learned by ear, and his singing made him a popular figure everywhere. He was the idol of the two nine-year-old boys, Ferd Morton and Sammy Davis. Tony was so outstanding that he seems to have been the rare exception to the rule that pianists had no place in the New Orleans bands. Roy Carew has a letter confirming this from the late veteran trumpeter Willie (Bunk) Johnson:

> Tony Jackson and I came up together and were razed up town in the 12th ward on Amelia Street and Tchoupitoulas St. N.O., La.
>
> "And Tony Jackson he started learning to play piano in the back of Adam Olivier's Bar Room now that was back in 1892 because I finish school in 1894 and Tony had only been on piano 2 years, but he really play, now he did not know anything about reading music at all, but Tony could play in any key on the piano so,

169

"That man Adam Olivier take Tony Jackson in his band because he had a good ear and that Olivier band it was my first band so that made Tony Jackson and I play in the same band in 1894 and I only played with that band one year, in 1895 I jumped the Olivier band and went with the King Bolden band because they did not fool with reading music and they only had one man in King Bolden band that could read a little, and that was the leader, that was Dada Brooks, now he was a violin player of Buddy Bolden's band, because they played all the music by head, and I did not like to read music because it was too much trouble.

"About Tony Jackson's age, I think he is a few years older than me—I was born December 27, 1879 and I'm 63 years old so you can come near Tony's age."

After the resolution instituting vice segregation, sponsored in 1897 by Alderman Sidney Story, set up the Storyville District immediately north of Canal Street and west of Basin, Tony and his contemporaries moved into the "houses." The choice spots, like the mansions of Gypsy Schaeffer and Antonia P. Gonzalez, were open to Tony. That he should have been a favorite musician of Madam Tonia is not to be wondered at after one peruses one of her professional ads from an issue of the New Orleans red-light directory called the *Blue Book:*

ANTONIA P. GONZALEZ
Corner Villere and Iberville Streets

The above party has always been a headliner among those who keep first-class Octoroons. She also has the distinction of being the only singer of Opera and Female Cornetist in the Tenderloin. She has had offers after offers to leave her present vocation and take to the stage but her vast business has kept her among her friends. Any person out for fun among a lot of pretty Creole damsels, here is the place to have it.

It is in this period that Roy Carew reports first hearing Tony Jackson play and the impression his music made. The

following description is excerpted from an article of his authorship in the *Record Changer* of February 1943:

"In the early years of the present century there stood,
at the downtown corner of Villere and Iberville Streets,
in that part of New Orleans known as Storyville, a frame
dwelling of the type descriptively called 'Camel-Back.'
This name was applied to those houses which had single
story in front but were of two stories in back. The house
rested upon a brick foundation a few feet high, and four
or five wooden steps led up to the front door, which faced
on Iberville Street. On the glass portion of the door was
painted the inscription 'GONZALEZ, FEMALE CORNETIST.'
There was no yard in front, nor at the side, and the brick
banquettes extended right up the side of the house. The
old Villere Street car line ran past the side of the house,
but few passengers got on or off in that neighborhood. It
was not a gaudy or noisy neighborhood; the dance halls
and flashy places were two or three blocks toward the
river, nearer Basin Street.

"One evening during the winter of 1904–05, I was
strolling aimlessly about downtown New Orleans, and in
the course of time I found myself approaching the corner
I have described. As I neared the front of the Gonzalez
establishment, I could hear the sound of piano playing
with someone singing, which my ears told me was coming
from the Villere side of the house. Always very fond of
popular music, I immediately walked to the side of the
house and got as close to the music as possible; with the
banquette going right up to the side of the house, I found
myself standing under one of the windows of what probably was Madame Gonzalez' parlor, listening to the 'professor' playing and singing. That night is about thirty-
eight years in the past now, but it is almost as clear in my
memory as if it were last night. It was the most remarkable playing and singing I had ever heard; the songs were
just some of the popular songs of that day and time, but
the beat of the bass and the embellished treble of the
piano told me at once that here was something new to me

in playing. And the singing was just as distinctive. It was a man's voice of very good quality which rang true on every tone; a vibrant voice that took each note with easy precision; a happy voice that had at times a sort of wild earnestness to it. High notes, low notes, fast or slow, the singer executed them all perfectly, blending them into a perfect performance with the remarkable piano style. As I stood there, I noticed another listener standing on the edge of the sidewalk a little ways away. I did not know who he was, but afterward found out that he was another local piano player, Kid Ross, I think. I never got to know the man, but I will never forget our very short conversation.

" 'Who in the world is that?' I asked, indicating the unseen player, as I stepped over to him. 'Tony Jackson,' he replied, 'He knows a thousand songs.' "

Tony made his first and perhaps only theatrical tour in 1904. Opportunities to join the traveling Negro companies were easy for a talented musician. A number of the groups originated in New Orleans. There was, for example, Bush's Ragtime Opera Company, a variety show that toured the South under the management of the New Orleans musician Joseph Palao. Ducournan Bros. Colored Southern Ministrel Company featured many Orleanians, with cornetist Andrew Kimble leading the brass band, and Albert Carroll was already on the road as musical director of the New Orleans Minstrels. In a column note in the *Stage*, April 23, 1904, two members of this company "send regards to Scott Joplin, Mr. and Mrs. Kersands, Bailey and Spiller."

When Albert Carroll returned to New Orleans in the summer of 1904, he and Tony signed with the Whitman Sisters' New Orleans Troubadours. The company was made up in that city, but the three singing sisters were from Lawrence, Kansas, where they had been schoolmates of Gèorge W. Walker. Carroll signed on as musical director, Tony as featured entertainer. By July 23 the *Stage* reports the troupe as appearing in the Jefferson Theater at Birmingham:

"This is the first time in the history of Birmingham, Alabama, that the colored people have been allowed seats in the dress circle and parquet. Credit is due to the clever management of Mabel Whitman who can safely say that she is the only colored woman managing her own company and booking them continuously in the leading Southern houses. . . .

"The singing of Tony Jackson was much appreciated. . . . Mabel, Essie and Alberta are decided favorites throughout the Southland. . . . The choruses, in fact the entire show was good under the direction of Albert Carroll of New Orleans, Louisiana."

When the company reached Louisville, Tony was already tired of the confinement and rigors of the traveling theatrical life. He left the Whitman Sisters to enter the musical world of that city of horseracing and mint juleps. There he met pianists like George Talbot, Jimmy Clark, and young Pete Givens, talented member of the Kentucky family from which Scott Joplin's mother, Florence Givens, had come. One who knew Pete before he died of dissipation in his twenties says: "He could read his can off and we couldn't, so he got the band jobs."

Tony also met the acknowledged leader of Louisville ragtime, "Piano Price" Davis, a real product of the period and of the scene in which Negro ragtime developed. He was a gambler and a sport, a dapper, tall, mustached thirty-year-old who wore a pearl-gray derby hat cocked on the side of his head. He had a popular and very different piano number of his own that he called *Piano Price Rag*. It was Glover Compton from Harrodsburg, then only twenty, who got most of the engagements that Price, engrossed at the gaming tables, would forget about. "White folks didn't understand Negro ragtime very well," says Compton, "so Price played mostly for colored sports who came from Frankfort, Lexington, and as far away as Indianapolis to hear him." Compton filled Price's shoes at the Cosmopolitan, Tom Pryor's back room, Jimmy Boyd's, the Ben Brush, named after the early Derby winner, and even

173

the top white sporting houses of Annette Winters and Madam Leo Belle.

Thirty-five years later Compton, playing at Harry's New York Bar in Paris, found white listeners more sympathetic to the Negro rags, and, for that matter, to the Negro himself; but in Price's day the Negro player often reserved his hottest music for listeners of his own race. Price Davis's end was in contrast with the later course of Glover's life. "He went to Pittsburgh about four years later and Polly Robison, a famous colored madam, made a pimp out of him, and from then on he was through." He left the playing in Pittsburgh to others. One of the most famous of the Pittsburgh ragtimers was a Negro woman known to all only as "Ragtime Mame."

When Tony Jackson met Glover Compton they immediately became friends. Compton got Jackson in to share his act with him for a while at Bill McHouton's Cosmopolitan. Tony, however, had already conceived the idea of settling in Chicago. That fall he returned to New Orleans, and the photograph of Tony that we reproduce was mailed to Glover (called Bill) from there. Jackson went to Chicago the next year, to return to New Orleans only once, in February 1914, when his mother died. His subsequent career was recounted in the preceding chapter.

Greatest of all the New Orleans pianists born after Tony Jackson was Ferdinand Joseph Morton, whose forbears were in New Orleans before the Louisiana Purchase. Morton's thin chiseled features, high cheekbones, and aquiline nose bespoke an ancestral strain that existed in America long before Columbus. Of the life stories of the great figures of ragtime and early jazz, that of Jelly Roll Morton is the most complete because he told it himself, together with that of the music he loved, in the eight-week series of documentary recordings that he made in 1938 for the Library of Congress.

The recorded interviews with curator Alan Lomax became long, fascinating monologues spoken over Morton's soft piano chords. These often digressed from his own life into the stories of other men, or were broken into by sudden flashing piano solos and songs. His descriptions ranged from an account of

174

the Robert Charles race riot in New Orleans to the flashy clothes and swaggering walk of the sports. He told of playing behind a screen in a "parlor" to shield the sensitive white paying guests and the naked dancing girls from racial "contamination." Then there was a deeply affecting account of a New Orleans funeral, beginning with his boyhood quartet that "specialized in spirituals" like *Steal Away*, through the feasting of the wake, the slow march through the streets to the brass-band dirge, and the return from the cemetery to the bright ragtime strains of *Oh, Didn't He Ramble*. He would play the "*Miserere*" from *Il Trovatore* like a concert pianist, superbly, and then rag it, or would convert *La Paloma* into a ragtime tango.

The Library of Congress records remain as a priceless musical, historical, and social document. Morton's saga is there, from his early days of "learning music," particularly from his idol Tony Jackson, on into the District to challenge the New Orleans greats and over the country to St. Louis, Memphis, Los Angeles, and Chicago. There are his early barnstorming days when he rode the freight-train rods, surviving less as musician than as pool shark and salesman for his own "consumption cure," concocted from Coca-Cola and salt. Then there is the middle period when he could meet the later St. Louis masters like Artie Matthews and Rob Hampton on their own terms, the period of his own most prolific tune-writing. There is the later time of his initial brilliant success in jazz, and the final one when he and the other authentic New Orleans masters of this music finally succumbed to money, to the onslaught of Paul Whiteman's "symphonic jazz" and the hundred and one other tawdry commercial imitations that white players made of a music that they could scarcely even play.

It was in these last years that Jelly Roll, not very old, but failing in health, sat at the mike in the staid Coolidge Auditorium to record the 116 record sides that make an American document second to none. These records, issued in the Circle limited edition, tell a sad story of great triumphs that were, and of triumphs greater still that never came. In the grooves there is material for a dozen books. One, in fact, is already written and published, Alan Lomax's moving biography of Morton called simply *Mr. Jelly Roll*.[1]

Born in 1885, almost simultaneously with Sammy Davis— "Our mothers carried us at the same time," says Sammy— Jelly Roll is the true connecting link between ragtime and jazz. No one need ever speculate again on how the Negro in America transformed white music into black: he can hear Morton play the celebrated transformation of an old French quadrille into *Tiger Rag* on the Circle documentaries. The introduction, the waltz, and the "mazooka" are shown metamorphosing into the syncopated strains that everyone knows so well. Nor is erudite musical analysis needed to differentiate ragtime from jazz when one has heard him play the *Maple Leaf* in the authentic St. Louis manner and then follow with his own complex stomped version "along the lines of jazz creation."

In Morton's fifty-six years, ended with his death in June 1941 in Los Angeles, are to be found the whole course of ragtime and jazz, their acceptance, their rejection, their triumphs, and their subtle spurious "improvement" by the music business, the swift alternations of the true masters between comparative riches and fame, and complete oblivion. There is the story here of a snobbish native intelligentsia that looks to Europe for its music, or else, like the Boston Pops, superficially dips into our native music and comes up with a performance of *Tiger Rag* that one river roustabout with his banjo could have put to shame.

But these are the sad overtones, the melancholy culminations that color the Library of Congress saga that Morton told. When he recalls the old New Orleans days the spell of memory is on Mr. Jelly Roll and, as though he were playing once more for the rough and ready longshoremen, levee men, and screwmen, for the touts, the gamblers, and the pimps, and for the St. Charles Avenue millionaires and their girls out for a night, his fingers recall the vanished ragtime magic or roll out the somber honkytonk blues.

"I happened to invade that section," he says, "one of the

[1] Alan Lomax: *Mr. Jelly Roll.* New York: Duell, Sloane & Pearce; 1950.

sections of the district where the birth of jazz originated. . . .
At that time, that was the year 1902, I was about seventeen
years old. I happened to go to Villere and Bienville, at that
time one of the most famous night spots after everything was
closed. It was only a back room where all the greatest pianists
frequented after they got off from work. All the pianists got off
from work in the sporting houses at around four or after unless
they had plenty of money involved, and they would go to
this Frenchman's—that was the name of the place—saloon—
and there would be everything in the line of hilarity there.
They would have even millionaires to come to listen to the
different great pianists, what would no doubt be their favorites, maybe, among 'em. They played every type of music.
Everyone no doubt had a different style.

"Well after four o'clock in the morning, all the girls that
could get out of the houses, they were there. There weren't
any discriminations of any kind; they all set at different tables
or any place they felt like sitting; they all mingled together as
they wished to; and everyone was just like one big happy
family. People from all over the country came there. This
place would go on from four o'clock in the morning at a tremendous rate of speed until maybe twelve, one, two, three
o'clock in the daytime. Of course when the great pianists
used to leave then all the crowds would leave.

"Among some of these great pianists," Jelly continues, "I
may mention some that I remember very well. Sammy Davis,
one of the greatest manipulators I guess that I've ever seen in
the history of the world on piano and the gentleman had a lot
of knowledge in music." The narrator then plays a short piece
demonstrating Sammy Davis's style of composition and playing. A minute or two of ragtime that had sparkled in the
Frenchman's back room long long years before, and then
Jelly almost sadly turns the page: "I don't know the name of
this tune. I only remembered a little bit of it. Of course it's
been years since I've seen Sammy."

One of Morton's greatest contemporaries is next to appear.
"Tony Jackson always frequented this place," Jelly relates.
"Tony was considered among all who knew him the greatest
single-handed entertainer in the world, his memory being

something like nobody's ever heard in the music world. There is no tune would ever come up from any opera, from any show of any kind, that was ever wrote on paper, that Tony could not play by memory." Tony, it should be remembered, was Jelly Roll's greatest rival for the acclaim and the largesse that famous, infamous Storyville bestowed on the "professor" who entertained in its gaudy palaces. Despite their rivalry, which must have been as keen as the rewards were large, it is evident that deep bonds of friendship existed between the two men. With each of them honest respect for the other's ability clearly outweighed envy.

Morton plays and sings *Pretty Baby*, Tony's well-remembered tune of the period, and a memorable, if short, performance it is, taken at the grateful, slow tempo of those years and full of affectionate nostalgia. This record side from the documentaries is like a tribute that even Jelly, most articulate of men, could not put into words.

As Morton talks on the records, the New Orleans piano generations appear. "In the Frenchman's we had Alfred Wilson and Albert Carroll, both great pianists, both of these boys, I'm telling you. Alfred Wilson did not care to work very much, neither did Albert Carroll. Sammy Davis was good and he knew it and he did not care to work. Well, poor Alfred Wilson, the girls taken to him and showed him a point where he did not have to work—that he could have as much money as he wanted without working. He naturally became to be a dope fiend. He got on hop, that is the plain name that they called it, which is taken for opium.

"Here's the way Albert Carroll would play for the girls. He played that stuff, I am telling you. It would sure sound good." Carroll's little tune is like the very beginnings of ragtime. Its close-chorded right hand sequences with their bitter-sweet dissonances are not unlike those of Louis Chauvin, but their more forceful, plunging rhythms echo the dancing of Congo Square. As he plays, Jelly speaks as the girls used to do: "Aw, play it, Mr. Carroll. He's not good looking but he's sure sweet."

The great New Orleans bass-player George (Pops) Foster describes Alfred Wilson as a handsome Creole nearly six feet in height, of a light copper color and with smooth, wavy hair. Before he died, in 1905, at about twenty-five years of age, he was a "real big shot," says George, "a bigger man than Jelly at that time." George says he was famous for his honkytonk blues and his ragtime, and his singing too, and that he had for a time the choice job at Lulu White's Mahogany Hall.

Then there comes to Jelly's mind the humbler players and singers of teeming New Orleans, who in their way had added to the richness, variety, and honest poetry of the music. All the world had forgotten these lesser ones, but Morton remembers. One, indeed, three-fingered Mamie Desdoumes, is destined for musical immortality because Jelly never forgot Mamie, his godmother's neighbor, and her simple folk blues. The melancholy archaic chords of Mamie's mutilated right hand over the rocking Spanish bass, and the haunting words she sang—all evoked with fidelity and love by the man who heard her as a child—are one of the authentic masterpieces of music. "She played a blues like this all day long when she would first get up in the morning":

> *I stood on the corner, my feet was dripping wet,*
> *Stood on the corner, my feet was dripping wet,*
> *I asked every man I met:*
>
> *Can't give me a dollar, give me a lousy dime,*
> *You can't give me a dollar, give me a lousy dime,*
> *Just to feed that hungry man o' mine.*
>
> *I got a husband and I got a kid man, too,*
> *I got a husband, I got a kid man, too,*
> *My husband can't do what my kid man can do.*
>
> *I like the way he cooks my cabbage for me,*
> *I like the way he cooks my cabbage for me,*
> *Looks like he sets my natural soul free.*[1]

Jelly Roll's memory moves now as in a dream. Old Buddy enters the Frenchman's room. "Old Buddy used to play some blues of his own. What is Buddy's last name? I don't remember

[1] From *Mamie's Blues*, by Jelly Roll Morton. Reprinted by permission of copyright-owners, Tempo Music Publishing Co.

—Buddy Bertrand, that's it." And here for a few seconds are Buddy and his levee camp holler, until they too fade into the long ago, the forgotten, and the lost.

A new wraith appears in the door, and Jelly, in his old role of master of ceremonies, introduces him: "One of the famous ones . . . Game Kid . . . one of the favorites in the Garden District, where the Robert Charles riot began. Here is one of his blues:

> *I could sit right here and think a thousand miles away,*
> *Since I had the blues, cannot remember my name.*

Game Kid wouldn't work. He was a man that really wouldn't work, just ragged as a pet pig, a big smile on his face, kind of nice-looking, sorta brown-skinned fellow. He just played the piano all day long, after he'd get up and just go around from one girl's house to another, not for any financial purpose at all, just to have a lot of fun. He did some of these hot honky-tonk numbers, such as these numbers like this." The music that follows is a "rush-on" of the period, so called because it was the cue for the high-stepping, brown-skinned "ponies" to get out on the stage.

One of the most fascinating parts of Jelly Roll's recorded saga is concerned with his early travels. He was only sixteen when he went to Biloxi, Mississippi, and then along the Gulf Coast through Mobile and as far as Pensacola, Florida. "At that time," says Jelly, "I was supposed to be a very good pool player and I could slip up on a lot of people playing pool, because I played piano and they thought I devoted all my time to the piano. I met players like Skinny Head Pete and Florida Sam," Jelly says. "They were among the best of the blues players, but they wouldn't work—were kept by women." At Gulfport Morton played for Mattie Bailey, a sporting-house madam. "Her place was for white people. She always carried a '38 special' pistol and I often closed up for her because it was so dangerous. Talk got around that there was something between Mattie Bailey and myself because I was always the last man out. I was threatened one night with lynching. She was white and they thought she was intimate with me. I decided this was a good time to leave." Jelly returned to New Orleans "feeling quite a man, and anytime I got broke, in a sporting house I would go."

In 1905, when he was twenty, Jelly went back to Mobile, where he met the great Florida pianists Baby Gryce of Pensacola and Frazier Davis, as well as Frank Rachel, "tops from Georgia." And it was down on the "famous corner" of St. Louis and Warren Streets in Mobile that Jelly made the acquaintance of Porter King, one of the greatest ragtime players in all the South. One of Morton's finest compositions, *The King Porter Stomp*, a perennial favorite, resulted from this meeting. It is a number that, like all of Morton's rags, is particularly adaptable to the jazz-band treatment. Morton later copyrighted the composition under his own name and explains in the saga that the name "King Porter" was intended as a tribute to Porter King. There is some reason to believe, however, that one or more of the themes are by King himself. Brun Campbell quotes a story to the effect that Porter King and Jelly wrote the manuscript of *King Porter Stomp*, sent it to Scott Joplin in St. Louis, and had him add to it and arrange it. "But from what Jelly and later Joplin told me," Campbell adds, "Jelly Roll rearranged it over again." *King Porter* was 4 copyrighted in 1906, but it was not until 1923 that the Melrose Brothers published it in Chicago.

In his saga Morton also describes the ragtime of the small string combinations or "serenaders" that were common in New Orleans. These little "orchestras," as Jelly calls them, were composed of mandolin, bass fiddle, and one or two Spanish guitars. They would stand on the banquette outside almost any Negro home at night and sing, and before long they would be invited in and an impromptu party would begin. Their rounds might last all night. They sang Creole numbers like *Les Ognons*, *Eh! La Bas*, and *Salée Dame*, songs on the order of *Hot Time in the Old Town Tonight*, *Wearing My Heart for You*, and *Bird in a Gilded Cage*, and, of course, ragtime specialties like *Mr. Johnson, Turn Me Loose.* "Their hot tunes were all ragtime," says Jelly. Many had no titles; some had "ragtime words," the meaningless, rhythmic syllables nowadays called "scat singing." And they sang the blues. The music and singing of typical "serenader" groups of this sort are preserved on Circle Records.

Finally, Morton tells of the great early trumpeters, Buddy Bolden and Freddie Keppard, who were "kings," first of band ragtime and then of band jazz. Jelly's story of Buddy's super-human horn is one of the great American legends. "Any time there was a quiet night at Lincoln Park . . . about ten or twelve miles from the corner where we used to hang out . . . he would just take his big trumpet and turn it around towards the city and blow this very tune . . . *I Thought I Heard Buddy Bolden Say* and the whole town would know that Buddy was there, and in a few seconds, why, the park would start to get filled." There is to this the simple, improbable truth of the real legend. Why, after all, should anyone question the miles that Buddy's horn could be heard on a quiet New Orleans night when, silent for thirty long years, it could still ring in one man's memory?

Those were the actors of the Storyville ragtime drama. All are dead and gone today, except one. Sammy Davis is still playing in Albany, New York, where he settled in the late 1920's, drawn there by the easy money from horserace gambling.

Jelly Roll Morton, the "winin' boy" that all New Orleans and later the whole country knew, died in 1941 in virtual poverty. But he left a treasure, copyright manuscripts and publications whose quantity is as staggering as their quality is amazing. Stomp rags, which are really ragtime jazz—like the *King Porter Stomp* and *Milneburg Joys*, named after the old dance resort on Lake Pontchartrain outside New Orleans—will never be forgotten. There are superb rags by the dozen, like *Frog-i-more Rag* and *The Pearls*, beautiful tangos like *Mama 'nita* and *The Crave*, as well as blues on the order of *Original Jelly Roll* and *Wolverine* that are played today by every jazz band.

Morton's phonograph records run into many hundreds and preserve the keyboard mastery, both individual and bril-liant, that few could match. Today's generation of pianists, with a few notable exceptions, laugh Jelly Roll off as corny and old-fashioned. His recorded playing remains a challenge, however, that not many care to meet as they dazzle a gullible public with wiggling scale work and a few cheap easy tricks.

In his memories recorded in the Folk Archives, Jelly did not forget the outstanding white ragtimer of Storyville. "We had Kid Ross, a white boy. Tommy (Kid) Ross was one of the outstanding hot players in this country, no question about it. He was a steady player at Lulu White's, one of the big mansions in New Orleans."

Tony Parenti, the New Orleans clarinetist, recalls other good players whose skin was white. He names several who were prominent in the generation after Morton left New Orleans. There were Irving Leclere, Roy Barton, and Tom Zimmerman, as well as Henry Ragas, who went north in 1916 with the group that became the Original Dixieland Jazz Band. Ragas was noted for his powerful "oompah" bass. Parenti recalls that the white players could command a choicer location than the colored. "The borderline was always there," he says. While Kid Ross might prefer the sporting houses, the others could play the cabaret "Tango Belt" around Iberville and Burgundy Streets in the French Quarter, spots that the Negro players could not even enter.

Roy Carew remembers a ragtime contest for whites only, held on Dauphine Street about 1914, with Leclere and Kid Ross among the entrants. Some unknown pianist won. His playing of Jay Roberts's *Entertainers Rag* elicited a storm of applause by its simultaneous counterpoint of *Dixie* and *Yankee Doodle*.

But the glory of New Orleans ragtime and jazz, with their common background of Gallic melody and African drum chant, came from their Negro originators, just as it was Scott Joplin and his group who gave the final form of classic syncopation to plantation melody and Anglo-American folksong. The knowledge of this and of how, when the accounts were eventually settled, these great creators were left without fame or, even, money was all in Jelly Roll Morton's heart as he turned from the piano in Washington to add his final comment. "That was when I was a little bit of fellow there," said Mr. Jelly Roll. "I guess times has changed considerable."

183

Chapter 10

RING-SHOUTS AND RENT-SHOUTS

TODAY'S traveler going westward from our Eastern seaboard passes through or flies above one range or another of the long Appalachian chain, the natural mountain rampart that extends from Quebec to Alabama. As he sits in comfortable train or pressurized plane cabin, or steers his modern motor car around the wide curves of mountain highways, he unreflectingly retraces the steps of our early American history. The modern traveler's mere hours or days were once painful years during which a young nation climbed the steep slopes and pushed heavy wagons through the rough passes to open up the West.

Once the mountain barriers were conquered late in the eighteenth century, expansion began. Through western Pennsylvania the emigrants poured and on into the Western Reserve—Ohio, Indiana. Then the frontier vanguard trekked on, opening up the Mississippi Valley, where only a few French trading outposts along the river, like St. Louis, had maintained the precarious French line from Canada to New Orleans.

The real highways of that day were the rivers that cleave to the plains. The new West lived in a comparative isolation from the old East, a separateness that was to last for nearly a century, until the railroads began to crisscross the continent. But it was once a far easier thing to go from Chicago to New Orleans than from Chicago to New York.

The basic culture that the emigrants carried west was British, from Puritan New England, from the Carolinas, and from Cavalier Virginia. Musically it had sprung from the madrigals and the rounds and old ballads and the hymn books of Calvin and Wesley. The English culture had subsisted, for example, for more than two centuries and a half in Virginia and the Carolinas and had grown wild and native, so to speak, in the Negro plantation music before it traveled with the settlers into the Tennessee, Missouri, and Arkansas areas.

In the Mississippi River country the large antebellum plantations arose. There the Negro music began to develop separately from that of the Eastern slave country. As it all more or less simultaneously emerged in the early unnamed ragtime of 1860–80, there were several principal ragtime areas, each with its own distinctive form of syncopated piano music.

We are now familiar with the classic folk ragtime of the area described by the great rivers, and with the stomp ragtime and archaic jazz piano of the French Delta land around New Orleans. There was ragtime behind the Appalachians, too. Today this music is called Harlem or rent-party piano because it first came to white attention after 1920 in New York's Harlem. Because of the lateness of its discovery, it was, in fact, not generally recognized as ragtime.

Eastern ragtime, however, has as long and honorable an ancestry as the others and comes from as folk-rich a soil. It focused at first in Virginia and the Carolinas, and then spread up into Maryland and down the coast into Florida, Georgia, and Alabama. From the Carolinas southward the ragtime currents crossed those of the blues as the latter spread out into the Mississippi Valley and later northward up the Atlantic seaboard. But the ragtime stream and that of the blues were always separate. If not from different layers of Negro society itself, they came forth at least as radically different musical expressions.

185

The blues are a strain so melancholy that some have believed that these laments come from the Ibo Negroes or "Calabars" in the Carolinas and Florida. Melville J. Herskovits in his book *The Myth of the Negro Past* quotes an old Haitian saying about this African tribe: "*Ibos pend' cor' a yo*— The Ibo hang themselves." There is no melancholy in ragtime. It developed from the joyous occasions of dancing and of plunking banjos and from group singing. Even where it carries over the strains of English folksong, the mournfulness of some of the old ballads is transmuted into gaiety.

The earliest ragtime—both East and Midwest—was a rocking music of medium tempo, though in the East this folk ragtime was called "slow drag." The ragtime of both sections consisted of syncopated pieces derived from the folk melodies and from the quadrilles and the schottisches. These rags were the four-themed compositions, including trios, with which we are familiar. While Scott Joplin developed this form through rising stages of complexity, he never deserted the essential dance quality or omitted his unfailing designations: "Slow March Tempo," or $\downarrow = 72$, or his familiar "Notice! Don't play this piece fast. It is never right to play 'Ragtime' fast." Joplin took the country dance form and developed it classically without losing the original character of the music.

The country ragtime of the East, moving in the 1880's into Baltimore, Washington, Philadelphia, and New York, underwent a different sort of development from that of the Midwest. In the cities its melodies took on sophistication and lost some of the charm of rural song, while a new rhythm and a quickened tempo came from the Negro church singing that stems back to the old ring-shouts. Thus both the blues and the final form of Eastern ragtime come from the music of the Negro church, the latter assuming the joyous abandon of the ring-shout and the spiritual as sung by the congregation, while the blues shaped its twelve-bar outcry from the melancholy of some of the early, minor-mode slavery spirituals. This sort of spiritual is described in the *Slave Songs of the United States* (1867). The editors, William Francis Allen, Charles Pickard Ware, and Lucy McKim Garrison, write: "At regular intervals one hears the elder 'deaconing' a hymn-book hymn which is sung two lines at a time and whose wailing cadences, borne on the night air, are indescribably melancholy."

Such a Joplin rag as *Pineapple* is filled with the feeling of folk-ballad, schottische, and reel, and the forceful rhythms of its concluding strains recall the buck and wing and the coonjine rag of the roustabouts. In an Eastern masterpiece like James P. Johnson's *Carolina Shout*, on the other hand, one can literally hear the high shout of one worshipper and the answering outburst of the ecstatic congregation. The Eastern shout is based on a different rhythmic beat from that used in the classic Midwestern ragtime. The two beats set up far different rhythmic tensions with the conventional ragtime bass. For this reason a shout is infused with a different spirit and has a different emotional effect from the classic ragtime of Scott Joplin and the other Missouri masters.

These subtle differences of Negroid rhythmic tensions work just as efficiently in hot music based on our melodies as in the original African music. In the latter there is a beat or a basic rhythmic figure to fit each of the many ceremonial, work, and entertainment functions. Our ears fail to detect any but the grossest differences in these, though with our training in harmony we can sense the subtlest chord colorations in our own music. The African on his side can barely distinguish our majors from our minors.

The ring-shout is an African dance that survived intact in this country, though used in a different context from that of the original ceremony. In Africa the shouters circled counter-clockwise around the deity, as it is tabu to present the right shoulder to the god. Although the reason for it is long forgotten, this formula is traditionally preserved in America whether the circle encloses the pulpit with its Bible, the leader of the religious chant, or, in the social form of the dance, one of the group "caught" in the ring.

The ring-shout was once a central feature of Negro social life and as important a part of church services as the sermon. It has been assumed that it had virtually disappeared, except perhaps in a tiny backwoods area here and there. But it is still danced in some of the churches of Harlem, the most sophisticated of all American Negro communities.

187

The Lion (Willie Smith), one of the famous Harlem pianists, is informative on this subject. "Shouts are stride piano —when James P. and Fats and I would get a romp-down shout going, that was playing rocky, just like the Baptist people sing. You don't just play a chord to that—you got to move it and the piano-players do the same thing in the churches, and there's ragtime in the preaching. Want to see a ring-shout? Go out to the Convent Avenue Baptist Church any Sunday."

In both the religious and the secular life of the Negro the incalculable power generated by the ring-shout rhythms brings about "spirit-possession," referred to in jazz as being "sent out of this world." This phenomenon is not fully understood, though modern psychologists know at least that this active yet trancelike state is as harmless to the individual as it is unrelated (though once it was thought to be) to hysteria and even epilepsy.

In *Slave Songs of the United States* we read: "The most peculiar and interesting of [Negro] customs is the 'shout.'" The authors then quote from the New York *Nation* of May 30, 1867 one of the earliest-known first-hand descriptions of this dance:

"The true 'shout' takes place on Sundays or on 'praise' nights through the week, and either in the praise-house or in some cabin in which a regular religious meeting has been held. Very likely more than half the population of the plantation is gathered together. Let it be the evening, and a light wood fire burns red before the door of the house and on the hearth. For some time one can hear, though at a good distance, the vociferous exhortation or prayer of the presiding elder. . . .

"The benches are pushed back to the wall when the formal meeting is over, and old and young, men and women, sprucely-dressed young men, grotesquely half-clad fieldhands—the women generally with gay handkerchiefs twisted about their heads and with short skirts— boys with tattered shirts and men's trousers, young girls barefooted, all stand up in the middle of the floor, and when the 'sperichil' is struck up, begin first walking and

by-and-by shuffling around, one after the other, in a ring.
The foot is hardly taken from the floor and the progres-
sion is mainly due to a jerking, hitching motion, which
agitates the entire shouter, and soon brings out streams of
perspiration.

"Sometimes they dance silently, sometimes as they
shuffle they sing the chorus of the spiritual, and sometimes the song itself is also sung by the dancers. But more
frequently a band, composed of some of the best singers
and of tired shouters, stand at the side of the room to
'base' the others, singing the body of the song and clapping their hands together or on the knees. Song and dance
are alike extremely energetic."

The authors of *Slave Songs of the United States* localized the
ring-shout as "probably confined to South Carolina and the
states south of it. It appears to be found in Florida, but not in
North Carolina or Virginia. . . . The term 'shouting' is
used in Virginia in reference to a peculiar motion of the body
not wholly unlike the Carolina shouting." The authors
distinguish between "sperichils" and "runnin' sperichils,"
the latter being the particular hymns to which the ring-shout
was danced. The description is amplified by further observations: "The shouting step varied with the tune; one could
hardly dance with the same spirit to 'Turn Sinner,' or 'My
body rock 'long fever,' as to 'Rock o' Jubilee,' or 'O Jerusalem, early in de morning.' The shouting is confined to the
Baptists; and it is, no doubt, to the overwhelming pre-
ponderance of this denomination on the Sea Islands that we
owe the peculiar richness and originality of the music there."

Lydia Parrish, who lived for years on the Sea Islands, has
given an extended description of the ring-shout in that lo-
cality, in her book *Slave Songs of the Georgia Sea Islands* (1942).
We quote briefly her description of characteristic bodily
postures in this ceremony:

"I shall never forget the night at the hall of the Queen
of the South Society when I first saw the ring-shout. . . .
Little had I suspected, when Margaret took care of my
room at the Arnold House years before, that she could

outdo the Ouled Nail Dancers of Biskra—if she wished. As it was, she wriggled her hips shamelessly, held her shoulder stiff—at the same time thrusting them forward— kept her feet flat on the floor, and with the usual rhythmic heel tapping, progresses with real style around the circle —goodness knows how. . . . As for Edith—every now and then she gives a stylized, angular performance as though copying the poses of the figures in Egyptian decorations. . . ."

James P. Johnson speaking of his childhood in New Brunswick, New Jersey, at the end of the last century, told us: "The Northern towns had a hold-over of the old Southern customs. I'd wake up as a child and hear an old-fashioned ring-shout going on downstairs. Somebody would be playing a guitar or jew's-harp or maybe a mandolin, and the dancing went to *The Spider and the Bed-Bug Had a Good Time* or *Susie, Susie*. They danced around in a shuffle and then they would shove a man or a woman out into the center and clap hands. This would go on all night and I would fall asleep sitting at the top of the stairs in the dark."

Although James P. was born only eight years before *Maple Leaf* was published, he was to write some of the most original masterpieces of Eastern ragtime—and there were many ragtime players before he was born. As with the first generation of ragtimers elsewhere—those born before the Civil War—only a handful of names survive today. A few are recalled by one of the oldest living players of the East, Walter Gould, known as One-Leg Shadow, who was born in Philadelphia in 1875.

"Old Man Sam Moore was ragging the quadrilles and schottisches before I was born," says The Shadow. "He was born 'way before the war. He doubled on bass and piano." The Shadow sits at the keyboard keeping time with his wooden leg like a pirate out of *Treasure Island* while he plays and sings *Sissie and Bob*. "This Virginia reel," he says, "is over ninety years old:

> *Sissie and Bob joined the wilderness,*
> *Prettiest little girl I ever did see—*
> *Oh, run on Bob, don't come near me.*

Run on, little Sissie, won't you marry me?
Bob, put your arms all round me—

All them sassy words you say.
Oh, run on Bob!
Oh, run on Sissie!
Bob, put your arms all round me.

Oh, they danced in them days and there was plenty ragtime."

The Shadow, stumping obscurely around Albany selling "numbers" (a report comes in as we write that he just "clicked a combo" for twenty thousand dollars) remembers names, while famous Eubie Blake, who was born in 1883, remembers more, and others still are gleaned from the memories of the remaining old-timers.

Shadow remembers "No-Legs" Cagey, ten years older than he, and another player of Old Man Moore's time is recalled by Louis N. Brown, the fine Washington ragtime pianist who now teaches the classics. This was Bud Minor, born in the 1850's. Louis says: "Bud was 'way up in his forties or near fifty when I began to learn my ragtime from him. That was around 1901, when I was twelve." Eubie Blake revives the memory of one more of the ragtime pioneers, "Old Man Metronome" French, who played the original banjo ragtime.

In the late 1860's an Eastern group began to be born that was to carry the slow-drag ragtime up to the cities. These were Jess Pickett, Sam Gordon, the fabulously named Jack the Bear, and others, real originators who went beyond the transformation of quadrilles to work out complete ragtime compositions. Pickett's most famous number was a really remarkable opus, *The Dream*, though a few claim that Jack the Bear wrote it. In any event, the latter derived his special fame from his playing of *The Dream* first fast and then slow-drag with blues. *The Dream* was called a Spanish number because of its tango bass. Nowadays, knowing this rhythm, the *Habanera*, to be of African origin, we are not surprised by the way it rocks in Pickett's piece, or for that matter in *Mama 'nita*, *Creepy Feeling*, and the other fine tangos of Jelly Roll Morton. The number was also called the *Ladies' Dream*, the

Bowdiger's Dream and the *Digah's Dream*, the latter titles having pornographic reference.

The Dream was never published, but it can be heard in two recorded versions, as an organ solo, *The Digah's Stomp*, by Fats Waller on a 1926 Victor, and a later twelve-inch Asch record by James P. Johnson and a small band. For anyone who has heard the superb piano versions played personally by Luckey Roberts, Eubie Blake, and James P. himself, these fine records still leave something to be desired. The composer of *The Dream*, Jess Pickett, whom Blake characterizes as "dark, heavy, medium size, gruff but fine, a gentleman gambler," died about 1922.

Sam Gordon of Trenton is named by all as a superb technician and reader, his work falling slightly more, perhaps, into a legitimate than a strictly ragtime vein. Two early Baltimore pianists whom Eubie Blake remembers are William Turk and Sammy Ewell.

Turk was born around 1866 and died about 1911. Almost six feet tall, he weighed more than three hundred pounds. Eubie says: "He had a left hand like God. He didn't even know what key he was playing in, but he played them all. He could play the ragtime stride bass, but it bothered him because his stomach got in the way of his arm, so he used a walking bass instead. I can remember when I was thirteen—this was 1896—how Turk would play one note with his right hand and at the same time four with his left. We called it 'sixteen'— they call it boogie-woogie now. His chords would jell even when he went into other keys by ear, and he often played in two keys, one key in one hand and one in the other, and the chords still jelled.

"The higher-class fellows who played things from the big shows looked down on this music. Nobody thought of writing it down. It was supposed to be the lower type of music, but now it is considered all right. I don't quite get that part of it."

Sammy Ewell was the patron saint of all the Baltimore Negro pianists who could not read music. "We would get around the bar," Eubie says, "and Sam played the songs until we got them. He had more clothes than Broadway Jones—

thirty-five pairs of pants and one room was just clothes. He played in sporting houses." In Eubie's childhood, around 1890, Big-Head Wilber and Jimmy Green were the march kings of Baltimore; they helped to develop the early style that contrasted the rhythms of straight march and syncopated ragtime.

A little older than Eubie was the man whom he considers the greatest ragtime player he ever heard. This was a Boston native from what must have been an accident-prone generation, One-Leg Willie Joseph. He is said to have had Boston Conservatory training before he went to Baltimore to take Eubie's place at the Goldfield Hotel. Joseph was a consistent winner of ragtime contests throughout the country. Eubie tells of one of the giant contests put on by Richard K. Fox and his *Police Gazette* in which Joseph entered through the maneuvering of Shep Edmonds. Fair-haired boy of the *Gazette* and habitual winner of these contests at Tammany Hall and the old Madison Square Garden was the white ragtimer Mike Bernard. To help assure his victories by audience acclamation, Mike always had the final spot. On this occasion, however, the brilliant Negro brought the house down with *The Stars and Stripes Forever* in march time, ragtime, and "sixteen." Hearing the applause, Mike hurriedly remembered a date elsewhere and disappeared.

The ragtime medals had golden plaques suspended by chains, each bearing the name of a city the champion had conquered. One-Leg Willie's medal finally reached an awe-inspiring length. At this point he began removing the cities one by one and pawning them, but his money never went into clothes. He was famous for his disreputable attire at a time when fancy dressers were the rule.

One-Leg was one of the technicians who developed the fast shout style. Slow-drag ragtime was already considered out of date by a new generation that emphasized the brilliant, fast techniques of the shouts, which utilize the ragtime bass, but in which the traditional trio is generally omitted. The shout piles one intricate theme on top of another and interrupts the "stride" with complex broken bass rhythms. Its effectiveness depends on a constant building up of tension and excitement to the sudden, staccato ending. Paradoxically, this is the expression of both the hectic sophistication of the new Negro urban life and the naïve fervor of the old ring-shouts. The easy-going plantation days were far behind, and the ragtime banjos of Old Man Metronome and the famous minstrel duo of the Bohee brothers were all but forgotten, yet the rhythms remained.

Jack the Bear and his contemporaries played in the older Negro districts of New York from the upper Twenties to the lower Thirties west of Sixth Avenue and on West Fifty-third Street, as well as in the area settled around 1900 by the influx of Negroes from Alabama and the so-called Geechees (or Gullahs) from the Charleston area. This last zone, called San Juan Hill, was between West Sixty-first and Sixty-third Streets around Tenth and Eleventh Avenues, near the Hudson. The fringes of this district, named the Jungle, were the haunts of men like The Bear, Jess Pickett, The Shadow, Fats Harris ("he laid down a terrific stomp"), and Abba Labba, and, a little later, of young James P. Johnson, Luckey Roberts, Willie Gant, The Lion (Willie Smith), and The Beetle (Stephen Henderson).

Many of the tricky broken basses of the shout came from a now almost legendary habitué of the Jungle haunts. Of uncertain origin, uncertain age, and uncertain end was Richard McLean, of the rhyming name Abba Labba, but his eccentric bass figurations can be found in the shout rags of Luckey Roberts, Eubie Blake, James P. Johnson, and Fats Waller.

In the Jungle and in the later uptown Harlem the house-parties or rent-shouts flourished. "The parties were good for everything," says The Lion. "A hundred people would crowd into one seven-room flat until the walls bulged. Food! Hog maws [pickled pig bladders] and chitt'lin's with vinegar—you never ate nothing until you ate 'em. Beer and gin. When we played the shouts, everyone danced."

The Lion is second to none as the sort of fantastic personality that was to be found by the dozen in the musical world of Harlem. Now over sixty he is faithful to the house-shout atmosphere in which he developed. He learned to play the organ in his childhood at his grandmother's on Minetta Lane in Greenwich Village. The old lady had once played banjo in the Primrose and West Minstrels, and while in her later years she opposed ragtime in theory, she gave it to him in fact. By twelve he was playing the *Maple Leaf Rag* on the wheezy old reeds and singing topical songs like

> *Don't you hit that lady dressed in green*
> *She's the best lover that you ever seen,*

which sprang up from nowhere—"just sayings that was got up in those days."

With this start, Willie (The Lion) Smith, born in Goshen, New York, as William Bertholff, became one of Harlem's most versatile performers and, with James P. Johnson and Fats Waller, a central figure of the rent-shouts of the period immediately after World War I. Incidentally, it was as a doughboy artilleryman, later sergeant, in France that Willie became The Lion. In his career Willie Smith has written many tunes that in the main are not shouts but atmospheric pieces featuring unusual rhythms and harmonies. Among these are *Echoes of Spring*, *Zig Zag*, *Contrary Motion*, and *Here Comes the Band*. The Lion has never seriously invaded society entertainment or show business. The house shout parties remain, and he remains with them. He says: "They're going to have rent parties as long as they have high rents in Harlem."

The shouts began to develop in the early period of Eastern ragtime, and during all this time the emphasis was on playing, with no thought of selling numbers for publication. Perhaps no two men could better illustrate this love of playing for its own sake than Paul Seminole and Donald Lambert, both born in 1904. Seminole's father was from Florida and true to his name part Indian. The family lived on Sharper Street in Philadelphia. For years father and son did an Indian act in vaudeville. Young Seminole was only five feet tall, slender, brown-skinned, with high cheekbones. He played the guitar left-handed, was a good xylophonist, and as a specialty played the piano with his right hand and the guitar with his left. Paul Seminole, who died in Asbury Park in 1932, was a player whom the greatest of them still remember with something like awe.

Eubie Blake first heard Seminole at Small's cellar place on Fifth Avenue near 135th Street. "If he played a tune twenty thousand times," says Eubie, "it was twenty thousand times different." The drummer, Hurley Diemer, says: "Every style was Seminole's. Just say Seminole and stop." When Seminole was in his early twenties he played with some of Luckey Roberts's society bands and also toured with a vaudeville act called Luckey and His Browns and Blues.

Seminole played a number of New Jersey spots and there met Don Lambert, with whom he formed a two-piano act. Although the part-Indian wizard left no records, his style is in many respects duplicated today in that of Lambert. Lambert, too, is a player who inspires awe. Four years after his birth, in Princeton, his mother, Alma, a local pianist and band-leader, began his piano lessons. To her he owes his command of the keys and harmony, but his technique is a highly individual thing. A diminutive man with hands almost as small as a woman's, he plays broken octaves and tenths so rapidly that he seems to be stretching them, and another of his tricks is to make rippling runs of rapid thirty-second notes entirely with his little finger.

Lambert's invention is as seemingly inexhaustible as that of Seminole was. Apparently discursive ideas lead him into themal transformations and abstract variations in remote keys, but there is a continuous musical logic. A specialty that Lambert shares with Seminole is the playing of semiclassics, first formally and then with a rush of shout-style syncopation. Another is his playing of two melodies in simultaneous counterpoint and often in different keys and yet in constant harmony. A part of the game is to allow his listeners to choose the melodies.

Lambert has never been a part of the Harlem scene. He dislikes New York, is disinterested in publication, has no drive for wealth or fame, and is only mildly interested in recording. He is a throwback to the unregenerate itinerant pianist of fifty years ago. At his small upright piano, with drinks sent by the bar patrons lined up on top, he will play thirty selections an hour. As his hands toss off some freshly conceived musical impossibility, he grins his toothy grin with a perverse, impish charm. He likes the feel of small fourth-rate bars where he can sit and play as he wishes. Lambert's work is to be heard on a few Bluebird and Circle records.

Four Eastern ragtime men—for their published works as well as for their other accomplishments—are destined for lasting fame. They are James Hubert Blake, Charles Luckeyeth Roberts, James Price Johnson, and Thomas Waller. Among them these men explored nearly all of the musical and entertainment fields.

Eubie Blake was born in Baltimore on February 7, 1883. At fifteen and a half years of age he was playing in the tenderloin. Far from approving of this, his mother did not even sanction any sort of secular music. As usual, the hard logic of economic necessity won out. Little Eubie, who cannot remember when he could not play, had a few lessons, but in the main he was self-taught. A neighbor told on him. "I heard someone playing, sounded just like little Hubie, at Aggie Shelton's bawdy house." His mother said: "It is not my boy. He goes to bed at nine every night." But Eubie had been getting up and into long pants and over the back fence.

Eubie was not one to fall for the lure of the red-light Bohemia. In a year he was fixing his sights on a goal that then seemed more easily attainable for the Negro, that of an equal participation with white in the theatrical world. And, as near as any Negro in America has ever been able to reach that goal, Eubie attained it.

Eubie was one of the first of the Eastern Negro ragtimers to get his instrumental pieces published, though his junior, Luckey Roberts, beat him by one year with his *Junk Man Rag*. Eubie had tried early enough to crash the Tin Pan Alley barriers. He would play a number like his early unpublished *Charleston Rag* or, a few years later, his *Black Keys on Parade* for Joseph W. Stern, and the publisher would say: "Sure it's good—it's wonderful—but who could play it but you and Luckey Roberts?"

Meeting the early tycoons of the music business, Eubie learned what was expected of the Negro: "None of us were supposed to know how to read music. They wanted folk stuff. If we could read, we had to pretend we couldn't. The day

197

before a show opened we'd get the music. They'd come to the spots after the show and hear us playing the tunes and say: 'Aren't they marvellous?' "

The house of Stern eventually published several Blake piano solos. The first two, appearing in 1914, were the melodic rags *Chevy Chase* and *Fizz Water*. The scores, greatly simplified at the publisher's request, give only a faint idea of the intricacy of these numbers as Eubie or James P. Johnson actually play them. *Bugle Call Rag* followed in 1916. Not the later, over-familiar jazz number, this is a rag of three strains in which over the ragtime bass the thumb of the right hand plays the bugle calls with the four fingers executing an independent counterpoint. Some of Eubie's finest solos remain unpublished chiefly because of their extreme difficulty of execution. Among these is a real syncopated masterpiece, *Troublesome Ivories*.

Eubie and Noble Sissle joined forced in 1915 to form the since famous team of Sissle and Blake. Tall, handsome, Indianapolis-born Sissle, gifted singer and entertainer and born lyricist, was like the diminutive, elflike keyboard wizard's alter ego. The composite personality, Sissle and Blake, made its mark as a composing-writing team on Broadway in 1921 in one of the outstanding musicals of that or any other day, *Shuffle Along*, premiered at the Sixty-third Street Theater, where it ran for eighteen months. The all-star Negro cast and the beautiful melodies captivated critics and public alike. Prima donna Lottie Gee, the enchanting Florence Mills, Sissle, and the team of Miller and Lyles, in their second-hand costumes (*Shuffle Along* cost a mere, almost unbelievable $700 to put on), scored a smash success. Eubie conducted, and his tunes—*I'm Just Wild about Harry*, *Love Will Find a Way*, *Bandanna Days*, and *Gypsy Blues*—became national hits. *Shuffle Along* with its various tours ran until 1924.

The next important Sissle and Blake collaboration was *Chocolate Dandies* of 1924, with its hits, *Manda*, *Thinking of Me*, and *Dixie Moon*. It ran at the Colonial Theater, Broadway at Sixty-first Street, and on tour for eight months.

A gala performance of *Shuffle Along* took place at Ford's Theater in Baltimore before the death of Eubie's mother. By special concession Negroes occupied boxes and balcony seats, and after the show old friends crowded backstage. Amid the congratulations Mrs. Blake stood aloof. When one well-wisher said to her: "Isn't Eubie's success wonderful?" she replied: "Some see it that way, but he might have done it all for Jesus instead."

Despite all his brilliant work for the stage, the folk strain is still in Eubie. He happens to think of old-timers whose sole instrument was the triangle. "What rhythms!" he says. "*There* is a lost art!" "What is a legitimate instrument?" he asks. "Why is it a drum and not a washboard? Give the finest drums in the world to a kid and they're only toys, but give a washboard to a drummer and you've got a rhythm instrument. And then those long metal cylinders, different lengths. The players wore gloves and would pull on them and make weird sounds like a Theremin."

In 1927 Sissle formed an orchestra, went to Paris for the American Legion convention, and remained abroad for several years. Blake continued on his own in New York, and in 1930 two musicals of his composition played in Manhattan. These were *Folies Bergere*, with book by Will Morrissey, produced at the Gansevoort in Greenwich Village, and Lew Leslie's *Blackbirds of 1930*, with Andy Razaf's lyrics, at the Royale Theater on Forty-fifth Street. The latter was another hit, starring Ethel Waters and the Berry brothers, with a brilliant cast.

By that time the Negro's day as independent writer and composer in the American theater was about over, though he has continued to make strides as an actor. The sound pictures too, in which the Negro never has had a real chance, were to a degree de-emphasizing the stage musical comedy. Today costs of production, pyramided to fantastic heights, frighten even the boldest angels away from the dark-skinned authors and composers. It is all a great pity, for the melodies, the singing and dancing, and the incomparable comedy of the Negro should still be a bright ornament to the American stage and screen. It is hoped that they will open up for him again. Today Eubie Blake studies the Schillinger system—as if any system of music manufacture could improve his superb gift of music-making—and lives in hopes.

199

It was Charles Luckeyeth Roberts who invaded society's upper four hundred. During the 1920's it was Luckey and his dinner-jacketed orchestras who played for the Astors, the Warburtons, the Wanamakers, the Vanderbilts, and the Goulds at Newport, Nantucket, and Narragansett, on Fifth Avenue and in Palm Beach. Jim Europe had pioneered in the upper crust, and Eubie Blake, James P. Johnson, and the remarkable woman shout-player Alberta Simmons had their dates in the drawing-rooms and the crystal-chandeliered ballrooms, but these were Luckey's special field. It was a long road up from Luckey's childhood in the early 1890's in Philadelphia, from his days as a child acrobat and his beginnings in music (when he ruined singers' voices with F sharp, the only key he then knew). From six dollars a week at barroom piano in the Baltimore dives to a thousand dollars and more a night among the millionaires was Luckey's long jump.

In the quarter century that intervened, he packed a world of activity into music and other fields, for short, vastly broad, and incredibly strong Luckeyeth Roberts is a powerhouse of energy. Born a Quaker, and a lifelong stranger to alcohol and tobacco, he recently appeared in an upper Manhattan precinct station dragging three young thugs who had thought the "old man" would be an easy hold-up. He has come through two major automobile accidents, in one of which both hands were shattered, to play more brilliant piano than ever. The day after an accident is his time to entertain his friends in the hospital room while doctors and nurses quietly give up and go away.

Luckey sits in the Rendezvous, the bar on St. Nicholas Avenue in Harlem that he now owns, calmly saying: "Peace has got to come first and eventually it will," as pandemonium reigns around him. Or, sipping orange juice, he will say: "Give these friends of mine the best Scotch in the house." Or, as his singing bartenders and waitresses, who include both operatic sopranos and blues singers, harmonize with the help of Columbia University students and other patrons, the vast hands that introduced tenths and twelfths into the ragtime bass are coaxing melodies from the keyboard. His mercurial playing is a thing of almost overpowering brilliance. Its range of volume, from a whisper to a thunderclap, almost stumped the Circle engineers when they recorded his only solo disks a few years ago. The piano itself is the innocent bystander. Braced to withstand his crashing chords, a string will suddenly snap under an unexpected and seemingly gentle flip of a finger. The final touch is supplied by the summer sign outside Luckey's Rendezvous. It reads: "Cooled by Air-Conditioned Typhoon."

Luckey's *Junk Man Rag* of 1913 was a big hit. It is surprisingly Joplinesque in score, but the composer's own playing reveals typical Eastern complexity. His other rags of pre-World War I vintage delineate his ranging versatility. *Pork and Beans*, one of the favorite shouts of the Harlem parlor-social pianists, has a trio famous for its rhythmic simulation of a rubber band stretching and then snapping. Its principal theme is a startling grotesquerie of dissonant chords of the kind that ragtimers call "crazy chords," based on the melancholy tonic triad of E minor. The effect of the discordant, jangling gaiety is somewhat akin in spirit to Ravel's *La Valse*, but there any resemblance ends, for the incantational rhythmic force of *Pork and Beans* is like voodoo.

The *Music Box Rag*, with its musical imitations, and *Shy and Sly* (a reconnoitering fox appears on the cover) reveal a delicately imaginative side that the composer keeps well hidden behind his ebullient façade. Luckey's many compositions include a number of beautiful songs and the rags *Palm Beach*, *Mo'Lasses*, and *Ripples of the Nile*. The last has a theme based on rapid triplets that were the despair of Luckey's pupils. As he played this movement over and over slowly for them, a beautiful melody emerged that he published separately and much later in song form. As *Moonlight Cocktail* this melody was one of the big hits of the 1930's. And not to be omitted from any list is Luckey's really superb, unpublished tango *Spanish Venus*.

Among Luckey's old programs and clippings are some telling of some of his public triumphs—his sensational success at a 1939 Carnegie Hall concert, one at Town Hall in New York in 1941, and the ovation a Robin Hood Dell audience accorded his *Whistlin' Pete—Miniature Syncopated Rhapsody* for piano and orchestra. The program notes: "In this composition Mr. Roberts stretches an octave and a fifth with both hands." Luckey was the first Negro to play nightly at the exclusive Everglades Club in Palm Beach. He was a favorite of the Prince of Wales, now the Duke of Windsor, when the Prince visited America, and played for him for nine consecutive nights. For years thereafter Luckey chose the hot records for Edward's collection.

The versatility of Luckey Roberts equals his prodigious energy. During the years that he played for the most exclusive society, he found time to write the music for no fewer than fourteen musical comedies, all of which were produced, although none scored the success that Sissle and Blake's *Shuffle Along* had attained. The earliest of Luckey's stage productions was *My People* (1911); his last two, *Go-Go* and *Sharlee*, were both produced by John Cort in 1923 at Daly's Sixty-third Street Theater, New York. Luckey today has two recently completed musical comedies, *Golden Brown* and *Emaline*, for which he is trying to secure backing. Both scores are full of beautiful melodies, such as the song *Exclusively with You* and a remarkably intricate four-themed rag called *The Park Avenue Polka*. This rag, geared to Luckey's own technical powers, could be played by few pianists.

Luckey's society services are used less often nowadays. The generation of grand dowagers and tycoons who were his patrons has passed on and the scions have other interests. As long as Franklin D. Roosevelt lived, however, he remembered Luckey, who had played so often at the old Gramercy Park house of his mother. Now and then, even today, Luckey will obey a telegraphed summons and with a hastily assembled orchestra board a plane for Florida. But most of the time Charles Luckeyeth sits in the Rendezvous as the Typhoon fans roar, fingering out intricate new melodies in haunting chord sequences that only a virtuoso could play—melodies that Tin Pan Alley and Hollywood cannot seem to use.

While Eubie Blake made stage history and Luckey Roberts invaded the Newport salons, young James Price Johnson was dreaming of conducting syncopated symphonies and of ragtime concerts played in brilliantly lit halls before a hundred-piece, tail-coated orchestra. His was a dream that, like the others' dreams, came true—for a while.

Jimmy was born in New Brunswick, New Jersey, in 1894. By the time he was twelve the Johnson family was living on Marcella Street in Jersey City. "It was an old-time honky-tonk street, but some nice families had to live there. We were a little out of line living there and we saw many things. Everyone who came to New York stopped in Jersey City first, and the city crowd came over to gamble.

"I heard these pianos in the houses, things like *Going Back to Cincinnati*, *Keep on Knockin' but You Can't Come In*, and other honkytonk specialties. I heard spirituals, too, but not on Marcella Street—my mother sang in the Methodist choir. I heard the brass bands in every campaign when they were out after votes. And I was only eleven when my brother got some free tickets for the New York Symphony and I got to hear them, too. All I heard was music—from the old ditties the pimps passed on from ear to ear up to the long-hair stuff.

"I was only a little kid when I picked up *Little Brown Jug*— that was the first tune I ever played on the piano, but of course I changed the chords around. When we moved to San Juan Hill in New York, I began to hear the real syncopators. When a new friend of mine, Ernest Green—my age—learned to play Joplin's *Gladiolus*, I knew I couldn't stop. My mother got me a Tway piano.

"I would hear the tunes and, to make sure, go home and 'woodshed' them in every key, put them in major and minor and all the ninth chords. Ernest's mother got opera lessons from old Professor Giannini by doing his housework, and she got him to teach me my harmony and counterpoint for just a dollar a lesson. He taught me for four years. I had to throw away my fingering and learn to put the right finger on the right note. I was on Bach, and double thirds need good fingering.

"I was on the job too, pounding piano from nine at night until seven the next morning. I never coasted—even if nobody was in, I played—and when I got in a hot groove, the piano was walking. And we had drummers then. Battle Ax worked tempos so fast with his foot that he played rolls on the bass

203

drum. Eugene Holland made a double contact each time the stick hit and it made an echo in the trap-drum rolls. But I never heard a drummer like Arthur MacIntyre—called 'Traps'—from Baltimore. He would build up a roll for three minutes until it tore the house down."

It was 1949: James P. turned to the piano in his plain, substantial house in Jamaica, New York, and played some of the many fine shouts he wrote—*Over the Bars*, *Caprice Rag*, *Keep Off the Grass*, and *Carolina Shout*. Then a beautiful waltz, *Eccentricity*, with a syncopated lilt that would make the *Blue Danube* sound as heavy-footed as wooden shoes.

"Scott Joplin was a great forerunner," James P. said. "Joplin was fifty years ahead of his time. Even today, who understands *Euphonic Sounds?* It's really modern.

"I've written some large pieces," he added simply, and brought out his scores. *Rhythm Drums* is scored for English horns, flutes, oboes, bassoons, four horns, trombones, trumpets, and many other instruments. Certain parts of this three-movement tone poem proceed in four-part counterpoint. His *Jasmine* (*Jazz-o-Mine*) *Concerto* is for piano and full orchestra. Its second movement is the classic theme and variations but a ragtime melody is used and the variations are characteristic: rhapsodic, classic blues, waltz, double syncopation, etc.

The *Harlem Symphony*, of four movements, written in 1932, ends with a majestic, syncopated passacaglia on the hymn *I Want Jesus to Walk with Me*. It was played at Carnegie Hall, the Brooklyn Academy of Music, and in other American cities, as well as in Germany, Peru, and Brazil. *Jasmine* was played at the Heckscher Foundation in Manhattan in 1943, as well as by the Brooklyn, Boston, and Philadelphia Symphonies. A long choral work, *Yamecraw*, was made into a movie short in the 1930's. These are long works with a feeling of breadth and sweep and with a racial pungency that Gershwin missed, and their African rhythms move with a forthright nobility. One feels none of these qualities as borrowed—they all reside in the dark, diminutive composer himself. The harmony, with its rich prolixity, seems strangely in contrast with that of moderns like Bartók and Stravinsky. They might, indeed, consider it old-fashioned.

But in this regard James P. said: "The atonal and twelve-tone systems become common and monotonous. I have done six-tone atonal work myself, but they haven't dug to the bottom of the old harmony yet. They've forgotten how to use it—there was a break somewhere—so they think it's all used up. Any harmony is only so many chords unless you have a real melody. And the Schillinger system—you are supposed to have emotional intent by science. This is impossible, because true inspiration is gone. Why do these composers, and the be-boppers, too, try to get away from melody? It shows a weakness. No melody is in them and they know it."

James P. had his chance, and his big works were heard a few times, but something happened and the whole thing vanished. White composers have their troubles too, of course, unless they belong to a small favored few—the memory of Bartók's obscure death in New York is still green. But it is an axiom that the Negro is first to go when jobs are scarce.

"When the sound films came in they hired white people," Jimmy explained. "There was no room for us. Radio and films changed things, the Negro lost out. When we performed personally in public, the Negro had a chance. When the medium is mechanical and they ship it out all over the country, we don't get a chance. The worst sections of the country pull the whole thing down.

"Even in ragtime we used to play our own stuff and the public liked us. But money got behind popular music, and the public believes what they read. So they began asking us for the stuff that was ballyhooed. Ten Top Tunes—what is that?"

Then Jimmy looked back from his symphonies to the music that they came from. "They're still playing ragtime now, or trying to, but they conceal and cover it up. It's considered certain traditional figures by some, but that's wrong, it's a rhythm that you feel and work with. They're just ashamed of a name."

A musical comedy called *Sugar Hill* was written in 1948 by Johnson and Flournoy Miller. It rehearsed in Harlem for a number of months and then opened in June 1949 at the Las Palmas Theater in Hollywood. The cast and entire production were Negro. After receiving fine reviews not only in local papers but also in the influential trade magazines *Variety* and *Billboard*, it ran for three months. The motion-picture industry showed no interest in show, music, or cast, though the high schools of southern California are being forever combed for the profound dramatic qualities of a new young face and a sexy figure. Nor could backing be found in New York, though in this very period new musicals were opening on Broadway, many of them closing almost immediately with the backers' loss for each running into six figures.

James P. Johnson was patient rather than bitter as he discussed these things. Most of all he seemed puzzled, as if all of them were beyond reasonable understanding.

In 1951 a stroke paralyzed this great artist. Finally, in 1955, death erased the man, but not his notes. They live unfaded in the scores, and also in the record grooves that guard forever the crisp delicacy and incomparable imagination of a playing that, like the ring-shout, sang while it danced. Our American heritage, it awaits our acceptance. His shouts, at last, may outrank James P. Johnson's symphonies. The best of them, like the best of Eubie Blake's, are among ragtime's top masterpieces.

Thomas (Fats) Waller was born on May 21, 1904 in New York, the youngest of four children. Like Eubie Blake, Luckey Roberts, and James P. Johnson, he entered ragtime over the objection of a respectable, middle-class Negro family. The Wallers were from Virginia. Thomas's grandfather, Adolph Waller, a noted violinist, had toured the South after the Civil War; his father, Edward Martin Waller, was deacon and then pastor of the Abyssinian Baptist Church in Fortieth Street (later in uptown Harlem); his mother, Adaline Locket Waller, played the piano and organ and had a good soprano voice.

The attachment between Fats—the public-school nickname that stuck with him—and his mother was strong. She continued to encourage his music even after he went into ragtime, which his father called "music from the Devil's workshop." Fats was six when his brother Robert bought a piano for him. He was eleven, and had played the organ at the church for a year, when he heard Paderewski. By fourteen he was organist at the Lincoln Theater in Harlem, and had already had years of classical study with Carl Bohm. Later in life he studied with Leopold Godowsky. He was fifteen when he wrote his first rag, for Fats was incorrigibly a hot player; seventeen when first married (and nineteen when married a second and final time); and only twenty when he recorded his first solos on the old Okeh label. In the nineteen remaining years of his life Fats was to play on nearly five hundred disks and a large number of player-piano rolls, and to copyright over four hundred musical compositions.

These prodigious figures fit the man, whose five-foot-eleven frame carried 285 pounds, whose appetite for life was even more avid than his famed capacity for food and liquor. His humor was vast, innocent, but sardonic; he kidded everything, everybody, and himself. Many phonograph records contain Fats Waller's hilarious spoofing. Some have become classics of American humor. Who does not remember, for example, the record on which he complains bitterly of his girl friend's oversized feet, or the other one in which, singing a song of Lil Armstrong's, he admonishes all and sundry to run their mouths while he runs his business?

Records like these employ the broad side of the blade of a wit that everyone loved. It had a sharp edge, too, that subtly lampooned the Tin Pan Alley and Hollywood film songs that RCA-Victor hired him to exploit. Waller owed his recording position to the fact that RCA had purchased the old Victor company and unceremoniously dropped the Victor jazz star Jelly Roll Morton, in 1930, as unamenable to the commercial point of view. Fats's treatment of banal material was unmerciful. Although he improved it instrumentally as far as possible, his vocal burlesques were outrageous—but they sold the product. And Fats insinuated a few masterpieces of band and piano solo into the list from time to time.

A natural humorist, Fats became a slapstick clown and world-renowned figure of popular music while inside, behind the buffoonery and the disingenuous irony, he kept himself intact. It is hard to measure his achievements and his compromises against those of Luckey Roberts or Eubie Blake, or against the achievements and frustrations of a James P. Johnson. One can only say that each fitted his life and his art

207

as best he could into the society in which he found himself.

The real triumphs that Fats cherished were not the public ones. Quiet backroom sessions with James P. and Willie the Lion and The Beetle, when the gin and creative inspiration flowed, remained in his memory as did his secret hours alone at the great organ consoles of many a theater and cathedral to which he gained after-hours access. The time that he and the Cathedral organist played alone in the loft of Notre-Dame in Paris was one such memory. When the reporters asked him about it, Waller would only say: "First Mr. Dupré played the God-box and then I played the God-box."

There are persistent rumors of grand organ records made for Victor that are said to begin with superb straight renderings of Bach chorales and to go into dazzling transformations in African ragtime rhythms. Victor has withheld the records, the rumors add, because of fear of insulting the long-hairs.

Fats wrote several successful musical revues. The first was *Keep Shufflin'*, produced in 1928 at the Sixty-third Street Theater, a good show but by no means another *Shuffle Along*. His *Hot Chocolates* opened in 1929 at Connie's Inn, the Harlem night club, to run for six months and then to move to Broadway in 1930. Its big hit was *Ain't Misbehavin'*. Just before his death Fats wrote the score for *Early to Bed*, a Broadway production with white cast. To mention only a few of his hit tunes, there were *I've Got a Feeling I'm Falling; Squeeze Me; Honeysuckle Rose; Ain't Misbehavin';* and *My Fate Is in Your Hands*. The serious side shows through in excellent piano shouts that include *Handful of Keys* and *Smashing Thirds*, and in the slow-drag blues *Numb Fumblin'*.

Fats made a number of movie shorts and was a featured player in the full-length film *Stormy Weather*, which starred the singer Lena Horne. His short sequence in a basement dive where he played, as blues-singer Ada Brown sang, was a riotous moment. One critic wrote that "Fats Waller lifted his left eyebrow and nearly stole the picture."

Fats Waller was only thirty-nine and at the height of his fame when he died of pneumonia on a train just pulling into Kansas City. He was headed east for a final night-club engagement that was to have been followed by his retirement to composing and an occasional piano concert. The memory of a much-loved man lives on, just as ragtime—all the vital transforming African rhythm—lived on in his music. Fats wore his laughing mask of clown without burnt cork, while inside the vast bulk of his body he laughed at the scene around him, "and under the sweet right-hand chords of the sentimental trash he had to play, the solid left rolled on like heat thunder on a summer day."

Just as classic New Orleans jazz represents the instrumental expansion -- or orchestration -- of piano ragtime, so Harlem ragtime fathered the big band jazz -- or swing -- of the 1930's. Its eastern form was initiated in the early 1920's by two stride pianists, Fletcher Henderson and Duke Ellington. It began as a cross between the keyboard shouts and theatre -- the songs of musical comedy. The southwest, or Kansas City, swing style is a crossing of eastern ragtime and the wailing blues -- the rough-gentle voices of deepwoods singers and the country guitars transforming plunging "double drive" train rhythms and "lonesome" night whistles into boogie. Unlikely as this hybrid might seem, it was effected by the ragtime delicacy and precision of Count Basie, pianist turned orchestra leader.

Always harmonically advanced, stride even helped to shape bop, the radical musical revolution of the 1940's, through the dissonant chord sequences and asymmetric rhythm patterns of a follower of James P. Johnson, Thelonious Sphere Monk.

Apart from its various orchestral catalyses, the Harlem piano style itself has never ceased evolving. Stride merged into modern jazz piano through the work of Art Tatum, but, in its own right, it has preeminently grown in rhythmic-melodic freedom and complexity with Earl "Fatha" Hines, a veteran of the Waller-Lambert-Basie generation. Hines' many innovations began in the middle 1920's. Today, in his sixties and at the height of his technical and inventive powers, Earl Hines impressively demonstrates the capacity of ragtime of any style to develop and evolve when its creative continuities have not been broken.

PAN-AM RAG

Composed by TOM TURPIN
Arr: by Arthur Marshall

Moderato

CALLIOPE RAG

MODERATO   JAMES SCOTT

D.S. ⅍ F.

THE ALASKAN RAG

SLOW MARCH TEMPO

JOSEPH F. LAMB

PEAR BLOSSOMS

SCOTT HAYDE[N]
Arr. by BOB DARC[H]

MODERATO

MISSOURI ROMP

SLOWDRAG TWO-STEP

MODERATO

ARTHUR MARSHALL

CENTURY PRIZE

MARCH and TWO-STEP

Tempo di marcia

ARTHUR MARSHALL

SILVER ROCKET

MODERATO

ARTHUR MARSHA

To the memory of
Harriet Janis

THE GOLDEN HOURS

ANDANTE MODERATO

MAX MORATH

ecial thanks to Max Morath for The Golden Hours especially composed for this edition.

One For Amelia

By MAX MORATH

Traditional ragtime tempo (*not fast*)

NOT FAST

OPERA HOUSE RAG

Respectfully Dedicated to Mr. Stanford Zucker

BY ROBERT R. DARCH

L.H.

TRIO

D. S. al Fine

BUSINESS IN TOWN

ANDANTE ma non troppo

DONALD ASHWANDER

Special thanks to Donald Ashwander for <u>Business In Town</u> especially composed for this edition.

FRIDAY NIGHT

ALLÉGRO MODERATO

DONALD ASHWANDER

GOTHENBURG RAG

ALLEGRO

PETER LUNDBERG

pecial thanks to Peter Lundberg for Gothenburg Rag especially composed for this edition.

BRUN CAMPBELL EXPRESS

ALLEGRO

THOMAS W. SHEA

CHESTNUT VALLEY RAG

.ALLEGRO

TREBOR JAY TICHENOR

CODA

CAKEWALK IN THE SKY

To BENJAMIN ROBERTSON HARNEY goes the credit for introducing ragtime to polite society—or perhaps one should say to polite male white society with wives included. The date was 1896, the place, as we have seen, a New York vaudeville theater. It was "jig-piano" then. Not until a year later was the music christened "ragtime" and the time ripe for the appearance of the first ragtime publications in Chicago.

Who was this slender, good-looking, twenty-five-year-old youth of medium height, who might have been a Negro, at least to judge by his authentically racial playing, singing, and dancing, and who in those early days teamed with Negro entertainers like Tom Mack and Strap Hill? Behind the man who scored such an instantaneous success at Keith's on the Rialto lay years of musical activities and tours, lay, in fact, a fascinating personal history.

Although Ben Harney came from Kentucky, where he had been born near Middleboro Post Office on March 1, 1871, he, like any of the itinerant players of that day, seemed a man of the present, a musical apparition materialized not out of our common past but suddenly in the calcium glare, a figure at a piano playing a new music few had ever heard. In those days, when ragtime was the newest new thing, its players were a new generation without a lineage that anyone recognized, seemingly spawned out of the novel and the strange.

Benjamin Robertson Harney is a little-known man today. Yet historically he is a figure of great importance, a white man who not only understood Negro music and could make that music like a veritable Negro, but who publicly pioneered it in an early day when Negroes themselves were cautious about presenting it full-strength to any but their own race. He was a seventeen-year-old student at a Kentucky military school when this music, to which he seemed so native, possessed him, and he began to search for someone to write out a song, later famous, that he had already created. At about this time he made a marriage that, like his association with ragtime, was to last as long as he lived. His bride, even younger than he, was a beautiful Kentucky girl, Jessie Boyce.

A few years later Harney is found playing in a saloon and dance hall on the southeast corner of Eighth and Liberty (then Green) Streets in Louisville. There he met a rich and prominent youth, one year his junior, named Bruner Greenup, scion of a prosperous Louisville merchant. Bruner is still living today. At seventy-seven he has written us about Harney. The letterhead, adorned with engravings of five Louisville stores, bears the name of the owners, Greenup & Whelan, Lovely Legs Shops. Bruner Greenup writes:

"Ben managed to sit at the piano with a cane in one hand or the other and did a sort of tap dance with one or both feet and the cane. He came to my store one day and asked me to publish a song that he had put together. The song, now historic, was *You've Been a Good Old Wagon But You Done Broke Down*. It was the 1st syncopated song to be published in America. That is absolutely true. . . . Ben had another song destined to be a hit, but claimed that Harry Green took it to Evansville, Ind. and published it under the name of *Mr. Johnson Turn Me Loose*.

"In the middle '90's after Ben had gone to New York to work, M. Witmark wrote and asked me if I would sell it to them saying they wanted it because it was the first

211

rag song on the market. I gave it to them, plates and all, for nothing, but they sent me a check for $25 which they thought would cover the costs of the plates. The work was done by Otto Zimmerman of Cincinnati. If there is a copy of it in existence I don't know of it.

"I started to buy the building and put a plaque on it in memory of Ben but my partner persuaded me not to. The plaque should be there because he was long before Paul Whiteman and Irving Berlin."

There *are* copies of Greenup's publication of *Good Old Wagon* in existence. They are filed in Washington and bear the date 1895. The publication is the first song scored as ragtime ever to appear, and it makes Benjamin Robertson Harney the first of the ragtime pioneers.

After trying for three or four years to get someone to help him put the song down, he finally found Johnny Biller in 1894, and shortly after the turn of the year Greenup brought it out with credit given to both men. No other tunes by Biller have been located, but Harney is credited by *Variety*, in an obituary article in March 1938, with the publication of nearly one hundred other compositions. Were this not enough, his next song, *Mister Johnson, Turn Me Loose*, as we have seen, establishes the Kentucky youth as having committed to paper the first archaic beginnings of the universal, migrant Negro lament that we now call the blues.

Ben and Jessie Harney led an active life as entertainers in the years before he scored his big hit at Keith's. Jessie, who survived her husband, recalled some of this period. The connection that Ben had made with Greenup enabled him to form an all-colored show, the *South Before the War*, which became one of the better-known traveling extravaganzas based on the black-face minstrels. Ben wrote all of the music for this show and played it at every performance. There were spots in which he and Jessie, as one of the earliest "Black and Hi Yaller" teams, did ragtime song-and-dance specialties to banjo accompaniment. About the time that the Chicago Exposition opened, Harney sold *South Before the War* to Whelan and Martell. Going to Chicago for the fair, Ben met the young

Negro ragtime player and entertainer Strap Hill, from Memphis. The Harneys and Strap formed a team. This is Jessie Harney's description of their act:

> "In the trio, Ben played for me to sing and dance and the name of the song was *I Love One Sweet Black Man*— Exit—Cartwheel. Ben opened the Act making his announcement, singing *Johnson* at the piano, Strap answering him from the gallery, came down on the stage and did his Hoss imitations, Ben doing his stick dance and playing at the piano made his exit for the finish. I blacking up, came back on the stage, all three together singing *I Love My Little Honey*, and did two-step off.

It was as a thoroughly accomplished entertainer, a man who in his native Kentucky had absorbed not only the folk melodies around him but also their spirit as well, and with years of experience with road shows and acts behind him, that Ben Harney came to New York with his sensational ragtime success in April 1896.

Like any man, Harney began to capitalize on his good fortune as best he could. Within three years at least a dozen of his ragtime songs were published, fine raggy tunes all of them, and of a true Negroid folk feeling, many with instrumental dance or cakewalk endings that play naturally with an early ragtime sound. Some, like *Mr. Johnson, Turn Me Loose*, were so generally accepted that they became, in effect, folksongs again; all have a robust, healthy, rural quality.

Ben was immediately booked into Tony Pastor's Theater and then into vaudeville's top circuits. For many years, headlined as "The Inventor of Ragtime," he toured the Percy G. Williams, Keith, and Orpheum circuits, as well as with the Howard Atheneum Star Specialty Show of Boston. After Harney's death his wife, Jessie, listed some of the shows in which her husband had taken part. Among these were the A. T. Pearson Stock Company, the Old Soldier Company, and Ben Harney's All Colored Minstrels, for all of which, she says, Ben wrote the music. In addition she said that Ben was with one of burlesque queen May Howard's shows, and with a

Flo Ziegfeld production featuring Anna Held, *The Cat and the Cherub.*

Parallel with Harney's new stage career as the famous ragtime man, a new development in ragtime had been started by his appearances at the famous Tony Pastor's in April 1896. As Harney brought down the house with his ragtime, Pastor's musical director, nineteen-year-old Mike Bernard, sat in the orchestra pit listening and watching every move that Harney made. Even if Ben had actually been the inventor of ragtime, a chain reaction was started over which he could have no control. Ragtime was now in the open for every quick opportunist to grab. Everything in the background of Mike Bernard, from New York Chinatown, was the antithesis of ragtime, and yet in a few years he was to travel the top circuits billed as "King of Ragtime" to counter Harney's claims to being its originator.

Opportunism had led Mike originally to Pastor's. "My original intention," he said in 1910, "was to become a concert player, but I gradually drifted into the line of work I am now doing. Perhaps I am better off though, financially at any rate." Mike had been something of a child prodigy. As the nine-year-old Barnett Bernard he had gone to Europe alone in care of the ship's captain and after two years at the Berlin Conservatory had played a command performance for the Kaiser.

As Mike Bernard listened to Ben Harney with one ear for the storms of applause, his next step was clear. He practiced secretly and within a few months made his appearance as the first of an army of pseudo-ragmen, players who brilliantly copied the externals of a native Negro music without capturing its true rhythms or understanding much of its spirit.

As Ben Harney was scoring another success with his all-colored spectacle show the *Ragtime Reception,* Mike was being designated "Rag Time King of the World" by a self-appointed musical authority, Richard K. Fox, owner of the *Police Gazette.* The mythical crown was won at a big Tammany Hall contest on January 23, 1900. It was the custom of the *Gazette* in that period to run public contests of every kind from quail-eating, pigeon-flying, and oyster-opening to boxing and

214

wrestling, in each of which the winner received a diamond-studded belt or some form of bejeweled medal.

"Many eyes are on the diamond-studded trophy," the *Police Gazette* explained in its January 20, 1900 issue. "The ragtime contest," it added, "will settle a much vexed question . . . since the coon melodies became popular." After making assurances that "in the first place the best man will win . . . an artist who belongs in an obscure country town has as much chance to win as anyone," the *Police Gazette* observed: "Acknowledged leader of the ragtime players is Mr. Michael Bernard, leader of the orchestra at Pastor's and whose fame as a manipulator of the ivories has spread throughout the land. If ever there was a champ, he is one."

Negro contestants were not even considered at this time, and the advance publicity effectually dissuaded many white would-be entrants. Almost any white itinerant "piano professor" of the underworld could have given Bernard real competition, but these, like Eddie (Sheet-Iron) Barnes and Brun Campbell, were occupied in their own world. One such in New York, however, raised his voice. Jake Schaefer, piano king of the New York bordellos, though persona non grata at Tony Pastor's, wrote to Fox's weekly as follows:

"I see where Mike Bernard is to give a ragtime contest and bills himself the champion of the world. I feel called upon out of duty to myself to respectfully dispute his claim to the title. I have played in contests all over the country and won first honors in every one in which I competed. I have played against the best of them and as I have never been defeated in open contest I was generally looked upon as the champion if there is such a thing among rag players. Has Mr. Bernard ever won any equitably conducted contests or has he competed against any of the leaders?

"I do not say I can defeat Bernard, but I would like a chance to prove whether I can or not. While I have had little trouble in defeating all my competitors of course there is no telling when you will rub up against your superior. If matters can be satisfactorily arranged, I will play against Bernard but not on his terms. He suggests that the judges be selected from the audience. It is just like a boxer with a traveling combination who is meeting all comers. When an outsider comes on the stage he is handicapped in that he is a stranger; the boxer with the company is not out to get the worst of it and the managers do not as a rule try to give him the bad end.

"While I do not say I would not get a fair deal under the proper conditions it is hardly a fair test to select judges from the audience. Out of all the spectators there might not be one who was able to judge the quality of the music or able to justly decide the winner. A man to judge ragtime must be able to play it. I would be glad to have a try at Bernard under the following conditions which all are bound to admit are fair:

"Each contestant to name two judges who can play ragtime music and have the four select a fifth; each one of the five to show his ability to judge by playing a number of selections. In that way both would get a fair show. I do not claim that I can play profound music as well as Bernard but with a set of competent judges I think I can add his name to my already long list. As a graceful suggestion, I might say that colored folk be selected as judges. . . ."

Unable to ignore so pointed a challenge, the *Police Gazette* printed Schaefer's letter and replied: "In regard to the judge question, those selected from an audience are all right from any standpoint," adding: "One of the judges in this case will be a representative of the *Police Gazette* and he will not be biased in favor of anyone. . . . If Mr. Schaefer don't get into the game on the 23rd at Tammany Hall, he misses his chance at the *Police Gazette* medal . . . which will be won by the best performer."

Mike Bernard won. Soon the new king was traveling the circuits, and whenever he and Harney met on the same bill, he had the tricks to win the audience. Harney's really Negroid ragtime and shouting excited the listeners; Bernard's sophisticated potpourri of light classicals and flashily dexterous syncopated showmanship overawed them. Ben would sing his famous songs like *The Cake Walk in the Sky*, with its fanciful description of a "crap-shootin' coon—doomed for below," who "sneaked in the other way and bluffed Peter at the Gate."

> *Now I'm goin' to show to each and ev'ry one of you*
> *That grand cake walk*
> *It will cause a talk,*
> *Now coons don't balk*
> *It's done on the earth and I will introduce it in the sky.*
>
> *Put a smile on each face*
> *Ev'ry coon now take your place—*
> *And then away they went*
> *All on pleasures bent.*
> *The harps were a-ringin'*
> *In ragtime they were singin'*
> *And they all bowed down to the king of coons*
> *Who taught the cake walk in the sky.*

Then he sang his extraordinary "jig words" to the chorus:

(RAG CHORUS *ad lib*):

> *Pugut agey smigule ogon egeache fagace evvery cagoon*
> *tagake yougora plagace.*
> *Agan wagay theygay wagant ogon plagasure begant*
> *Wigith hargarps reginging gin ragag tigime theygay*
> *werger saginging*
> *Agan theygay agaul bowgowd dogon togo thege kingying*
> *agove cagoons.*
> *Whogo tagot thege cagake wagauke gin thege skigi.*

Everyone shouted and clapped hands and laughed until the tears ran down their faces. "He's the inventor of ragtime all right, yes sir!"

Then Mr. Bernard, dapper, citified, confident, put the audience in its place with his *Fantasy on the Pilgrim's Chorus from Tannhäuser and the Finale to Rubinstein's E Flat Concerto.* No shouts and laughter from the audience now. Then a medley of Tin Pan Alley songs with stilted brittle syncopation, the weak left hand covered up by the fireworks in the right. Here's something new: the audience is watching now. Then for the wind-up, a musical description that was Mike's specialty, the *Battle of San Juan Hill:* bugle calls, drumbeats, *Dixie, Marching through Georgia,* and the *Star-Spangled Banner.* Rifle fire, the boom of cannon, the music gets softer—taps (it's very sad), *Yankee Doodle,* and the music dies out softly on the strain of "The girl, the pretty little girl, the girl I left behind me."

Then the applause. "Maybe this Harney invented it, but this boy Bernard can sure play it—why, he makes it real classical." Richard K. Fox knew his public.

Tin Pan Alley was in the ragtime business now, grinding away. Chicago can't get away with the ragtime business. Where do St. Louis and Detroit get off, anyway? Here's where the money is. Get busy, boys, lay off the Irish and the Jewish stuff for a while. Let's have some rags.

Ted Snyder, Jean Schwartz, Irving Berlin, as well as a whole army of copyists, arrangers, and mere hacks were ready. The inundation began. The mills of the Alley gods grind swiftly and they grind exceeding coarse:

> *That Lovin' Rag*
> *That Tired Rag*
> *That Pleasin' Rag*
> *That Tuneful Rag*
> *That Fascinatin' Rag*

> *Sweet Pickles Rag*
> *Sour Grapes Rag*
> *Chocolate Creams Rag*
> *Red Peppers Rag*
> *Chewin' the Rag*

> *Ragtime Skedaddle*
> *Ragtime Chimes*
> *Ragtime Violin*
> *Ragtime Joke*
> *Ragtime Insanity*

Mop Rag
  Doll Rags
    Shine or Polish Rag
      Smash-up Rag
        and—
          Alexander's Ragtime Band

Read 'em and weep!

Chicago publishers moved to New York; Detroit publishers moved to New York; big publishers gobbled up some of the little ones, and most of the others died on the vine. Publishers merged, and then the mergers merged. Vaudeville and theater were put under control; Smith Corporation's tunes were plugged, and Jones & Company's were inexplicably side-tracked. Performers were subsidized and even the singing waiters at Coney Island got "a buck to put this new song over." Jones & Company held on anyway, so Smith put cheap editions on ten-cent-store counters and lent their pluggers free to the stores. Finally Jones went on the block; the creditors got ten cents on the dollar; and Smith got the Jones copyrights at bankruptcy prices. Smith moved to a tower suite where platoons of pretty-legged girls guard the big boys. E. B. talks to J. C. in the office next door by intercommunicating system; typewriters click; Western Union boys rush in and rush out; accountants work overtime; and life is just one conference after another.

Amid this bedlam John Stark, ragtime pioneer, opened a New York office. He made only one mistake, but that was fatal. He brought with him music instead of merchandise.

There is no denying the power of the music business; it grows as the business grows. It is not generally recognized, however, that this power operates in fields not ordinarily considered the province of manipulation by money. The objective of the music business by and large is the making of money. Nevertheless, its centralization ultimately works out into public censorship on the one hand and a coercive direction of creative talent on the other. To be explicit: with the sources of distribution controlled by Tin Pan Alley and with the public trained no longer to make its own music, the public

219

takes the pap that it is fed and can make its real wishes felt only by slow, indirect, and partly effective means. The composer himself has little choice but to give the music moguls what they think will sell most readily, for in this realistic age it is no longer the fashion to starve in a garret. Giving the public what it wants is the time-worn excuse for giving it the cheap and trivial. The average mental age-level of the public has been as ruthlessly charted as insurance life-expectancy tables. If public taste is bad, it becomes steadily worse, for deterioration is as real a process as improvement. The public is not merely like a child kept in the same school grade year after year; its education is actually a regression.

Power is one thing, its use another. When Ford and General Motors decided to give the public Bach and Beethoven, hiring the finest artists and conductors to broadcast classical music over vast radio networks, even to tiny hamlet and lonely farmhouse, the American taste for classical music developed with a speed and to a degree hardly short of amazing. Unfortunately at this time it might be hard to convince advertising executives and public-relations men that the American Negro has ever created anything that might lend prestige to the vast, serious business of making and selling motor cars.

While Tin Pan Alley was squeezing ragtime dry, a few people made a lot of money and a great number of people made a little. Many of the good white ragtimers adapted themselves to the new business set-up, in which, however, there was little place for the Negro ragtime composer. Percy Wenrich, for one, did well. It is a useless irony to point out that his biggest hits, songs like *Put On Your Old Grey Bonnet*, are really Missouri folk music that his publishers took under strong protest after Wenrich had made a name for himself.

George Botsford did well, too, and stuck to composing good ragtime as long as he could. *Buckeye Rag* and *Incandescent Rag* and several others came out in 1913, the year in which his excellent rag song *Sailing Down the Chesapeake Bay* was published. And even in 1916, when ragtime was almost at its end, he wrote *Boomerang Rag*.

Henry Lodge, a competent rag-composer in a good tradition, wrote a half-dozen rags almost on a par with his popular

Temptation Rag of 1909, and he wrote rags by the dozen even up to 1923.

Another genuine rag-composer, who has fitted himself very well into music business and the movies, is J. Russel Robinson, of Indianapolis. When Robinson was thirteen years of age— he was born in 1892—his home city was a lively center of ragtime. It was then that Russel, who had had a bare year of piano lessons, teamed with his drummer brother to play ragtime for lodge dances and various social functions. They became a well-known duo that competed successfully with adult musicians.

On the Indianapolis scene at that time were a number of competent composers. There was the Negro Russell Smith, still living in Indianapolis today, who is remembered for a number of excellent rags, including *The Princess*, *Microbe Rag*, and *That Demon Rag*, published there by the Seidel brothers.

Indianapolis was an especially staunch stronghold of good white ragtime. The earliest published were May Aufderheide and Paul Pratt. May's father, the loan broker J. H. Aufderheide, went into music publishing as a sideline to handle the rags of these two. May Aufderheide's first numbers are *Dusty Rag* of 1908 and *The Thriller* of 1909. Thirty-five years after their publication the great New Orleans trumpeter Bunk Johnson could play both from memory, so popular had they been with the early New Orleans jazz bands. May's publications run through 1911, and include *Blue Ribbon*, *A Totally Different Rag*, and *Novelty Rag*, as well as waltzes and songs written with Paul Pratt and others.

Pratt himself was an excellent pianist, who later traveled with road shows of New York plays which formed in Chicago. Although he published comparatively few rags, his *Hot House* and *Springtime Rag* belong near the top.

Cecil Duane Crabbe was another excellent Indianapolis player and a commercial artist as well, who drew the covers for such of his own rags as *Klassicle Rag*, published by Aufderheide in 1910, and *Trouble Rag*. Later he formed one of the early outdoor-advertising firms.

Busy as the Indianapolis scene was, it seemed dull to J. Russel Robinson. He was not fifteen when he and his brother conquered parental objections to their traveling alone by getting their parents to accompany them on a tour of the South. For four years they were in Macon, Georgia, where their nickelodeon accompaniment to the early movies was highly complimented. Some patrons complained, indeed, that they "spent all their time watching those fool musicians." In 1909 Russel Robinson wrote *Sapho Rag* and sent it to Stark, who immediately bought it. Robinson's second publication was *Dynamite Rag*, brought out by the Southern California Music Company in 1910. Stark followed with *The Minstrel Man* and *Whirlwind Rag* a year later. The Seidels published Russel's arrangement of an old New Orleans song, *Te-na-na*, and *That Eccentric Rag* in the same year. The latter is probably Robinson's finest. After *Eccentric* Robinson's output conforms more and more to the Tin Pan Alley norm.

The attitude of many of the good ragtimers who moved into Tin Pan Alley is well summarized in remarks of Emil Seidel. When we interviewed him, his first concern was that "the real originators like Scott Joplin and James Scott should get the credit. No matter what has happened to me, I am still an Ozark hillbilly at heart, and I have great reverence for the creators of ragtime."

A composer of a different sort who fitted himself into the Tin Pan Alley set-up was Abe Holzmann, who is remembered for his fine cakewalks *Smoky Mokes*, *Hunky Dory*, and *Bunch o' Blackberries*. The *New York Herald* of January 13, 1901 tells the Holzmann story, a sidelight on the fantastic picture of the American music business. Excerpts from the *Herald* article follow:

GERMAN COMPOSER WHO WRITES AMERICAN CAKEWALK MUSIC

There is in this country at the present time a celebrated writer of classical music whose propensity for composing darky dances has given him an international reputation. His name is Abe Holzmann and he is a German of high musical education. His knowledge of bass and counterpoint is thorough and his standard compositions bear the stamp of harmonic lore which makes his proclivity for the writing of the popular style of music the more remarkable. Still he continues to compose the latter, and with such unqualified success that his name has now become associated with the leading successes in this line in the country.

When John Philip Sousa raised his baton to the opening measures of Composer Holzmann's famous *Smoky Mokes* last season the noted bandmaster's audience was non plussed. Then surprise gave way to delight and vociferous applause. Persons in the audience consulting their programs discovered a new genius in their midst. From that hour the name of Holzmann was a byword for American cake walks and *Smoky Mokes* re-echoed upon the pianos of a million music lovers.

The biggest of all cakewalk hits, however, came not from Holzmann's pen but from that of a regular Tin Pan Alley denizen, Kerry Mills. In the midst of pouring out one sentimental song after another Mills found time to write the outstanding *At a Georgia Camp Meeting* in 1897. The most tuneful and popular strain of this number is an adaptation of the old Civil War song *Our Boys Will Shine Tonight*.

There are other cases when Tin Pan Alley clicked. Jean Schwartz's *Whitewash Man* and Ted Snyder's *Wild Cherries Rag*, for example, are highly competent and melodious rags. Such exceptions, however, occurred mainly before 1910, when Tin Pan Alley seemed to have killed the golden goose.

It was Irving Berlin who gave the dying egg-layer a transfusion with his *Alexander's Ragtime Band*, published in 1911, the year that Scott Joplin was straining his financial and mental resources to publish his opera *Treemonisha*. The market in spurious rags increased so effectively with Berlin's catchy but musically mediocre song that many people now believe that ragtime began with it.

The damage to real ragtime was done. Working unknowingly together, musical snobbery, moral prudery, and Tin Pan Alley commercialism had done a thorough job. The serious Negro musician found himself back again very close to the point at which he had started. The great Negroes already in the field kept on as best they could, but few new figures came

223

in after 1913 except in the later-developing Eastern shout style.

The pseudo ragtime of Mike Bernard set up a style of playing distinct from that of the Negroes and began a split between the two kinds of ragtime which widened steadily. The schools are best compared by contrasting a white player from each. The Ragtime Kid, Brun Campbell, learned his syncopation from Scott Joplin himself and, being imbued with the real ragtime spirit, never lost its proper style. For Mike Bernard, on the other hand, the Negro might as well never have existed. Mike's conspicuous success was due to the fact that his reduction of Negro musical thinking to the flashy cliché was exactly suited to public taste as it was being conditioned by Tin Pan Alley. The difference is as basic as this: Negro ragtime could transform Mendelssohn's *Spring Song* into something African, but *Maple Leaf* played by Bernard was only a white conservatory piece.

There were many followers of the Mike Bernard school in New York and elsewhere. Pete Wendling, born in 1888 in Manhattan, was one. He became a leading Tin Pan Alley figure through song hits like *Oh What a Pal Was Mary* and the Al Jolson feature, *Yacka Hula Hickey Dula*. There were Lee S. Roberts and Max Kortlander, active with Q. R. S., the piano-roll manufacturers in Chicago. Kortlander later became owner of this company in New York. The Q. R. S. recording artists included a few Negroes like Luckey Roberts, James P. Johnson, and Fats Waller, but mainly featured players of the Bernard school, like Frank Banta, Victor Arden, Lee Ohman, Zez Confrey, Charlie Straight, and Roy Bargy.

There must always be the exception to the rule, and the exception in this case is The Schnozzle, Jimmy Durante. Before World War I, Jimmy at fifteen was playing ragtime at Kerry Walsh's in Coney Island and around Fourteenth Street and the Bowery. He recently told us: "My perfesser tried to make me play *Poet and Peasant*. I played *Maple Leaf, Popularity*, and *Wild Cherries*. I couldn't do nuttin' else den, and I can't do nuttin' else today." The beloved comedian was an inexplicable throwback to Negro ragtime. Only Pete Wendling could even begin to approach Jimmy's natural rhythm. Something in Jimmy made the "Great Profile No. 2" feel rhythm as the Negroes do. Even today the ragtime lilt is still there— "I kept me attitude," he says.

The course of white ragtime composition and playing from 1912 on was toward mere digital speed, dexterity, and fanciful piano embroidery, while melodic originality and rhythmic force progressively disappeared. Compositions that show this progressive deterioration are Les Copeland's *French Pastry*, Confrey's *Kitten on the Keys*, and the *Rufenreddy* of Bargy and Straight. In the late twenties and early thirties the final stages of deterioration were reached with things like Rube Bloom's *Soliloquy* and *Sapphire*. A new generation, which had never heard real Negro ragtime and had been weaned on jazz, rejected the tinkling ridiculous music of the white ragsmiths, and by the early 1930's its course was run.

Mike Bernard, who during his successful years had developed an unreasonable and fantastic arrogance, began to slip. The big time was through with him. In 1936 the man whom the *Police Gazette* had once crowned Rag Time King of the World was playing obscurely in the Gay Nineties night club in Manhattan. In June of that year his death at the age of fifty-nine occasioned only a few newspaper lines.

Ben Harney at least packed some adventure into the years of ragtime's decline. His widow told of their travels to England and the Pacific islands, and Harney himself is quoted concerning these in the *Louisville Herald* of April 23, 1916. Harney says that he made "three trips around the big globe" and that he "was a little bit doubtful at first just how some countries would take to his jig-time music, but after he had given them one snatch of his raggy goods, he found everybody calling for more, and he gave it to them as long as his wind held out."

He captured Britain, the *Louisville Herald* says, and even China: "The Chinamen caught onto his quirks and were soon singing his songs, even if they did sound funny." The Fiji Islands fell too: "The natives there took to his ragtime songs and jig steps like a duck takes to water. The whole island went wild over Harney's songs and he was a little king while he remained there." But if Ben Harney could conquer the rest of

225

the world with ragtime, he could not reconquer his native country.

The year 1916 was enlivened by a controversy between Harney and the veteran entertainment team of McIntyre and Heath as to who originated ragtime. James McIntyre stated in an interview that a buck dance with handclapping to the tune of an old "rabbit" song he had learned from Southern Negroes was ragtime. This dance he had brought to Tony Pastor's in New York in 1879. Harney, who was becoming a bit touchy on the whole subject of ragtime, took up the issue and offered to pay a forfeit of one hundred dollars and to bow out of the profession if he could be shown a piece of ragtime music antedating his two songs *You've Been a Good Old Wagon* and *Mr. Johnson*. The controversy, of course, was on unsound grounds from any point of view. Nevertheless it elicited some interesting facts. McIntyre, for example, stated that ragtime originated with the Negroes and that it was taught to him in the South while he was working with Billy Carroll in a circus in the 1870's. An old Negro taught him a song that his grandfather had brought from Africa, an African chant in true ragtime syncopation. McIntyre made some interesting observations regarding Negro dancing. He claimed that the anatomy of the Negro made dances like the buck and wing and the Virginia Essence almost impossible for the white dancer to imitate correctly.

In a later interview Harney retreated for a moment from the claim that he had invented ragtime to a more tenable position. "Real ragtime on the piano, played in such a manner that it cannot be put in notes," he said, "is the contribution of the graduated Negro banjo-player who cannot read music." He expanded this with some pertinent observations. "On the banjo there is a short string that is not fretted and that consequently is played open with the thumb. It is frequently referred to as the thumb string. The colored performer, strumming in his own cajoling way, likes to throw in a note at random, and his thumb ranges over for this effect. When he takes up the piano, the desire for the same effect dominates him, being almost second nature, and he reaches for the open banjo-string note with his little finger. Meanwhile he is keeping mechanically perfect time with his left hand. The hurdle with the right-hand little finger throws the tune off its stride, resulting in syncopation. He is playing two different times at once."

Ragtime controversies, however, were taking on the character of post-mortem arguments. In a year or so, after the controversy with McIntyre, Harney began playing in lesser theaters. In the early 1920's his large posters with their huge photographic blow-up of his likeness and the bold legend: "Ben Harney—World Famed Creator of Rag Time," were to be seen outside the small neighborhood houses. Over the years, however, Harney had published a large number of really excellent rag songs, though strangely enough it seems never to have occurred to him to write piano solos. His piano style was unquestionably an advanced one. His long-time friend Roscoe Peacock says that the Harney style closely resembled that of Fats Waller. Among his many songs, in any event, were ones like *You Can Go but This Will Bring You Back, The Hat He Never Ate* (a campaign song written for Carter H. Harrison in Chicago), *The Only Way to Keep Her Is in a Cage*, and *The Sporting Life Is Sure Killin' Me*. Others were *If You've Got Any Sense You'll Go, That Ever Lovin' Rock Pile*, and *Tomahau*, one of the earliest of the Hawaiian songs, which he wrote on the ship coming back from Honolulu. Then there was his song *Tell It To Me*:

> I had a lot of hard luck for awhile,
> > Until my Baby greets me with a smile.
> I have been dealing in bones with those Japs—
> > Didn't know what it was to shoot crap—
> Until at Delmonico's I said Babe, we'll dine.
> > Well, sir, I walked into a crap game.
> The dice lay in my hand. Shake, rattle and roll,
> > Foh to beat the band
> And the system I've got, there ain't losses,
> > Foh the ringers were hosses.
> Oh, Babe just tell it to me.

227

CHORUS:

> *Sealskin sacks, diamong rings,*
> *Everything I ask;*
> *Yachts, aeroplanes, automobiles*
> *All my hard luck is past.*

In 1923 unfortunately Ben Harney's hard luck was just beginning. In that year he suffered a heart attack and could make only rare stage appearances. By about 1930 Jessie and he had retired and were living in an upstairs flat at 1510 North Gratz Street in Philadelphia. The house, owned by one Ludwig Pfundmayr, is the only one of white occupancy in its block, at the center of an area of squalid tenements in which the segregated Negroes live.

The story of Harney's last years is pieced together partly from Pfundmayr's brief account. The Harneys lived on relief money eked out by checks from the Actors' Fund. They kept very much to themselves in the poor flat, which did not even boast of a piano on which the "Creator of Ragtime" might play. Ben and Jessie kept actors' hours, sleeping all day and sitting up all night, talking and talking. During the evenings Harney's figure, now gaunt, might be seen slipping out to the grocery to bring in a little food, a can or two to heat up over the gas plate.

In their long midnight dialogues the Harneys dwelt on the triumphs they had once shared, for there was only the past to look at in the Gratz Street flat. But memories, no matter how bright, could not give Harney his health again. He was a sick man. In February 1938 the illness became grave, but Harney refused to go to a hospital or even to see a doctor. On March 1 he died in his wife's arms; he was buried in an unmarked grave.

Only Jessie accompanied the coffin to Fernwood Cemetery. Although in the late years she spoke a great deal of Ben's relatives as the socially prominent and distinguished Harney family in Kentucky, none of them appeared. Pfundmayr says that Harney's last relative, a sister, had died in Boston several years before his death. Bruner Greenup relates that Ben Harney was "raised on Madison Street here in Louisville in a neighborhood of good families. His sister, Lizzie Harney, married one of Louisville's finest surgeons, Dr. Louis Frank, now dead, and his brother Selby married into the prominent Long family." In any event, the years had wrought many changes, and after the poor funeral of the man who believed that he had invented ragtime, Jessie went back to Gratz Street and a life of almost unbearable loneliness. This was somewhat lightened a little later by a fortunate and almost accidental contact with Roscoe Peacock, an old acquaintance and admirer of Harney's.

Peacock at that time was circulation manager of Curtis Publications. A sister of Peacock in Philadelphia had clipped and saved a Harney obituary notice from a local paper and sent it to him. Peacock wrote to Jessie. In one of her first letters she wrote: "When the Harney ship comes in, I am in hopes to have a headstone for my Precious." Peacock immediately got together with the late Isidore Witmark of the firm that had published Harney's work, and a music magazine was induced to campaign for a fund to provide the headstone. Both Witmark and Peacock contributed generously to this fund.

While the money was being raised, lonely Jessie took flowers by day and sat by the unmarked grave and between times wrote long letters to her only friend. "I am on my way to get a bouquet," she wrote to Peacock, "and I think I'll swing and sway out to Fernwood today." In another she wrote: "I should like to see you and visit with you. I get the jumpin' jivin' jitters. I just hate to be alone." In another letter she would reminisce of Harney and the life they had had together: "As you know, my Fancy Man, Ben, was a very sympathetic nature, and did certainly enjoy life as did I. Did we have thousands or a dollar, fifty-fifty at all times. 'United we stand, divided we fall' is the motto of Kentucky." Then she quoted a refrain from a song Harney often sang to her:

> *I loves my little honey,*
> *Yes indeed I do.*
> *I loves my little honey,*
> *To her I'll be true.*

I'm goin' to love my little honey,
Until the day I die.

She dwelt, too, on the fact that Harney had died in obscurity. Her desire to obtain recognition for his life and accomplishments became almost obsessive. "Every music publisher that heard him play," she wrote, "tried to grab his ideas. But they said he never played anything twice alike, which was the truth. That was the reason it took so many years for them to get the swing of Ragged Rhythm Harneian."

Alone, she marked the calendar from the date of Ben's death, figuring the time elapsed. In one letter she writes to Peacock: "It is just two years and eight months since my big Fancy Man Ben passed to the great beyond."

Then in 1941 the headstone arrived and was set in place. Jessie wrote: "The headstone is here and it is very lovely." The inscription, carved in the granite, reads:

In Memory of My Beloved Husband
BEN R. HARNEY
Creator of Ragtime
Born March 6, 1871
Died March 1, 1938

The inscription remains unchanged today, although the same grave now holds Jessie too. For a few years after the memorial stone that she had so passionately wanted had been set in place, Jessie lived on at Gratz Street, supported only by her relief checks. The long midnight talks were now only her own lonely monologues. One morning Pfundmayr found Ben Harney's widow seated in her shabby old chair near an open gas jet. In the official Philadelphia records is the statement: Jessie Boyce Harney—death accidental.

Chapter 12

TREEMONISHA

Ⅶⅇ ⱳⅇⱤⅇ runnin' friends for years," says Arthur Marshall of the close bond of his friendship with Scott Joplin in the Sedalia and St. Louis days. And it was to friends like Arthur that Joplin turned after his separation from Belle Hayden in 1906. For the first part of the year, after leaving St. Louis, he was in Chicago. For about three weeks he stayed with the Marshalls at 2900 State Street on the second floor over Beau Baum's saloon. "He went downtown to see some publishers," Marshall relates. "He said they received him cordially and asked further contact with him. Perhaps they didn't talk to suit him, so he never said more, but he received many letters from Von Tilzer and others. Mr. Joplin was very eager to go to New York. This was the last time I ever saw him."

Joplin did not make the change immediately, though it is probable that he made a quick trip east during this time. For some months he stayed on in Chicago at 2840 Armour Avenue. Toward the end of the year he went back to St. Louis and until well into 1907 lived with the Tom Turpins at 2221 Market. Then he finally made the move east.

Before this, however, during the difficult year of 1906 Joplin managed to get only two compositions finished for publication, both by his old patron. Stark issued the 6/8 march *Antoinette* in 1906. A year later he released the fruit of Joplin's last visit with Chauvin, the haunting *Heliotrope Bouquet* with it thirty-two short measures saved from the prodigality of a heedless, wastrel genius.

Joplin did not immediately set up a permanent New York residence. Determining upon a life of more varied activity, he embarked upon a series of vaudeville tours, carrying on his composition in boarding houses and hotels en route. He also set about making contacts with the New York publishers. He evidently felt that his classical rags needed his personal missionary work as well as the exploitation of the large publishing houses. He realized that the original impetus of the *Maple Leaf* hit could carry him only so far, and his plans were ambitious. Perhaps, too, a vaudeville life on the road suited the unaccustomed restlessness with which he had been left by his infant daughter's death, the break with Belle, and her death.

6   At this time Joplin recorded a number of piano rolls of his own compositions. These are the only known recordings to give an idea of his playing. As was the method of that early period, they reproduce his actual performances without editing, and are made to be played by the old-fashioned Pianola. This was a portable mechanism in a cabinet that one moved up to a piano. It included the tracker bar for the player roll. Bellows actuated by foot pumps operated the hammers, which moved up and down. The operator sat in front of this mechanism to work it, and in turn its hammers, functioning like fingers, hit the keys of the piano, from which the music emerged in a chain reaction from operator to cabinet to piano. The mechanism had a sixty-five-note spread, the remainder at the top and bottom of the standard eighty-eight-note keyboard being beyond its range. Early rolls can be identified by the label designation "65 note," later rolls played on the more familiar type of internal-mechanism player piano being marked "88 note."

Experience with operating player pianos can lead to a surprisingly accurate control of touch and dynamics through the pressure exerted on the pedals. Some player-piano enthusiasts believe that this is more true of the early sixty-five-note

Pianola than of the later eighty-eight-note type. In any case, a player piano operated by a musical person has very little of the mechanical sound of the electrically pumped models that were once commonly heard in the penny amusement arcades and the cheaper nickelodeons.

To remove doubt that Joplin played these rolls, most of them are designated as "played by Scott Joplin." Several are in the collection of Dr. Hubert S. Pruett of St. Louis. They include *Maple Leaf Rag* on Connorized Roll No. 148 (also converted to eighty-eight-note on many other labels), *Original Rags* on Connorized No. 843, *Weeping Willow Rag* on Connorized No. 10277, *Gladiolus Rag* on Standard No. 76836, and several others.

Joplin's vaudeville tours went on intermittently for several years. He had good billing on the pioneer Percy G. Williams Circuit, presented as "King of Ragtime Composers—Author of *Maple Leaf Rag*." His playing was still excellent in those years, still the legato, singing style that was so musical and that, if not flashy, had a quiet, forceful rock. Joplin, so serious and reserved, made the impression of a celebrity playing serious music rather than a vaudeville performer trying to put over his act.

About 1909 Joplin married Lottie Stokes in New York, and his second marriage provided a companionship that the first had not. Lottie was good for Joplin. Although not markedly musical, she supported him sympathetically in his work and, recognizing that music was his deepest love, did not try to replace it. Giving him the privacy of his own thoughts, she provided for his material wants and his need for an affection without demands. For some time after the marriage Lottie and Scott traveled together, and when they finally settled down in New York she made a good home for the composer. They moved into their first house, at 252 West Forty-seventh Street, and remained there until the general migration of the Negroes uptown. On Forty-seventh Street Joplin began once more to teach. Lottie set up the accustomed boarding house, whose transient occupants were musicians and theatrical people. Many former Joplin guests remember the Forty-seventh Street menage or the later one at 163 West 131st

Street. Somewhere a piano would be going—Joplin giving lessons or, with his infinite, patient care, working over a phrase from a new composition. Lottie would be busy with meals, the care of the house, or the collecting of bills—not too precise a procedure the last, for one of the most cherished memories of the Joplin hospitality is the way those "at liberty" were "carried."

In this wonderful world of live and let live the Joplins moved like colored cousins of the Sangers in *The Constant Nymph*. Scott was finishing a new opera to succeed the unpublished *Guest of Honor*. This was *Treemonisha, an Opera in Three Acts*, which Joplin copyrighted and published at his own expense in 1911.

In the four years before the publication, Joplin's pen was not idle. Some nineteen numbers had appeared, in addition to the Chauvin collaboration, *Heliotrope Bouquet*, of 1907. Stark brought out *Nonpareil (None to Equal)*. Some of the octave bass passages in the scherzo-like third strain of this rag are similar to those which later became a characteristic feature of Jelly Roll Morton's style. J. W. Stern published *Search Light Rag* and *Gladiolus Rag*. The former, too, foretells Morton. Its last theme is very raggy and its title is a subtle compliment to Tom and Charlie Turpin, referring to their gold mine near Searchlight, Nevada. *Gladiolus* is based in part on the *Maple Leaf* harmonies, but with variant melodies.

The Boston firm of Joseph M. Daly issued *Rose Leaf Rag*, a number that must be accounted one of Joplin's most successful pieces and probably one of his masterpieces. In the four themes of this unostentatious rag the composer has achieved a blending of his prevailing tendency toward the classical style proper to ragtime and the original melodic sources of his inspiration. The first theme employs parallel and contrary motion with fine effect; the second has a light, lilting dance rhythm; the trio is of a Missouri folk character and is largely in thirds; and the final strain is an exposition of honkytonk chords. The whole is a compressed picture of the many-sided folk world from which ragtime sprang.

Arthur Marshall's *Lily Queen*, with Joplin rearrangement, also appeared in 1907 under their joint names with the New

York imprint of W. W. Stuart; Universal Music of St. Louis brought out a Joplin song, *Snoring Sampson*, with lyrics by Harry La Mertha.

The following year saw the Stark publication of *The School of Ragtime* études and *Fig Leaf Rag*, echoes of the trio of which can be heard in a half-dozen subsequent Tin Pan Alley songs, while Seminary Music of New York issued *Pineapple Rag* and *Sugar Cane*. The three rags have very fully chorded and "eccentric" rhythmic strains that, recalling the steps of the buck and wing, also anticipate the forceful rhythms of band jazz.

Six Joplin numbers appeared in 1909, all published by Seminary. Four are rags: *Paragon*, *Wall Street*, *Country Club*, and *Euphonic Sounds*. A ragtime waltz, *Pleasant Moments*, and a Mexican serenade, *Solace*, complete the list. *Wall Street*, an excellent rag, has descriptive headings over the themes: "Panic in Wall Street"; "Brokers Feeling Melancholy"; "Good Times Coming"; "Good Times Have Come"; "Listening to the Strains of Genuine Negro Ragtime Brokers Forget Their Cares." *Solace* is a most unusual tango for the period: it avoids the minor mode, and its melodies are rather anticipatory of those of the Brazilian maxixe, which was to be introduced a few years later. In 1911 *Felicity Rag*, the Joplin–Hayden collaboration, reached publication.

Euphonic Sounds is of course one of Joplin's masterpieces. The title may have suggested itself to the composer from a sentence in the Monroe Rosenfeld eulogy that had appeared years before in the *St. Louis Globe-Democrat*. In this article one of Joplin's numbers was referred to as euphonious. *Euphonic Sounds*, a difficult number, was a challenge to the Eastern shout pianists. It became the kind of test piece that, years earlier, *Maple Leaf* had been. Lonnie Hicks of Philadelphia and James P. Johnson were noted for their mastery of its intricacies. The piece is remarkable for its daring use of advanced harmonies and the classic concept of the whole. It could scarcely have been a good investment for the publishers.

It was in 1907 that young Joseph Lamb went into the New York office of John Stark to buy some rags. He was already known as such a good customer that he was regularly given a discount. Lamb tells about what happened on this occasion.

235

"There was a colored fellow sitting there with his foot bandaged up as if he had the gout, and a crutch beside him. I hardly noticed him. I told Mrs. Stark that I liked the Joplin rags best and wanted to get any I didn't have. The colored fellow spoke up and asked whether I had certain pieces which he named. I thanked him and bought several and was leaving when I said to Mrs. Stark that Joplin was one fellow I would certainly like to meet.

" 'Really,' said Mrs. Stark. 'Well, here's your man.' I shook hands with him, needless to say. It was a thrill I've never forgotten. I had met Scott Joplin and was going home to tell the folks.

"Mrs. Stark told him I had sent in a couple of rags for their approval. I had, all right, and they had come back two days later. Joplin seemed interested and asked if he could walk up the street with me. We walked along Twenty-third Street and into Madison Square Park and sat on a bench.

"Mr. Joplin asked if my rags were really good. I said: 'To me they seem all right—maybe they are not, I don't know.' He invited me to bring them over to his place. Needless to say, I didn't waste time.

"I went to his boarding house a few evenings later and he asked me to play my pieces on the piano in the parlor. A lot of colored people were sitting around talking. I played my *Sensation* first and they began to crowd around and watch me. When I finished, Joplin said 'That's a good rag—a regular Negro rag.' That was what I wanted to hear.

"Then I played my two other numbers, *Dynamite Rag* and *Old Home Rag*. There is a place in the first strain of *Dynamite* where the bass and treble originally went upward together. At Joplin's suggestion I made the bass move down in contrary motion to the treble. Joplin liked *Sensation* best of my first three rags."

At this first meeting Joplin offered to present *Sensation* to Stark personally. Lamb remembers that Joplin said: "We will put on along with your name: 'arranged by Scott Joplin.' People do not know you, and my name might sell the rag." Joplin was as good as his word. "He wanted to get me going," Lamb says. "A week later a letter came from Stark offering

me twenty-five dollars and an equal sum after the first printing of one thousand was sold. He could have had it for nothing
—I wanted to see it published. I got the other twenty-five
dollars in a month. Then I brought in *Ethiopia* and *Excelsior*
together. After that he took any rag I wrote."

Joplin's help had been decisive once again. James Scott and
Joseph Lamb, two men he assisted, rank in that order as rag-
time composers just below him, and the work of Marshall and
Hayden as well as Chauvin's only rag survive because of him.

Joseph Francis Lamb is one of the phenomena of ragtime.
Born in the East with little or no Negro music in his environment, he became one of the few white men to write rags that
are thoroughly Negroid and worthy to stand with the very
best. He did this without copying and while giving vent to
his own original inspiration on a purely musical plane before
he met Joplin. He simply liked ragtime, and that of Joplin
best, and wanted to compose music of that sort.

It was not quite so simple as that, of course. Many had tried
to copy Joplin with little enough success. Although this distinction may at first seem shadowy, the young white man emu-
lated rather than copied the master. Joseph Lamb was able
to do this because he possessed a rare ability. He could pene-
trate to the very sources of the developed and personal style
of the other man. To this ability he added another perhaps
even rarer: that of channelizing his own great creative powers
into that style without in any way limiting his flow of ideas.
That this was so can mean only one thing. What Lamb had to
say—though his own—was so thoroughly American and so
thoroughly of his time that classic ragtime was the one best
medium for its expression.

The musical career of Joseph Lamb conclusively points up
two facts. One is that classical ragtime, though of Negro
origin, had become with Joplin a music for all America. The
other was that ragtime showed itself capable of developing a
strong and healthy tradition. Just as in European music, the
ragtime tradition must be one in which composer succeeds
composer, each working with individuality, yet carrying a
homogeneous development onward.

Until we located Joseph Lamb, he was considered by most

ragtime followers to have been a Negro. He was the hardest of all the ragtime survivors for us to find. Literally no one in the music world had ever met him. At one stage of our search we were almost forced to accept a current theory that his name was a Joplin pseudonym. Acceptance balked, however, at the indubitable fact that the Lamb rags, though delightfully Joplinesque, exude a personality of their own. The reason for Joseph Lamb's obscurity became evident when, finally, he talked with us.

In the modest little frame house in Brooklyn near Coney Island, where he has lived since 1911, Joe Lamb told his story with a kind of quiet amazement that what had happened so long ago could possibly interest anyone today.

"I was born December 6, 1887, in Montclair, New Jersey. I was fourteen when I went to college in Canada at a town called Berlin, later changed to Kitchener during the war. My mother hoped I would become a priest, but I thought I wanted to be an electrical engineer. I got far enough to pass the entrance exams for Stevens Institute. But in the summer I got a job in New York and I said: 'What the hell,' and never went back. It was in a fabric house, and I've been there ever since.

"I had two sisters who were classical pianists, but I never took any lessons. I guess I just had inborn talent. At college I wrote waltzes and songs. The Harry H. Sparks Company in Toronto gave me five dollars for my *Celestine Waltzes*, named for one of my sisters. Then they asked me to set poems to music. I wrote a couple dozen. I would read the poem over and get the rhythm of the words—maybe it was a ballad, a comical song, or a novelty. The music would always come—especially if the poem affected me.

"It was in 1907 that ragtime hit me and I began to write it. I thought I was good—anybody figures his own music is good. But I wanted to find out. Scott Joplin's music was the kind I liked, so I thought of Stark and sent some rags in. A few days later I got a polite refusal. It was after that when I went in and met Mr. Joplin.

"I wrote heavy rags, the way I wanted whether it was hard to play or not. Chords might strike me first, or a melody, or a conjunction of chords and melody. I kept working it over until

I got something. With my *Ragtime Nightingale*, it was the name that struck me first. You may have noticed that in the beginning of the trio I use a little part of Ethelbert Nevin's *Nightingale Song*. I saw it in an *Etude* magazine of my sisters'. I usually got one complete strain finished and the others would follow, but the strains have to fit with each other.

"I didn't want to be in the music business—I hardly met any musicians except Scott Joplin—I wanted to keep my music in my private life. I didn't want to make any money on my things. I only wanted to see them published because my dream was to be a great ragtime composer.

"John Stark always impressed me more like a Western farmer or ranchman. He did not look like a music publisher. He was an honest man. Around 1909 he and Joplin had a disagreement. Stark said that he couldn't afford a royalty deal on new numbers. He wanted to buy them outright, but Joplin insisted on royalties—said that was the way that *Maple Leaf* had been handled—but Stark explained that business had fallen off. Joplin never sold him any more music. I was sorry about this. Both felt they were right. I didn't know about the falling out until I took in a rag that Joplin and I wrote together, a very good rag. Stark liked it very much, but said he would never buy anything more with the name Joplin on it.

"I wrote *Contentment Rag* for a wedding anniversary of the Starks, and Mr. Stark had a cover design made of an old couple sitting by a fire. But before publication Mrs. Stark took sick and he took her back to St. Louis, where she died. He brought the number out years later with the picture of an old man sitting alone smoking his pipe.

"I feel as if I knew James Scott and Arthur Marshall and Artie Matthews—you have a common bond in music. I have always felt that *American Beauty*, *Topliner*, and *Patricia* are my best rags. Stark changed the names of a few of my numbers. My name for *Topliner* was *Cottontail*.

"Stark published my rags as long as rags sold. The last one was *Bohemia* in 1919. It was in a difficult key, and Stark wrote to me to transpose it. Then he liked it in the original key better, anyway.

"In the twenties I took a number of things up to Mills;

they were the type of classic rags. Mills said to write some that were more novelettes, like *Nola*. He took my first one and wanted four more. Fifty dollars was all he would give me. He ordered ten more, and when I took them in he would only give thirty-five dollars for the lot. Finally I said: 'All right, I want to see them published.' But they have never come out.

"I have written nothing since. I live here with my family, and my children and grandchildren are near. That was all a long, long time ago."

On top of the dusty pile of music that Lamb had brought up from the basement was a manuscript. Looking at it we were struck by the florid hand-lettered title. Lamb glanced at it, laughed, and said: "I wrote that when I was just a kid." The manuscript was dated 1900, and the title read:

COONTOWN FROLICS

Two-Step by J. Francis Lamb
"One of Lamb's Famous Hits"

Stark's Eastern venture was not going well. Neither the Missouri pioneer nor his classic ragtime, the composers of which made no concessions to mere popular taste, fitted into the Tin Pan Alley world. Stark's country-peddler shrewdness was offset by his missionary zeal for the classic ragtime music he had chosen to champion and by a personal concept of honesty that drew a distinct line between the shrewd and the sharp. Neither ruthlessness nor compromise was a part of his strong nature. He came from a generation that believed that business thrived on fair competition rather than on its crushing, a generation that gave a place to the little businessman.

Stark fought back at Tin Pan Alley's methods as well as he could. The following is excerpted from one of many trade circulars he sent to the retail dealers:

"Hulla-gee! did you hear something 'drap'?

"We wonder if all the music dealers are wise to the chaos just now existing in the music trade. Has the legitimate music dealer begun to realize that he is just now in that interesting condition known in history as 'between the devil and the deep blue sea?'

"Well, it's like this. Some time ago the Whitney-Warren Co. (Remick) impatient with the publishing business alone, conceived the idea of appropriating to himself the retail business of the country also. To this end he began buying up stands of the department stores.

"Sol Bloom and others followed suit and soon there was a merry war on in retail prices. The 'hits' have been persistently advertised at 9 cts. But this is not quite half the evil to the retail dealer-legitimate. Leo Feist—nettled at seeing a competitor's 'hits' going faster than his own filled up the Woolworth 5 and 10 ct. stores with music on sale. S. H. Knox of Buffalo was induced to put music in his 68 5 and 10 ct. stores scattered throughout the country. The New York Music Co (Albert Von Tilzer) actually sends a man to these 10 ct. stores to sing and push their pieces. It is said that Chas. K. Harris sold Knox 50,000 pieces at one order.

"Just how the regular music dealer is amusing himself during this war of the publishers we are curious to know . . . anyone can buy one of the 'hits' lower than he as a dealer can buy it in dozen lots.

"And yet, after all, the regular dealer has it in his power to make or break any publisher.

"There is no salesman so helpless that he cannot sell a good thing whether it is called for or not.

"No one can tell what the end of this foolish greed will be. Were it not for the copyrights all music would be dragged to the level of cost for paper and printing.

"Fortunately as it is each publisher can only degrade his own publications. We will try to protect the dealer in a profit on our prints and hope we will not be dragged into junk-shop methods. It will be some time yet before our prints are found on sale in barber shops and livery-stables."

After the death of his wife, Sarah Ann, in November 1910, John Stark returned to New York, but he was sick of cut-throat competition and he soon wrote off the Manhattan venture and closed the offices. He went back to St. Louis, to

241

the plant that *Maple Leaf Rag* had built, and to a home with Etilmon and his family.

That Scott Joplin had had a rupture with Stark was indicative of two things. One was his growing obsession with the new opera, which incidentally Stark had turned down. *Treemonisha* dominated Joplin's thoughts to the exclusion of almost all else. As early as 1908 he had played parts of it for Joseph Lamb and dwelt on his dream of its production. Its scoring and printing—the published piano version of 1911 runs to 230 pages—had made heavy demands on the composer's slim purse. For the badly needed extra money from royalties he was constrained to break with Stark.

But the quarrel with his long-time supporter was more deeply symptomatic of something else. A slow and serious change in Joplin himself was beginning to worry Lottie and the friends of long standing. Once a man of remarkably even temperament, Joplin was becoming more and more subject to alarming changes of mood that would suddenly veer from black depression verging sometimes on apathy to a hectic, almost feverish elation in which his energy was seemingly boundless and his concentration razor-sharp.

Nor was this all. The old Joplin, trusting and confident, was changing, becoming the prey of gnawing suspicions. The Joplin of Sedalia, who with Hayden and Marshall had made a league of "all for one and one for all," could now entertain thoughts that his friends were betraying him and that the world was against him. He began to believe that his compositions were being stolen and that the kingpins of Tin Pan Alley were waxing rich on piracies from his work. Joplin, of course, knew that a great deal of ragtime composition had leaned heavily on his work for years, but this was something different; it was not a question of his influence on others, but of what he believed to be outright theft.

In his periods of depression the old-time skill deserted him. He was like a child learning to play the piano. He would come to a halting stop, audibly correct himself, start again, and stop again. Those who had not known him laughed at the spectacle of a man who could compose *The Maple Leaf Rag* but could not even play it. Some even doubted that he had written the compositions that bore his name, and groundless rumors were rife that he had stolen the work of others. "I had heard so much about Scott Joplin," said one Eastern rag-timer, "but I had never heard him play. A club in Washington wired for him to appear and he told the guests 'I don't play,' but they wouldn't believe it and they kept after him until he gave in. It was pitiful to hear."

All of this, however, was a little later. The signs were appearing in 1911, but only as fateful intimations of what was to come. The periods of elation were long and fruitful, and Joplin vigorously prosecuted his plans for *Treemonisha*. Amid his labors on the opera he found little time for other composition. In 1910, the year before the opera's publication, only one new Joplin number had appeared. This was *Stoptime Rag* published by Stern. The title page bears the instructions: "To get the desired effect of 'Stoptime' the pianist should stamp the heel of one foot heavily upon the floor, wherever the word 'Stamp' appears in the music."

In 1911, in addition to *Treemonisha*, *Felicity Rag*, Joplin's collaboration with Scott Hayden, was brought out by Stark, having been purchased some years before. Stern published the solitary number to appear in 1912, *Scott Joplin's New Rag*, the final theme of which, in E minor, is very serious in cast. The following year there were no rags, the only Joplin copyright being a separate entry for *A Real Slow Drag* from *Treemonisha*. *Magnetic Rag* appeared in 1914 with the black-and-white engraved cover typical of classical publications and bearing the imprint: Scott Joplin Music Publishing Co. It is a heavy, serious work that no New York publisher would have touched. The G minor theme is in the pathetic vein, and that in B-flat minor has a grave cast. The intimations of *Euphonic Sounds* begin to be realized here in the use of ragtime syncopation to express more profound musical thoughts. Outside of another *Treemonisha* excerpt, *Frolic of the Bears*, copyrighted in 1915, and the posthumous publication by Stark of a rag bought earlier, this is the last work from Joplin's pen. *Magnetic Rag*, however, tragically indicates the potential musical development that was broken off soon after its publication.

The yellow-bound score of *Treemonisha* is a large work, the

230 pages mentioned previously. The score is for eleven voices and piano accompaniment. A preface, written by Joplin, runs from page one through page three:

TREEMONISHA

Opera in Three Acts

Words and Music By
SCOTT JOPLIN

(*Story Fictitious*)

ACT I—*Morning*   ACT II—*Afternoon*   ACT III—*Evening*

* * *

PREFACE

The scene of the Opera is laid on a plantation somewhere in the State of Arkansas, Northeast of the Town of Texarkana and three or four miles from the Red River. The plantation being surrounded by a dense forest.

There were several Negro families living on the plantation and other families back in the woods.

In order that the reader may better comprehend the story, I will give a few details regarding the Negroes of the plantation from the year 1866 to the year 1884.

The year 1866 finds them in dense ignorance, with no one to guide them, as the white folks had moved away shortly after the Negroes were set free and had left the plantation in charge of a trustworthy Negro servant named Ned.

All of the Negroes but Ned and his wife Monisha were superstitious, and believed in conjuring. Monisha, being a woman, was at times impressed by what the more expert conjurers would say.

Ned and Monisha had no children, and they had often prayed that their cabin home might one day be brightened by a child that would be a companion for Monisha when Ned was away from home. They had dreams, too, of educating the child so that when it grew up it could

244

teach the people around them to aspire to something better and higher than superstition and conjuring.

The prayers of Ned and Monisha were answered in a remarkable manner. One morning in the middle of September 1866, Monisha found a baby under a tree that grew in front of her cabin. It proved to be a light-brown-skinned girl about two days old. Monisha took the baby into the cabin, and Ned and she adopted it as their own.

They wanted the child, while growing up, to love them as it would have loved its real parents, so they decided to keep it in ignorance of the manner in which it came to them until old enough to understand. They realized, too, that if the neighbors knew the facts, they would some day tell the child, so, to deceive them, Ned hitched up his mules and, with Monisha and the child, drove over to a family of old friends who lived twenty miles away and whom they had not seen for three years. They told their friends that the child was just a week old.

Ned gave these people six bushels of corn and forty pounds of meat to allow Monisha and the child to stay with them for eight weeks, which Ned thought would benefit the health of Monisha. The friends willingly consented to have her stay with them for that length of time.

Ned went back alone to the plantation and told his old neighbors that Monisha, while visiting some old friends, had become mother of a girl baby.

The neighbors were, of course, greatly surprised, but were compelled to believe that Ned's story was true.

At the end of eight weeks Ned took Monisha and the child home and received the congratulations of his neighbors and friends and was delighted to find that his scheme had worked so well.

Monisha, at first, gave the child her own name; but, when the child was three years old, she was so fond of playing under the tree where she was found that Monisha gave her the name of Tree-Monisha.

When Treemonisha was seven years old Monisha arranged with a white family that she would do their washing and ironing and Ned would chop their wood if the lady of the house would give Treemonisha an education, the schoolhouse being too far away for the child to attend. The lady consented and as a result Treemonisha was the only educated person in the neighborhood, the other children being still in ignorance on account of their inability to travel so far to school.

Zodzetrick, Luddud and Simon, three very old men, earned their living by going about the neighborhood practicing conjuring, selling little luck-bags and rabbits' feet, and confirming the people in their superstition.

This strain of music is the principal strain in the Opera and represents the happiness of the people when they feel free from the conjurors and their spells of superstition.

The Opera begins in September 1884. Treemonisha, being eighteen years old, now starts upon her career as a teacher and leader.

Scott Joplin.

Treemonisha contains twenty-seven complete musical numbers, including overture and a prelude to Act III. The plot, involving Treemonisha's abduction by the conjurors, her rescue, and her acceptance, at her people's insistence, of leadership of them, is a simple folk tale. *Treemonisha* like the tales of Uncle Remus, is a fable. Its subject is the Negro race, its moral that the Negro—like any man—must rise above superstition and ignorance to enlightenment in order to be fully a man and to exercise his own gifts. Joplin contrasts the superstitions of the conjuror—the goofer-dust man—and the lust for revenge on his band by those he has wronged, with the reasoned charitableness of Treemonisha.

> *Sweep not de dust from yo' cabins at night,*
> *For some of yo' neighbors surely will fight.*
>
> *If yo' nose should itch while you sit in yo' room,*
> *An unwelcome neighbor will visit you soon.*
>
> *If you are eatin' food wid ease,*
> *And drawin' pleasant breath,*

> *Be careful you do not sneeze,*
> *Because 'tis sign of death.*

To ward off these imagined evils the voodoo man sold his little bags of charms. In reply Treemonisha sings:

> *There's need of some good leader,*
> *And there's not much time to wait,*
> *To lead us in the right way,*
> *Before it is too late.*
>
> *For ignorance is criminal,*
> *In this enlightened day;*
> *So let us all get busy,*
> *When once we've found the way.*

With Treemonisha elected leader, the people all get together at the end to do *A Real Slow Drag.*

DIRECTIONS FOR THE SLOW DRAG.

1. The Slow Drag must begin on the first beat of each measure.
2. When moving forward, drag the left foot; when moving backward, drag the right foot.
3. When moving sideways to right, drag left foot; when moving sideways to left, drag right foot.
4. When prancing, your steps must come on each beat of the measure.
5. When marching and when sliding, your steps must come on the first and the third beat of each measure.
6. Hop and skip on second beat of measure. Double the Schottische step to fit the slow music.

In this, the Negro's own ragtime dance, he is, in Joplin's own words:

> *Marching onward, marching onward,*
> *Marching to the lovely tune;*
> *Marching onward, marching onward,*
> *Happy as a bird in June.*

Sliding onward, sliding onward,
Listen to that rag!

Hop and skip,
Now do that slow—do that slow drag.

Dance slowly, prance slowly,
While you hear that pretty rag.

Unlike the earlier *Guest of Honor*, *Treemonisha* is not called a ragtime opera. Joplin attempted in the later work to combine ragtime and folk music in more time-honored forms. It is difficult to judge *Treemonisha's* value as a dramatic vehicle, but the score reveals that it is full of beautiful music. Missouri and the ragtime country, the sights and sounds of a vanished time, echo in its measures. If *The Green Pastures* was a picture of a God who was a Negro and of a heaven made for the dark of skin, then *Treemonisha* is the legend of a Negro Eden.

To hear the chorus, from Act I, of the Corn-Huskers in the distance is to walk among the fruitful rows of the rolling Missouri fields, mellow in the autumn light. To hear the eight bears singing "OO-ar! OO-ar!" and to visualize their clumsy frolic in the Ozark forest is to be transported still farther back to the faery world of animal legends that Uncle Remus once borrowed from far-away Africa.

With the herculean task of publication accomplished, Scott Joplin set about the even more formidable tasks of orchestrating and writing out the instrumental parts and attempting to secure backing for the opera's production. His hopes ran high. During the long productive periods he worked on the score, got more pupils, whose fees would help to finance the activity, and gave private auditions for potential backers.

Sam Patterson helped with the orchestration. He and Joplin would work all day in the basement apartment of the 131st Street house, Sam copying parts from the pages of the orchestral master score as Joplin finished them. At noon Lottie would bring their lunch in to them.

Sam describes a typical lunch: "Joplin said, 'Let's knock off, I hear Lottie coming.' Just then the phone rang and I went to answer it. When I came back, there were fried eggs on the table and Lottie was opening a bottle of champagne some folks she worked for had given her. I said, 'These eggs are cold,' and Scott said, 'Look, Sam, if they're good hot, they're good cold.' "

Finally, the score finished, Joplin began auditioning a cast. He had determined to put on one performance at his own expense to test public reaction, and perhaps to attract a backer, too. "Joplin got his whole cast set up," Patterson tells. "He worked like a dog training them."

A single performance finally took place in a hall in Harlem in 1915. The performance was by full cast, but without scenery or orchestra. Joplin played the orchestral parts on the piano. The musical drama made virtually no impression. Without scenery, costumes, lighting, or orchestral backing, the drama seemed thin and unconvincing, little better than a rehearsal, and its special quality in any event would surely have been lost on the typical Harlem audience that attended. The listeners were sophisticated enough to reject their folk past, but not sufficiently to relish a return to it in art. Nor have they, it may be remarked, reached that stage even today.

Scott Joplin never recovered from the blow that completely crushed the hopes of a lifetime. The progress of his infirmity accelerated as though all inner resistance were gone. His physical co-ordination grew more uncertain, his periods of depression darker and of more frequent occurrence. And yet there were intervals in which he brightened and would begin once more to scribble scores on an envelope or any scrap of paper that was handy. The time came at last when even Lottie had to face the fact that the mind that had conceived *Maple Leaf Rag* was all but gone.

In the fall of 1916 Scott Joplin was removed to the Manhattan State Hospital on Ward's Island in the East River along the strait called Hell Gate. Lottie relates that even at the hospital there were moments when the composer began once more feverishly jotting notes on bits of paper. But the flashes were dimmer and dimmer, and at length all was dark. On April 1, 1917 Scott Joplin died.

For one day Scott Joplin was a famous man even in Harlem. That was the day of his long and impressive funeral. A legend has since grown up that the mourners' carriages each bore a banner with the name of a Joplin composition. The legend adds that the first carriage displayed a banner the black letters of which spelled *Maple Leaf Rag*. Lottie disproves the legend. Nevertheless, as the composer's widow rode in the leading carriage on the long ride to St. Michael's Cemetery on Long Island, it was the *Maple Leaf Rag* that filled her mind.

Before the funeral Lottie remembered a request that her husband had made years before. "Play *Maple Leaf Rag* at my funeral," he had said. But when the time finally came she said no. "How many, many times since then," she says, "I've wished to my heart that I'd said yes."

Chapter 13

MISSOURI AUTUMN

Wहेन news of the death of Scott Joplin reached John Stark in St. Louis, he compacted into two lines of obituary much of the significance of the life of this one Negro man:

"Scott Joplin is dead. A homeless itinerant, he left his mark on American music."

Late that year Stark & Company brought out from their files an unpublished number and issued it under the name: *Reflection Rag—Syncopated Musings* by Scott Joplin. This is the last piece by the king of ragtime composers ever to appear. A number of unpublished Joplin manuscripts remained in the company files for many years. When the firm moved its plant from Laclede to Vandeventer Avenue in 1935, eight years after John Stark's death, these, together with the manuscripts of others, were destroyed. At this time the choice part of the catalogue was assigned to the Melrose brothers in Chicago. John, Jr., the grandson, then dropped music entirely to concentrate on trade printing.

In 1912, when the founder of the Stark fortunes returned to St. Louis and moved in with the Etilmon Starks in Maplewood, a residential suburb south of the city, he was embroiled in a controversy. Earlier in that year Mrs. William Stark had written a tune to be used in the campaign of Missouri's favorite son for the presidential campaign. The boom for Champ Clark, Speaker of the House, was assuming formidable proportions before the Republican convention was held. Mrs. Stark's song, which consists of her own verse to a hillbilly chorus from the Arkansas Ozarks, was called *They Gotta Quit Kickin' My Dawg Around*. Published under the pseudonym of Cy Perkins it was an immediate hit of such proportions that Witmark offered Stark ten thousand dollars for it, and the offer was accepted.

The contract called for a down payment and the balance later in the year. The first payment came in two checks before Stark left New York. Early the next morning John went with the first check to one bank and his son-in-law Jim Stanley, singer husband of Eleanor, took the second to another. They waited until the banks opened, and cashed them. Hours often counted in the life of a popular hit, and their hunch proved correct; when shortly afterwards the Clark boom collapsed on the convention floor, *They Gotta Quit Kickin' My Dawg Around* collapsed with it. When the subsequent notes fell due, Witmark did not meet them. Stark filed suit in the Chicago courts and, acting as his own lawyer, got a settlement in full, with costs, including, the family says, a sizable fee for the services of John Stark, attorney.

William Stark's marriage had been the culmination of a ragtime romance. In the early years of Stark & Son, William did the outside promotion work, going to the music stores and introducing the new publications to the buyers. On his periodical visits to the Boston Department Store in St. Louis, he became aware that his attention was wandering from the promotion of the Stark line to the bouncy, vivacious, good-looking girl who plugged the tunes in the music department. Carrie Bruggeman was a girl who, over and beyond the call of duty, simply loved to play ragtime. Today, several years after William's death, she says: "*Maple Leaf Rag* brought us together," and though a grandmother, she can still play the old classic with the true verve of the ragtime period.

For the next few years after John Stark's return to St. Louis, his publications kept coming out at a good pace. James Scott and Joseph Lamb had replaced Joplin as headliners, and their works replaced his as well as any could. The Stark catalogue by now occupied a special category in the music field. Stark's insistence on publishing difficult numbers and his propaganda for the best ragtime as a classic music, while it had failed to convince serious music-lovers, had to some extent conditioned its acceptance in the ragtime world itself. There Joplin, Scott, and Lamb were now the acknowledged old masters. An advertisement of the St. Louis house in a 1915 *Rag Time Review* read as follows:

"We have advertised these as classic rags and we mean just what we say. They are the perfection of a type. They have lifted ragtime from its low estate and lined it up with Beethoven and Bach."

In the same publication a month before, editor Axel Christensen had written of John Stark:

"He is the pioneer of ragtime sheet music—real ragtime we mean—and when one hears him talk of his favored subject, namely ragtime, one is bound to be impressed with the fact that ragtime is on a par with the best music that ever was written. He is one of the greatest champions that ragtime has ever had, or ever will have."

Stark himself was his own tireless and best propagandist. While in New York, he had aired his views on many subjects in the letter columns of nearly every metropolitan daily, and in St. Louis he continued the practice. His salty opinions were expressed in aphorism and epithet, and supported by poetic and Biblical quotation. In one instance he wrote:

"It is a maxim among publishers that the best songs never make what is known as a 'hit.'

"The pieces that rage at picture shows and cafes are songs with a catch phrase or an imitation of dog barks, cat calls, or auto or boat whistles and like a stale joke, are dead when heard twice.

"Many of them are unfit to be seen on your piano or to be sung to your friends.

"The methods of selling them are wide of our own conception of how the 'art divine' should be dispensed. They

253

are hurled across the country with a whoop and hurrah, while the songs that teach and thrill the purer souls too often lie silent on the shelf.

> *Full many a gem of purest ray serene*
> *The deep unfathomed caves of ocean bear,*
> *Full many a flower was born to blush unseen*
> *And waste its fragrance on the desert air.*
>
> *Full many a mushy, gushy song—and vile*
> *Is sold by methods—sure the devil's own,*
> *Full many a gem of art and love—the while*
> *Lies silent, sadly waiting to be known.*

Although the Stark rags were the accepted classics of the ragtime world, outside it the controversy still raged. One writer felt that the music itself should convert the die-hards, not envisioning, however, the methods by which they were to be induced to listen. He wrote: "Take for instance, the *Ragtime Nightingale*. This really beautiful rag can be handled in such a way that the most obstinate old anti-ragtimer in the world could be converted for keeps inside of ten minutes."

John Stark himself took up the cudgels against prejudice once more in a 1916 issue of the *Rag Time Review:*

RESPECTABILITY OF RAGTIME

I note that the controversy still goes on as to the respectability of ragtime. In the first place the name no doubt was a handicap. Then there were quite a number of fairly good players that could not play it and of course these were against it and again there were and are yet a large number of people who have no other way of showing culture and good taste (as they think) but to berate ragtime.

And last there were quite a number of good souls who really believed that there is something evil lurking somehow in ragtime. All these people have cultivated these ideas until it has taken possession of their wills. The mind of man consists of a will and an intellect. The will is a silent partner and is all powerful. The intellect is a puppet slave hustling around to find ways and means to justify the decision of the will.

Jesus said: If they believe not Moses and the prophets neither would they believe though one rise from the dead.

Mohammed said: If we should open a window in heaven and show you the angels you would say 'our eyes deceive us' ye would not believe.

Shakespeare makes kind Henry IV say: The wish was father to that thought, Harry.

And an old saw among the people has it:

> Convince a man against his will
> He's of the same opinion still.

New names were appearing in the Stark composers' list. The publisher, of course, had always bought a number of rags that, though in the best tradition, might be called minor. In 1906–8, for example, three rags by Clarence H. (Cad) St. John were brought out; several by Ed Mellinger, head of the Christensen schools in St. Louis, appeared a little later. A Stark publication of 1911 was Arthur Sizemore's *The Climbers Rag*, dedicated to Miller Huggins and one of the St. Louis ball clubs. During this period Stark published Will Held's *Chromatic Rag* (1916), and of course there were periodical publications by his son E. J. Stark. Etilmon, who was a practicing legitimate musician, has several good rags to his credit. Earliest is the *Kyrene* of 1904. His *Chicken Tango* is dated 1914, and the *Gum Shoe Fox Trot*, 1917. Under the pseudonym of Bud Manchester, his *Brain Storm Rag* appeared in 1907, *Clover Blossoms Rag* in 1912; and Etilmon is in addition author of several waltzes, as well as a campaign song, his first publication in 1896, entitled: *Bryan and Sewell—Free Silver*.

Added to the Stark roster of white ragtime writers in this period was Paul Pratt, a player active in Indianapolis. His *Hot House Rag* (1914) and *Springtime Rag* (1916) are very fine, just short of a top ranking. Stark's earliest Pratt publication (1912) was a song, *That Gosh Darn Hiram Tune*, with words by J. Will Callahan. In the catalogue of 1917 appears Pratt's instrumental *On the Rural Route*. Pratt's earliest rags, including

Vanity Rag (1909) and *Walhalla* (1910), were brought out by the Indianapolis loan-broker and amateur music publisher J. H. Aufderheide.

The composing bug even bit Old John Stark himself. In 1913 he composed and copyrighted an operetta, *The Vital Question*, with libretto by Etilmon. It was never produced and seemingly never printed. The Missouri touch appears in some of the operetta song titles: *The Rubes of New York*, *The Wise Old Hen*, and the old folksong, now forgotten, *Weevily Wheat*. John Mason Brown (not the present-day writer), evoking memories of the old slave songs in an article in *Lippincott's Magazine* of December 1868, wrote of this beautiful old Negro air: "Who could hear without a responsive tapping of the foot and unbending of the wrinkled brow:

> *I won't have none of your weevily wheat*
> *I won't have none of your barley.*"

If one excepts a group of teaching pieces published under the pseudonym of Julius Wichman, John Stark's Opus 2 was a war song of 1917, *He's All Shot to Pieces—by the French Girls' Eyes*. His career as composer continued in 1919 when he apostrophized his personal physician's orders with the song *John Barleycorn, Goodbye*, and closed in 1920 with Opus 4, *Oh, You Tommy (Reminiscent of Tom Moore)*. The parenthetical clause refers to the use of *The Last Rose of Summer* as chorus, while the verse is acknowledged as being adapted from Scott Joplin, the source being *The Entertainer*.

The classic side of the new Stark publications came, however, from Lamb and Scott and from three new Negroes, Artie Matthews, Robert Hampton, and Charles Thompson. This trio of composers were the chief figures in the new St. Louis school that had arisen since 1907.

The work of Rob Hampton, self-taught and remarkable pianist from Little Rock, first appears with *The Dogin' Rag* of 1913, a song with words by Frank Gray. The later hit *Walking the Dog* by Shelton Brooks is said to be derived from this number. *Cataract Rag* bears the date 1914 and *Agitation Rag* 1915. The second and third strains of *Cataract*, alternating raggy sections with flowing passage work in thirty-second and sixty-fourth notes, are of a strongly classical European feeling. No such obvious derivations as the *Spring Song* or *Melody in F* are their inspiration. Parts of the third theme, for example, seem to echo a Brahms chamber work of the late Bad Ischl period.

Of the more than forty numbers that Rob Hampton composed, only the three published by Stark are known to remain.

Artie Matthews, who today heads the successful Cosmopolitan Conservatory of Music in Cincinnati, remembers the later years of St. Louis ragtime as brilliant ones. And so they were. But there was a hurrying tempo, a hectic quality to their brilliance, which betokened the rapidly approaching end of the ragtime vogue. Born in Minonk, Illinois, in 1888, Artie Matthews was brought up in Springfield. He played no ragtime when he went to St. Louis for the fair in 1904 at the age of sixteen during the golden period of Joplin, Chauvin, Turpin, and the rest. It was in Springfield during the two following years that he learned piano syncopation from one Banty Morgan, a "hophead" in the local tenderloin, and from Art Dunningham, who played at the Lisle and the Solace Clubs. From then on, Artie earned his way, at first by street serenading with his trio—steel guitar, mandolin, and violin—and later by playing the Washington Street wine rooms and the private upstairs *couchés*, pronounced "cow cheese" in Springfield. When Artie settled in St. Louis, around 1907, only Joplin and Turpin remained from the old school of players.

Most of the district jobs were impermanent, or perhaps it is more accurate to say that the players liked to roam, hated to stay put. They met at the cafés, especially Turpin's Rosebud, to pass the time and learn the new tunes while waiting for calls to come in. "We weren't competitive," says Artie. "Anyone who learned a new number taught it to everyone else. There was plenty of work and it was no question of how much could you make, but what did you want to make. If you just needed a dollar you didn't have to wait for a piano job—you could take a guitar and a camp stool and sit on the sidewalk outside a hotel and make it in half an hour."

There were new faces at the Rosebud and "down the line."

There were the honkytonk characters like Dollar Bill and Scopec and players like Sonny Anderson, Can-Can (Paul Sedric), George Reynolds, Walker Farrington, and Owen Marshall. In a few years Charley Thompson, Rob Hampton, and Conroy Casey joined the crew. There were brilliant women pianists, too, playing the district—Gertrude (Sweety) Bell, Louella Anderson, and Theodosia Hutchinson, later the first Negro woman allowed to join the musicians' union—but they did not as a rule frequent the Rosebud. Besides work in the wine rooms and the sporting-house parlors, there was work for all to be had at the many rent parties that St. Louis Negroes call Buffet Flats, and there were the Negro clubs, finest of which was the Modern Horseshoe of the gambler Ollie Jackson, whose diamond-horseshoe tie pin, Charley Thompson says, "was big enough for a Shetland pony."

Across the Mississippi River in Illinois about three miles above East St. Louis was the little town of Lovejoy, called Brooklyn by the sporting set. The not inappropriately named Lovejoy was an all-Negro town that ran wide open twenty-four hours a day. Around 1917, in the closing days of the ragtime period, the big place there was Aunt Kate Gryder's "cabaret," where Thompson, Hampton, and the others earned huge tips from the out-of-towners who crowded the village every night. The St. Louis singing entertainer Webb Owsley could often be heard at Aunt Kate's, as could the pianist Mike Jackson from Louisville via Terre Haute. Mike was a great inventor of songs. One of his favorite songs, a hit at the time, went as follows:

> Mrs. Trice had a restaurant
> She had a restaurant grand;
> She thought she'd open it up
> Just for the working man;
> The meals she served
> Were just immense—
> You got the whole darned business
> For fifteen cents.
>
> She served rice and gravy
> And gravy and rice,

Sauce seasoned very high
With spice,
She had egg in the omelet,
Egg in the shell—
The hen that laid them
Never was well.

She had bread pudding hot
Bread pudding cold
Bread pudding from one
To nine days old;
Her chicken and dumpling
Were just immense—
You had the whole darned business
For fifteen cents!

In later years Mike was a familiar figure in New York's Harlem, entertaining with an accordion and still making up songs. One ditty that he sang in bars kept him in drinks to the end in 1947. It was called *Man, Knock Me a Drink*, and a recent hit song, *Baby, Knock Me a Kiss*, is said to have come from the Jackson tune.

Around 1911 Jelly Roll Morton blew into town. He had heard talk of the prowess of the St. Louis ragtimers. "The time that I came into St. Louis," he said, "I was afraid that I'd meet somebody that could top me a whole lot . . . so I claimed that I was a singer. I was hired at a club called the Democratic Club—the proprietor's name was Noah Warrington.

"They had a singer there, his name was Speck. Speck had a rough, oh, a terrible voice. I had a bad voice myself, but not as bad as Speck's. But Speck was a real favorite. He used to sing some kind of a song about the doctor's application, what's good for you.

"Speck didn't come to work until late, since I went to work at nine o'clock and Speck didn't get off until twelve or one o'clock at the other job he was working, and we stayed on until four or five in the morning.

"So of course," Jelly continued, "George was a little bit chesty—that's the piano player—because all the girls was around, trying to make eyes at him. So I asked George to play me a tune and he didn't seem to want me to be working in the place. So he played the tune, didn't look like he was very much particular about playing it.

"I told him, I said, 'You don't play that right.' I said, 'I'd like to have a little more pep in this thing here because it helps me out a bit.'

"He says, 'Well, if you don't like the way I'm playing it, there's the piano, play it yourself,' not knowing I could play. So I got up and played the tune, and where I told him the mistakes were, he found I was really telling the truth.

"Immediately he had a great, big, broad smile on his face— he wanted to make friends with me. He had a lot of music lined up on the piano and he asked me did I read music and I told him a little bit.

"Of course he gave me the different difficult numbers, and they were all simple to me because I knew 'em all anyway, and I played everything he had. By that time he started getting in touch with different piano-players around that was supposed to be good readers.

"So they finally start to bringing me different tunes. They brought me all of Scott Joplin's tunes; I knew 'em all by heart anyhow, at that time; so I played 'em all. They brought me James Scott's tunes; I knew 'em all. They brought me Artie Matthews' *Pastimes;* in fact, Artie himself brought them down, but I didn't know it. I had played his tunes so he decided to find out whether I could really play piano or not and could really read. Artie was supposed to be the best reader of the whole St. Louis bunch.

"So Artie brought me down things like *Humoresque.* I knew 'em all anyway, so he decided to bring down *Martha*, an overture. *Martha* was something that I had been remembering for years, so that was all O.K.

"Finally they brought me *Poet and Peasant.* It seems like in St. Louis if you was able to play *Poet and Peasant* correctly you was really considered the tops. I had known this tune for years and they placed this number in front of me and I started looking at it like I never seen it before—which I had rehearsed it maybe two months before I was able to play it.

"And I start playing this number, and I had to turn the page over, but it was impossible due to the fact that the passage was so fast. I couldn't turn it over even though I knew the tune, and Mr. Matthews grabbed the tune from in front of me and said, 'Hell, don't be messing with that guy, he's a shark.'

"And I told them, 'Boys, I been kidding you all the time. I knew all these tunes, anyway.' "

It was in 1911, while he was in St. Louis, that Jelly Roll wrote one of his outstanding ragtime numbers, *Bert Williams*. The great Negro comedian heard Jelly playing it and was greatly taken by the dancelike qualities of its themes. As the result of his praise, the number bears his name.

St. Louis ragtime playing of the final period was more a cosmopolitan than a regional style. It reflected the influences of other parts of the country, most notably the incisive rhythms and brilliant figurations of the Eastern shout style that was just then developing. The playing of Charley Thompson, for example, combines the solid attributes of traditional St. Louis ragging with the graceful treble passage work of the great New York players. This stylistic infiltration began, in fact, rather early. Artie Matthews, while in Cincinnati in 1912, arranged *Junk Man Rag* for the great Eastern player Luckey Roberts, and this accounts for the Joplinesque quality of the *Junk Man* score, which is so markedly at variance with Luckey's shout playing of this tune.

Charley Thompson met James P. Johnson, another leader of the New York school, in Cleveland in 1919. They became close friends, and Charley's playing ever since has shown the effects of their association. Thompson, like the other St. Louisians, is a prolific composer, though only one of his rags has ever been published. Besides *The Lily Rag*, brought out by Syndicate Music, St. Louis, his work includes a number of very fine syncopated pieces. *Ragtime Humming Bird* ranks melodically with *The Lily; Deep Lawton* is a remarkable synthesis of ragtime and the barrel-house or boogie-woogie bass. Other Thompson rags are *Hop Alley Dream, Mound City Walk Around*, and *Buffet Flat Rag*.

Around 1913 in St. Louis there was much activity in the

production of small tabloid musicals and variety shows. Charlie Turpin's Booker T. Washington Theater put on a new show with a different theme—African, cowboy, Egyptian, and so on—each week. At this time both Tom Turpin and Artie Matthews wrote music for these shows. Some of the instrumentals and songs were of high caliber, but all were thrown away at the end of the week. Ragtime contests were a weekly feature of this theater for many years, and attracted long rosters of fine players. This house later became a prominent stopover on the old T. O. B. A. circuit (Theatre Owners Booking Association, Negro vaudeville circuit), with the appearance of such artists as Ethel Waters, Butterbeans and Susie, Bessie Smith, Ma Rainey, Ida Cox, Josephine Baker (who had previously been a waitress at Turpin's dance palace, Jazzland), and most of the other leading Negro performers of the day.

The Booker T. Washington shows were on a high professional level, as were those at the Princess roadhouse. Matthews composed numbers for these, and the owners of the Princess published several in 1913, including *The Princess Prance*, *When I'm Gone*, and *Lucky Dan—My Gambling Man*. Artie also wrote music for the weekly local talent shows that were interludes between pictures at a nickelodeon called Barrett's Theatorium.

Someone, probably William Stark, heard Artie Matthews playing and came back with an offer of fifty dollars a tune. The result was the publication of the remarkable series of *Pastime* rags. *Pastime Rag No. 1* and *No. 2* were brought out in 1913. *No. 1* embodies a very early appearance of the barrelhouse walking bass in a printed score. Another "first" belonging to Matthews is that of arrangement of the first number to bear the name "blues" in a musical sense. (Earlier numbers had appeared in which "The Blues" figured as a regimental name.) This is *Baby Seals Blues*, published in August 1912. The *Dallas Blues* of Hart A. Wand appeared one month later, W. C. Handy's *Memphis Blues* about three weeks later still. The vaudeville team of Seals and Fisher traveled the old T. O. B. A. The priority of *Baby Seals Blues* is pointed out by Abbe Niles in the revised 1949 edition of Handy's *A Treasury of the Blues*, but he qualifies the acknowledgment by implying that Baby Seals may have learned *his* blues from *Mister Crump*, the unpublished 1909 campaign song by Handy that later became the *Memphis Blues*. Niles's alternative suggestion is far more likely: namely, that Seals picked it up from the widespread folk sources from which Handy's own blues were taken.

Artie Matthews's ability to write scores enabled him to prepare the rags of others for publication by Stark. He is known to have set down Rob Hampton's *Cataract* as well as *The Lily Rag* (1914) of Charley Thompson. In 1915 John Stark announced to his composers that he wanted a blues number to compete with the fast-selling *St. Louis Blues* of W. C. Handy. In the competition Artie's number was chosen, and it was published the same year with the title *Weary Blues*. It became a hit, and Stark, after paying fifty dollars plus royalties for it, gave Artie a later bonus of twenty-seven dollars "to buy a suit." Matthews is financially successful today, but he still remembers John Stark's payment for this number as exceedingly generous for that period. He still receives heavy royalties for *Weary Blues*, which has been a standard jazz number ever since its publication.

The year the *Weary Blues* was published the District was closing in St. Louis, and Artie Matthews decided it was time to get out of ragtime. He took a job as organist in Chicago at the Berea Presbyterian Church. By 1918 he was settled in Cincinnati. He has never returned to St. Louis. Today, a successful teacher of the classics, he has never rejected the ragtime idea, and his playing is as phenomenal as ever. One can sit in one of his studios and listen to his remarkable "double-stride bass" and his thundering octaves, while over the transom from the next studio comes the *fugato* of a Bach *Invention*.

Pastimes 3, 4, and *5* were published by Stark after Matthews left for Chicago. Matthews did not even know that the last two had been printed. *No. 3* came out in 1916; oddly enough, *No. 5* was issued in 1918, and *No. 4* not until 1920. All five are thoroughly in the classic manner, with much feeling of Joplin and James Scott, but with highly original touches of

Matthews's own. Besides the walking bass already mentioned in *No. 1*, *No. 5* uses a tango treble most originally in conjunction with a ragtime bass.

As Artie Matthews departed, a quarter century or more of St. Louis ragtime was drawing to a close. The District was shuttered like most of the districts everywhere. Some of the players scattered. Of those who remained, some in a few years were playing for small wages where they could, while others eventually got out of music altogether. It had been a lot of fun; it had been a brilliant and productive time, but it was over.

When Tom Turpin died, on August 13, 1922, the ragtime days were through. Indeed, that 1917 April when Joplin breathed out his last dark moments, the month that America went to war, is the symbolic date when the ragtime vogue was virtually ended. Not because its great figures were dying, but because public interest itself was dying. As long as that interest might have sustained it, James Scott, Joseph Lamb, and Artie Matthews could have continued, and new figures would have arisen to bring about the even greater developments implicit in ragtime ever since *Maple Leaf Rag* had been published.

But, like autumn, the last colors were fading. One looks around today at the survivors of that golden St. Louis harvest. There is Arthur Marshall retired in Kansas City, Sam Patterson a union delegate in New York, Joe Jordan in business in Tacoma. Charley Thompson is proprietor of a prosperous little bar at 3005 Lawton Boulevard in St. Louis. Like the others, Charley can still play beautifully with free invention—"I've always been a make-up player," he says—but a juke box makes the music at Charley's place. Look for the old players in the old places everywhere, and in almost every spot where the piano once stood is the juke box collecting its nickels.

In 1943 Rob Hampton was playing in a small place in a neighborhood of fifteen-cent hotels. When jazz critic William Russell visited him, Hampton was living in a small room on Laclede, furnished with little more than a cot. He was a bitter old man at fifty-two. "I can't play 60 degrees, not even 45, let alone 90 anymore," said Hampton, referring to wide-compass playing on the keyboard. A year or so later the man who had once written the intricate and beautiful *Cataract* wandered off to California to die. But on that June day when Russell was leaving him, Hampton had said: "Nobody knows today how difficult the old rags were. If old man Stark were around he would still be publishing them."

But old man Stark was not around. It had been sixteen long years since the straight soldier's figure had last been seen walking into the old office on Laclede Avenue. All of John Stark's last fifteen years were lived in the home of Etilmon, his son named after the brother who had raised him as an orphan so many years before in Kentucky. Although he was eighty-six when he died, John Stark kept his vigor and alertness to the very end. One scarcely thinks, indeed, of pioneers of John Stillwell Stark's generation as dying; it is rather that they decide at last to quit living.

He had his own room at Etilmon's, and his real companion there was not his son or his daughter-in-law, but his little granddaughter, Margaret Eleanor, whose middle name recalled the mother whom he had lost in early childhood. Margaret Eleanor saw eye to eye with the old man, matched his ever youthful enthusiasms with her own, and understood him as his own sons had never quite been able to.

In the evenings he would play his old Kentucky guitar and sing *Jump Jim Crow* or *Weevily Wheat* or perhaps one of his Civil War songs:

> *Our boys will shine tonight,*
> *Our boys will shine.*
> *Our boys will shine tonight,*
> *All down the line.*
>
> *They've washed their faces too,*
> *Out for a time;*
> *When the sun goes down*
> *And the moon comes up,*
> *Our boys will shine.*

Or he would sing the nonsense song that was Margaret Eleanor's special delight, consisting merely of the singing of the names of four of his sisters:

> *Angelica Sardinia*
> *Arbelia Tyrene*
> *Effie Arcada*
> *Atlantas America Livada.*

As Margaret Eleanor grew older, her grandfather helped with her lessons, and when she reached high school they would rush through them to save the precious evening hours. These they spent in the attic, far from the disapproving eyes of Mr. and Mrs. Etilmon, delving into John's enthusiasms—philosophy, Greek mythology, or, especially, comparative religion. Through Talmud, Koran, and *Science and Health with Key to the Scriptures* they waded together, feeling holy and learned.

Every morning at six John Stark was off to the office, disturbing the household and much to the annoyance of his daughter-in-law. To the last he seemed to hope that by some miracle America's ears would be opened once more to the music in which he had believed. But sales were getting smaller and publications fewer. *Maple Leaf* still sold well, and more than ever the early Scott Joplin masterpiece supported the Stark venture. In 1920 the house published only three numbers, one by James Scott; in 1922 four, in 1923 two. From then on until John Stark's death only reprints came off the Laclede presses.

By then Margaret Eleanor had moved to New York. With the independence her grandfather had taught her she ventured out on her own to find a place in the business world. She lived with her aunt and uncle Eleanor and Jim Stanley until she got a job. Years before, when she had been chafing under parental restrictions, John had sagely advised her: "Your parents can dictate to you only because you depend on them for money. Earn your own."

John Stark kept in correspondence with his granddaughter. Margaret Eleanor has saved the letters. It was the summer's end of 1926 in Missouri with the Indian corn man-high in the rich bottom lands, the full ears waiting to be garnered, when he wrote: "I hope you will be able to land something that will be sufficient to cover all necessary expenses . . . as for myself I am bruising along about as usual getting enough orders to make me safe from age decrepitude and besides old Uncle Sam raised my pension $15 per month, so it looks like I should have no fears for the future."

The crisp Missouri autumn air was loud with the songs of the husking bees, the frosts were flushing the pumpkins, the blue-ripe persimmons were dropping to the ground, and along the Mississippi banks the cottonwood yellow and maple scarlet were dimming, when next he wrote: "I am afraid I have been a little dilatory in answering your letter. . . . I will not throw in laconic or cryptic squibs to show off my education, nor will I invade Greek mythology to show off my vast knowledge of the world. But I am vain enough to believe that the spice of these have been effective in my circular matter, in my success in coming from a farm and competing with the well organized music trade of this country." Then he exclaims: "I can't dance the Charleston or Jump Jim Crow but I have been equal to all requirements up to the present."

In the meantime John Stark had divided what was left of his fortune between his sons and daughter. On November 5, 1926 he writes: "I was not aware that I owed you two letters but I have been so busy and worked up about the new *Maple Leaf* copyright that I could hardly think about anything else for it has been my principal income. However, my rights last to it until the 18th of next September and perhaps that is as long as I will last. . . ."

Autumn was long vanished and deep winter lay on the prairies when the last letter came. "My health has been much better than I thought it possible through the winter," John Stark wrote. "I think I will be ready for the strawberries when they get here."

The fat, red strawberries came and were gone; spring passed into summer, and summer ripened yellow, and there was one more autumn. John Stark lived to see Lottie Joplin make the renewal that, under the law, is the sole privilege of the composer or his heirs, and assign the *Maple Leaf* rights back once more safely to its original publishers. It was only a short while after, on November 20, 1927, as autumn's end faded on the hills, when John Stillwell Stark decided that his work was done.

There was still the classic of all ragtime classics. Scott Joplin wrote it, and for John Stark it was a flaming sword, and together, Negro and white man, they fought the good fight. Surely it is no more than the small part of justice that the *Maple Leaf Rag* should outlive them both.

POSTLUDE

In 1927, when John Stark died, the word "ragtime" had become little more than a quaint obsolescence. It had been a name that helped to launch an almost unparalleled musical craze. Then—as the name of jazz did later—it helped to bar serious acceptance of Negro syncopated music. Finally in our time it became approximately synonymous with the term "corn." Yet ragtime itself has never ended; without the name, it still goes on in many places and in many ways.

In its broadest sense of a racial rhythm, ragtime is in all truly Negroid music today and in a great deal of white music too. It is in Negro speech, in Negro preaching, and in the syncopated surge of the shouting spiritual. It is in Negro song and Negro jazz. It is so basically of the race, whatever its environment, that one might say that ragtime rhythm infuses Negro motor activity itself, activating both work and play. Fortunately the vast majority of American Negroes are still a long way from rejecting their own sources of music-making and musical inspiration.

In its broadest sense, as a music for all Americans, the rhythms of ragtime have lost not a whit of their power to captivate and charm. Whenever the movie-makers wish to enliven and lend authenticity to the dance-hall and honky-tonk scenes of period pictures or Westerns, they give the symphony orchestras that are always on call a holiday and summon an old-time ragtime pianist. To the moguls, this is hokum. But the audiences, who would not dream of using a horse and wagon, leave the theaters humming and whistling the old tunes. Ragtime is not outmoded like the horse and buggy; it is not an artifact; it has the currency and continuity of a developing and irrepressible thing. Its effectiveness in the film context too is owing to its stark presentation. Hollywood has not got around to glorifying ragtime.

Ragtime in the movies is not yet a central theme. The music functions as background. In its pure idiomatic form, however, it is still being used in its original, functional way. Throughout the country, in small bars and obscure roadhouses, are hundreds of ragtime players—one never knows where they will be encountered. On a dance night Charley Thompson can be heard in St. Louis; Glover Compton plays at his own small South Side club in Chicago; and in Walnut Creek, out in California, one can hear Sid Le Protti, Glover's old pal from Purcell's Barbary Coast dive. In Albany, New York, Sammy Davis is not hard to find; in San Francisco the white ragtimer Paul Lingle holds forth; and at Sheepshead Bay in Brooklyn one can see and hear the entertaining antics of Fred Burton, "The Human Pianola." In Movieland the visitor is apt to run into Eddie (Sheet Iron) Barnes, quondam ragtime champion who defeated the British contender Phil Stebbins many years ago in an international contest. In Long Beach, the Ragtime Kid, Brun Campbell, will play *Maple Leaf* at the drop of a hat; and in Kansas City, Arthur Marshall will do likewise. Around Manhattan, James P. Johnson, Luckey Roberts, The Lion, and Eubie Blake play frequently; and over in New Jersey, Donald Lambert holds forth in his favorite neighborhood bar. And so it goes—along the Gulf Coast, in New Orleans, in Fort Worth, and all through the country the old-timers still perform. The spotlight on the "professors" is dimmer and the tips that support them smaller, but the music is worth looking for.

A general revival of ragtime is just beginning, spurred on by

an awakening interest both serious and popular and imple-
mented by a host of brilliant young white players just arising.
It is a gratifying fact that this is coming about while there are
so many of the old veterans left to share in it. It is inevitable
that this revival should take place, for ragtime, with all its
aspects of a past fad, is inextricably interwoven with American
life. Like any truly native music, it is more than just a song;
it is a part of our speech.

There is strong lasting quality and a continuing con-
temporaneity in a music that lives for more than half a
century. It was in the year of the *Maple Leaf Rag* that Rupert
Hughes wrote his remarkably clear sighted "Eulogy of Rag
Time." We wrote to the famous novelist fifty-one years later,
asking him to state his opinions today. We quote from his
letter, which bears the date February 17, 1950:

"It is both surprising and flattering to have you bring
back to memory my ancient article on ragtime. I can say
nothing about it now except that, for all the critical contempt of ragtime among the intellectuals, it was a revolutionary phase of musical evolution, and it has had a profound influence in all subsequent music.

"It swept Europe and thrilled millions, and it was
strangely so difficult to master that many of the harshest
critics of it could not play it. It required a new technique
in rhythm and fingering, and I saw many a snooty conservatory trained expert, get his fingers all tangled up as
he tried to do what thousands of Negroes and their
imitators did naturally and with ease."

The conservatory experts are not trying ragtime at the
present, though Jose Iturbi may be expected to do so at any
moment. The matter is being well taken care of outside the
conservatories by a group of extraordinarily talented young
white players. As long ago as 1941 young Wally Rose of San
Francisco left the conservatory in which he was studying to
master the ragtime idiom. Soon, with his rhythmically sound,
smooth, and well-articulated playing, he was delighting a new
generation with old classics like Joplin's *Pineapple*, Scott's
Sunburst, and Artie Matthews's *Pastimes*.

271

More fiery is the ragtime of Ralph Sutton, who came to New York from St. Louis. Like Wally Rose, Sutton is still in his twenties. His childhood training in St. Charles, Missouri, was with the sort of teacher that, presumably, is only to be found in Missouri. "She would send me home," Ralph says, "with a Bach fugue under one arm and *Maple Leaf* under the other." Sutton's playing, like that of the Negro ragtimers, supplements the sheet music with brilliant added variations of his own, which re-emphasize the fact that ragtime has always been a music primarily of playing rather than composing. Sutton and Rose are the leaders of a whole new generation of white ragtimers who may succeed in making this music once more a field in which Negroes will find an artistic and economic foothold. It is to be hoped that this can be achieved on a level of mature appreciation without the dubious agencies of Tin Pan Alley.

Ragtime is undeniably America's music, a part of our folksong and a part of our art. Whenever we shall tire sufficiently of the synthetic, the temporal, the vulgar, the banal, and the cheap, it is right here in our midst, ready once more to "hypnotize dis nation, and shake de earth's foundation."

CHRONOLOGY OF IMPORTANT
RAGTIME DATES

1841. *John Stark born in Shelby County, Kentucky.*

1847. *La Bamboula—Danse Nègre composed by Louis Moreau Gottschalk from African themes heard in Congo Square, New Orleans.*

1848. *Blackface minstrel idea grows.* The Dandy Broadway Coon *published in Christy Minstrels songbook.*

1868. *Scott Joplin born in Texarkana, Texas.*

1876. *Tony Jackson born in New Orleans.*

1885. *Jelly Roll Morton born in New Orleans.*

1886. *James Scott born in Neosho, Missouri.*

1887. *Joseph Lamb born in Montclair, New Jersey.*

1893. *Chicago World's Fair. Ragtime players congregate in Chicago; African music of Dahomeans impresses musicians and public.*

1894. *James P. Johnson born in New Brunswick, New Jersey.*

1895. *Ben Harney's* You've Been a Good Old Wagon *published by Greenup in Louisville (January).*

1896. *Cakewalk craze begins. Coon-song craze continues. Harney's success at Keith's, New York, starts public acceptance of ragtime.*

1897. *Ragtime publication begins with Krell's* Mississippi Rag *(January). First Negro rag,* Turpin's Harlem Rag, *published (December).*

1899. *Joplin's first rag,* Original Rags, *published (March). His* Maple Leaf *published by Stark in Sedalia (September).*

1900. *John Stark moves from Sedalia, begins music publication in St. Louis. Joplin follows.*

1903. A Guest of Honor, *ragtime opera, composed by Scott Joplin and presented in St. Louis.*

1904. *St. Louis World's Fair and National Ragtime Contest.*

1905. *John Stark opens New York offices.*

1907. *Scott Joplin moves to New York.*

1911. *John Stark returns to St. Louis. Scott Joplin publishes his opera* Treemonisha.

1917. *Scott Joplin dies as ragtime vogue wanes and jazz craze begins.*

1921. *Tony Jackson dies.*

1922. *Tom Turpin dies.*

1927. Maple Leaf *copyright renewed. John Stark dies.*

1938. *Ben Harney and James Scott die. Jelly Roll Morton records his saga for Library of Congress archives.*

1941. *Jelly Roll Morton dies, as interest in ragtime begins to revive.*

THE PIONEERS MOVE ON

1950	Harry P. Guy dies
	Charles L. Johnson dies
1952	Percy Wenrich dies
1953	S. Brunson Campbell dies
1955	Sam Patterson dies
1959	Artie Matthews dies
1960	Joseph F. Lamb dies
1962	Donald Lambert dies
	Paul Lingle dies
	Etilmon Justus Stark dies
1963	G. Tom Ireland dies
	J. Russel Robinson dies
1964	Charley Thompson dies
	Glover Compton dies

LISTS OF MUSICAL COMPOSITIONS

General Notes:

In the lists of musical compositions below, each title is followed by a code symbol indicating publisher and/or copyright-owner. This symbol is followed by the name of the lyricist, if any, and the name of the composer. When only one name is given it is that of the composer; when two names separated by *and* are given they are those of joint lyricists or of joint composers. When names are separated by a dash, those before th• dash are lyricists, thcse after the dash are composers. With instrumental compositions, only the composer's name is listed. The final numerals indicate date of copyright.

Section I contains works of the leading ragtime composers listed separately under the composers' names. In this section Scott Joplin, James Scott, and Joseph Lamb are listed first; the other composers follow in alphabetical order beginning with Eubie Blake. Under each composer's name the compositions are listed in chronological order. The composers in this section were chosen not for prolific output or hit successes, but for merit.

Section II contains a general alphabetical listing of compositions (other than those in Section I) referred to in the text, as well as many of allied interest from the ragtime period. This section is selected from various types of compositions, being intended as a cross-section of the musical activity of the period. In this section all compositions are for piano unless otherwise noted.

AAC	Alfred & Company	**BM**	Brokaw Music, St. Joseph, Mo.		Williams Music Compa New York
AAR	Andino & Ruehl, New York	**BMC**	Ball Music Company, Carthage, Mo.	**CWF**	Clarence Woods, Fort Worth
AB	A. Burke	**BMCB**	Brooks Music Company, Brooklyn	**CWH**	Charles W. Held, New York
ACM	Acme Music Company	**BMCNY**	Broadway Music		
AD	Arnett-Delonais, Chicago		Corporation, New York	**DAH**	Danton & Haskins, N York
AE	A. Elie, New Orleans	**BMCO**	Barth Music Company		
AEH	A. E. Henrich, Mt. Vernon, Ind.	**BPH**	Belmont Music Company, Philadelphia	**DDG**	Dumars Music, and Dumars, Gammon Mu Company, Carthage, M
AEO	A. E. Ostrander	**BRH**	Ben R. Harney, Chicago		
AF	Alb. Fox, Bridgeport, Conn.			**DHM**	De Haviland Music Company, New York
AGA	Attucks Music, and Gotham-Attucks, New York	**CAC**	Craig & Company, Chicago	**DMC**	Drumheller Music Company, St. Louis
AKH	A. K. Houck Piano Company, Nashville	**CAH**	Cohan and Harris, New York	**DNY**	Dunn, New York
AMC	Albright Music Company, Chicago	**CAL**	Carlin & Lennox, Indianapolis	**EAJ**	Emmett & Johns
AMCC	Allen Music Company, Columbia, Mo.	**CAS**	Chapman & Smith	**EBM**	Edward B. Marks, New York
AMCNO	Ashton Music Company, New Orleans	**CC**	Cable Company	**ECR**	Eugene Clarence Ramsdell, Boston
AMS	Atwill's Music Saloon, Baltimore	**CD**	C. Duane Crabb, Indianapolis	**ED**	E. Derville
APS	A. P. Severin, Moline, Ill.	**CF**	Carl Fischer, New York	**EEC**	Enoch et Cie, Paris
AS	Arthur Siebrecht, Lexington, Ky.	**CGNY**	Conner & Gillis, New York	**EHB**	Elias Howe, Boston
		CH	Carl Hoffman, Kansas City	**EJD**	E. J. Denton & Compa New York
ASC	Arling Shaeffer, Chicago	**CHC**	Charles Himmelman, Chicago	**ELB**	Euday L. Bowman, Ft. Worth
ATM	American Standard Music Publishing Company	**CHSL**	Charles Humfeld, St. Louis		
AWC	Axel W. Christensen, Chicago	**CKH**	Charles K. Harris, Milwaukee and New York	**EM**	Enterprise Music, New York
AWP	A. W. Perry & Son, Sedalia, Mo.	**CLJ**	Charles L. Johnson, Kansas City	**ENF**	Eva Note Flennard
				ES	Edward Schuberth & Company, New York
AWT	Arthur W. Tams, New York	**CLR**	C. Luckeyeth Roberts, New York	**ETP**	E. T. Paull, New York
		CM	Central Music Company, St. Louis	**EWB**	E. W. Berry Music Company, Kansas City
BAB	Backman & Backman, New York	**CMP**	Canton Music Publishing Company, Chicago		
BAD	Belcher & Davis, Detroit				
BAG	Bush & Gerts, Dallas	**CMPC**	Chicago Music Publishing Company, Chicago	**FAF**	Feist & Frankenthaler, New York
BAS	Broder & Schlam, New York	**CMPNY**	Consolidated Music Publishing Company, Chicago and New York	**FAH**	Firth & Hall
				FAM	F. A. Mills, New York
BAT	Barron & Thompson Company, New York	**CNB**	C. N. Buchanan, Cairo, Ill.	**FBH**	F. B. Haviland, New Y
BB	Brehm Bros., Erie, Pa.	**CON**	Con Conrad, New York	**FC**	Frank Clark Music Company, Chicago
BC	Buck & Carney, Chicago	**CR**	C. Ricordi, New York	**FCS**	F. C. Schmidt
BD	Brooks & Denton, New York	**CS**	Charles Shackford, Boston	**FDB**	F. D. Benteen, Boston
BFB	B. F. Bares & Company, Philadelphia	**CT**	Charles Turpin, St. Louis	**FDHU**	Francis, Day & Hunter London
		CTF	Charles T. French, New York	**FGF**	Frank G. Fite, Nashvill
BFF	Bennett F. Fritch, St. Louis	**CW**	Williams & Piron, Chicago, & Clarence	**FHC**	Fred Heltman, Clevela
BGM	Greenup Music Company, Louisville, Ky.			**FJH**	Fred J. Hamill

	Publisher
	Ferdinand Joseph Morton
HHK	F. K. Harding, New York
	Frank K. Root, Chicago and New York
HHST	F. Meyer, Chicago
HJW	Forster Music Publisher, Inc., Chicago
HMC	F. O. Gutmann, Cleveland
	Firth & Pond, New York
HMCC	Gould & Company
HMP	Gates & Jacobson, Cincinnati
	Grasmuk & Schott, New York
HNW	George Botsford, Centerville, Iowa, and New York
HPC	Giles Brothers, Quincy, Ill.
	Geraldine Dobyns, Memphis
HPMC	George D. Meares, Raleigh, N. C.
	Gus Edwards Music Publishing, New York
HPV	George Faberg Music Company, Cincinnati
HRM	George L. Spaulding, New York
HS	George. W. Meyer Music Company, New York
Y	Georgia Music, New York
HSG	G. Nichols Company
	Guckert Publishing Company, Bucyrus and Toledo, Ohio
HSW	G. Satterlee, Brooklyn
HVT	George Southwell, Kansas City (C)
	G. W. Setchell, Boston
HWM	G. W. Warren Company, Evansville, Ind. (NC)
HWMC	H. A. French, Nashville
	Homer A. Hall
HUN	Hurtig & Seamon, New York
	Harry Coleman, Philadelphia
HVS	H. C. Washington, Cincinnati
	H. F. Harding
IB	Harry Graul, Detroit
ICS	Hamilton S. Gordon, New York (Y)
IS	Howley, Haviland, and Howley, Haviland &

Code	Publisher
	Dresser, New York
HHK	H. H. Kratz, Minerva, Ohio
HHST	Harry H. Sparks, Toronto
HJW	Hy J. Wehrman, Chicago
HMC	Henning Music Company, Chicago
HMCC	Home Music Company, Chicago
HMP	Head Music Publishing Company
HNW	H. N. White, Cleveland
HPC	Hitchcock Publishing Company
HPMC	Hakenjos Piano Manufacturing Co., New Orleans
HPV	Henry P. Vogel, Albany, New York
HRM	Harold Rossiter Music Company, Chicago
HS	Herald Square Music Publishing Company, New York
HSG	Hamilton S. Gordon, New York
HSW	Harry S. Webster
HVT	Harry Von Tilzer, New York
HWM	Harry Williams Music Company, New York
HWMC	Hy Wehrman and N. J. Clesi, New Orleans
HUN	Joseph F. Hunleth, St. Louis
HVS	Hugo V. Schlam, New York
IB	Irving Berlin, New York
ICS	I. Cohen & Son, Baltimore
IS	I. Seidel, and Seidel Music Company, Indianapolis
IWCI	I. Whiteson, Chicago
JA	Joseph Armbruster
JAS	Jerome & Schwartz Publishing Co., New York
JBE	J. R. Bell, Leavenworth, Kansas
JCC	John Church & Co., Cincinnati
JD	Jimmy Durante
JDNY	Joe Davis, New York
JEA	J. E. Agnew, Des Moines
JF	Joseph Flanner, Milwaukee
JFAC	Jesse French & Company, Nashville
JFH	J. Fred Helf

Code	Publisher
JFP	J. F. Perry, Boston
JHA	J. H. Aufderheide, Indianapolis
JHB	Joseph H. Barrett
JHK	John H. Keyser, New Orleans
JJK	J. J. Kaiser & Company, New York
JKM	Joseph Krolage Music Company, Cincinnati
JLH	J. Leubrie Hill, New York
JLP	J. L. Peters
JMD	Joseph M. Daly Music Company, Boston
JMNY	Jewell Music Publishing Company, New York
JMP	Joseph Morris, Philadelphia and New York
JOS	John O. Sheatz, Philadelphia
JPJ	James P. Johnson
JRF	J. R. Fuller, Temple, Texas
JSAS	John Stark & Son, Sedalia, St. Louis and New York
JTH	John T. Hall, New York
JWJ	J. W. Jenkins Music Company, Kansas City
JWP	J. W. Pepper Company, Philadelphia
JWS	Joseph W. Stern & Company, New York
KJ	Keithley-Joy Music Company, Des Moines
KP	Keith Prowse & Company, London
KSG	S. G. Kiesling
LAB	H. Lesser & Brother, New York
LBG	Lee B. Grabbe, Davenport, Iowa
LBS	Leiter Brothers, Syracuse
LEB	Leo E. Berliner, New York
LF	Leo Feist, Inc., New York
LG	Gruenewald, New Orleans
LGC	London Gramophone Company
LM	Lester Melrose, Chicago
LPG	Lucien Porter Gibson, St. Louis
LR	Lew Roberts, Nashville
MAA	Martin & Adams Music Company, Wichita, Kansas
MAF	McCarthy & Fisher Inc., New York

CODE SYMBOLS OF PUBLISHERS

MB	Myll Bros. New York	PMP	Philadelphia Music Publishing Company, Philadelphia	SCMC	Southern California M Company, Los Angeles
MBMC	Melrose Brothers Music Company, Chicago			SCSF	Sherman Clay, San Francisco
MBNY	Miller Music, New York	PMU	Popular Music Publishers, Cleveland	SEW	Secie E. Wyatt
MBR	Millard Bryant	PP	Paull-Pioneer, New York	SF	Sam Fox, Cleveland ar New York
MC	Moffett, Cleveland	PPC	Puderer Publishing Company, New Orleans		
MCK	McKinley Music Company, Chicago	PPCC	Pekin Publishing Company, Chicago	SG	Spaulding, Gray, New York
MDS	M. D. Swisher, Philadelphia	PRM	P. R. McCargo, Boston	SJMC	Scott Joplin Music Company, St. Louis an New York
MLM	M. L. Mantell, Syracuse	PTW	P. T. Wayne, New Orleans		
MMC	Mills Music Company, New York			SMC	Success Music Compan Chicago
MMCNY	Mayfair Music Corp., New York	RAB	Rogers and Roberts, New York	SMCC	Sunlight Music Compa Chicago
MMPC	Maryland Music Publishing Co.	RAS	Richard A. Sallfield, New York	SMCNY	Seminary Music Compa New York
MMSF	Model Music Company, San Francisco	RB	Robert Bircher, St. Louis	SMLO	Southern Music, New Y and London
MMU	Millet's Music Saloon	RBM	Rogers Brothers Music Publishing Company, New York	SMP	Standard Music Publishing, Chicago
MRMC	Maurice Richmond Music Company, New York			SMSL	Syndicate Music Company, St. Louis
MS	Maurice Shapiro, New York	RDY	Robert De Yong & Company, St. Louis	SNY	G. Schirmer, New Yor
MWAS	M. Witmark & Sons, New York	RE	Robbins-Engel, New York	SS	Stanford & Sundelson, Philadelphia
		RGB	Richard G. Behan Music Company, Newark, N. J.	SSL	S. Simon, St. Louis
		RGC	Roger Graham, Chicago	SSSL	Shattinger Piano Company, St. Louis
NMC	National Music Company, Chicago	RH	Robert Hoffman, New Orleans	SZM	S. Z. Marks, Des Moir
NMU	Nicholas Music Company, New York	RL	Ralph Larsh, Chicago		
NNE	N. Nelson, Chicago	RLC	Roger Lewis, Chicago		
NW	N. Weinstein, New York	RMC	Robbins Music Corporation, New Vork	TAS	Treat & Shephard Company, New Haven, Conn.
		RR	Richmond-Robbins, New York		
OD	Oliver Ditson, Boston	RRH	R. R. Hogue, Knoxville, Tenn.	TBH	T. B. Harms & Compa Inc., New York
OES	O. E. Sutton, Rochester	RS	Robert Smith, Temple, Texas	TBNY	Theron C. Bennett, Ne York
OJDM	O. J. DeMoll & Company, Washington, D. C.	RSP	R. S. Peer, New York	TBP	T. Bahnsen Piano Manufacturing Compa St. Louis
OSSL	Owen Spendthrift, St. Louis	RW	Rudolph Wurlitzer, Cincinnati		
				TM	Tempo Music Compan Washington, D. C.
PAH	Pryor & Higgins, New York	SAB	Stewart & Bauer, Philadelphia	TMCC	Thompson Music Company, Chicago
PAS	J. Placht & Son	SAF	Seals and Fisher, St. Louis		
PB	Perry Bradford, New York	SAS	Schuster & Son, New York	TMM	Theodore Morse Music Company, New York
PBC	Princess Publishing Company, St. Louis	SAY	Stortchz & Yout, Little Rock, Ark.	TMU	Triangle Music, New Y
PBU	Paul Burmeister, St. Louis	SB	Sol Bloom, Chicago	TP	Theo. Presser, Philadel
PC	W. C. Polla Company, Chicago	SBC	Shapiro, Bernstein & Company, and Shapiro, Bernstein & Von Tilzer, New York	TS	Thiebes-Stierlin, St. L
PE	Paul Eno, Philadelphia			TSB	Ted S. Barron, New Y
PK	Philip Kussel, Cincinnati			TSNY	Ted Snyder, New York
PMC	Pacific Music Company, San Francisco	SBNY	Santly Brothers, New York	UM	University Music
PMCO	Pacific Music Company, Oakland, Calif.	SBS	S. Brainerd's Sons, Chicago and New York		Publishing Company, Louis

S Union Music Company, Cincinnati

Van Alstyne and Curtis

Val A. Reis, St. Louis

Victor Kremer, Chicago

Vandersloot Music, Williamsport, Pa., and New York

C Vinton Music, Boston and Chicago

Vivian Music Publishing Company, Boston

Villa Moret, San Francisco

W. A. Evans, Boston

William A. Pond, New York

V Welch & Wilsky Music Publishers, Philadelphia

Wood, Boston

Willard Bryant, Detroit

William B. Gray, New York

WBS Waterson, Berlin & Snyder, New York

WCH W. C. Handy, New York

WCS William C. Stahl, Milwaukee

WCW W. C. Williams, New York

WCWI Warren C. Williams, Indianapolis

WES Will E. Skidmore

WFB Will F. Burke

WGH Walter G. Haenschen, St. Louis

WHC Wenrich-Howard Company, New York

WJ Walter Jacobs, Boston

WJD W. J. Dyer & Brother, St. Paul

WJNY Werner Janssen, New York

WL Will Livernash, Kansas City

WM Will Morrison, Indianapolis

WMC Windsor Music Company, Chicago and New York

WMD Walter M. Davis, Chicago

WMH William Haskins, New York

WP Walton Publishing Company, New York

WPC Wand Publishing Company, Oklahoma City

WRC Will Rossiter, Chicago and New York

WSM White-Smith Music Publishing Company and White, Smith & Terry, Boston

WW Willis-Woodward, New York

WWR Whitney-Warren, and Remick Music Company, Detroit and New York

WWS W. W. Stuart, New York

WWWI W. W. Willis & Company, Cincinnati

YMP York Music Publishing, New York

SCOTT JOPLIN

RAGS (*Piano Solo*):

Original Rags CH 1899
Maple Leaf Rag JSAS (copyright renewed 1927—present editions
   erroneously state 1926) 1899
Peacherine Rag JSAS 1901
The Easy Winners SJMC 1901
A Breeze from Alabama JSAS 1902
Elite Syncopations JSAS 1902
The Strenuous Life JSAS 1902
The Entertainer JSAS 1902
Weeping Willow VAR 1903
Palm Leaf Rag—A Slow Drag VK 1903
The Favorite AWP 1904
The Sycamore—A Concert Rag WRC 1904
The Cascades JSAS 1904
The Chrysanthemum—An Afro-American Intermezzo JSAS 1904
Leola Two-Step (American Music Syndicate) 1905
Eugenia WRC 1905
The Ragtime Dance—Two Step JSAS 1906
Search Light Rag JWS 1907
Gladiolus Rag JWS 1907
Rose Leaf Rag JMD 1907
The Nonpareil (None to Equal) JSAS 1907
Fig Leaf Rag JSAS 1908
Sugar Cane—A Ragtime Classic SMCNY 1908
Pineapple Rag SMCNY 1908
Wall Street Rag SMCNY 1909
Solace—A Mexican Serenade SMCNY 1909
Country Club SMCNY 1909
Euphonic Sounds SMCNY 1909
Paragon Rag SMCNY 1909
Stoptime Rag JWS 1910
Scott Joplin's New Rag JWS 1912
Magnetic Rag SJMC–MMC 1914
Reflection Rag—Syncopated Musings JSAS 1917

INSTRUCTION BOOK:

School of Ragtime   JSAS   1908

OPERAS:

A Guest of Honor—A Ragtime Opera, Book by Scott Joplin—unpublished 1903

Treemonisha—Opera in Three Acts, Book by Scott Joplin   SJMC   1911

SYNCOPATED WALTZES:

Bethena—A Concert Waltz   TBP   1905
Pleasant Moments   SMCNY   1909

SONGS:

I'm Thinking of My Pickaninny Days (words by Henry Jackson)   TS   1902
The Rag Time Dance (words by Scott Joplin)   JSAS   1902
Little Black Baby (words by Louise Armstrong Bristol)   SMC   1903
Maple Leaf Rag Song (words by Sydney Brown)   JSAS   1904
Sarah Dear (words by Henry Jackson)   TBP   1905
When Your Hair Is like the Snow (words by Owen Spendthrift)   OSSL   1907
Pineapple Rag Song (words by Joe Snyder)   SMCNY   1910
A Real Slow Drag (from *Treemonisha*)   SJMC   1913
Frolic of the Bears (from *Treemonisha*) Bass with Mixed Chorus   SJMC   1915

RAGS WRITTEN IN COLLABORATION WITH OTHERS:

Swipesy Cake Walk (with Arthur Marshall)   JSAS   1900
Sunflower Slow Drag (with Scott Hayden)   JSAS   1901
Something Doing (with Scott Hayden)   VAR   1903
Heliotrope Bouquet (with Louis Chauvin)   JSAS   1907
Lily Queen (with Arthur Marshall)   WWS   1907
Felicity Rag (with Scott Hayden)   JSAS   1911
Kismet Rag (with Scott Hayden)   JSAS   1913

MISCELLANEOUS:

A Picture of Her Face—Waltz Song   LBS   1895
Please Say You Will—Waltz Song   MLM   1895
The (Great) Crush Collision March—Piano Solo   JRF   1896
Combination March—Piano Solo   RS   1896
Harmony Club Waltz—Piano Solo   RS   1896
Augustan Club Waltzes—Piano Solo   JSAS   1901
March Majestic—6/8 March Piano Solo   JSAS   1902
Cleopha Two Step—Piano Solo   SSL   1902
Rosebud March—6/8 March Piano Solo   JSAS   1905
Binks Waltz—Piano Solo   TBP   1905
Antoinette—6/8 March Piano Solo   JSAS   1906
Silver Swan Rag (found on piano roll, 1970)

ARRANGEMENTS:

Snoring Sampson (ragtime song by Harry La Mertha)   UM   1907
Sensation Rag (by Joseph F. Lamb)   JSAS   1908

281

MUSICAL COMPOSITIONS

SURVIVING UNPUBLISHED MANUSCRIPTS:

Pretty Pansy Rag (incomplete song)   . . . .
Confidence Rag (incomplete song)   . . . .
Confidence Rag (piano arrangement from song)
Treemonisha (orchestrations)   . . . .
For the Sake of All (incomplete ragtime song)   . . . .
Magnetic Rag (incomplete song)   . . . .
Pretty Pansy Rag (incomplete song orchestration)   . . . .
Search Light Rag (incomplete orchestration)   . . . .
Recitative Rag (incomplete orchestration)   . . . .
Morning Glory (incomplete song)   . . . .
Stoptime Rag (incomplete orchestration)   . . . .

JAMES SCOTT

RAGS (*Piano Solo*):

A Summer Breeze—March and Two Step   DDG   1903
The Fascinator—March   DDG   1903
On the Pike—March and Two Step   DDG   1904
Frog Legs Rag   JSAS   1906
Kansas City Rag   JSAS   1907
Great Scott Rag   AMCC   1909
The Ragtime Betty   JSAS   1909
Sunburst Rag   JSAS   1909
Grace and Beauty   JSAS   1910
Hilarity Rag   JSAS   1910
Ophelia Rag   JSAS   1910
Quality—A High Class Rag   JSAS   1911
The Ragtime Oriole   JSAS   1911
Climax Rag   JSAS   1914
Evergreen Rag   JSAS   1915
Honeymoon Rag   JSAS   1916
Prosperity Rag   JSAS   1916
Efficiency Rag   JSAS   1917
Paramount Rag   JSAS   1917
Rag Sentimental   JSAS   1918
New Era Rag   JSAS   1919
Troubadour Rag   JSAS   1919
Princess Rag   JSAS   1919
Peace and Plenty Rag   JSAS   1919
Dixie Dimples—Ragtime Fox Trot   IS   1919
Pegasus—A Classic Rag   JSAS   1920
Modesty Rag—A Classic   JSAS   1920
Don't Jazz Me—Rag (I'm Music)   JSAS   1921
Victory Rag   JSAS   1921
Broadway Rag—A Classic   JSAS   1922

SONGS:

She's My Girl from Anaconda (words by Dumars)   DDG   1909
Sweetheart Time (words by Dumars)   DDG   1909
Take Me Out to Lakeside (words by Ida Miller)   BMC   1914
The Shimmie Shake (words by Cleota Wilson)   JSAS   1920

WALTZES:

Hearts Longing Waltzes   JSAS   1910
Suffragette Waltz   JSAS   1914
Springtime of Love, Valse   IS   1919

ORCHESTRAL ARRANGEMENT:

The Fascinator—March and Two Step (arranged by E. W. Berry)   EWB   1912

JOSEPH LAMB   *Selected List of Compositions*

RAGS (*Piano Solo*):

Sensation—A Rag (arranged by Scott Joplin)   JSAS   1908
Excelsior Rag   JSAS   1909
Ethiopia Rag   JSAS   1909
Champagne Rag—March and Two Step   JSAS   1910
American Beauty Rag   JSAS   1913
Cleopatra Rag   JSAS   1915
The Ragtime Nightingale   JSAS   1915
Contentment Rag   JSAS   1915
Reindeer—Ragtime Two Step   JSAS   1915
Patricia Rag   JSAS   1916
Top Liner Rag   JSAS   1916
Bohemia Rag   JSAS   1919

WALTZES:

Celestine Waltzes (Piano Solo)   HHST

SONGS:

Gee, Kid! But I Like You (words by Jos. F. Lamb)   MS   1908
Love in Absence (words by Mary A. O'Reilly)   1909
I'll Follow the Crowd to Coney (words by Mrs. G. Satterlee)   GS   1913
I Want to be a Birdman (words by Mrs. G. Satterlee)   GS   1913
   Note: There are many other songs by Joseph F. Lamb

UNPUBLISHED RAGS WRITTEN FROM 1907 to 1914:

Alabama—A Characteristic Two-Step
Bee Hive Rag
Blue Grass Rag (incomplete)
Dynamite Rag
Good and Plenty Rag
Greased Lightning
Hyacinth, A Rag

MUSICAL COMPOSITIONS

Jersey Rag, The
Old Home Rag, A Syncopated Characteristic
Rag Time Special, The—A Slow Drag Two Step (*Respectfully dedicated to my Friend, Scott Joplin*)
Rapid Transit—A Slow Drag
Sunset, A Ragtime Serenade
Symphonic Syncopations (incomplete)
Toad Stool Rag

RAGS BOUGHT BY MILLS MUSIC BUT UNPUBLISHED
(All the following MMC)

All Wet
Apple Sauce
Banana Oil
The Berries
Brown Derby
Chime In
Cinders
Crimson Ramblers
Knick Knacks
Ripples
Shooting the Works
Soup and Fish
Sweet Pickles
Waffles
   Note: There is one more in this series, title unknown.

EUBIE BLAKE   *Selected List of Compositions*

RAGS (*Piano Solo*):

Charleston Rag (copyright 1917)   circa   1899
Chevy Chase   JWS-EBM   1914
Fizz Water   JWS-EBM   1914
Troublesome Ivories   Unpublished   circa   1914
Bugle Call Rag   Unpublished   1916
Black Keys on Parade   WCH   1935

SONGS: (*words by Noble Sissle*):

It's All Your Fault (words by Sissle and Eddie Nelson)   MMPC   1915
I'm Just Wild About Harry   MWAS   1921
Love Will Find a Way   MWAS   1921
Bandanna Days   MWAS   1921
Gypsy Blues   MWAS   1921
Manda   TBH   1924
Thinking of Me   TBH   1924
Dixie Moon   TBH   1924

284

GEORGE BOTSFORD: *Selected List of Rags*

The Katy Flyer—Cakewalk Two Step GB 1899
Black and White Rag WWR 1908
Klondike Rag DAH 1908
Pianophiends Rag WMH 1909
Texas Steer Rag WWR 1909
The Big Jubilee—March and Two Step WWR 1909
Old Crow Rag WWR 1909
Wiggle Rag WWR 1909
Fat Men on Parade WWR 1909
Chatterbox Rag WWR 1910
Grizzly Bear Rag (words by Irving Berlin) WWR 1910
Lovey-Dovey Rag TSNY-MMC 1910
Hyacinthe Rag WWR 1911
Honeysuckle Rag WWR 1911
Royal Flush Rag WWR 1911
Eskimo Rag (words by Jean C. Havez) GB 1912
Buckeye Rag—Stoptime Dance Unpublished 1913
Incandescent Rag WWR 1913
Rag, Baby Mine WWR 1913
Universal Rag Unpublished 1913
Sailing Down the Chesapeake Bay—Rag Song (words by Jean C. Havez) WWR
    1913
Boomerang Rag WWR 1916

THOMAS E. BROADY:

Mandy's Broadway Stroll—A Genuine Ragtime March HAF 1898
A Tennessee Jubilee HAF 1899
Whittling Remus HAF 1900

LOUIS CHAUVIN

RAG (*Piano Solo*):

Heliotrope Bouquet (in collaboration with Scott Joplin) JSAS 1907

SONGS:

The Moon is Shining in the Skies (in collaboration with Sam Patterson) SZM
    1903
Babe, It's Too Long Off (words by Elmer Bowman) MWAS 1906
Dandy Coon—Musical Revue (in collaboration with Sam Patterson)
    Unpublished 1903

ROBERT HAMPTON

RAGS (*Piano Solo*):

The Dogin' Rag—Ragtime Song (words by Frank Gray) JSAS 1913
Cataract Rag JSAS 1914
Agitation Rag JSAS 1915

285

MUSICAL COMPOSITIONS

BENJAMIN ROBERTSON HARNEY

RAGTIME SONGS: (*Words and Music by Ben R. Harney unless otherwise noted*)

You've Been a Good Old Wagon But You've Done Broke Down (arr. by Johnny Biller) BGM—1895 MWAS—1896
Mr. Johnson (Turn Me Loose) FKH 1896
Mr. Johnson Turn Me Loose MWAS 1896
I Love My Honey MWAS 1897
There's A Knocker Layin' Around FAM 1897
You May Go But This Will Bring You Back FAM 1898
If You Got Any Sense You'll Go MWAS 1898
Draw That Color Line FAM 1898
The Cake-Walk in the Sky MWAS 1899
Tell It to Me MWAS 1899
The Hat He Never Ate (words by Howard S. Taylor) HMCC 1899
The Black Man's Kissing Bug MWAS 1899
The Only Way to Keep Her is in a Cage JJK 1901
T.T.T. ("Treat, Trade or Travel") HHD 1903
There's Only One Way to Keep a Gal (arr. by W. R. Dorsey) BRH Unpub. 1914
Cannon Ball Catcher (arr. by W. R. Dorsey) BRH Unpublished 1914

INSTRUCTION BOOK:

Ben Harney's Rag Time Instructor SB-MWAS 1897

ORCHESTRAL ARRANGEMENT:

I Love My Little Honey (arranged by W. H. Mackie) MWAS 1899

RAGTIME SONGS (*publishers and copyright dates unknown*)

I Love One Sweet Black Man
The Sporting Life is Sure Killing Me
That Ever Lovin' Rock Pile
Tomahau
Li Hung Chang
While in Chicago
If the Gal Was Mine
Wissahickon

SCOTT HAYDEN:

See Scott Joplin. All Hayden rags are in collaboration with Joplin.

CHARLES H. HUNTER

Tickle to Death—Ragtime March and Two Step FGF 1899
A Tennessee Tantalizer HAF 1900
'Possum and 'Taters—A Ragtime Feast HAF 1901

286

Cotton Bolls FGF-AKH 1901
Queen of Love—Two Step HAF 1901
Just Ask Me FGF 1902
Why We Smile FGF 1903
Back to Life CKH 1905
Seraphine Waltzes JSAS 1905

TONY JACKSON *Selected List of Compositions*

RAGS (*Piano Solo*):

The Naked Dance (c. 1902, recorded by Jelly Roll Morton on General and Circle Records)
Michigan Water (exists only in arrangement by Jelly Roll Morton on Circle and General Records)
Pick-It Boy (mentioned in *Rag Time Review*, 1917, MS. never found)

SONGS:

The Clock of Time (1904, Louisville, Ky.) in collaboration with Glover Compton Unpublished
You're Such a Pretty Thing (circa 1915) Unpublished
Pretty Baby, in collaboration with Egbert Van Alstyne, (words by Gus Kahn) WWR 1916
Miss Samantha Johnson's Wedding Day (words by Tony Jackson) FKR 1916
I've Got 'Em (words by Jack Frost) FKR 1916
Waiting at the Old Church Door (words by Tony Jackson) FKR 1916
I've Been Fiddle-ing, in collaboration with Egbert Van Alstyne (words by Gus Kahn) WWR 1917
Some Sweet Day (with Abe Olman and Ed Rose) FMP 1917
Don't Leave Me in the Ice and Snow WRC 1917
Why Keep Me Waiting So Long WRC 1917
When Your Troubles Will Be Just Like Mine (unpublished, MS. never found) 1917
I'm Cert'n'y Gonna See 'Bout That CW 1921

CHARLES L. JOHNSON *Selected List of Compositions*

RAGS (*Piano Solo*):

Scandalous Thompson—Cake Walk JWJ 1899
Doc Brown's Cake Walk JWJ 1899
Black Smoke—Dance Characteristic CH 1902
Beedle-um-Bolo Slow Drag (as Raymond Birch) SB 1903
Dill Pickles Rag WWR-MMC 1906
Fine and Dandy AD-WWR 1907
All the Money (as Raymond Birch) CLJ 1908
Porcupine Rag MWAS 1909
Apple Jack (Some Rag) VM 1909
Lady Slippers Rag (as Raymond Birch) CLJ 1910

Yankee Bird (as Raymond Birch)   CLJ   1910
Golden Spider Rag   VM   1910
Cum-Bac Rag   WWR   1911
Melody Rag (as Raymond Birch)   CLJ   1911
Barber Pole Rag   GNC   1911
Tar Babies Rag   CLJ   1911
Swanee Rag   SF   1912
Hen Cackle Rag   JWJ   1912
Crazy Bone Rag   FMP   1913
Peek-a-boo Rag   FMP   1914
Pink Poodle   FMP   1914
Alabama Slide   FMP   1915
Blue Goose Rag (as Raymond Birch)   FMP   1916
Teasing the Cat   FMP   1916
Fun on the Levee—Cake Walk   FMP   1917
Snookums Rag   FMP   1918

INDIAN INTERMEZZOS:

Iola (words by Jas. O'Dea)   WWR   1906
Silver Star   JWJ   1911

SYNCOPATED WALTZ:

Tobasco—Rag Time Waltz   WWR   1909

SONGS:

It Takes a Coon to Do the Rag Time Dance (words by Robert Penick)   GPC
1899
I'm Goin', Goodbye, I'm Gone (words by Charles L. Johnson)   FMP   1912
Sweet and Low (words by J. Stanley Royce)   FMP   1919

JAMES P. JOHNSON   *Selected List of Compositions*

RAGS (*Piano Solo*):

Caprice Rag   MMC   1914
Daintiness Rag   MMC   1916
Harlem Strut   MMC   1917
After Hours   MMC   1923
Jungle Nymphs   MMC   1924
Carolina Shout   CW   1925
Keep Off the Grass   CW   1926
Jingles   CW   1926
Scouting Around   PB   1927
Toddlin' (Home)   PB   1927
You've Got to be Modernistic   CW   1930
Riffs   ACM   1930
Over the Bars (or Steeple Chase)   CW   1936
Just Before Daybreak   MMC   1942

SYNCOPATED WALTZ:

Eccentricity Waltz CW 1926

BLUES:

Mama and Papa Blues FBH 1916
You Can't Do What My Last Man Did (words by A. Moore) JPJ 1923
Snowy Morning Blues PB 1927

SONGS:

Stop It Joe (words by William Farrell) FBH 1917
Old Fashioned Love (words by Cecil Mack) TBH 1923
Charleston (words by Cecil Mack) TBH 1923
If I Could Be With You One Hour Tonight WWR 1926
Slippery Hips (words by Andy Razaf) JDNY 1930
Aintcha Got Music (words by Andy Razaf) WCH 1932

SYMPHONIC AND CHAMBER WORKS:

Yamecraw, for Orchestra with Chorus and Soloists AAC 1928
Harlem Symphony RMC 1932
Jasmine (Jazz-o-Mine) Concerto MMC 1935
Old Time Suite MMC 1942

PIANO ARRANGEMENTS FROM SYMPHONIC WORKS:

Reflections—Tone Poem MMC 1935
Jasmine Concerto—Second Movement MMC 1949

JOE JORDAN *Selected List of Compositions*

RAGS (*Piano Solo*):

Double Fudge—Ragtime Two Step HUN 1902
Nappy Lee—A Slow Drag JEA 1903
Pekin Rag, Intermezzo PPCC 1904
J.J.J. Rag PPCC 1905
Salome Dance Unpublished 1908
The Darkey Todalo—A Raggedy Rag HVT 1910

SONGS:

Oh Say Wouldn't It Be a Dream (words Earl C. Jones) CKH 1905
Sweetie Dear PPCC 1906
I'm Going to Exit WRC 1907
Rise and Shine PPCC 1908
Oh Liza Lady PPCC 1908
Dixie Land PPCC 1908
Lovie Joe (words by Will Marion Cook) HVT 1910
That Raggedy Rag—Ragtime Dance Song HVT 1910
Brother-in-law Dan Unpublished
Dat's Ma Honey Sho's Yo' Born WRC 1912

289

MUSICAL COMPOSITIONS

HENRY LODGE   *Selected List of Compositions*

Ole South—Plantation Dance for Piano   VMBC   1909
Skylark—An Intermezzo for Piano   NW   1909
Temptation Rag   MWAS   1909
Sneaky Shuffles Rag   WWR   1910
Sure Fire Rag   VK   1910
Red Pepper—Spicy Rag   MWAS   1910
Roulette Reel   MWAS   1911
Black Diamond Rag—A Rag Sparkler   MWAS   1912
Moonlight Rag   MWAS   1913
Pastime Rag   MWAS   1913
Oh! You Turkey—A Rag Trot   MMC   1914
Demi-Tasse   WBS-MMC   1914
Hill and Dale—Syncopated Fox Trot   MRMC   1915
Silver Fox—A Raggy Fox Trot   WWR   1915
Wireless Wavelets—An Electrical Musical Novelty   MMC   1923
Bunny Hug   MWAS   1928

SYNCOPATED WALTZES:

Fascination Waltz   MMC   1914
The Boston Stop—Hesitation Waltz   WBS   1914

ARTHUR MARSHALL

RAGS (*Piano Solo*):

Kinklets—Two Step   JSAS   1906
Ham and—Rag   JSAS   1908
The Peach—Ragtime Two Step   JSAS   1908
The Pippin Rag   JSAS   1908
Silver Arrow Rag   Unpublished—Copyright A. Marshall   1950
National Prize Rag   Unpublished—Copyright A. Marshall   1950
Missouri Romp—A Slow Drag   Unpublished—Copyright A. Marshall   1950

RAGS WRITTEN IN COLLABORATION WITH SCOTT JOPLIN:

Swipesy Cake Walk   JSAS   1900
The Lily Queen   WW   1907

ARTIE MATTHEWS

RAGS (*Piano Solo*):

Pastime Rag No. 1   JSAS   1913
Pastime Rag No. 2   JSAS   1913
The Weary Blues   JSAS   1915
Pastime Rag No. 3   JSAS   1916
Pastime Rag No. 5   JSAS   1918
Pastime Rag No. 4   JSAS   1920

290

SONGS:

Give Me, Dear, Just One More Chance (words by Ford H. Hayes) TS 1908
Twilight Dreams (words by H. Inman) AGA 1912
Wise Old Moon (words by George S. Tiernan) AGA 1912
Everybody Makes Love to Someone (words by P. Franzi) AGA 1912
Lucky Dan, My Gamblin' Man (words by Chas. A. Hunter) PBC 1913
The Princess Prance (words by Chas. A. Hunter) PBC 1913
When I'm Gone (words by Chas. A. Hunter) PBC 1913
Old Oak Tree by the Wayside (words by T. Hiibren Schaefer) PBC 1913
Everything He Does Just Pleases Me JSAS 1916

ARRANGEMENTS:

Baby Seals Blues SAF 1912
Well, If I Do, Don't You Let It Get Out—by Baby Seals SAF 1912

FERDINAND (JELLY ROLL) MORTON *Selected List of Compositions*

(Note: Many Morton compositions were composed a number of years before being copyrighted.)

RAGS (*Piano Solo*):

Superior Rag Unpublished circa 1915
Frog-i-more Rag FJM-TM 1918–46
The Pearls MBMC 1923
Grandpa's Spells MBMC 1923
Kansas City Stomps MBMC 1923
King Porter Stomp MBMC 1924
Milenberg Joys (with Leon Rappolo and Paul Mares) MBMC 1925
Shreveport Stomps MBMC 1925
Midnight Mama MBMC 1925
Chicago Breakdown MBMC 1926
Black Bottom Stomp MBMC 1926
Ham and Eggs TMU 1928
Boogaboo MBMC 1928
Freakish SMLO Unpublished 1929
Seattle Hunch SMLO Unpublished 1929
Turtle Twist SMLO Unpublished 1930
Ponchartrain SMLO Unpublished 1930
Fickle Fay Creep SMLO Unpublished 1931
Fat Frances SMLO Unpublished 1931
Pep SMLO Unpublished 1931
Gambling Jack SMLO Unpublished 1932
Crazy Chords SMLO Unpublished 1932
Sweet Peter SMLO Unpublished 1933
Mister Joe TM Unpublished 1939
The Naked Dance (arr. of a Tony Jackson rag) TM Unpublished 1939
The Finger Breaker TM Unpublished 1942

MUSICAL COMPOSITIONS

Bert Williams FJM Estate Unpublished 1948
Albert Carroll's Blues (Rag) FJM Estate Unpublished 1949
Crazy Chord Rag FJM Estate Unpublished 1949
Buddy Carter's Rag FJM Estate Unpublished 1949
The Perfect Rag FJM Estate Unpublished 1949

INSTRUMENTAL BLUES:

The (Original) Jelly Roll Blues WRC 1915
Wolverine Blues (also as song, words by Spikes Bros.) MBMC 1923
London Blues MBMC 1923
New Orleans Blues MBMC 1925
Sidewalk Blues MBMC 1926
Cannonball Blues MBMC 1926
Deep Creek Blues SMLO Unpublished 1930

VOCAL BLUES:

The Winin' Boy TM Unpublished 1939
Buddy Bolden's Blues TM Unpublished 1939
Don't You Leave Me Here TM Unpublished
Mamie's Blues TM 1948

INSTRUMENTAL TANGOS:

The Crave TM Unpublished 1939
Creepy Feeling TM Unpublished 1944
Spanish Swat FJM Estate Unpublished 1948
Mama 'nita FJM Estate Unpublished 1949

SONGS:

Mr. Jelly Lord MBMC 1923
My Home is in a Southern Town TM 1938
Sweet Substitute TM 1938
I'm Alabama Bound FJM Unpublished 1939
Anamule Dance TM Unpublished 1939
Jazz Jamboree Unpublished circa 1938

PAUL PRATT *Selected List of Compositions*

RAGS (*Piano Solo*):

Vanity Rag JHA 1909
Walhalla—A Two Step Rag JHA 1910
Colonial Glide JHA 1910
Hot House Rag JSAS 1914
Everybody Tango MCK 1914
Springtime Rag JSAS 1916
On the Rural Route JSAS 1917

SONGS:

That Ever Lovin' Bearcat Prance (words by Paul Pratt) JHA 1911
Moontime is Spoontime (words by Paul Pratt) JHA 1911
That Gosh Darn Hiram Tune (words by J. Will Callahan) JSAS 1912
Gasoline (words by J. Will Callahan) FKR 1913
I'm Going Back to Birmingham (words by J. W. Callahan) FKR 1913

LUCKEY ROBERTS *Selected List of Compositions*

RAGS (*Piano Solo*):

Junk Man Rag JWS 1913
Pork and Beans JWS 1913
Music Box Rag JWS 1914
Palm Beach JWS 1914
Shy and Sly CR 1915
Helter Skelter CR 1915
Ripples of the Nile
Mo'Lasses SBC 1923
Park Avenue Polka CLR 1949

PIANO SOLOS—MISCELLANEOUS:

Spanish Venus—Tango Unpublished
Railroad Blues VAC 1920

SONGS:

Rockaway with Howard Johnson and Alex Rogers LF 1917
Billy Boy (words by Lester A. Walton) WP-JWS 1917
Go-Go Bug (words by Alex Rogers) SBC 1923
Leaping Leopards (words by Alex Rogers) SBC 1923
Mo'Lasses (words by Alex Rogers) SBC 1923
Magnolia (words by Alex Rogers) RAB 1926
Moonlight Cocktail (words by Kim Gannon) JMNY 1941
Massachusetts MBNY 1942
Exclusively With You CLR 1949

SYMPHONIC WORKS:

Whistlin' Pete—Miniature Syncopated Rhapsody for Piano and Orchestra
   Unpublished circa 1939
Spanish Suite:
                Spanish Venus
                Spanish Fandango
                Porto Rico Maid
                     For Piano and Orchestra Unpublished circa 1939

J. RUSSEL ROBINSON *Selected List of Compositions*

RAGS (*Piano Solo*):

Sapho Rag JSAS 1909
Dynamite Rag—a Negro Drag SCMC 1910

MUSICAL COMPOSITIONS

The Minstrel Man—Ragtime Two Step JSAS 1911
Whirlwind Rag JSAS 1911
Erratic Rag MMC 1911
Daphne Two Step CKH 1911
That Eccentric Rag IS-MMC 1912

SONGS:

On the Eight O'Clock Train (words by M. Kendall) IS 1912
Te-Na-Na (words by M. Kendall) IS 1912
Margie, written with B. David and Con Conrad WBS-MMC 1920
Aggravatin' Papa (words by R. Turk) MMC 1922
St. Louis Gal WBS 1923

RUSSELL SMITH

RAGS (*Piano Solo*):

Princess—Two Step Oriental WM 1908
That Demon Rag IS 1912
Everybody Knows I Love Him IS 1918

E. J. STARK *Selected List of Compositions*

RAGS (*Piano Solo*):

Trombone Johnsen JSAS 1902
Darktown Capers JSAS
Kyrene JSAS 1904
Brainstorm Rag (as Bud Manchester) JSAS 1907
Clover Blossoms Rag (as Bud Manchester) JSAS 1912
Billiken JSAS 1913
La Mode—Dance Sensation (in collaboration with V. R. Whitlow) JSAS
    1913
Chicken Tango JSAS 1914
Gum Shoe Fox Trot JSAS 1917

SONGS:

Bryan and Sewell—Free Silver (words by E. J. Stark) JSAS 1896
We Are Coming, Uncle Sammy (words by John Stark) JSAS 1917

WALTZ:

Valse Pensive JSAS 1913

LIGHT OPERA:

The Vital Question (book by E. J. Stark, music by John Stark) JSAS 1913

CHARLES THOMPSON

RAGS (*Piano Solo*):

The Lily SMSL 1914
Rag Time Humming Bird Unpublished

Deep Lawton   Unpublished
Hop Alley Dream   Unpublished
Mound City Walk Around   Unpublished
Buffet Flat Rag   Unpublished

TOM TURPIN

RAGS (*Piano Solo*):

Harlem Rag   RDY-JWS   1897
The Bowery Buck   RDY   1899
A Ragtime Nightmare   RDY   1900
St. Louis Rag   SB   1903
The Buffalo Rag   WRC   1904
Siwash, Indian Rag Intermezzo   Unpublished   1909
Pan-Am Rag (arr. by Arthur Marshall)   Unpublished   1914
When Sambo Goes to France (arr. by J. H. Harris)   Unpublished   1917

THOMAS (FATS) WALLER   *Selected List of Compositions*

RAGS (*Piano Solo*):

Wildcat Blues (Rag)   CW   1923
St. Louis Shuffle (with Jack Pettis)   RE   1927
Valentine Stomp   SMLO   1929
Handful of Keys   SMLO   1930
Smashing Thirds   SMLO   1931
Fractious Fingering   SF   1938
Bach Up to Me   SF   1938
Black Raspberry Jam   SF   1938
Latch On   SF   1938
Paswonky   SF   1938
Happy Feeling   GMU   1940
China Jumps   GMU   1941
Sneakin' Home   GMU   1941
Palm Garden   GMU   1941
Wandrin' Aroun'   GMU   1941
Falling Castle   GMU   1941

PIANO BLUES:

Chinese Blues   MMC   1926
Numb Fumblin'   SMLO   1935

ORGAN SOLOS:

The Rusty Pail   RSP   1927
Lenox Avenue Blues   RSP   1927
Hog Maw Stomp   RSP   1928

SONGS:

Squeeze Me (with Clarence Williams)   CW   1925
Darkies' Lament   AGA-MMC   1927

Come On and Stomp Stomp Stomp (with Chris Smith and Irving Mills) MMC
1927
(What Did I Do to Be So) Black and Blue (with Andy Razaf and Harry Brooks)
MMC 1929
Blue, Turning Grey Over You (words by Andy Razaf) JDNY 1929
My Fate Is In Your Hands (words by Andy Razaf) SBNY 1929
I've Got a Feeling I'm Falling (with Billy Rose and Harry Link) SBNY 1929
Ain't Misbehavin' (with Andy Razaf and Harry Brooks) MMC 1929
Honeysuckle Rose (words by Andy Razaf) SBNY 1929
I'm Crazy 'Bout My Baby (words by Alexander Hill) JDNY 1931
Stealin' Apples (words by Andy Razaf) MMC 1936

SUITES:

London Suite LGC 1948
Harlem Living Room Suite:

> *Functionizin'* MMC 1935
> *Corn Whiskey Cocktail* Unpublished
> *Scrimmage* Unpublished

PERCY WENRICH *Selected List of Compositions*

RAGS *(Piano Solo)*:

Ashy Africa—An African Rag BC 1903
Peaches and Cream Rag WWR 1905
Noodles—A German Rag AD 1906
Chestnuts—Rag Medley AD 1906
The Smiler—A Joplin Rag FMP 1907
Fun Bob AD 1907
Sweet Meats Rag AD 1907
Dixie Darlings—Rag Two Step MCK 1907
Bom Bay WRC 1907
Flower Girl AD 1907
Crab Apples—Rag Two Step BB 1908
Persian Lamb Rag—Pepperette WJ 1908
Memphis Rag MCK 1908
Ragtime Ripples MCK 1908
Ragtime Chimes WWR 1911
Sunflower Rag WWR 1911
Whipped Cream—A Rag WHC 1913
Steeple Chase MCK 1916

SONGS:

Wabash Avenue After Dark (words by James O'Dea) Unpublished 1903–5
Put On Your Old Grey Bonnet (words by Stanley Murphy) WWR 1909
Alamo Rag (words by Ben Deely) WWR 1910
Red Rose Rag (words by Edward Madden) WWR 1911
Kentucky Days (words by Jack Mahoney) WHC 1912

Ragtime Turkey Trot (words by Julian Eltinge and Jack Mahoney)   WHC
   1913
When You Wore a Tulip and I Wore a Big Red Rose (words by Jack Mahoney)
   LF   1914
Come Back, Dixie (words by Jack Mahoney)   1915
Sweet Cider Time, When You Were Mine (words by Joe McCarthy)   LF   1916
Where Do We Go From Here (words by Howard Johnson)   LF   1917
What's the Matter With the Mail (words by Fred J. Hamill)   FJH

MISCELLANEOUS INSTRUMENTAL:

L'Inconnu—6/8 Two Step   SB   c.   1897

CLARENCE WOODS   *Selected List of Compositions*

RAGS (*Piano Solo*):

Meteor March   DDG   1903
Slippery Elm Rag   CWF   1912
Graveyard Blues (words by John S. Caldwell) Song   WL-JWS   1917
Sleepy Hollow Rag   WL   1918

SECTION ONE -- ADDENDA FOR THIRD EDITION

SCOTT JOPLIN   (In collaboration with Joseph F. Lamb)
"Scott Joplin's Dream" (first published in this edition) Copyright by
Mrs. Joseph F. FLamb and Robert R. Darch

JAMES SCOTT
"Calliope Rag" (circa 1910) Copyright by Robert R. Darch. Note: Darch
reports that this rag in incomplete MS was given him by a sister of Scott,
with the information that "Scott played it on the steam calliope at Lakeside Park, between Carthage and Joplin, Mo." The score was completed
by Darch and edited by Donald Ashwander.

SCOTT HAYDEN
"Pear Blossoms" (1899-1900) Copyright by Robert R. Darch. Note: Darch
reports this rag, from Hayden's Sedalia highschool days, was given him
by the late Tom Ireland. In MS, it was thematically complete but only
partly harmonized and without a bass part. The score was completed by
Darch and edited by Donald Ashwander.

JOSEPH F. LAMB
Note: These posthumous addenda fill out the Lamb piano oeuvre as now
known. (There are 51 known unpublished songs, not listed here.)
Copyright symbols: JFL—Joseph F. Lamb; RD—Robert Darch; ALRD -
(Mrs.) Amelia Lamb and Robert Darch.

MUSICAL COMPOSITIONS

RAGTIME TREASURES

An album of Lamb rags published posthumously by Mills Music Inc. in 1964. Mostly of early composition, 1908-1914, Lamb reworked them late "Alabama Rag" -- "Bird-Brain Rag" -- "Blue Grass Rag" -- "Chimes of Dixie" -- Cottontail Rag" -- "Firefly Rag" -- "Good and Plenty Rag "Hot Cinders" -- "The Old Home Rag" -- "Ragtime Bobolink" -- "Thoroughbred Rag" -- "Toad Stool Rag." -- "Arctic Sunset."

ADDITIONAL PIANO SOLOS

Note: unpublished except as noted. Dates in parenthesis are those of composition; other dates are those of publication.
"Alaskan Rag" (first published in this edition) RD 1959
"Chasin' the Chippies -- Characteristic Two-Step" (1914) ALRD 1961
"Doin' the Lonesome Slow Drag" (arranged by Eubie Blake) n.d.
"Don't You Be Lonely" (arranged by Eubie Blake) n.d.
"Florentine Waltzes" (published) HHST 1906
"Florida" (1905) ALRD 1962
"Golden Leaves -- Canadian Concert Waltzes" (1903) ALRD 1961
"I'd Like You To Love Me" (arranged by Eubie Blake) n.d.
"Ilo-Ilo" (arranged by Eubie Blake) ALRD 1962
"I'm Going To Go Somewhere" n.d.
"I Should Have Known" n.d.
"Joe Lamb's Medley Overture No. 1." (1908) ALRD 1962
"Joe Lamb's Medley Overture No. 2." ALRD 1962
"Joe Lamb's Old Rag" (original title: "Dynamite Rag") RD 1959
"Le Premier -- French-Canadian March - Two Step" (1903) ALRD 19
"The Lilliputians' Bazaar" (published) HHST 1905
"Lorne Scots on Parade" (1904) ALRD 1961
"Mignonne -- Valse Lente" ("Inscribed to my Mother") (1901) ALRD
"Muskoka Falls -- Indian Idyl" (1902) ALRD 1961
"My Queen of Zanzibar -- A Serenade" (piano version 1904) ALRD 19
"Rapid Rapids Rag" (1905) ALRD 1962
"Red Feather -- March Intermezzo" (1906) ALRD 1961
"Since You Took Your Heart Away" ALRD 1961
"Sourdough March" (1906) ALRD 1962
"Spanish Fly Rag" (1912) ALRD 1962
"22nd Regiment March" ALRD 1962
"Walper House Rag" (1903) ALRD 1962

RAGTIME SINCE 1950: A SELECTION

JOHN ARPIN

"Centennial Rag" (on Canadian themes) JA 1964

298

DONALD ASHWANDER

"Business in Town" (Composed for this edition) DA 1966
"Friday Night -- A Piano Rag" (first published in this edition) DA 1966
 "Ragime Pierrot" DA 1965

JAKI BYARD

"Harlem Femininity" n.d.
"Just Rollin' Along" JB 1963
"European Suite for Piano and Orchestra" (1965) includes the
     following piano ragtime sections:
"Galop" (1960); "One Step" (1957); "Ragtime Waltz" (1957-58)

ROBERT DARCH

(unless otherwise noted published by Ragtime Music Publishing Co.,
Virginia City, Nev.)

"Arctic Circle Cakewalk" n.d.
"Calico Queens" n.d.
"Capitol Saloon Rag" n.d.
"Carson City Rag" n.d.
"Cedar Street Rag" n.d.
"Chapeaux Bas March-Two Step" n.d.
"Delta Saloon Rag" n.d.
"Eads Bridge Rag" n.d.
"Flicker Red" Cornish Music n.d.
"Old Washoe Club Rag" n.d.
"Sandy Bowers' Mansion" n.d.
"That V & T Railroad Rag" n.d.
"Foolin' Around" n.d.
"Hastings Street Rag" n.d.
"Nickels and Dimes" n.d.
"Port the Helm" n.d.
"Profanity Hill Rag" n.d.
"South Franklin Street Rag" n.d.
"Stir the Porridge" n.d.
"That Seward Rag" n.d.
"The Swisher" n.d.
"The Kobuk Maiden" Cornish n.d.
"Suicide Table Rag" n.d.
"That Virginia City Rag" n.d.
"Opera House Rag" (arr. by Jos. F. Lamb) (in this edition) n.d.

TEDDIE BETH HARDY

"The Good Years" Hollis Music Inc., New York 1964

MUSICAL COMPOSITIONS

PETER LUNDBERG

"Gothenburg Rag" (composed for this edition) PL 1966
"Hippocampus Two-Step" Hollis Music Inc., New York 1964
"Lundberg Special" PL 1965
"Smorgasbord Rag" copyright by Robert Darch n.d.

JORGE D. MILLS

"Danse Orientale" JDM 1964
"Krazy Kat" JDM 1964
"The Carousel" JDM 1964

MAX MORATH

"Cakewalkin' Shoes" (song) Hollis Music Inc., 1964
"Gold Bar Rag" Hollis Music Inc., 1964
"The Golden Hours" ("To the memory of Harriet Janis")
    (composed for this edition) Hollis Music Inc., 1966
"One For Amelia" Hollis Music Inc., 1964
"Polyragmic" Hollis Music Inc., 1964
"Tribute to Joplin" (based on Joplin themes) Hollis Music Inc., 1964

TONY PARENTI

"Moonlight In New Orleans" (song) TP 1952
"Picture of Love" (song)   TP 1953
"Praline" (piano -- composed 1947) TP 1953
"Praline" (song -- words by James P. Johnson) TP 1952
"The City of the Blues" Art Masterpiece Society 1952
"Tony's Rag" Art Masterpiece Society 1952
"Vieux Carre NOLA" Art Masterpiece Society 1952
(The following earlier Parenti compositions are included here for
completeness)
"Cabaret Echoes" (composed 1924) TP 1925
"Creole Blues" (composed 1924) TP 1925
"French Market" (composed 1924) TP 1925
"My Plea For Love" (composed 1928 -- song) TP 1929
"Crawfish Crawl" TP 1947

THOMAS W. SHEA

"Black Mike's Curse" n.d.
"Corinthian Rag" TS 1964
"Hasty Pudding" n.d.
"Johnny Walker Rag" n.d.
"Little Wabash Special" n.d.

"Oliver Road Rag" TS 1964
"Pegtown Patrol" n.d.
"Prairie Queen" n.d.
"R.F.D." n.d.
"Rosebud Rag" n.d.
"Spasm Rag" n.d.
"Storyville Sport" n.d.
"Trillium Rag" Hollis Music 1964
"Venial Sin" n.d.
"Brun Campbell Express" (first published in this edition) TS 1966

BILLY TAYLOR

"Evolutionary Rag" (composed for television) BT 1953
"Ragtime Piano Solos and How To Play Them" (Instruction
    Manual) Charles H. Hansen, New York 1950

TREBOR JAY TICHENOR

"Bucksnort Stomp" n.d.
"Missouri Autumn" TB 1965
"Missouri Breeze" TB 1962
"Missouri Country Rag" n.d.
"Missouri Rambler" TB 1962
"Old Levee Days" TB 1963
"Ozark Rag" n.d.
"Pierce City Rag" n.d.
"Ragtime In the Hollow" n.d.
"Show-Me Rag" n.d.
"Chestnut Valley Rag" (first published in this edition) TB 1966

COLLECTIONS

Ann Charters, editor: "The Ragtime Songbook" Oak Publications,
    N.Y. 1965
Joseph F. Lamb: "Ragtime Treasures" (13 posthumously published
    rags) Mills Music Inc., New York 1964
Max Morath, editor: "Max Morath's Guide to Ragtime" Hollis Music 1964
Max Morath, editor: "100 Ragtime Classics" Don Printing, Denver 1963
"Ragtime Piano" (A collection of 16 rags) Mills Music, Inc. N.Y. 1963
"34 Ragtime-Jazz Classics for Piano" Melrose Music, New York 1964

A-Blowin' Down de Line—A Colored Cyclone in Rag Time HSG Karl Kennett—Lyn Udal Song 1898

Across the Continent, March SBC Jean Schwartz 1900

African Beauty, An—Two Step PAH Arthur Pryor BAND 1899

African Beauty, An—Two Step JWP Arthur Pryor 1903

African Pas—Rag Time Two Step JSAS Maurice Kirwin 1902

After the Cake Walk—March-Cakewalk VM Nathaniel Dett 1900

Aggravation Rag WJ George L. Cobb 1910

Ain't Dat a Shame HHD John Queen—Walter Wilson Song 1901

Alabama Barbecue MMC Benny Davis—J. Fred Coots Song 1936

Alabama Cake Walk—Rag Time Cakewalk George D. Barnard 1899

Alabama Cake Walk O. J. De Moll 1897

Alabama Coon's Jubilee—Rag-Time-Two Step HG Chauncey Haines 1899

Alabama Hoe Down—Rag Two-Step SBS R. J. Hamilton 1899

Alabama Hop JHB Joseph H. Barrett 1902

Alabama Jigger—Character Rag JWS Edward B. Claypoole 1913

Alabama Jubilee, An MC C. C. Moffett 1898

Alabama Rag Time—Cake Walk HMC J. E. Henning 1898

Alabama Shuffle OJDM Joseph Ott 1903

Alabama Tickle, An GSKC George Southwell BAND 1899

Alagazam Cake Walk, March and Two Step LF Abe Holzmann 1902

Alagazam (also published as an instrumental) LF Abe Holzmann Song 1903

Alexander's Rag Time Band IB Irving Berlin Song · 1911

All Coons Look Alike to Me MWAS Ernest Hogan Song 1896 Instr. 1897

All the Candy JWJ E. H. Kelly 1907

Ambolena Snow SBS Bodine—Maywood Song 1896

And the Song Came Back JSAS Clarence H. (Cad) St. John Song 1922

Anti-Rag-Time-Girl WWR Elsie Janis Song 1913

Apeda Rag WBS–MMC Dave Harris 1913

Ape Man CMPC James Blythe 1928

Appetite Pete Rag HHK–DHM H. H. Kratz 1909

April Fool Rag WWR Jean Schwartz 1911

Arabian Rag SCSF G. Gould 1917

Arizona Kicker, The FAM John A. O'Keefe 1896

At a Coffee-Colored Party—Ragtime Two Step CMP   O. S. Wald   1899
At a Darktown Cake Walk—Characteristic March BPH   Chas. Hale   1899
At a Georgia Camp Meeting FAM   Kerry Mills   1897
At the Ball, That's All JLH-WWR   J. Leubrie Hill   1913–14
At the Rag Time Jamboree AWT   Dan Packard—Ed J. Simwes   SONG
      1898
Aunt Dinah's Cake Walk—Ragtime March AF   William Weidenhammer
      1899

Baby Let Your Drawers Hang Down—Traditional Honkytonk Rag Song
      Unpublished
Baby, Won't You Please Come Home? CW   Charles Warfield and Clarence
      Williams   SONG   1919
Bachelor's Button—Rag Time Intermezzo JWJ   William C. Powell   1909
Ballin' the Jack JWS   Chris Smith and James Reese Europe   SONG   1914
Baltimore Buck Ragtime Two-Step VMBC   Harry Brown   1905
Bamboula, La—Danse Nègre   Louis Moreau Gottschalk, Op. 2   1847
Bananier, Le—Chanson Nègre   Louis Moreau Gottschalk, Op. 5
Banjo—Grotesque Fantaisie   Louis Moreau Gottschalk, Op. 15
Banjo Rag Time ASC   Arling Shaeffer   BANJO   1899
Banjo Twang—Danse Nègre for Piano DMC-VAR   Charles Drumheller
      1893
Baptisin' Down at Dixon's Pool, De MWAS   Charles Lovenberg   SONG
      1897
Barnyard Rag HRM   Billy Johnson—Chris Smith   SONG   1911
Basin Street Stroller TM   Roy J. Carew   1941
Battle of San Juan Hill, Grand Descriptive Military Fantasia CF   Albert C.
      Sweet   ORCHESTRA   1909
Beeswax Rag VM   Harry J. Lincoln   1911
Belle Creole, La—Quadrille des Lanciers Americain AE   Basile Barès   1866
Belle of Blackville Lane, The WBG   Irving Jones   SONG   1899
Belle of the Cake Walk WB   F. C. Lowder and W. M. Lind—L. B.
      O'Connor   SONG   1898
Belle of the Creoles—Cake Walk and Two Step WAE   Harry P. Guy   1899
Bennett's Raggedy Rag, (Rube) WBS   Rube Bennett   1914
Bill Bailey, Won't You Please Come Home? HHD   Hughie Cannon   SONG
      1902
Bird in a Gilded Cage SBC   Arthur J. Lamb—Harry Von Tilzer   SONG
      1899–1900
Black and Blue Rag SF   Hal G. Nichols   1914
Black Bawl, A PC   Harry C. Thompson   1905
Black Beauty Rag WWR   Jean Schwartz   1910
Black Canary Rag TSNY-MMC   Harry Austin Tierney   1911
Black Cat Rag WWR   Frank Wooster and Ethyl B. Smith   1905
Black Four Hundred's Ball, The HHD   Billy Johnson—Bob Cole   SONG
      1896

Black Hand, A—Rag-time Two Step JHK   Robert Hoffman   1908
Black Laugh, The AMC   C. Seymour   1904
Black Venus—Cake Walk VMP   G. M. Blandford   1899
Blackville Strutters Ball, The HAS   Williams and Walker   SONG   1900
Black Wasp Rag (A Stinger) VM   H. A. Fischler   1911
Blaze Away March LF   Abe Holzmann   1901
Blue Blazes Rag VK   Arthur L. Sizemore   1909
Blue Ribbon Rag JHA   May Aufderheide   1910
Boardin' House Johnson—Cake Walk JWS   Sadie Koninsky   1899
Bolo Rag WWR   Albert Gumble   1908
Boom-e-Rag—Characteristic March and Two Step AWT   Warner Crosby
   1898
Bon Bon Buddy, the Chocolate Drop AGA   Alex Rogers—Will Marion Cook
   SONG   1907
Boone's Rag Medley No. 1 AMCC   Blind Boone   1908
Boone's Rag Medley No. 2—Strains from Flat Branch AMCC   Blind Boone
   1909
Bos'n Rag WWR   Fred S. Stone   1899
Bouncing on the Keys MMC   Ed B. Claypoole   1924
Bowery Gals EHB   From *Christy Minstrels Ethiopian Glee Book*   SONG   1849
Bowery Spielers, The SBS   Wm. H. Krell   1900
Break Away, Mr. Coon AWT   Irving Jones—Tom Logan   SONG   1898
Breakin' the Piano MMC   Billy James   1922
Bric-a-Brac Fox Trot Novelette WJNY   Werner Janssen   1926
Bric-a-Brac Novelty Fox Trot WBS   Clifford Hess   1915
Bric-a-Brac Rag VMBC   Maurice Porcelain   1906
Bridal Cake Walk HNW   Anthony L. Maresh   1899
Buddy Bertrand's Blues (as played by Jelly Roll Morton on Circle Records)
   c. 1905
Bud Rag SF   R. L. Cross   1909
Buff Rag   Robert Bircher   1904
Bugle Call Rag MMC   Pettis and Meyers and Schoebel   1923
Bugle Calls in Rag Time WWR   Val Marconi   1921
Bully's Wedding Night, De   J. W. Cavanaugh   SONG   1896
Bunch O' Blackberries FAF   Abe Holzmann   1900
Bunch of Rags, A HHD   Arr. by Ben M. Jerome   1898
Bundle of Rags, A PK   Robert S. Roberts   1897
Bunny Hug Rag WBS-MMC   H. De Costa   1912
Buzzard's Lope—A Characteristic   unpublished   R. Emmett Kennedy
   1906
Buzzer Rag JHA   May Aufderheide   1909
By the Beautiful Sea SBC   Harold R. Atteridge—Harry Carroll   SONG
   1914
By the Light of the Silvery Moon GE   Edward Madden—Gus Edwards
   SONG   1909
By the Watermelon Vine, Lindy Lou MMC   Thomas S. Allen   SONG   1904

Cactus Rag JSAS Lucian Porter Gibson 1916
Cake Walk of the Day, The (with Rag-Time Chorus) SS Tony Stanford
    SONG 1899
Cake Walk Patrol SBS Wm. H. Krell 1895
Cake Walk to the Sky WW Cad L. Mays SONG 1897
Calico Rag RGB R. G. Behan 1909
Calico Rag EAJ Lee B. Grabbe 1905
Calico Rag FMP Nat Johnson 1914
Camel Walk BMCNY Chris Smith and Bob Schafer—Tim Brymn and
    Cecil Mack SONG 1925
Camel Walk, The JSAS Ebon Gay SONG 1919
Campin' on de Ole Suwanee VM Lee Orean Smith SONG 1899
Camptown Races (De), Gwine to Run All Night FDB Stephen Collins Foster
    SONG 1850
Candied Cherries JWJ Lucien Denni 1911
Candy Rag, The RB Robert Bircher 1909
Cannonball, The VK-WRC-PP Jos. Northup Arranged by Thos. R.
    Confare 1905
Can't Stop—Two Step GAC Pete Washington 1913
Captain of de Coontown Guards, De MWAS Dave Reed, Jr. 1897
Carbarlick Acid—Two Step GBQ-WWR Clarence C. Wiley 1904
Carnival of Venice J. B. Arban
Carolina Cake Walk, A TBH Max Dreyfus 1898
Carolina Cake Walk, The GDM George D. Mears 1899
Carpet Rags—Characteristic March and Two Step JMP Raymond W. Conner
    1903
Carrie's Gone to Kansas City—included in *Boone's Rag Medley No. 2*
Carry Me Back to Old Virginny JFP James Bland SONG 1878
Castle House Rag JWS-EBM James Reese Europe 1914
Cauldron Rag, The AWC Axel W. Christensen 1909
Chanticleer Rag WWR Albert Gumble 1910
Checker Board Rag MMC Harry Austin Tierney 1911
Checkers Rag VM Harry J. Lincoln 1913
Chestnut Street in the 90s S. Brunson Campbell unpublished
Chewin' the Rag MMC J. Gart 1934
Chicken Charlie PC Ashley Ballou 1905
Chicken Chowder WWR Irene M. Giblin 1905
Chile Sauce Rag VM H. A. Fischler 1910
Chills and Fever SF Theron C. Bennett 1912
Chippewa Rag WWR Myrtle Hoy 1911
Chloe VMSF Gus Kahn—Neil Moret SONG 1927
Chocolate Creams—Cake Walk WFB Will Burke 1901
Christensen's Instruction Books for Vaudeville Piano Playing—Books 1 to 5 AWC
    Axel W. Christensen 1912
Chromatic Chords ELB Euday L. Bowman 1926
Chromatic Rag JSAS Will Held 1916
Chromatic Rag WBS-MMC Pete Wendling—Ed Gerhart 1916

305

Cincinnati Rag   AD   W. C. Powell   1909
Cinders—Novelty Two Step   JEA   T. Fred Henry   1905
Circus Solly   EAJ   G. C. Stone   1905
Clarinet Marmalade   LF   Larry Shields and Henry W. Ragas   1918
Climbers Rag, The   JSAS   Arthur Sizemore   1911
Clorindy, The Origin of the Cake Walk   MWAS   Will Marion (Cook)   **Piano**
    arr. by F. W. Meacham   1899
Clover Leaf Rag   AMC   C. Seymour   1909
Cock-a-doodle-doo   CKH   Wm. D. Hall—Ernest Hogan and Joe Jordan
    SONG   1905
Cohan's Rag Babe—New Kind of Step   CAH   George M. Cohan   SONG
    1908
Cole Smoak Rag   JSAS   Clarence H. St. John   1906
Collars and Cuffs Rag   JSAS   Clarence H. St. John   1907
College Rag, The   HS   Wm. Hunter   1910
Colonial Rag   WWR   Ernest R. Ball and Julius Lenzberg   1914
Colored 400, The   H. G. Wheeler—J. W. Wheeler   SONG   1890
Colored Elks—Cake Walk   HHD   M. Bernard   1896
Come Down, Ma Honey, Do   TBH   J. H. Wagner—Gustave Kerker   SONG
    1894
Come, Thou Fount   HYMN
Comus Rag   JSAS   Carrie Bruggeman   (Mrs. William Stark)
Congregation Will Please Keep Their Seats, The   MWAS   Ernest Hogan
    SONG   1900
Contagious Rag   JSAS   Ed. J. Mellinger   1913
Contrary Motion   "The Lion"   (Willie Smith)   unpublished   1949
Coon Band ("Half Shot") Playing Rag Time—Descriptive   ED   (E.) Derville
    1905
Coon Band Contest, A   Arthur Pryor
Coon Band Parade   SB   James Reese Europe   1905
Coon! Coon! Coon!   SB   Gene Jefferson—Leo Friedman   SONG   1900
Coon Hollow Capers   CGNY   W. Murdoch Lind—Frank Gillis   1899
Coon-Jine   Fred Mack   1898
Coon's Day in May   FAM   Chris Smith—Theo. Bowman   SONG   1898
Coons' Frolic, The   GSKC   George Southwell   BAND   1897
Coontown Capers—A Negrosyncrasy   HHD   Paul Dresser—Theo F. Morse
    SONG   1897
Coontown Carnival   MB   Louis Myll   INSTR. AND SONG   1898
Coontown Chimes—March and Two Step   HSW–MWAS   Harry F. Webster
    1899–1902
Coontown Frolic, The   ETP   Charles Jerome Wilson   1899
Coontown Jubilee   SB   Leo Friedman   1898
Coontown's Merry Widow—A Rag Time Arrangement of the Famous Opera   TSB
    Edward Laska—Charls Eliott   1908
Corrugated Rag   JSAS   Ed. J. Mellinger   1911
Cotton Blossoms—March Comique   JCC   Milton H. Hall   1898
Cottonfield Dance   NMC   Monroe H. Rosenfeld   1892

Cotton Patch Ragtime, A   jwj   C. Tyler   1902
Crappy Dan, The Sporting Man   Chas. Trevathan   Song   1897
Crawfish Crawl   Tony Parenti   unpublished   1948
Crazy Chord Rag   tm   Albert Carroll   (as played by Jelly Roll
    Morton on Circle Records)   (*c.* 1904)   1949
Crazy Joe   mmc   Harry F. Reser   Piano and Banjo   1922
Creole Belles—March Two Step   wwr   J. Bodewalt Lampe   1900
Creole Pieman's Song, see *Hush Little Baby, Don't You Cry*
Crimson Rambler   tsny-mmc   Harry Austin Tierney   1911
Cullered Cokett, De   ehb   From *Christy Minstrels Ethiopian Glee Book*   Song
    1848

Daisy Rag   sf   Fred Heltman   1908
Dakota Rag   sbs   O. H. Anderson   1909
Dallas Blues   wpc-mmcny   Lloyd Garrett—Hart A. Wand   Song   1912
Dandy Broadway Swell, The   ehb   From *Christy Minstrels Ethiopian Glee
    Book*   1848
Dardanella   maf   Fred Fisher and Felix Bernard—Johnny S. Black
    Song   1919
Darkey's Barbecue, The   mwas   Vess L. Ossman   Banjo   1896
Darkey's Mardi Gras   fbh   Theodore Wenzlik   1906
Darkey Tickle, The   hfh   E. B. Hunt   1892
Darkies' Delight   bfb   Henry B. Green   1895
Darkie's Dream, The   nmc   G. L. Lansing   1889
Darkies' Masquerade   dmc   Maurice Kirwin   1899
Darkie Volunteer, The   sab   Vess L. Ossman   Banjo   1899
*Dark Sett, The—Celebrated Negro Quadrilles as Played by All the Quadrille
    Bands*   fp   1848
Darktown Belles—Rag Time March and Dance   cf   Alfred Paulsen   1898
Darktown Is Out Tonight (From *Clorindy*)   mwas   Paul Laurence Dunbar
    —Will Marion Cook   Song   1897
Darktown Schottische   asc   Arling Shaeffer   Banjo   1899
Darktown Social—Two Step Polka Cake Walk and March   bmcb   B. B.
    Brooks   1901
Darktown Swell, The—March   oes   O. E. Sutton   1899
Dar's a New Coon Wedding   wsm   A. S. MacKenzie   Song   1892
Dar's Rag Time in de Moon   fam   Maurice Schapiro—Seymour Furth
    Song   1898
Dat Blackville Wedding—Characteristic March and Two Step   mwas   Robert
    Cone   1898
Dat Gal of Mine   hnw   Ben Shook   1902
Dat's It   hpmc   Sebastian Lutz   1903
Dat Lovin' Rag   hhd   Victor A. Smalley—Bernard Adler   Song   1906
Dat Mornin' in de Sky   ch   Blind Boone   Song   1899
Dat's de Way to Spell "Chicken"   mwas   Sydney L. Perrin and Bob Slater
    Song   1902

Daylight ("*Tom Will Now Play for You His Idea of Daylight*") SBS Blind Tom 1866

De Banks ob de Mississippi EHB From *Ethiopian Glee Book of the New Orleans Serenaders* 1848

Devilish Rag, The LR Lew Roberts 1908

Digah's Stomp, see *Dream, The*

Dinah Doe and Mr. Crow EHB From *Christy Minstrels Ethiopian Glee Book* 1848

Dinah's Jubilee—Characteristic March and Two Step HHD Jacob H. Ellis 1897

Dinah's Wedding Day From *Christy's Melody Book* SONG 1852

Dingle Pop Hop TSNY Harry Austin Tierney 1911

Dingy's Serenade, The—A Rag Two Step CAL Roy Mullendore 1898

Dis Evenin', dis Mornin', So Soon ("The Handout Song") Jeff La Mont—Fred W. Busch SONG 1898

Dixie (originally published as *Dixie's Land*) FP Dan Decatur Emmett (arr. by W. S. Hobbs) SONG 1860

Dixie Doodle—Rag and Cake Walk CNB C. N. Buchanan 1899

Dixie Queen CC Robert Hoffman 1906

Dixie Flyer AEH A. E. Henrich 1901

Does You Love Me as You Used to, Miss Jane? HVT Avery and Hart—Chris Smith SONG 1904

Dogizity Rag MMC B. Taylor 1910

Doll Rags HAH Homer Hall 1906

Don't Go Way, Nobody AMCNO Percy Cahill (music by) "P.A.G.T." SONG 1906

Dora Dean, the Hottest [Sweetest] Gal You Ever Seen BAS Bert Williams SONG 1895

Down among the Sheltering Palms LF James Brockman—Abe Olman SONG 1915

Down Home Rag WRC Wilbur Sweatman INSTR. 1911 SONG 1913

Down in Honky Tonk Town BMCNY Charles McCarron—Chris Smith SONG 1916

Down in Jungle Town FBH Ed. Madden—Theo Morse SONG 1908

Down South—Rag Time March and Two Step WWR C. A. Grimm 1907

Downtown Rag MMC G. Carrozza—Frank Signorelli 1923

Dream, The Jess Pickett unpublished

Dusky Dinah—Cake Walk and Patrol CS Dan J. Sullivan 1899

Dusky Dudes Cake Walk SBC Jean Schwartz 1899

Dusky Maiden—Two Step or Cake Walk HHD Spencer—Morse 1903

Dustin' the Piano LM James Blythe and Buddy Burton unpublished 1928

Dusty Rag JHA May Aufderheide 1908

Dusty Rag Song JHA J. Will Callahan—May Aufderheide 1912

Early in de Mornin' JLP Wm. Shakespeare Hayes 1877

Easy Money—Rag Time Sonata FCS A. H. Tournade 1905

Easy Money Rag wcs Will D. Moyer 1915
Easy Pickins' wrc–lf Egbert Van Alstyne 1902
Echoes from the Snowball Club—Syncopated Waltz wbd Harry P. Guy
   1898
Echoes of Spring rmc "The Lion" (Willie Smith) 1935
Eh! La Bas—Traditional Creole Song
El Capitan March jcc John Philip Sousa 1896
Elephant Rag wwr Malvin M. Franklin 1913
Eli Green's Cake Walk jws Sadie Koninsky 1898
Empire City Rag smcc–mmc Frank Broekhoven 1911
Encore Rag akh Tad Fischer 1912
Entertainers Rag, The pmco Jay Roberts 1910
Essay in Ragtime S. Brunson Campbell unpublished
Everybody Two Step wwr Earl C. Jones—Wally Herzer Song 1912
Every Darkey Had a Raglan On jws Allen Brown 1901
Every Race Has a Flag but the Coon jws Heelan and Helf Song 1900
Exhortation sny Alex Rogers—Will Marion Cook Song 1912

Fanatic Rag tsny–mmc Harry Austin Tierney 1911
Fas', Fas' World aga Alex Rogers—Bert Williams Song 1907
Fidgety Feet lf D. J. LaRocca and Larry Shields 1919
First Wench Done Turned White, The fam Ed Rogers 1897
Fleur de Lis Rag jws Harry Austin Tierney 1911
Florida Cracker, A—Rag Two Step sbs Ellis Brooks 1899
Fluffy Ruffles cd C. Duane Crabb(e) 1907
Fluffy Ruffles—Slow Drag kj Frank Keithley 1908
Foolishness Rag—Buck Dance hrm Mort Weinstein 1911
Four Little Curly Headed Coons nmc J. W. Wheeler Song 1889
Franco-American Rag wwr Jean Schwartz 1910
Frank A. Daniels March ptw Laurent Comes 1894
Frankie and Johnnie—Traditional ballad
Freckles Rag pc Larry Buck 1905
Fred Heltman's Rag sf Fred Heltman 1918
French Pastry Rag wwr Les Copeland 1914
Frozen Bill—Rag cf Arthur Pryor 1909
Full Moon, The—An Original Rag ppc Roy Carew 1909
Funny Folks Rag pc W. C. Powell 1904

Game Kid Blues (as played by Jelly Roll Morton on Circle Records) *c.*
   1904
Georgia Camp Meeting See *At a Georgia Camp Meeting*
Georgia Giggle Rag is Will Livernash 1918
Give Me Back dem Clothes fam Irving Jones Song 1899
Glendy Burk, The Stephen Foster Song 1860
Glen Oaks Rag awc Axel W. Christensen
Go Down, Moses—Spiritual
Going Back to Cincinnati Honkytonk rag unpublished

Gold Dust Twins Rag FMP Nat Johnson 1913
Golden Wedding, De JFP James Bland 1880
Golliwog's Cake-Walk Claude Debussy
Goodby, My Honey, I'm Gone—Schottische PRM H. M. Rosenfeld 1888
Goodby, My Lady Love—Cake Walk MMC Joe E. Howard 1904
Good Gravy MMC Mike Bernard 1925
Gravel Rag WWR Charlotte Blake 1908
Greenwich Witch MMC Zez Confrey 1921
Guess That Will Hold You for a While HHD Smart and Williams SONG
   1897

Halley's Comet VM Harry J. Lincoln 1910
Ham Tree Barbecue, The WWR-MMC William Jerome—Jean Schwartz
   SONG 1905
Handy Andy SB Leo Friedman 1900
Happy Cotton Pickers' Dance—A Rag Time Two Step AMC Sol Green 1899
Happy Days in Dixie FAM Kerry Mills 1896
Happy Heine—Two Step WWR J. Bodewalt Lampe 1905
Happy Little Nigs—Rag Two Step DAB George Elliott 1898
Happy Sammy—A Teasing Rag F. C. Schmidt 1906
Harmony Rag SF Hal G. Nichols 1911
Havana Rag JSAS Maurice Kirwin 1904
Heebie Jeebies CMPNY Boyd Atkins and Richard M. Jones SONG 1926
Hello, Ma Baby TBH Howard and Emerson SONG 1899
Hen on the Nest, A WRC Geo. L. Spalding 1904
Here Comes the Band "The Lion" (Willie Smith)
He's All Shot to Pieces by the French Girls' Eyes JSAS John S. Stark SONG
   1917
Hezekiah Lee, Don't You Fool with Me JTH Frank Montgomery—Ernest
   Hogan and William J. Carle SONG 1905
Hiawatha—A Summer Idyl WWR Neil Moret (Charles N. Daniels)
   INSTR. 1901 SONG 1903
High Society CW A. J. Piron 1929
High Society March EJD Porter Steele 1901
High Society March and Two Step SEW Secie E. Wyatt 1906
High Society One Step FKR Tom Lemonier and Clarence M. Jones 1914
High Society Rag Joe Oliver, arr. by Lillian Hardin (unpublished)
   copyright 1923
His Rag-Time Walk Won the Prize HVS Nathan Bivins 1899
Holy Moses Rag AD C. Seymour 1906
Honey, I'll Be Your Man—Ethiopian Proposal with Rag Time Chorus MMSF
   L. S. Ramsdall SONG 1898
Honey on de Rag HCP Alonzo F. Burt ORCHESTRA 1898 PIANO 1899
Honky-Tonky Monkey Rag TMCC Chris Smith unpublished SONG
   1911
Honky Tonk Rag Charles N. Daniels (Neil Moret)
Horseshoe Rag JHA Julie Lee Niebergall 1911

Hot Chestnuts HS   Rag Medley arr. by G. J. Trinkhaus 1910–11

Hot Coon from Memphis FAM   Bob Cole and George W. Walker 1897

Hot Rag, A—Two Step SBS   S. R. Lewis 1900

Hot Stuff Rag BAB   D. E. Maharb 1911

Hottest Coon in Dixie MWAS   Paul Laurence Dunbar—Will Marion (Cook) SONG

Hottest Ever, The—Cake Walk and Polka CKH   Jas. O'Dea—Chas. B. Brown SONG 1898

Hot Time in Mobile—Cake Walk JWS   Stanley Carter 1899

Hot Time in the Old Town Tonight HHD   Joe Hayden—Theo. A. Metz 1896

Humoresque Antonin Dvořák

Humpy's Buck   Charles Humfeld   unpublished   1914

Hunky-Dory—Characteristic Cake Walk March FAF   Abe Holzmann 1901

Hurricane Rag WRC   F. G. Johnson 1911

Hush, Little Baby, Don't You Cry, or The Creole Pieman's Song   Alphonse Sirefaire (The Pieman Himself) SONG 1895

Hysterics Rag WWR   Paul Biese—F. Henri Klickman 1914

I Ain't Got Nobody CAC-FKR   Roger Graham—Charles Warfield and Spencer Williams SONG 1916

I Can't Lose My Home and My Pork Chops Too HHD   Ernest Hogan SONG 1899

Icycles—Rag Two Step WWR   Jas. E. C. Kelly 1907

Ida, Sweet as Apple Cider   Eddie Leonard and Eddie Munson SONG 1916–19

I Don't Like No Cheap Man JWS   Williams and Walker Arranged by Will H. Tyers SONG 1897

I Don't Like That Face You Wear HHD   Ernest Hogan SONG 1898

I Don't Play No Favorites FAM   Al Johns SONG 1898

I Don't Understand Rag Time JWS   Irving Jones SONG 1899

I Don't Want Nobody to Ball the Jack in Here CT   Joe Golphin SONG 1914

If the Man in the Moon Were a Coon WRC   Fred Fisher SONG 1902

If You Go, Why This Will Bring You Back HHD   Smart and Williams SONG 1898

I Guess That Will Be About All FAM   Al Johns 1899

I Hope These Few Lines Will Find You Well HHD   Cole and Johnson SONG 1897

I Know Darn Well I Can Do without Broadway (But Can Broadway Do without Me?) JD   Jimmy Durante SONG 1928

I'll Be Ready When the Great Day Comes SBS   James S. Putnam 1882

I'll Break Up This Jamboree MWAS   Al Brown—Sydney L. Perrin SONG 1898

I Love Dat Man (with added Rag Time Chorus) MB   Dan Packard—E. J. Simnes 1898

I Loves My Little Honey Best of All HHD   Ernest Hogan SONG 1898

I Love You Sunday   FMP   Charley Straight   1920

I'm a Cooler for the Warmest Coon in Town   JWS   Williams and Walker
  SONG   1898

I'm Afraid to Come Home in the Dark   WWR   Harry Williams—Egbert Van
  Alstyne   SONG   1907

I'm Alabama Bound—included in *Boone's Rag Medley No. 2;* also see Jelly
  Roll Morton listing

I'm Alabama Bound—*Ragtime Two Step*   RH   Robert Hoffman   1909

I'm Certainly Living a Rag-Time Life   SB   'Gene Jefferson—Robert S.
  Roberts   SONG   1900

I'm Goin' to Ease Back (to My Happy Home)   SAY   Will E. Skidmore   SONG
  1903

I'm Going to Live Anyhow until I Die   Shepard N. Edmonds

I'm Livin' Easy   FAM   Irving Jones   SONG   1899

I'm Old Enough for a Little Lovin'   JWS   Marshall Walker—Will E.
  Skidmore   SONG   1917

Impecunious Davis—Characteristic Cake Walk   FAM   Kerry Mills   1899

Imperial Rag   WMD   Walter M. Davis   1910

If I Ever Cease to Love   Connolly

Imperial Rag   BAG   Billie Talbot   1914–15

I'm So Glad My Mama Don't Know Where I'm At   SMSL   William Twosweets
  SONG   1915

I'm Sorry I Made You Cry   LF   N. J. Clesi   SONG   1916

In Chinatown   HHD   Mike Bernard   1900

In Dahomey   HHD   J. W. Johnson   SONG   1898

In Jolly Junktown—A Hot Rag Time and Cake Walk Two Step   CF   Emil
  Ascher   1899

In My Merry Oldsmobile   MWAS   Gus Edwards   SONG   1905

Innocent Rag   MMC   Harry Austin Tierney   1911

In the Evening by the Moonlight   HPC   James Bland   SONG   1880

Invitation Rag   WWR   Les Copeland   1911

Irmena Rag   AWC   Axel Christensen   1908

It Takes a Long Tall Brown-Skin Gal to Make a Preacher Lay His Bible Down
  JWS   Will E. Skidmore   SONG   1917

I Ups to Him and He Ups to Me   JD   Jimmy Durante   SONG   1929

I've Got Chicken on the Brain   JWS   Elmer Bowman—Al Johns   (arr. by
  Will H. Tyers)   SONG   1899

Ivoryland   MMC   Les Copeland   1925

I Want a Real Lovin' Man   JHA   Paul Pratt—May Aufderheide   SONG
  1911

I Want Jesus to Walk with Me—HYMN

I Want to Linger   WWR   Stanley Murphy—Henry I. Marshall   SONG
  1914

I Wish I Could Shimmy like My Sister Kate, see *Sister Kate*

I Wonder What Is That Coon's Game   HHD   Bob Cole and J. W. Johnson
  SONG   1898

Ja Da LF Bob Carleton SONG 1918

Jagtime Johnson's Ragtime March MCK Ryder 1901

Jamaica Jinger Rag WWR Egbert Van Alstyne 1912

Jasper Jenkins, de Cake Walk Coon HPV Henry P. Vogel 1898

Jasper Johnson's Jubilee—Cake Walk and Two Step HHD Paul Rubens 1899

Jasper's Dream WRC Warren Beebe 1897

Jay Roberts Rag FMP Jay Roberts 1911

Jelly Roll WBS Henry W. Santley and Pete Wendling 1915

Jim Along Josey FAH Edward Harper (sung in *The Free Nigger of New York*) SONG 1840

Jinx Rag LPG-JSAS Lucian Gibson 1911–15

John Barleycorn, Goodbye JSAS John S. Stark SONG 1919

Johnson Rag RMC Guy Hall and Henry Kleinkauf 1917

Jolly Darkey, The From *Christy Minstrels Ethiopian Glee Book* 1848

Joy Rag FMP Jay Roberts 1911

Joyeux Nègres—Cake Walk (à Philip Sousa) EEC Rodolphe Bergere 1903

Jump Jim Crow Thomas "Daddy" Rice SONG 1828–9

Jungle Jamboree Rag JWS Chris Smith 1913

Jungle Time—A Genuine Rag APS E. Philip Severin 1905

Just Because She Made dem Goo-Goo Eyes HHD Hughie Cannon SONG 1900

Just Give Me Ragtime Please IB-MMC Maceo Pinkard SONG 1916

Kangaroo Hop, A WWR Fred S. Stone 1903

Keep on Knockin' but You Can't Come In—Traditional honkytonk rag song unpublished (a version copyrighted by Dale E. Brown 1924)

Keystone Rag Willy Anderson 1921

Kitten on the Keys MMC Zez Confrey 1921

Klassicle Rag JHA C. Duane Crabbe 1911

Knice and Knifty SF Roy Bargy and Charley Straight 1922

Lafayette, The—Two Step WRC Mike Bernard 1897

'Lasses Candy One Step LF D. J. La Rocca, arr. by J. Russel Robinson 1919

Last Rose of Summer, The Thomas Moore

Leg of Mutton (Le Gigot)—One Step, Two Step and Turkey Trot JWS Sigmund Romberg 1913

Lemon Drops JM Mike Bernard 1910–11

Let's Dance—A Rag Turkey Trot WWR Wally Herzer 1913

Levee Rag, The GAJ Fred E. Gates 1914

Levee Rag, The WRC Charles Mullen 1902

Levee Revels—An Afro-American Cane-Hop MWAS Wm. Christopher O'Hare 1898

Liberty Bell March JCC John Philip Sousa 1893

Lime Kiln Club, The WRC Bogart—O'Brien 1893

Lindy Lou, see *By the Watermelon Vine*

Lingard Quadrille, The WAP David Braham 1868
Listen to the Mocking Bird Richard Milburn Arranged by Alice
  Hawthorne (Septimius Winner) 1855
Little Alabama Coon ww Hattie Starr SONG 1893
Little Brown Jug Traditional
Louisiana—Intermezzo Unique WWR L'Albert (C. N. Daniels) 1907
Louisiana Rag TMCC Theo. H. Northrup 1897

Mackinac March Fred S. Stone 1896
Mad House Rag, The FAM Edgar Leslie—Freddy Watson (arr. by
  Will H. Tyers) SONG 1911
Ma Ebony Belle RBM Ed Gardinier—Maurice Levy SONG 1901
Mah Jong MMC Sid Reinherz 1924
Make Me a Pallet on the Floor—Traditional Song (There is an
  arrangement by W. C. Handy, 1923)
Mama's Gone, Goodbye CW Peter Bocage and Armand Piron 1924
Mammy's Little Pickaninny Boy MWAS Williams and Walker SONG 1896
Mammy's Little Pumpkin Colored Coons MWAS Eugene Hillman and Sidney
  Perrin SONG 1897
Ma Mobile Babe—Rag Time Cake Walk JCC John N. Klohr 1899
Mando Rag JSAS R. G. Ingraham 1914
Mandy's Ragtime Waltz SF J. S. Zamecnik 1912
Man in the Moon Is a Coon HHD George M. Cohan 1897
Man, Knock Me a Drink Mike Jackson SONG unpublished,
  uncopyrighted
Man That Broke the Bank at Monte Carlo, The Fred Gilbert SONG
Maori—A Samoan Dance AGA Will H. Tyers 1908
Maple Leaf Waltz AWP Florence Johnson 1897
Ma Rag Time Baby WWR Fred S. Stone 1898
Ma Rag Time Queen John F. Barth 1902
Mardi Gras—Intermezzo-Two Step VK Robert Hoffman 1910
Martha, Overture to Friedrich von Flotow 1847
Ma Tiger Lily MWAS A. Baldwin Sloane 1900
May Irwin's Bully Song WSM Charles Trevathan SONG 1896
Meddlesome Rag JSAS Clarence H. St. John 1908
Medicine Man, The JWS Williams and Walker SONG 1899
Meet Me in St. Louis, Louis FAM Andrew B. Sterling—Kerry Mills
  SONG 1904
Me Heart Breaker "Rags" WWR Eddie Dustin—Charles N. Daniels
  SONG 1903
Melancholy (later issued as *My Melancholy Baby*) TBNY George A.
  Norton—Ernie Burnett SONG 1911
Melancholy Baby, see *Melancholy*
Melancholy Mose Ben M. Jerome 1897
Melody in F Anton Rubinstein
Memphis Blues, The WCH J. Russel Robinson—W. C. Handy SONG
  1912

Ménestrels (Minstrels)   Claude Debussy
Merry-Go-Round Rag   RL   Ralph Larsh   1918
Midnight Rag   FMP   Gus Winkler   1912
Minnesota Rag, The   AWC   Axel Christensen   1913
Minstrels of Annie Street, The   Melvin (Turk) Murphy   unpublished
Miserable Rag   WBS-MMC   Malvin M. Franklin   1915
Miserere from *Il Trovatore*   Giuseppe Verdi
Miss Brown's Cake Walk   SBS   Bert Williams   1896
Mississippi Rag   SBS   Wm. H. Krell   1897
Mississippi Side Step—Cake Walk   LEB   Leo. E. Berliner   1899
Missus Johnson's Rent Rag Ball   NMC   Fred (Stasia) Hammil and D. A.
   Lewis   INSTR. and SONG   1897
Mistah Police, Don't 'Rest Me   CH   N. C. Smith   SONG   1896
Mr. Black Man—March and Two Step—With Vocal Trio   WWR   Arthur
   Pryor   1904
Mister Crump   W. C. Handy   1909
Mister Johnson, Turn Me Loose   GWWC   Haering and Green   SONG   1896
Mobile Buck-Wing Dance, The   WSM   Dan J. Sullivan   1899
Modulations, or Stepping on the Keys   WRC   Clarence M. Jones   1923
Monkey Rag   AKH   Wheatley Davis   1911
Monkey Rag, see *Honky-Tonky Monkey Rag*
Moon Face   SF   Abe Olman   1907
Moonshine Rag   JSAS   Edward Hudson   1916
Mop Rag   WWR   Helen S. Eaton   1909
Mopsy Massy of Tallahassee—Plantation Song and Rag Time Dance   SSSL
   Anita Comfort   1898
Morte, La   OD   Louis Moreau Gottschalk, Op. 60   1869
Movie Rag   SF   J. S. Zamecnik   1913
Movie Trot   FMP   Harry H. Raymond   1916
Moving Day   HVT   Andrew B. Sterling—Harry Von Tilzer   SONG   1906
Mrs. Trice's Restaurant   Mike Jackson   SONG   unpublished,
   uncopyrighted
My Black Venus   SB   Barney Fagan   SONG   1897
My Body Rock 'Long Fever   Traditional Spiritual
My Brudder Gum   FP   Stephen Foster   SONG   1849
My Coal Black Lady   MWAS   W. T. Jefferson   SONG   1896
My Gal Sal   JWS   Paul Dresser   1905
My Little Ala Gooslum—Cake Walk   HGNY   Alonzo F. Burt   1899
My Melancholy Baby, see *Melancholy*
My Rag Time Lady   CH   Albert Brown—Charles N. Daniels   SONG
   1898

Nellie Bly   FP   Stephen Foster   SONG   1850
Never Let No One Man Worry Your Mind   WES   Will E. Skidmore   SONG
   1919
New Coon in Town   SB   J. S. Putnam   1883

New Orleans Honky Tonk TM Roy J. Carew 1945

Nicodemus and His Banjo—Rag Time and Cake Walk Two Step GAS Emil Ascher 1899

Nightie Night MMC Axel W. Christensen

Nightingale Rag WCWI Lester Sill 1914

Nightingale Song Ethelbert Nevin

Night on the Levee, A SB Theo H. Northrup 1897

1915 Rag CTF Harry Austin Tierney 1913

Ninth Battalion on Parade, The MWAS Ernest Hogan and Bert Williams SONG 1896

Nitric Acid Rag JSAS Ed Hudson 1922

Noble de Game of Craps HHD Wendell P. Dabney and Gussie L. Davis 1898

Nobody AGA Alex Rogers—Bert A. Williams SONG 1905

Nobody Knows We're Lovin' but You and the Moon JSAS S. G. Rhodes SONG 1911

Nola SF Felix Arndt 1922

No More Will I Ever Be Your Baby HHD Ernest Hogan SONG 1899

Nonette Rag WRC H. Spencer 1912

Nonsense Rag—A Ragged Sensation JWS R. G. Brady 1911

Not a Coon Came Out the Way That He Went In JWS Williams and Walker SONG 1898

Notoriety Rag—Two Step WWR Kathryn L. Widmer 1913

Novelty Rag JHA May Aufderheide 1911

Oceana Roll WWR Roger Lewis—Lucien Denni SONG 1911

Ognons, Les—Creole Serenade, Traditional (An arrangement by Nicholas and Barker has been published)

Oh, Didn't He Ramble JWS-EBM Will Handy pseudonym for Cole and Johnson SONG 1902

Oh, Honey, Ain't You Sorry—included in *Boone's Rag Medley No. 2*

Oh I Don't Know or I Thought I Was a Winner SBS Bert Williams 1896

Oh! I Don't Know, You're Not So Warm! SBS Bert Williams SONG 1896

Ohio Flo JSAS Herbert W. Willett SONG 1913

Oh, Mr. Coon From *Christy Minstrels Ethiopian Glee Book* 1848

Oh! What a Pal Was Mary WBS Edgar Leslie and Bert Kalmar—Pete Wendling SONG 1919

Oh, You Beautiful Doll WWR A. Seymour Brown—Nat D. Ayer SONG 1911

Oh! You Devil Rag Ford Dabney 1909

Oh, You Tommy JSAS John S. Stark SONG 1920

O Jerusalem, Early in de Morning Traditional Spiritual

Old Dan Tucker MMU Daniel Decatur Emmett SONG 1843

Old Folks Rag JWS Wilbur Sweatman 1914

Old Kentuck—Rag Time Two Step WJD Frank Schmuhl 1898

Old Man, Your Hair Is Turning Gray JSAS S. G. Rhodes SONG 1912

Old Time Jubilee Cakewalk—Music of the Original Melodies from the Memories of Billy Kersands, Harry P. Guy, Dan Polk GPC   Piano arrangement by J. A. Noble   1900

Old Time Rag, The FBH   Edward Madden—Theodore Morse   SONG   1908

Old Zip Coon   Traditional   See *Zip Coon*

Ole Time Cake Walk, De W. Moody—Lee B. Grabbe   SONG   1898

Ole Virginny Barbecue AAR   J. E. Andino   1899

On Emancipation Day—Characteristic Negro March and Two Step HVT   Paul Laurence Dunbar—Will Marion Cook   SONG   1902   INSTR.   1902

One o' Them Things—Rag CAS   James Chapman and Le Roy Smith   1904

Operatic Rag WWR   Julius Lenzberg   1914

Original Dixieland One Step EBM   Original Dixieland Jazz Band and Joe Jordan   1917

Paloma, La   Sebastián Yradier   SONG

Panama   Will H. Tyers

Panama Rag AMU   C. Seymour   1904

Parade of the Shake-Rag Militia RRH   R. R. Hogue   1898

Passing of Rag-time, The CGC   Arthur Pryor   1902

Pathetic Rag AWC   Axel W. Christensen   1913

Patrol Comique CF   Thomas Hindley   1890

Peaceful Henry—A Slow Drag CH-WWR   E. H. (Harry) Kelly   1901

Pearl of the Harem—Oriental Rag and Two Step MBR   Harry P. Guy   1901

Peek-A-Boo Rag   Warren Edwards   1905

Pegasus—March and Two Step JSAS   Robert B. Stirling   1908

Phantom Rag JFH   Al W. Brown—Violinsky   1911

Pianoflage SF   Roy Bargy   1922

Pianola MMC   Frank Westphal   1923

Pianola Concert Rag, The ATM   Otto Welcome   1921

Piano Price Rag   Price Davis   unpublished   *c.* 1900

Pickaninny Christening, A EM   Winthrop Wiley   1902

Pickaninny Rag SF   Irene M. Giblin   1908

Pickles and Peppers—A Rag Oddity JF   Adeline Shepherd   1906

Piffle Rag JHA   Gladys Yelvington   1911

Pious Peter—Cake Walk LF   Egbert Van Alstyne   1909

Plantation Echoes—Rag Two Step SB   Theo H. Northrup   1897

Play Dat Rag Time, Play It Right FM   Fred Meyer   SONG   1898

Playful Willie JA   Laurent L. Comes, Op. 38   1903

Please Let Me Sleep HVT   Jas. T. Brymn   1902

Poet and Peasant Overture   Franz von Suppé

Poison Ivories RR   Walter G. Haenschen and Harry Akst   1923

Policy King—A Popular Two Step WRC   Charles B. Brown   1905

Policy Sam—Two Step and Cake Walk TBH   Joseph Gioscia   1899

Poor Jim—Rag Time Two Step PAS   James Chapman   1903

Popularity March and Two Step FAM   George M. Cohan   1906

Popular Rag, The MAA Webb Long 1912
Possumala WW Irving Jones 1894
Possum Barbecue, The SBS John Martin 1899
Possum Hall·Rag BFF Bennett F. Fritch ORCHESTRA 1899
Possum Hunt, De (*Coon Song in Rag Time*) JOS Harvey Johns SONG
   1899
Possum Hunt—Two Step SAS C. Van Baar BAND 1896
Possum Rag GD Geraldine Dobyns 1907
Poster Girl March, The CH Charles N. Daniels 1899
Prancing Picaninnies TBH Max Dreyfus 1899
Pray for the Lights to Go Out JWS Will E. Skidmore SONG 1916
Press Club Rag AWC Axel W. Christensen 1912
Pride of Bucktown PK Robert S. Roberts 1897
Prize Cake Walk of the Blackville Swells Walter V. Ullner 1898
Put Your Arms around Me, Honey YMP Junie McCree—Albert Von
   Tilzer SONG 1905

Quand Patate la Cuite na va Mangé Li Traditional New Orleans Creole
   Song
Queen of the Raggers—March Rag Time or Cake Walk TS A. Bafunno
   1898
Queen of the Rag Time—A Syncopated Two Step BAD Harry Powers 1899
Queen Rag, The JKM Floyd Willis 1911
Queen Raglan AH-HAF A. E. Henrich 1902

Radium Dance, The WWR Jean Schwartz 1904
Rag-a-lin WWWI Emil Ebann 1901
Rag-a-Muffin Rag and Two Step SF W. T. Pierson 1913
Rag Baby Rag VM F. H. Losey
Rag Bag Rag VM Harry J. Lincoln 1909
Ragged Raglets RW James M. Fulton 1902
Ragged Raglets JBE D. Jefferson Thomas and Loren E. Taylor 1903
Ragged Rastus—Two Step SBS O. H. Anderson 1900
Ragged Thoughts CF J. Von Der Mehden, Jr. 1908
Ragged William EJD Frank P. Banta 1899
Ragging the Scale BMCNY Ed. B. Claypoole 1915
Raggy Raggers, The DNY Howard Lipson 1899
Raggy Military Tune RLC Roger Lewis—Jay Roberts SONG 1912
Rag-Ma-La IWCI A. Shaw and A. Anderson SONG 1897
Rag Man's a Coming, De TS Nettie Gehr SONG 1898
Rag Medley MWAS Max Hoffman 1897
Rag Medley MWAS-SBNY Max Hoffman 1897
Rag Melodies MWAS Medley arranged by W. H. Mackie 1898
Rag Pickers Rag—Two Step UMUS Robert J. O'Brien 1901
Rag Pickings MWAS Geo. L. Lansing BANJO 1898
Rags, Bottles and Old Iron HHD Louis Tocaben and F. W. Meacham
   1901

Rags to Burn JWJ Frank X. McFadden 1899
Ragtime Cadets CHC J. Martin 1901
Rag Time Chimes WRC Egbert Van Alstyne 1901
Ragtime Cowboy Joe FAM Grant Clarke—Lewis F. Muir and Maurice Abrahams SONG 1912
Rag Time Dance, De CMPNY Arranged by Dreyfus from Harry Von Tilzer's Song *When You Do de Rag Time Dance* 1898
Ragtime Dream, The LF Joe Goodwin—Lew Brown SONG 1914
Rag-Time Drummer KP J. Leubrie Hill 1903
Ragtime Engineer JWS Sam Lewis—Clay Smith SONG 1912
Rag Time Goblin Man, The HVT Harry Von Tilzer 1912
Ragtime Guards—Characteristic March SBS Walter E. Petry 1899
Ragtime Insanity PMP Chris Praetorius 1900
Ragtime Instruction Books AWC Axel S. Christensen 1903-6-7-8-9-27-31-33-36-37
Ragtime Intermezzo—A Syncopated Symphony FAM Maxwell Silver 1900
Ragtime Jimmie's Jamboree HHD Ned Wayburn SONG 1899
Ragtime Joke, A AB Andy L. Burke 1905
Rag Time Jubilee TAS James W. Seeley 1901
Rag Time Laundry VK W. C. Powell 1902
Ragtime Liz MWAS Richard Carle—Alfred E. Aarons SONG 1898
Rag Time March WRC Warren Beebe 1897
Rag-Time Pasmala—Characteristic Two Step GLS Paul A. Rubens 1899
Ragtime Patrol ETP Charles Jerome Wilson 1899
Ragtime Patrol, The NMC R. J. Hamilton 1897
Rag-Time Queen, The FAF Irving Jones SONG 1901
Ragtime Reception, A—Cake Walk GF Irwin L. Sperry 1902
Ragtime Reel KSG S. G. Kiesling 1902
Ragtime Revels—Schottische FAM E. S. Phelps 1899
Ragtime Rifles—Two Step MDS Martina Mattingly 1901
Ragtime Rings the Bell AWC Axel Christensen 1918
Ragtime Showers—March and Two-Step RAS Kathryn Athol Morton 1902
Ragtime Skedaddle, A JWS George Rosey 1899
Ragtime Violin, The TSNY Irving Berlin SONG 1911
Ragtime Wedding March AWC Axel W. Christensen 1902
Rag Town Lancers JWP Samuel Hosfeld 1899
Ragtown Rags MWAS arr. by Max Hoffmann 1898
Rambling Mose—Characteristic Slow Drag HNW J. F. Barth 1903
Ramshackle Rag MMC Ted Snyder 1911
Rastus Honeymoon PE J. Lloyd Meacham 1897
Rastus on Parade FAM Kerry Mills 1895
Razzazza Mazzazza CF Arthur Pryor 1906
Recreation Rag No. 1 Roy J. Carew unpublished 1949
Recreation Rag No. 2 (Get Over, Dirty) Roy J. Carew unpublished 1949
Red Devil Rag WSM Lucien Denni 1904
Red Head Rag LF Irene Franklin and Burt Green 1910

319

Red Wing—An Indian Intermezzo FAM (also published as a song) **Kerry** Mills 1907

Reuben Fox Trot JWS Ed. B. Claypoole 1914

Rhapsody Rag MS Harry Jentes 1911

Richmond Rag JHA May Aufderheide 1908

Ring-Tum-Diddie—A Boston Rag PMU Fred Heltman 1912

Rock o' Jubilee Traditional Spiritual

Rocky Rags IS Isidore Seidel 1911

Roll Out! Heave Dat Cotton OD Wm. Shakespeare Hayes SONG 1877

Roustabout Rag LG Paul Sarebresole 1897

Row Row Row HVT William Jerome—James V. Monaco SONG 1912

Rubber Plant Rag—A Stretcherette WJ Geo. L. Cobb 1909

Rufenreddy SF Roy Bargy and Charley Straight 1922

Rufus Rastus Johnson Brown HVT Andrew B. Sterling—Harry Von Tilzer 1905 See *What You Goin' to Do When the Rent Comes 'Round*

Safety Pin Catch TMCC Luis Fuiks 1909

Salée Dame Traditional Creole NMU Albert Nicholas and Danny Barker 1948

Salute to Sam Johnson—Cake Walk JWP O. E. Sutton 1899

Sambo out o' Work—Cake Walk WMAS J. A. Silberberg 1899

Sandella Rag JSAS Edward Hudson 1921

Sandpaper Rag JSAS H. E. Ellman and S. Lew Schwab 1909

Sapphire TMU Rube Bloom 1927

Saskatoon Rag RGC Phil Goldberg 1915

Sassafrass Rag AD J. Levy 1905

Satisfied—An Emotional Drag VK Theron C. Bennett 1904

Scarecrow Rag JHA Will B. Morrison 1911

Schultzmeier Rag JSAS B. R. Whitlow 1914

Second Hungarian Rhapsody Franz Liszt

Shake Yo' Dusters or Picaninny Rag SBS Wm. H. Krell SONG 1898

Shamrock Rag ELB Euday Bowman 1916

Shave 'Em Dry—Rag-Blues-Trot JSAS Sam Wishnuff 1917

She's a Thoroughbred—Coon Song à la Ragtime WSM Ned Wayburn SONG 1898

She's Getting More like White Folks Every Day SBC Williams and Walker SONG 1901

She's Got a Good Pussy Traditional Honkytonk Song unpublished

Shew Fly Quadrille WSM C. A. White 1869

Shifty Shuffles—Buck Dance ENF-WAW Eva Note Flennard 1897

Shine or Polish Rag FHC Fred Heltman 1914

Shout, Sister, Shout CW Tim Brymn—Clarence Williams SONG 1930

Shuffling Coon, The JWS John Rastus Topp 1897

Shuffling Jasper—Rag-Time Two Step JCC W. H. Scouton 1899

Silence and Fun—A Rag Time Essence WRC Charles Mullen 1904

Simplicity Rag SMP Eugene Ellsworth 1912

Sissie and Bob Traditional

Sister Kate—Cake Walk cw   A. J. Piron   1919
Skidding—Novelty Solo MMC   Ed Claypoole   1923
Skidmore Guard, The WAP   Ed Harrigan—David Braham and William Carter SONG   1874
Slippery Place, A—Comic Rag March WWR   P. M. Hacker, arr. by J. Bodewalt Lampe   1911
Slivers—Eccentric Rag CM   Harry Cook   1909
Smash-Up Rag WWR   Gwendolyn Stevenson   1914
Smoky Mokes—Cake Walk—Two Step   Abe Holzmann   1899
Smokin' Charley—Two Step and Cake Walk BD   Ed Lincoln   1901
Snake Rag   Joe Oliver—Alphonse Picou   1923
Snappin' Turtle Rag WWR   Chas. L. Cook   1913
Snap Shot Sal FAF   Williams and Walker SONG   1899
Snipes—Two Step Characteristic CH   Mamie E. Williams   1909
Snowball—Intermezzo MWAS   Lee S. Roberts   1912
Snow Ball Rag WWR   Nellie M. Stokes   1907
Soliloquy TMU   Rube Bloom   1926
Sonata Appassionata   Ludwig van Beethoven
S.O.S. Musician's Distress JSAS   Bradshaw and Joe McGrade   1919
So They Say—included in *Boone's Rag Medley No. 2*
Soup and Fish Rag GM   Harry Jentes and Pete Wendling   1913
Sour Grapes Rag   W. B. Morrison
South Car'lina Sift—Wing Dance WSM   George Lowell Tracy   1897
South Car'lina Tickle—Cake Walk TP   Adam Geibel   1898
Southern Blossoms—A Darktown Two Step PAH   Arthur Pryor   1898
Southern Smiles JWJ   E. H. Kelly   1903
Southern Snowballs—Rag Two Step VMBC   La Rue E. Black   1907
Sparkler Rag, The VK   H. S. Wilson   1908
Sparkles—Rag Time Two Step WIL   Charles B. Ennis
Spider and the Bed Bug Had a Good Time, The   Traditional
Spring Song   Felix Mendelssohn
Squee-Gee, The—Characteristic Two Step March AGA   Will H. Tyers   1904
Squirrel Rag—Slow Drag WRC   Paul Biese—F. Henri Klickman   1913
Star and Garter—Rag Time Waltz AWC   Axel Christensen   1910
Steal Away   Traditional Spiritual
Steamboat Rag SMSL-JSAS   Ernie Burnett   1914
Steeple Chase—Pigeon Walk WBS   Milton Ager and Pete Wendling   1915
St. Louis Blues WCH   W. C. Handy   1914
St. Louis Rag LBG   Leo Grabbe   1899
St. Louis Ripple Rag, The PBU   Paul Burmeister   1912
St. Louis Society Dance, The WGH   Walter G. Haenschen   1911
St. Louis Tickle, The VK   (words in Song Version: James O'Dea)— Barney and Seymore   1904–5
St. Patrick's Day Is a Bad Day for Coons SB   Irving Jones SONG   1901
Stinging Bee—Characteristic WRC   Mike Bernard   1908
Stompin' the Bug RSP   Mercedes Gilbert—Phil Worde   1927
Stone's Barn Dance WWR   Fred S. Stone   1908

Stop Dat Knocking EHB Coon Song From *Christy Minstrels Ethiopian Glee Book* 1848

Stumbling LF Zez Confrey (Edward Elzear Confrey) 1922

Stuttering Coon, The MWAS H. Y. Leavitt SONG 1898 INSTR. 1899

Sunshine Capers SF Roy Bargy 1922

Susie, Susie Traditional

Swanee Rag CKH Phil Kussel 1904

Swanee Ripples—A Rag Novelette FC-HWM Walter Blaufus 1912

Sweet Kentucky Babe WSM Richard H. Buck—Adam Geibel SONG 1896

Sweet Pickles—Characteristic Two Step VK George E. Florence 1907

Sweet Potatoes SMC Justin Ringleben 1906

Swellest Dressed Gal in Town, De HWNC N. J. Clesi—Hy Wehrmann 1898

Sympathetic Jasper—A Drag Rag E. L. Catlin 1905

Sympathetic Rag AS Arthur Siebrecht 1911

Syncopated Sandy BAS Ned Wayburn and Stanley Whiting SONG 1897

Take It Easy MMC Axel W. Christensen 1924

Take Me Back, Babe GWS T. Barrett McMahon SONG 1898

Tanglefoot Rag VM F. H. Losey, Op. 300 1910

Tango Rag JMP Abe Olman 1914

Tar-Heeler's Dream—Cake Walk ICS William J. Rahley 1899

Tennessee Shout—Southern Jubilee March and Two Step for Band R. M. Brand 1898

Texas Teaser—Wing Dance WSM George Lowell Tracy 1898

That Aeroplane Rag WWR Fred C. Roegge—Berte C. Randall 1911

That Banjo Rag WJ A. J. Weidt 1912

That Banjo Rag WWR Earl C. Jones—Neil Moret SONG 1912

That Baseball Rag WRC C. Jones SONG 1913

That Candy Rag RBSL Robert Bircher 1909

That Chopstick Rag JAS Grant Clark—Jerome and Schwartz SONG 1912

That Fascinating Rag JWJ Walter Rolfe 1911

That Fussy Rag FBH Victor H. Smalley 1910

That Futuristic Rag MMC Rube Bloom 1923

That International Rag WBS Irving Berlin SONG 1913

That Irresistible Rag JTH E. R. Wright—Paul Eugene SONG 1913

That Left Hand Rag CHSL-JSAS Charles Humfeld, "Musical Architect" INSTR. and SONG 1912

That Lovin' Johnson Rag, See *Johnson Rag*

That Lovin' Rag FDHU Bernie Adler 1913

That Lovin' Rag Time Man TMM D. A. Esrom—Theo. F. Morse SONG 1912

That Mesmerizing Mendelssohn Tune TSNY SONG Irving Berlin 1909

That Mysterious Rag TSNY Irving Berlin—Ted Snyder SONG 1911

That Peculiar Rag TSNY-MMC E. Erdman—F. M. Fagan SONG 1910

That Pleasin' Rag HRM Fred J. O'Connor 1911

That Puzzlin' Rag   DHM   Elmer Bowman—Chris Smith   SONG   1912
That Rag Time Dancing   FAM   H. J. Breen—T. Mayo Geary   SONG
    1898
That's a Plenty   WR   Bert Williams   SONG   1909
That's a Plenty   JMP   Lew Pollack   1914
That's Why They Call Me Shine   AGA   Cecil Mack—Ford Dabney   SONG
    1910
That Ticklin' Rag   CKH   Mike Bernard   1910
That Tired Feeling—A Slow Drag   JMP   Joe Arzonia   1906
That Tired Rag   WWR   Charlotte Blake   1911
That Tuneful Rag   SMCC   Beul B. Risinger   1911
That Whistling Rag   ES   Cecil Macklin   1913
That Will Bring You Back   MWAS   Shepard N. Edmonds   SONG   1899
There's No Coon That's One Half So Warm   SB   James O'Dea—M. B.
    Garrett   SONG   1897
They Gotta Quit Kickin' My Dawg Around   JSAS-MWAS   Webb M. Oungs—
    Cy Perkins (Mrs. Wm. Stark)   SONG   1912
This Coon Is Just the Card   HHD   J. H. Russell   SONG   1898
Thoroughbreds—March and Two Step   IS   Emil Seidel   1912
Thriller Rag, The   JHA   May Aufderheide   1909
Tickle the Ivories   WWR   Walley Herzer   1913
Tiger Rag   LF   The Original Dixieland Jass Band   1917
Timbuctoo March—Ragtime Dream   ECR   E. C. Ramsdell   1899
Toboggan Rag   SF   John F. Barth   1912
Tom and Jerry Rag   JSAS   Jerry Cammack   1917
Tom Boy Rag—Two Step   AD   W. F. Bradford   1907
Too Much Mustard   ES   Cecil Macklin   1911
Totally Different Rag, A   JHA   May Aufderheide   1910
Très Moutarde, see Too Much Mustard
Trilby Rag   JWS   Cary Morgan   1915
Trip to Coontown, A   HHD   Billy Cole and J. Weldon Johnson—Bert
    Williams   SONG   1898
Trombone Rag   Melvin   (Turk) Murphy   unpublished
Trombonium   AEO   A. E. Ostrander   1927
Turkey in the Straw, See Zip Coon
Turkey in the Straw—A Rag Time Fantasy   LF   Otto Bonnell   1899
Turkish Towell Rag   (*A Rub Down*)   Thomas S. Allen   1912
Turn, Sinner   Traditional Spiritual
12th Street Rag   SBC   Euday Bowman   1914
Two Happy Coons   PMC   Theo. H. Northrup   1891
Two Key Rag   LAB   Joe Hollander   1916

Uncle Jasper's Jubilee—Cake Walk   ETP   E. T. Paull   1898
Uncle Moses, Culud Ge'm'man—Two Step   AWP   Benjamin R. Smith   1898
Underneath the Cotton Moon   GM   Sam M. Lewis—George W. Meyer
    SONG   1913
Under the Bamboo Tree   JWS   Bob Cole   1902

Valse, La   Maurice Ravel
Venetian Rag   MMC   Donald Heywood   1922
Virginia—Two Step and Hot Rag Swing   WMC   Harry C. Mincer   1899
Virginny's Black Daughter   EHB   From *Christy Minstrels Ethiopian Glee Book*
    1848
Voodoo Man, The   HAS   Williams and Walker   SONG   1900

Wagner Couldn't Write a Rag Time Song   JAS-MMC   W. Jerome—Jean
    Schwartz   SONG   1913
Waiting for the Robert E. Lee   FAM   L. Wolfe Gilbert—Lewis F. Muir
    SONG   1912
Walkin' fo' de Great White Cake   MWAS   M. Petravsky   1894
Walking for Dat Cake   WAP   Ed Harrigan—David Braham   SONG   1877
Walkin' the Dog   WRC   Shelton Brooks   1916
Warmest Coon in Town, The   RDY   Rem Shields—Jas. Murray   INSTR.
    1896   SONG   1897
Warmin' Up in Dixie, A   ETP   E. T. Paull   1899
Warm Proposition, A—Cake Walk   CWH   Paul Knox and Monroe H.
    Rosenfeld   1899
Washington Post March   HCP   John Philip Sousa   1889
Watermelon   (from *Rufus Rastus*)   CKH   Wm. D. Hall—Ernest Hogan
    and Joe Jordan   SONG   1905
Watermelon Dance, The   Charles Wilson   1893
Watermelon Rag   FOG   E. F. Dillebar   1898
Watermelon Trust, The   HAT   Harry C. Thompson   1906
Weather Bird Rag   Louis Armstrong   1923
Weaving Around Rag   SF   Lawrence A. Mitchell   1913
Webster Grove Rag   AWC   Axel Christensen   1915
What Am You Gwine to Tell Massa Peter?   BAS   Ernest Hogan and Billy
    Kersands   SONG   1893
What You Goin' to Do When the Rent Comes 'Round   HVT   Andrew B. Sterling
    —Harry Von Tilzer   1905
When Miss Maria Johnson Marries Me   SG   Williams and Walker   SONG
    1896
(When Steve Plays That) Early Morning Rag   Eddie Raye   unpublished
    1912
When the Band Plays Rag Time   JWS   J. W. Johnson—Bob Cole   SONG
    1902
When Uncle Joe Plays a Rag on His Old Banjo   TMM-MMC   D. A. Esrom—
    Theo. Morse   SONG   1912
When You Ain't Got No Money, Well, You Needn't Come 'Round   MWAS
    Clarence S. Brewster—A. Baldwin Sloane   SONG   1898
When You Do de Ragtime Dance—March and Two Step—Schottische   GAS
    Harry Von Tilzer   1898
Whistling Coon   WAP   Sam Devere   1888
Whistling Rufus   FAM   Kerry Mills   1899
Whitewash Man, The   CAH   Jean Schwartz   1908

Whoa! You Heifer—Cowboy Intermezzo HPMC Al Verges 1904
Who Dat Say Chicken in Dis Crowd? MWAS Paul Laurence Dunbar—Will
 Marion (Cook) 1898
Who'll Win de Cake Tonight?—Ethiopian Schottische GLS Walter Hawley
 1897
Wild Cherries Rag—Characteristique Rag TSNY Ted Snyder 1908

Yacka Hula Hickey Dula WBS E. Ray Goetz and Joe Young—Pete
 Wendling SONG 1916
Yaller Gal Dance, The—Levee Dance Grotesque HJW John Harding 1896
Yaller Gals EHB From *Christy Minstrels Ethiopian Glee Book* 1848
Yankee Doodle words anonymous folk tune 1782
You Can't Fool All of the People All of the Time JWS Shepard N. Edmonds
 SONG 1913
You Got to Play Rag Time MWAS Jean C. Havez—A. Baldwin Sloane
 SONG
You're Talking Rag Time TBH Beaumont Sisters SONG 1899
You Tell Me Your Dream, I'll Tell You Mine VMSF Gus Kahn—Chas. N.
 Daniels (Neil Moret) SONG 1928

Zig Zag "The Lion" (Willie Smith) 1949
Zip Coon AMS claimed by Bob Farrell and also by a Mr. Dixon 1834
 (included in *Christy Minstrels Ethiopian Glee Book* EHB 1848)

(Note: This list is selected from the many known rolls. For valuable help in assembling it, thanks are due to Len Kunstadt, editor of Record Research, *and also to Dr. Hubert S. Pruett, Mike Montgomery, Trebor Jay Tichenor, and Russ Cassidy.)*

A LIST OF PLAYER-
PIANO ROLLS

Key to Label Abbreviations

AE	Aeolian Grand	MEL	Mel-O-Dee
AM	American Piano Co.	MET	Metrostyle
AMP	Automusic Perforating Co.	MT	Metro Style
AN	Angelus		Themodist
AR	Artempo	MU	Music Note
ART	Arto	NA	National
AU	Autopiano	OW	Owen Player
AUT	Autograph		Roll Co.
CA	Capitol	PE	Perfection
CB	Chase & Baker	PMR	Perforated Music
CE	Cecilian		Roll Co.
COL	Columbia	QRS	QRS
CON	Connorized	RE	Recordo
DA	Duo-Art	REP	Republic
DO	Dominant	RH	Rhythmodik
EL	Electra	RO	Royal
FS	88 Note Full Score	ST	Standard
HE	Herbert	STA	Starr Piano Co.
IM	Imperial	SU	Supertone
KI	Kimball	UN	Universal
LH	Lyon & Healy	UNI	Uni-Record
MA	Metro Art	USM	U. S. Music
MAS	Master Record	VIR	Virtuoso
ME	Melographic	VO	Vocalstyle

The symbol "pl" followed by a name indicates the pianist who played, i. e. recorded, a specific roll. All early rolls were mechanically cut.

SCOTT JOPLIN

(Note: rolls definitely known to have been played by Joplin are preceded by *)
Cascades, The CON-430; CON-6047; included in medley CON-854; QRS-30088

Chrysanthemum, The CON-6076

Entertainer, The CE-6046; CON-6046; QRS-X3087; QRS-30358

Euphonic Sounds included on medley rolls:　AN-90193, MET-102302, UN-77987, UN-92715

Favorite, The CON-4173; QRS-X3345

Felicity Rag (Joplin-Hayden) KI-B6781; USM-65050B

Fig Leaf Rag QRS-03073; QRS-30141

Gladiolus Rag AM-12623; AN-90002; EL-76896; KI-C6529; MT-79513; MT-92261; QRS-30162; ST-76836; UN-77769D; UN-92265

Kismet Rag (Joplin-Hayden) KI-B-6793; USM-5819

*Magnetic Rag CON-10266　pl Scott Joplin

*Maple Leaf Rag CON-10265; MA-202704; UNI-202705;　all pl Joplin

Maple Leaf Rag EA-8440; AM-493; in medley　AM-4066; AM-95101; AN-90080; AR-9976 pl Steve Williams; ART-8440; CA-95101; CON-148; CON-4028; in medley CON-2966; in medley KI-F6154; ME-0369; ME-1731; MEL-89965; MT-89961; PE-8440; QRS-X3817; QRS-30900; QRS-7308 pl J. L. Cook; QRS-100419 pl Max Kortlander; STA-8057; SU-10029; UN-8440; UN-89965; USM-1368; USM-61368B; in medley USM-65399F

Nonpareil, The (None to Equal) CON-4401

Original Rags AE-20428; AMP-4051; CON-843; CON-4051; ME-0370; QRS-3268

Palm Leaf Rag—A Slow Drag QRS-X3034; QRS-30342

Paragon Rag in medley USM-75378

Peacherine Rag CON-6047

Pineapple Rag in medley AN-90193; LH-6067; in medleys MET-102303, UN-77987, UN-92715

*Pleasant Moments—A Ragtime Waltz CON—pl Scott Joplin

Ragtime Dance, The QRS-X3626

Rose Leaf Rag CON-1336

Scott Joplin's New Rag AE—; AM-11263; AN-90806; CON-2121; KI-C-6132; QRS-31282; STA—; UN-79527; UN-99365

Searchlight Rag QRS-X3866; QRS-30595

*Something Doing (Joplin-Hayden) CON-10278 pl Scott Joplin

Something Doing (Joplin-Hayden) CON-4433; QRS-30396; QRS-30786; RO-3389; USM-6055

Stoptime Rag QRS-30786

Strenuous Life, The CON-4090

Sugar Cane—A Rag Time Classic CON-4421

Sunflower Slow Drag (Joplin-Hayden) AE-8479; AM-1072; CON-844; CON-4082; UN-8479

Swipesy Cake Walk (Joplin-Marshall) CON-4087; QRS-30328

Sycamore, The—A Concert Rag CON-4320; QRS-30395

Wall Street Rag MAS-653

*Weeping Willow CON-10277 pl Scott Joplin

Weeping Willow CON-400; CON-4411; QRS-30404 (30304?)

Note: the following is the only known roll recorded by Joplin of a composition by another composer:
*Ole Miss Rag (W. C. Handy)   CON—pl Scott Joplin

JAMES SCOTT

Climax Rag   AN-91333; AR-1857 pl Steve Williams; MET-104364;
 MET-301036; UN-100797; UN-301037
Efficiency Rag   MET-303152; UN-303153; USM-8397
Evergreen Rag   QRS-32269; USM-7278
Frog Legs Rag   CON-582; CON-4301; EL-76202; KI-B-5132; in medley
 KI-F6154; ME-0804; ST-76202; USM-1255; USM-61255
Grace and Beauty   AN-90969; CON-20460 pl W. Arlington; FS-80260;
 KI-B6317; MET-102604; MET-300118; in medleys QRS-S3026,
 QRS-31388; ST—; UN-79839; UN-300119; USM-3294; USM-5162;
 USM-63294; in medleys USM-5399, USM-65162
Great Scott Rag   QRS-31138
Hilarity Rag   AN-91069; in medley KI-F6154; ME—; MET-103174;
 MET-300278; in medley QRS-31379; UN-100017; UN-300279;
 USM-5399; USM-64542B; in medley USM-65399F
Honeymoon Rag   AR-9935 pl Steve Williams; MA-203008 and UN-203009
 pl Felix Arndt; USM-8143
Kansas City Rag   CON-1560; CON-4334; QRS-30566
Prosperity Rag   USM-7905 (7205?)
Quality Rag   in medley KI-C6778; QRS-32226; in medley QRS-32346;
 USM-5270
Rag Sentimental   MU-1075
Ragtime Oriole   AN-91182; AR-1898 pl Steve Williams; CON-10311 pl
 W. Arlington; FS-80353; KI-C6787; MET-103672; MET-300642;
 QRS-32228; STA—; UN-100345; UNI-300643; USM-5311; USM-65311
Sunburst Rag   KI-B6794; USM-2261; USM-62261

JOSEPH LAMB

American Beauty Rag   AE—; AN-91255; AR-1878 pl Ernest Stevens;
 MET-104054; MET-300874; QRS-100299 pl Max Kortlander; RO—;
 UN-100595; UN-300875; USM-6312; in medley USM-7065
Champagne Rag   USM-4523; USM-64523
Cleopatra Rag   in nickelodeon medley roll ST-A1273
Contentment Rag   AR-2815 pl Steve Williams; USM-7050
Excelsior Rag   USM-2255; USM-62255B
Ragtime Nightingale   AR-3855 pl Steve Williams; MEL-303003; MET-302002;
 in medley ST-A1273; UN-302003; USM-7373
Reindeer Rag   USM-7272; in medley USM-7345
Sensation Rag   CON-1303; QRS-30845
Top Liner Rag   AR pl Howard Lutter; MA-202626 pl Felix Arndt;
 USM-7671; in medley USM-8007

GEORGE BOTSFORD

Black and White Rag AN—; MT-98712; USM—; UN-75569
Buckeye Rag UNI-300559
Chatterbox Rag CON—; QRS-30915; UN-78565; USM-4618; USM-64618
Grizzly Bear Rag CON-1533; CON-3671; KI—; MT-93081; UN-77815
Honeysuckle Rag QRS-31172
Hyacinth Rag QRS—; ST—; USM-65189-B
Incandescent Rag AN—; KI-B-6495; QRS-31390; ST—; UN-300176; USM—
Pianophiends Rag in medley MET-94711; ST—; UN-78475
Royal Flush Rag QRS-30992; in medley UN-78717
Sailing Down the Chesapeake Bay KI-86448; SU-10034
Universal Rag AE—; AN—; UN-100019
Wiggle Rag QRS-30847

CHARLES L. JOHNSON

Apple Jack Rag—Some Rag QRS-32329
Butterflies—Caprice USM—
Cloud Kisser in medley USM-470
Crazy Bone Rag AM—; AU—; HE—; ST—; USM-65903-B
Cum-Bac Rag AE—; AN—; CON-2215; QRS—; ST—; UN-98565
Dill Pickles Rag COL-95120; USM—
Fine and Dandy QRS-30168
Golden Spider Rag QRS-30929; ST—; USM—
Melody Rag USM-64808-B
Porcupine Rag CON-1544; CON-4502; QRS-30756
Scandalous Thompson AM-2922
Silver King Rag Two Step USM-62354
Tar Babies Rag ME—; QRS-31233; USM—
Tobasco—Ragtime Waltz UN-77259

HENRY LODGE

Black Diamond Rag KI-C6441; QRS—; ST—
Boston Hop—Hesitation Waltz USM-66425
Demi-Tasse—One Step or Castle Walk USM-66426
Pastime Rag HE—
Red Pepper, A Spicy Rag SU-10034; UN-8507
Roulette Reel—A Parisian Prance AN—; CON—; UN—
Silver Fox—A Raggy Fox Trot CON—; DO-10396
Temption Rag in medley KI-F-6154; UN-76615; USM-3047
Tokio Rag AE—; QRS—; UN—; UNI—

PERCY WENRICH

Alamo Rag AE—; ST—; UN-78615; UN-78659
Chestnuts Rag USM-61071-B
Clover Land—Peck o' Pickles USM-66452
Cotton Babes Rag QRS-30802

Crabapple Rag   QRS-30684
Dixie Blossoms   MEL-0879
Dixie Darlings   QRS-43860
Flower Girl   UN-83477
Jack o' Lantern Moon—Peck o' Pickles   USM-66451
Noodles Rag   CON-579
Peaches and Cream Rag   UN-75485
Persian Lamb Rag   QRS-30647
Ragtime Chimes   QRS-31046
Red Rose Rag   ME—
Skeleton Rag   AE—; STA—; UN—; in medley USM-65306-F
Smiler, The   DA-5551; UN-3361
Sugar Boon (Wenrich and Botsford)   AN—
Sunflower Rag   QRS-31063; ST—; USM—
Whipped Cream Rag   AN—; CON-4748; CON-2541; RH— pl Pete Wendling;
     ST—

ROLLS HAND-PLAYED BY EUBIE BLAKE

Arkansas Blues (Lada-Spencer Williams)   MEL—
Boll Weevil Blues (Hess)   MEL-4259
Broadway Blues (Morgan)   MEL-5153
Crazy Blues (Perry Bradford)   MEL—
Dangerous Blues   MEL—
*Fizz Water (Sissle-Blake)   ST—
*Gypsy Blues (Eubie Blake)   REP—
Home Again Blues (Berlin-Akst)   MEL-S-2949
Memphis Blues (Handy)   MEL-4371
Negro Spirituals: *Go Down Moses; I'm A-Rolling; Nobody Knows De
     Trouble I'se Seen; I Got Shoes*   DA-10091
Strut Miss Lizzie (Creamer and Layton)   MEL-4241
Ten Little Fingers and Ten Little Toes   MEL-S-3003
Wang Wang Blues (Mueller-Johnson)   MEL-S-2985

JAMES P. JOHNSON

*(Note: A selection of this artist's hand-played rolls of his own compositions, as well
as several Eubie Blake tunes.)*
Baltimore Buzz (Sissle-Blake)   QRS-1738
Caprice Rag   UN-203177; MA-203176
Carolina Shout   QRS-100999
Charleston   RE-M-611790
Daintiness Rag   MA-203106; UN-203107
Don't Tell Your Monkey Man   QRS-1338
Eccentricity Waltz   QRS-101000
Fascination   MA-203226; UN-203227
Gypsy Blues (Sissle-Blake)   QRS-1674
He's My Man Blues   QRS-3676

If I Could Be With You One Hour Tonight with Waller QRS-3818
If You've Never Been Vamped by a Brown Skin Gal (Sissle-Blake) QRS-1644
Innovation MA-203254; UN-203255
It Takes Love to Cure the Heart's Disease QRS-1339
Mama's Blues AR—; duet with Wilson UN-2355
Runnin' Wild Medley: Charleston, Old-Fashioned Love, Open Your Heart,
    Love Bug QRS-101027
Steeplechase Rag MA-203178; UN-203179
Stop It MA-203204; UN-203205
Twilight Rag, duet with Wilson MA-203274
Wasn't It Nice QRS-3996

ROLLS HAND-PLAYED BY JELLY ROLL MORTON

Dead Man Blues (Morton) QRS-3674
Grandpa's Spells (Morton) VO-50487
King Porter Stomp (Morton) VO-50480
London Blues (Morton) VO-50479
Midnight Mama (Morton) QRS-3675
Mr. Jelly Lord (Morton) VO-12973
Original Jelly Roll Blues QRS-32351
Shreveport Stomp (Morton) VO-50481
Stratford Hunch (Morton) VO-50485
Sweet Man (Morton) CA-1334
Tin Roof Blues (New Orleans Rhythm Kings) VO-12974
Tom Cat Blues (Morton) OW—; VO—

PLAYER ROLLS—A SELECTED GENERAL LISTING

African Beauty, An (Pryor) AM-1884
Agitation Rag (Hampton) AR-3027 pl Dave Kaplan
Alabama Tickle—Cake Walk (Southwell) UN-8125
Alagazam (Holzmann) AM-483; UN-60677
Alexander's Ragtime Band (Berlin) AE—; CON—; ME—; ST—; USM—
All Coons Look Alike to Me in medley ST-76142
All That Lovin' I Had For You Is Gone, Gone, Gone (Chris Smith) USM—
Apeda Rag (Harris) RH— pl F. A. Schmitz
Apple Sass Rag (H. Belding) CON-20377 pl W. Arlington
April Fool Rag (Jean Schwartz) USM—
At a Georgia Camp Meeting (Mills) AE-20295; AM-481; UN-8105
At a Ragtime Reception (Jerome) AM-1948; UN-4241
At the Ragtime Ball (Monaco) AE—; AN—; UNI—

Baboon Bounce—A Rag Step Intermezzo (George L. Cobb) USM—
Ballin' the Jack (Chris Smith) DO-10306
Bamboula, La (Gottschalk) AE-40576
Banana Peel Rag (Winkler) HE—
Banjo—Grotesque Fantasie (Gottschalk) UN-4204

Banjo Rag (Bennett) UN-77445
Barbed Wire Rag (Spencer) UN-77829
Barnyard Rag (Chris Smith) ME—; QRS—; USM—
Bell Hop Rag (Bryan) QRS—; STA—; UNI— pl Paul Paris
Black and Blue Rag (H. G. Nichols) USM-66370
Black Beauty Rag (Schwartz) included on MET-94711
Black Cat Rag (Wooster and Smith) UN-71855
Black Laugh, The (Seymour) AM-629
Blame It on the Blues—A Weary Blue Rag (C. L. Cooke) USM-66403
Blue Ribbon Rag (Aufderheide) QRS-30930
Boardwalk Parade (Al Johns) AM-480
Bohemian Rag (Hall-Barton) QRS—
Borneo Rag (Neil Moret) CON—; QRS—; USM—
Bowery Buck (Tom Turpin) AM-676; CON-4044; UN-8355
Bunch o' Blackberries (Holzmann) AM-2022
Bunch o' Rags (Jerome) AM-470; UN-8628
Bunny Hug Rag (H. De Costa) AE—; ST—; UN—; UNI—
Buzzer Rag (May Aufderheide) QRS-03359; QRS-30910

Caberavings Rag (R. Whiting) USM-66436
Calico Rag (Nat Johnson) HE—
California Sunshine Rag (Harry Jentes) USM—
Cannonball, The (Northup) included on KI-F-6154; UN-74357; USM—
Carbarlick Acid Rag (Wiley) UN-77299
Carolina Fox Trot (Will H. Vodery) DO-10304
Castle House Rag (James R. Europe) HE—; USM-66448
Castle Lame Duck Waltz (Europe-Dabney) CON-5581; CON-2758;
    USM-66598
Castle Maxixe—Brazilian Maxixe (Europe-Dabney) CON-2736; CON-5574;
    USM-66533
Castle Perfect Trot (James Reese Europe) USM-66567
Castles' Half and Half (James Reese Europe) USM-66488
Castles' Innovation-Tango (Europe) USM-66534
Castles' Modern Dances (Europe) ST—
Cataract Rag (Rob Hampton) AR-1863 pl Steve Williams
Checkers Rag (Harry J. Lincoln) USM—
Chicken Chowder (Giblin) UN-73595
Chili Sauce Rag (Fischler) UN-78645
Chimes—Novelty Rag (Homer Denny) AU-93495; MT-93941; MT-100121
Cinders Rag (Henry) UN70817
Classic Rag (Neil Moret) USM—; included on ME-77667
Clef Club March (James Reese Europe) HE—
Clorindy—or The Origin of the Cakewalk, Medley (Will Marion Cook)
    UN-4278
Cohan's Rag Babe (Neil Moret) USM—
Coon Band Contest, A (Pryor) AM-2078; UN-8320

Coon Band Parade (Europe) UN-69805
Corrugated Rag (Mellinger) STA—
Cotton Blossoms—Cake Walk (Milt Hall) AM-907
Cotton Patch Ragtime, A (Tyler) AM-476
Cotton Time Rag Two Step (C. N. Daniels) USM-4592; USM-64592
Creole Belles (Lampe) AE-8351; UN-8351

Dallas Blues—Syncopated Melody (Wand) CON—; USM—
Darkey Todalo (Jordan) UN-78529
Dat's Harmony (Bert Williams) USM—
Desecration Rag (Felix Arndt) AN—; UN—
Dischord Rag (Tennessee Blues) Tango (A. Stone) USM-66380
Dockstader Rag (Copeland) AE—; AN—; ST—; UN—
Down Home Rag (Sweatman) ST—; UNI-200869 pl Felix Arndt
Down in Honky Tonk Town (Chris Smith) CON-20398 pl William Axtman
Down in Jungle Town (Theo. Morse) UN-76607
Down South—Ragtime March (Grimm) VIR-5287
Dusky Dudes (Schwartz) AM-2146
Dusty Rag (May Aufderheide) CON-315; ST-76152
Dynamite—A Noisy Rag (F. Henri Klickman) USM—

Edward J. Mellinger's Rag (Mellinger) USM—
"1863" March Medley (E. C. Calvin) CON-4273
Elephant Rag (Malvin Franklin) CON-4723; HE—; RH— pl by Franklin
Entertainers Rag (Jay Roberts) CON—; IM-54290 pl Jack Clyde; RH— pl
  Mabel Wayne; ST—; USM—
Ethiopia—African Intermezzo (Al Johns) AM-2204
Evolution Rag (Thos. S. Allen) ST—; USM—

Fanatic Rag (H. A. Tierney) ME—; UN-78679; USM—
Fiddlesticks Rag (Olney) CON—
Florida Rag (Lowry) AM-662; UN-72559
Flying Arrow—Intermezzo Indienne (Holzmann) UN-71445
French Pastry Rag (Copeland) MA-202652
Frisky Picks—Cake Walk (L. M. Teichman) AM-2253
Frozen Bill—Rag (Pryor) UN-75557
Funeral Rag, The (Morawski-Kortlander) USM—
Futurist Twirl (Burch) AN—

Georgia Grind (Ford Dabney) UNI—
"Get This"—Slow Drag (Walter Blaufuss) USM-66421
Gold Dust Twins Rag (Nat Johnson) HE—; RO—; USM—
Good Gravy Rag (H. Belding) CON—; USM-65979-B
Gravel Rag (Blake) UN-78067
G-Whiz Rag Two-Step (Sam H. Ewing) USM-4508; USM-65508

Hanky Panky—Slow Drag Rag (Robinson-Adams) USM-66575

Haytian Rag (Ford Dabney)   CON—; USM-4613; USM-64613
Hiawatha—A Summer Idyl (Moret)   AM-851
High Jinks (Rudolf Friml)   USM—
Honeymoon Rag (Olman)   USM-64234
Horseshoe Rag (Niebergall-Alferd)   ME-02187
Humpty-Dumpty—Novelty Rag (Chas. Straight)   CON—; HE—;
    ST—; UNI—; USM-66369
Hypnotic Rag (Mahoney)   AE—; AN—; ST—; UN—

Impecunious Davis (Mills)   AM-2343
Invitation Rag (Copeland)   AE-79199
I've Got the Finest Man (Creamer-Europe)   AN—
I Want a Ragtime Bungalow (Bert Kalmar)   USM—
I Wonder Where My Easy Rider's Gone (Shelton Brooks)   USM—

Jag Rag, The (Arthur C. Morse)   USM—
Jamaica Jinger Rag (E. Van Alstyne)   AE—;   AN—
Jay Rag (Roberts)   QRS—
Jay Roberts Rag (Roberts)   QRS—
Jogo Blues (The Memphis Itch)—Rag (W. C. Handy)   CON-2733;
    CON-4765; USM—
Jungle Jamboree Rag (Chris Smith)   AN—
Junk Man Rag (Luckey Roberts)   MT-6140; ST—; STA—; UNI-200985
    pl Felix Arndt

King Chanticleer (Ayer)   QRS-41133
King of Rags (Swisher)   MET-6274
Kinklets Rag (Arthur Marshall)   QRS-30519
Klassicle Rag (C. Duane Crabbe)   USM—

Lady of Quality—Waltzes (Fred S. Stone)   AM-2418
La Rumba—Tango Argentine (Tim Brymn)   USM—
Last Waltz (Ford Dabney)   UNI— pl Paul Paris
Lemon Drops Rag (Mike Bernard)   CON—
Live Wires Rag (Shepherd)   ME-01901; UN-78697
Louisiana Rag (Northrup)   AE-8190
Lovie Joe (Joe Jordan)   UN-78209; USM-4548; USM-64548

Maori—A Samoan Dance (Tyers)   UN-75459
Ma Ragtime Baby (Fred S. Stone)   AE-8207
Ma Ragtime Queen (Barth)   AE-8445; UN-8445
Maurice Rag (Penn)   ST—
Medic Rag—Ragtime Two Step (Woolsey)   AN—;   QRS-03362; QRS-30913;
    ST-77857; UN77857
Melancholy Mose (Jerome)   QRS-4509
Melody Rag (Birch)   ME—; QRS—

334

Melrose Rag (H. Bauersachs)   con-20861 pl Sybil Court
Memphis Blues Rag (W. C. Handy)   an—; un—
Midnight Whirl (Hein)   an—
Ministrel Man Rag (J. Russel Robinson)   usm-65156-b
Mr. Black Man (Pryor)   am-2548; un-63497
Mr. Johnson Turn Me Loose (Harney)   ae-40167; in medleys st-76142, un-9803
Mizzoura Mag's Chromatic Rag (Fariss)   un-70409
Mobile Prance, The—Cake Walk (Brown)   pmr-d-520
Mockingbird Rag (Walsh-Straight)   sta—
Monkey Rag (Chris Smith)   ae-79475; an—; st—; un—
Movie Rag (Zamecnik)   rh— pl Franklin; st—
Music Box Rag (Luckey Roberts)   ae—; an—; con-2890; do-10336; ma—
Mutt and Jeff Rag (P. L. Eubank)   con-2600; con-4762; usm—
My Coal Black Lady (Jefferson)   ae-40202

Nat Johnson Rag (Nat Johnson)   he—
1915 Rag (Tierney)   ae—; rh—; st—; un—
Nonsense Rag (R. G. Brady)   qrs—; usm—
Notoriety Rag (Kathryn L. Widmer)   st—; usm—

Oh That Beautiful Rag (Snyder)   st-76314
Old Folks Rag (Wilber Sweatman)   an—; usm-66547
Ole Miss Rag (Handy)   pl Scott Joplin

Palm Beach (Luckey Roberts)   qrs-31772
Panama (Tyers)   ae—; con—; qrs-31091
Panama Rag (Seymour)   un-68287
Pastime Rag No. 1—A Slow Drag (Artie Matthews)   usm-66071-b
Peaceful Henry (Kelly)   un-63525
Pearl of the Harem—Oriental Rag (H. B. Guy)   am-2653
Pele Mele Ragtime Hesitation (Malvin Franklin)   rh— pl Malvin Franklin
Pickles and Peppers (Shepherd)   un-75449
Pork and Beans (Luckey Roberts)   usm-66186-b
Porto Rico Rag (Dabney)   con—
Possum Hall Rag (Fritch)   qrs-30492
Possum Rag (Dobyns)   un-75619
Powder Rag (Birch)   un-78697; un-77975 included on ki-f-6154

Rag-a-Muffin Rag and Two Step (W. T. Pierson)   usm—
Raggedy Rag (Henry)   me—; sta—
Ragging the Scale (Claypoole)   mt-302196
Ragtime Arabian Nights (S. Romberg)   na—; un—
Ragtime Cowboy Joe (Muir)   rh— pl composer; st—
Ragtime Dream (Goodwin and Brown)   usm—
Ragtime Engineer (Smith)   met-101694; sta—

335

Ragtime Eyes (Schwartz) AN—
Rag Time Goblin Man (Von Tilzer) RH— pl Melville Morris; UN—
Ragtime Mephisto (Glen C. Leap) HE—
Ragtime Nightmare, A (Tom Turpin) CON-4149
Rag With No Name (Warren Camp) USM—
Rambling Mose (Barth) AN-25306
Ramshackle Rag (Snyder) AE—; AN—; CON—; ME—; ST—; USM—
Rastus on Parade (Mills) AE-20079; UN-8434
Razzazza Mazzazza (Pryor) UN-72685
Red Head Rag (Franklin and Green) USM-3617
Red Onion Rag (Oleman) QRS—
Red Wing (Mills) UN-75077
Rig A Jig Rag (Ayer) AE—; RH— pl composer; UN-30015;
    UN-79735
Rigmarole Rag (Kendall) CON—
Rufus Rastus Johnson Brown (Von Tilzer) AM-597

St. Louis Rag (Turpin) CB-2150-J; CON-1460; CON-4143
S. Louis Tickle (Barney and Seymore) AM-519; CON-461; UN-70947
San Antonio Swing (J. W. Buford) USM-66595
Sapho Rag (J. Russel Robinson) QRS-80781
Scarecrow Rag (Will B. Morrison) USM-66387
September Eve—A Trot (Will H. Dixon) USM—
Shovel Fish Rag (H. C. Cooke) CON-4364
Silks and Rags Waltzes (Fred S. Stone) AM-2956
Sky Rockets Rag (Severin) ST—
Slippery Elm Rag (Clarence Woods) USM—
Smokey Mokes (Holzmann) AM-2965; MET-6208; UN-8091
Snappin' Turtle Rag (C. L. Cooke) QRS-31389
Sour Grapes Rag (Morrison) CON-2539; CON-4747
Springtime Rag (Paul Pratt) MET-302454; MT-302454
Squeeze Me (Waller) pl by Fats Waller
Squirrel Rag—Slow Drag (F. Henri Klickman) USM—

Tantalizing Tingles—Rag Two Step (Violinsky) USM—
That Beautiful Rag (Berlin and Snyder) AN-35764; KI—; ME-4693;
    MET-79903; UN-780490
That Demon Rag (Russell Smith) QRS-31145
That Devil Rag (Madden-E. Van Alstyne) VO-9038
(That) Eccentric (Rag) (Robinson) DO—; QRS-31211
(That) International Rag (Berlin) AM—; CON; UNI-300659; UNI-201065 pl
    Felix Arndt; USM—
That Irresistible Rag (F. Parker) USM-66383
That Mysterious Rag (Berlin and Snyder) CON—
That Peculiar Rag (Fagan) ME-4904; QRS—; ST—
That Rag (Browne) AE-75709; UN-75709

That Raggedy Rag (Hodgkins-Coogan) QRS—
That's a Plenty (Lew Pollack) NA—
That Scandalous Rag (E. F. Kendall) RH— pl Kendall; ST—
That Stop Time Rag (Ernie Erdman) HE—
That Tango Rag (C. Roy Larson) USM-66459
That Teasin' Rag (Jordan) QRS-40795; included on MET-77667, UN-77667
That Ticklin' Rag (Mike Bernard) ME-4683; UN-78215
Thrity-Eighth Street Rag (Copeland) AN—
Those Ragtime Melodies (Gene Hodgkins) CON—; STA—
Thriller Rag, The (Aufderheide) AN-25770; ST-77727; UN-77727
Tickled to Death (Hunter) AM-745; CON-20349 pl W. Arlington; ST-8189;
   UN-88625
Tickle the Ivories Rag (Herzer) MT-301154
Tiger Rag (Original Dixieland Jass Band) QRS-5353 pl J. Lawrence
   Cooke
Too Much Mustard (Macklin) AE—; UN—
Totally Different Rag (Aufderheide) QRS-03380
Triangle Jazz Blues (Rag) (Leclere) QRS-100631 pl Max Kortlander
Trilby Rag (Morgan) PE-86508 pl Gertrude Baum
Trouble Maker Rag (Claude Messinger) USM-66582
Twentieth Century Rag (Maurice Abraham) AN—; HE-88465; UN—;
   USM-66382
Two Key Rag (Hollander) MT-302848

Vanity Rag (Paul Pratt) QRS-30708; USM—
Variety Rag (Tierney) ST—

Wailana Rag (Pratt) USM-7917-B
Warmin' Up in Dixie—Cake Walk (E. T. Paull) UN-2072
Wash Day—Rag Two Step (Charles Goeddel) USM-66618
Weary Blues (Artie Matthews) MET-302382
Weird Rag (Jean Schwartz) QRS—
Whistling Rufus (Kerry Mills) UN-8059
Whitewash Man—Rag Two Step (Jean Schwartz) USM-61151
Wild Cherries Rag (Snyder) UN-77479; USM-61137
Winter Garden Rag (Oleman) AUT— pl Phil Schwartz; STA—
Wriggley Rag, The (David and Arthurs) USM—

Yama Yama Man (Hoschna) included on UN-76467
You've Been a Good Old Wagon (Harney) included on ST-76142

A SELECTED LIST
OF PHONOGRAPH RECORDS

Key to Record Label Abbreviations

AM	American Music	DO	Dot
AS	Asch	DOH	Down Home
B & W	Black and White	GE	Gennett
BB	Bluebird	GTJ	Good Time Jazz
BER	Berliner	HA	Harmony
BN	Blue Note	JC	Jazz Classic
BR	Brunswick	JI	Jazz Information
BRUN	Brun (Campbell)	JM	Jazz Man
CA	Capitol	JR	Jazz Record
CAM	Camden	ME	Mercury
CAS	Castle	NA	National
CE	Century	PE	Perfect
CI	Circle	RI	Riverside
CL	Climax	SD	SD
CMS	Commodore	VE	Verve
CO	Columbia	VI	Victor
DE	Decca	WC	West Coast

(*All records 10" unless otherwise indicated*)

78 RPM RECORDS

Ain't Misbehavin' (Waller) Fats Waller VI-22108; Jelly Roll Morton
  CI-JM-44
Alabama Jubilee (Cobb-Yellen) John Maddox DO-1023
Alexander's Ragtime Band (Berlin) Victor Military Band VI-17006
At a Georgia Camp Meeting (Mills) Columbia Band CO-A86; Lu Watters
  Band JM-4; Sousa's Band VI-16402; from Pianola roll CI-5009

Baby, Won't You Please Come Home (Warfield-Williams) All Star Stompers
  with Chippie Hill CI-1024
Battle of San Juan Hill Mike Bernard CO-A-1266
Bert Williams (Morton) Jelly Roll Morton CI-JM-45
Black and White Rag (Botsford) Prince's Orchestra CO-A-711;. Wally
  Rose JM-1

338

Blaze Away March (Abe Holzmann) Mike Bernard CO-A-2577
Bowery Buck (Turpin) from Pianola roll CI-5008
Buddy Bolden's Blues (Morton) Nicholas-Ewell-Dodds CI-1039; Jelly Roll Morton CI-JM-77, CMS-489
Buffalo Rag (Turpin) banjo Vess L. Ossman VI-16779

Calico Rag (Nat Johnson) Frank Banta, Howard Kopp CO-A-2441
Caprice Rag (Johnson) James P. Johnson BN-26
Cascades Rag (Joplin) Wally Rose GTJ-27; Ralph Sutton DOH-10
Cataract Rag (Hampton) Parenti, Sutton, Wettling CI-1054
Carolina Shout (Johnson) James P. Johnson OK-4495; Fats Waller VI-27563
C'est l'Autre Can-Can Jelly Roll Morton CI-JM-81
Chestnut Street in the 90s (Campbell) Brun Campbell WC-113
Chicken Chowder (Giblin) Ossman-Dudley Trio CO-A-220
Climax Rag (Scott) George Lewis New Orleans Stompers CL-101; Jelly Roll Moton and His New Orleans Jazzmen BB-B10442
Coon Band Contest (Pryor) Arthur Pryor's Band VI-16079
Cotton Blossoms Cake Walk (Hall) (7″ disk, 1898) BER-1482
Crave, The (Morton) Jelly Roll Morton CI-JM-31, CMS-589
Crawfish Crawl (Parenti) Parenti, Sutton, Wettling CI-1056
Crazy Bone Rag (C. L. Johnson) John Maddox DO-1005; U. S. Marine Band VI-35380
Crazy Chord Rag (Albert Carroll) Jelly Roll Morton CI-JM-50
Creepy Feeling (Morton) Jelly Roll Morton CI-JM-29/30
Creole Belles (Lampe) from Pianola roll CI-5011

Delmar Rag (Thompson) Charley Thompson AM-528
Derby Stomp (Thompson) Charley Thompson AM-527
Digah's Stomp (Pickett) Fats Waller VI-21358
Dill Pickles Rag (C. L. Johnson) Arthur Pryor's Band VI-16482; John Maddox DO-1057; Ralph Sutton CI-1053
Dixie Belle (Wenrich) from Pianola roll CI-5007
Dixie Blossoms (Wenrich) Thomas Mills CO-A-224
Down Home Rag (Sweatman) Kid Ory's Creole Jazz Band JM-24
Dream, The (Pickett) James P. Johnson and Band AS-551-1 (12″)
Dusty Rag (Aufderheide) Bunk Johnson's Jazz Band JI-14

Easy Winners (Joplin) Wally Rose with rhythm WC-113; Wally Rose GTJ-28
Echoes of Spring (Smith) Willy (The Lion) Smith CMS-521
Eh, La Bas (Creole Traditional) The Creole Stompers AM-513; Conrad Janis Band CI-3006; Paul Barbarin's New Orleans Band CI-J-1077
Entertainer, The (Joplin) Mutt Carey and Band CE-4007; from Pianola roll JC-534
Entertainer's Rag (Jay Roberts) Parenti, Sutton, Wettling CI-1054

Essay in Ragtime (Campbell) Brum Campbell WC-114
Euphonic Sounds (Joplin) James P. Johnson and Band AS-551-1 (12″)
Everbody Two Step (Herzer) Mike Bernard CO-A-1266
Excelsior Rag (Lamb) from Pianola roll CI-5004

Fantasy on Mendelssohn's Spring Song and Rubinstein's Melody in F; Pilgrim's Chorus from Tannhäuser and Finale to Rubinstein's E Flat Concerto Mike Bernard CO-A-1276
Fig Leaf Rag (Joplin) from Pianola roll JC-533
Fingerbuster (Morton) Jelly Roll Morton JM-12
Florida Rag (Lowry) Van Eps Trio VI-17308
Freakish (Morton) Jelly Roll Morton CI-JM-71
Frog-i-More Rag (Morton) Jelly Roll Morton SD-103; Armand Hug GTJ-20

Grace and Beauty Rag (Scott) Tony Parenti CI-1030; from Pianola roll CE-4022; Ralph Sutton DOH-10
Grandpa's Spells (Morton) Jelly Roll Morton GE-5218
Grizzly Bear Rag (Botsford) Arthur Collins CO-A-844; Pryor's Band VI-5802

Handful of Keys (Waller) Fats Waller VI-V-38508
Heebie Jeebies (Atkins) Louis Armstrong Hot Five CO-35660
Heliotrope Bouquet (Joplin-Chauvin) Lee Stafford CAS-10
Hiawatha (Moret) Tony Parenti's Ragtimers CI-1031
High Society (Steele) Kid Rena Jazz Band CI-1037; 6 and ⅞ Band CI-5002
Hilarity Rag (Scott) from Pianola roll CI-5003
Hot House Rag (Pratt) Wally Rose JM-17
House Rent Rag Dixieland Jug Blowers VI-20420
Hunky Dory (Holzmann) Vess L. Ossman (recorded 1901) CO-290
Hysterics Rag (Biese-Klickman) Tony Parenti's Ragtimers CI-1029

If I Ever Cease To Love (Connolly) Original Zenith Brass Band CI-1005
I'm Alabama Bound (Morton) Jelly Roll Morton CI-JM-67/68
I've Got a Feeling I'm Falling (Waller) Fats Waller VI-22092

Jingles (Johnson) James P. Johnson BR-80032
Jungle Blues (Morton) Jelly Roll Morton CI-JM-46
Junk Man Rag (Roberts) Luckey Roberts CI-1026

Kater Street Rag Benny Moten's Kansas City Orchestra OK-8227
Keep Off the Grass (Johnson) James P. Johnson OK-4495
King of Rags, The (Swisher) Arthur Pryor's Band VI-16821
King Porter Stomp (Morton) Jelly Roll Morton CI-JM-23, CMS-591 and GE-5289; Wally Rose GTJ-28

Lily Rag (Thompson)   Parenti, Sutton, Wettling CI-1056; Charley Thompson AM-527
Lovie Joe (Jordan)   Arthur Collins CO-A-953

Magnetic Rag (Joplin) Pianola roll played by Scott Joplin CI-5012
Mama 'Nita (Morton)   Jelly Roll Morton CI-JM-25
Mamie's Blues (Morton)   Jelly Roll Morton CI-JM-49, CMS-487
Maori (W. H. Tyers)   Mike Bernard CO-A-1427
Maple Leaf Rag (Joplin)   Art Hodes' Chicagoans BN-505; Brun Campbell BRUN-1 and WC-112; Elmer Schoebel's Dixieband NA-9113; Half Way House Orchestra CO-476 D; Hank Duncan Trio B & W-31; Jelly Roll Morton (St. Louis and New Orleans versions) CI-JM-21/22; Kid Ory's Jazz Band JM-28; Lu Watters Jazz Band JM-1 and WC-114; New Orleans Rhythm Kings GE-5104; Ralph Sutton with Condon Orchestra DE-27035; Pianola roll played by Scott Joplin CI-5003; Vess L. Ossman CO-A-228
Margie (Robinson)   Original Dixieland Jass Band VI-18717
Michigan Water (Tony Jackson)   Jelly Roll Morton CI-JM-58 and CMS-588
Milenberg Joys (Morton)   New Orleans Rhythm Kings GE-5217
Minstrels of Annie Street (Turk Murphy)   Lu Watters Jazz Band WC-110
Mr. Black Man March (Pryor)   Arthur Pryor's Band VI-16668
Mr. Freddy's Rag (Shayne)   J. H. Shayne CI-1011
Mr. Jelly Lord (Morton)   Jelly Roll Morton CI-JM-3; Jelly Roll Morton with New Orleans Rhythm Kings GE-5220
Music Box Rag (Roberts)   Luckey Roberts CI-1027

Naked Dance (Tony Jackson)   Jelly Roll Morton CI-JM-85, CMS-588
1915 Rag (Mike Bernard) CO-A-1427
Nonsense Rag (Brady)   Parenti, Sutton, Wettling CI-1055
Notoriety Rag (Widmer)   Van Eps Trio VI-17601
Numb Fumblin' (Waller)   Fats Waller VI-25338 and VI-V-38508

Ognons, Les (Nicholas-Barker)   Nicholas, Barker, James P. Johnson, Foster CI-1019
Original Rags (Joplin) from Pianola roll CI-5006 and JC-534; Jelly Roll Morton CMS-587; Wally Rose WC-112

Pastime Rag No. 5 (Matthews)   Wally Rose WC-118
Peaceful Henry (Kelly)   Columbia Orchestra CO-A-144
Pearls, The (Morton)   Jelly Roll Morton GE-5323, CI-JM-41/42; Wally Rose GTJ-26
Pep (Morton)   Jelly Roll Morton CI-JM-43
Perfect Rag (Morton)   Jelly Roll Morton GE-5486
Persian Lamb Rag (Winchester)   Vess L. Ossman VI-16127
Pineapple Rag (Joplin)   Wally Rose WC-110, GTJ-27
Policy King March (Brown)   Vess L. Ossman CO-220

Pork and Beans (Roberts)   Luckey Roberts   CI-1027
Pretty Baby (Tony Jackson)   Jelly Roll Morton   CI-JM-47

Quality Rag (James Scott) from Pianola roll   CI-5005

Ragging the Scale (Claypoole)   Fred Van Eps   VI-18085
Ragtime Drummer (Lent)   drum solo James I. Lent   VI–17092
Ragtime Engineer (Chris Smith) from Pianola roll   CI-5010
Ragtime Nightingale (Lamb)   Johnny Witwer   JM-20
Ragtime Oriole (Scott) from Pianola roll   CE-4022
Railroad Blues (Roberts)   Luckey Roberts   CI-1026
Ramshackle Rag   (Synder)   Arthur Pryor's Band   VI-17021
Randall's Rag (George Reynolds)   Jelly Roll Morton   CI-JM-21
Razzazza Mazzazza (Pryor)   Arthur Pryor's Band   VI-35040
Red Head Rag (Franklin & Green)   Tony Parenti Trio   CI-1055
Red Pepper Rag (Lodge)   Fred Van Eps   VI-17033; Wally Rose   GTJ-26
Ripples of the Nile (Roberts)   Luckey Roberts   CI-1028
Rocky's Rag (George L. Cobb)   Joe "Fingers" Carr   CA-1311
Russian Rag   Jim Europe's Orchestra   PE-1410

St. Louis Tickle (Barney & Seymore)   from Pianola roll   CI-5010; John
    Maddox   DO-1005;   Vess L. Ossman   CO-A-937
Sapphire (Bloom)   Rube Bloom   CO-1195
Scott Joplin's New Rag (Joplin) from Pianola roll   JC-533
Scouting Around (Johnson)   James P. Johnson   OK-4937
Sensation Rag (Lamb, arr. Joplin)   Mutt Carey and Band   CE-4007
Shy and Sly (Roberts)   Luckey Roberts   CI-1028
Slippery Place Rag (Hacker)   Victor Military Band   VI-17006
Smashing Thirds (Waller)   Fats Waller   VI-V-38613 and VI-25338
Smiler Rag (Wenrich)   Vess L. Ossman   CO-A-972
Smokey Mokes (Holzmann)   Columbia Orchestra   CO-A-150;   Lu Watters
    Jazz Band   JM-3
Snake Rag (Oliver-Picou)   Claude Luter et ses Lorientais   CI-1045;   King
    Oliver's Creole Jazz Band   GE-5184
Snowy Morning Blues (Johnson)   James P. Johnson   AS-350-3, CO-14204-D;
    Art Hodes   B & W-I
Soliloquy (Bloom)   Rube Bloom   HA-164
Spanish Swat (Morton)   Jelly Roll Morton   CI-JM-26
Squeeze Me (Waller)   Louis Armstrong Hot Five   CO-35661;   James P.
    Johnson   DE-23596;   Mildred Bailey and Band   DE-18109
Sunburst Rag (James Scott)   Wally Rose   WC-103
Sunflower Slow Rag (Joplin-Hayden) from Pianola roll   CI-5004;   Tony
    Parenti's Ragtimers   CI-1029
Swipesy Cake Walk (Joplin-Marshall)   Tony Parenti's Ragtimers   CI-1031

Tantalizing Tingles (Bernard)   Mike Bernard   CO-A-1386

Temptation Rag (Lodge)   Prince's Military Band   co-A-854;   Wally Rose
  JM-7
(*That*) *Eccentric* (*Rag*) (Robinson)   All Star Stompers   ci-1023;   Art Hodes
  JR-1004;   New Orleans Rhythm Kings   GE-5009
That Peculiar Rag (Fagan)   Mike Bernard   co-A-1313
Thriller Rag (Aufderheide) from Pianola roll   ci-5007;   Bunk Johnson's
  Jazz Band   JI-11
Tickled to Death (Hunter)   Prince's Band   co-A-972
Tiger Rag (Original Dixieland Jass Band)   Jelly Roll Morton   ci-JM-1/2;
  Original Dixieland Jass Band   vi-18472;   The 6 and 7/8 Band   ci-
  5001
Toddlin' (Johnson)   James P. Johnson   ok-4937
Trip Across the Pond (Bernard)   Mike Bernard   co-A-1590
Trombone Rag (Turk Murphy)   Lu Watters Jazz Band   wc-103
12th Street Rag (Euday Bowman)   Richard M. Jones   GE-5174

Valentine Stomp (Waller)   Fats Waller   vi-v-38554

Weary Blues (Matthews)   Kid Ory's Creole Jazz Band   ci-12002 (12″);
  Kid Rena's Delta Jazz Band   ci-1038
Weather Bird Rag (Louis Armstrong)   Louis Armstrong, Earl Hines
  co-36375;   King Oliver's Creole Jazz Band   GE-5132
Weeping Willow Rag (Joplin) from Pianola roll played by Joplin   ci-5005
Whistling Rufus (Mills)   banjo solo   co-A-229
Whitewash Man (Schwartz)   Ralph Sutton   ci-1052;   Fred Van Eps
  co-A-1118
Winin' Boy (Morton)   Jelly Roll Morton   ci-JM-60, ci-JM-90
Wolverine Blues (Morton)   Jelly Roll Morton   GE-5289, ci-JM-55/56

You've Got to be Modernistic (Johnson)   James P. Johnson   BR-80032

Zig Zag ("The Lion" Smith)   Bob Wilber's Jazz Band   ci-1064

33 1/3 r.p.m. LONG PLAYING MICROGROOVE RECORDS
(12″ Records except where noted - (S) Stereo)
Compiled by David A. Jasen

ARPIN, JOHN: Concert in Ragtime. Scroll 101
    The Other Side of Ragtime. Scroll 103
    Ragtime Piano. Harmony 6026 (S)
ASH, MARVIN: Marvin Ash. Jazz Mann 335 (10″)
    Honky Tonk Piano. Capitol T-188
ASHWANDER, DONALD: The New View. Jazzology JCE-71
ATWELL, WINIFRED: Double 7. London 1573
BALES, BURT: They Tore My Playhouse Down. GTJ 12025
BARBER, CHRIS: Elite Syncopations. Col. 33 SX 1245

BLAKE, EUBIE: The Wizard of the Ragtime Piano. 20th Century
    Fox 3003
    The Marches I Played On the Old Ragtime Piano. Fox 3039
    Golden Reunion in Ragtime. Stereoddities 1900 (S)
    The Eighty-Six Years of Eubie Blake. Col. C2S-847 (S)
BOCAGE, PETER: The Living Legends. Riverside 379
BOLLING, CLAUDE: Original Ragtime. Philips 70.341
BOWMAN, EUDAY: The Professors Vol. 2. Euphonic 1202
BUSCH, LOU: Honky Tonk Piano. Capitol T-188
    (Joe Fingers Carr - pseud.)
CAMPBELL, BRUN: The Professors Vol. 1. Euphonic 1201
    The Professors Vol. 2. Euphonic 1202
CARR, JOE FINGERS: Bar Room Piano. Capitol T-280
    Rough-House Piano. Capitol T-345
    And His Ragtime Band. Capitol T-443
    Plays the Classics. Capitol T-649
    Mister Ragtime. Capitol T-760
    Honky Tonk Street Parade. Capitol T-809
    The Hits of Joe Fingers Carr. Capitol T-2019
    The World's Greatest Ragtime Piano Player. Warner Bros. 1386
    Brassy Piano. Warner Bros. 1456
CHARTERS, ANN: Essay in Ragtime. Folkways 3563
    A Joplin Bouquet. Portents 1
    Treemonisha. Portents 3
DARCH, BOB: Ragtime Piano. United Artists 3120
    Gold Rush Daze. Stereoddities 1901 (S)
DAVIS, PETE: Ragtime Piano. Saydisc 118
DELANO, LOIS: The Music of Joe Jordan. Arpeggio 1205
DICKIE, NEVILLE: Ragtime Piano. Saydisc 118
    Creative Ragtime. Euphonic 1206
    Introducing Neville Dickie. Major Minor 5039 (S)
    I Love a Piano. Major Minor 5054 (S)
DUGAN, AL "SPIDER": Please Don't Put Your Empties On The
    Piano. Warner Bros. 1329
THE DUKES OF DIXIELAND: Piano Ragtime. Audio Fidelity 5928 (S)
DUNCAN, HANK: Hot Piano. Ri-Disc 4
EWELL, DON: Pianist. Windin' Ball 101 (10")
    Piano Solos of King Oliver Tunes. Windin' Ball 103
    Music To Listen To Don Ewell By. GTJ 12021
    Grand Piano. Exclusive 501 (S)
GLOVER, JOE: That Ragtime Sound. Epic 3581
GOLD, HARRY: Pieces of Eight. London 337 (10")
The Golden Age of Ragtime. Riverside 110
HANDY, PETE: Honky Tonk Piano. Mercury 20344
HUG, ARMAND: Plays Rags and Blues. Golden Crest 3064
JACKSON, CLIFF: Hot Piano. Ri-Disc 5
JASEN, DAVID A.: Creative Ragtime. Euphonic 1206
JOHNSON, DINK: The Professors Vol. 1. Euphonic 1201
    The Professors Vol. 2. Euphonic 1202

JOHNSON, JAMES P.: Rare Solos. Riverside 105
    Backwater Blues. Riverside 151
    Father of the Stride Piano. Columbia 1780
    Yamekraw. Folkways 2842
    The Jazz Makers. Swaggie S-1211
    James P. Johnson. Xtra 1024
    New York Jazz. Stinson 21
    Jazz of the Forties Vol. 1. Folkways 2841
    James P. Johnson. Edited Mike Montgomery.
        Biograph 1003Q
JONES, HANK: This Is Ragtime Now! ABC Paramount 496
JOPLIN, SCOTT: Scott Joplin. Biograph 1005Q
JORDAN, JOE: Golden Reunion in Ragtime. Stereoddities 1900
KOVACS, STEPHEN: Tiger on the Keys. Elektra 111
KRENZ, BILL: Oh Willie, Play That Thing. MGM E-184 (10")
LAMB, JOSEPH: A Study in Classic Ragtime. Folkways 3562
LINGLE, PAUL: Vintage Piano. Euphonic 1203
    They Tore My Playhouse Down. Good Time Jazz 12025
MADDOX, JOHNNY: Authentic Ragtime. Dot 102 (10")
    The World's Greatest Piano Rolls Vol. 1. Dot 25321 (S)
    " Vol. 2 Dot 25476 (S)
    " Vol. 3 Dot 25477 (S)
    " Vol. 4 Dot 25478 (S)
MANDEL, ALAN: Gottschalk - 40 Piano Works. Desco 6470-73
MITCHELL, BILL: Vintage Piano. Euphonic 1203
MORATH, MAX: A Scintillating Program. . .Epic LN 24066
    Oh, Play That Thing. Epic BN 26106 (S)
    The Entertainer. Arpeggio 1204 (S)
    At The Turn Of The Century. RCA LSO-1159 (S)
MORGAN, RUSS & EDDIE WILSER: Kitten on the Keys.
    Decca 8746
MORTON, JELLY ROLL: Classic Piano Solos. Riverside 111
    Jelly Roll Morton. Edited Mike Montgomery.
        Biograph 1004Q
    Library of Congress Recordings. Circle 14001-12
    Piano Solos. Mainstream 56020
    Jelly Roll Morton. Swaggie S-1213
    The Incomparable JRM. Riverside 128
    Jelly Roll Morton. Gaps 010
    The King of New Orleans. RCA LPM 1649
    King of the Piano. Brunswick 58003
    Stomps and Joys. RCA LPV 508
    Hot Jazz, Pop Jazz. . .RCA LPV 524
    Mr. Jelly Lord. RCA LPV 546
    I Thought I Heard Buddy Bolden Say. RCA LPV 559
    Classic Jazz Piano Styles. RCA LPV 543
MURPHY, TURK: The Music of Jelly Roll Morton. Col. 559
THE NEW ORLEANS RAGTIME ORCHESTRA: Pearl 7
NICHOLS, RED: Blues and Old-Time Rags. Capitol 2065 (S)
O'TOOLE, KNUCKLES: Plays The Greatest All Time Ragtime
    Hits. Grand Award 373

PARENTI, TONY: Ragtime. (Orig. Circle masters) Jazzology 15
    Ragtime Jubilee. Jazzology 21
PARKET, KNOCKY. Knocky Parker Trio. Dixie 101 (10")
    The Complete Works of Scott Joplin. Audiophile 71/72
    The Complete Works of James Scott. Audiophile 76/77
    The Complete Works of Jelly Roll Morton. Audiophile 102-105
    Golden Treasury of Ragtime. Audiophile 89-92
    Old Rags. Audiophile 49
Parlor Piano (historic piano rolls): Edited Mike Montgomery.
        Biograph 1001Q
PEMBERTON, BROOKE: The Ragtime Kid. Warner Bros. 1235
THE PIANO ROLL: Edited Rebor J. Tichenor. RBF 7
Piano Roll Ragtime. Sounds 1201
Pianola Jazz. Saydisc 117
Pianola Ragtime. Saydisc 132
A Programme of Ragtime. Vintage Jazz Music VLP 1
Ragged Piano Classics. Origin 16
Ragtime - A Recorded Documentary. Piedmont 13158
Ragtime, Cakewalks & Stomps. Saydisc 210
Ragtime Piano Roll Classics. Riverside 126
RASCH, CHARLIE: Ragtime Down the Pike. Ragtime Society 4
RIFKIN, JOSHUA: Piano Rags by Scott Joplin. Nonesuch 71248 (S)
ROBERTS, LUCKEY: Harlem Piano. Good Time Jazz 12035
ROSE, WALLY: Ragtime Classics. Good Time Jazz L-3 (10")
    Ragtime Piano Masterpieces. Columbia CL 6260 (10")
    Ragtime Classics. Good Time Jazz 12034
    Cakewalk to Lindy Hop. Columbia 782
    The Music of Jelly Roll Morton. Columbia 559
    Rose on Piano. Blackbird 12007
RYAN, SLUGGER: Plays Honky Tonk Piano. Judson 3015
ST. LOUIS RAGTIMERS: Vol. 1. Audiophile 75
    Vol. 2. Audiophile 81
SAN FRANCISCO HARRY: 30 Barbary Coast Favorites.
    Fantasy 3270
SHEA, TOM: Classic & Modern Rags. Ragtime Society 1
    Prarie Ragtime. Ragtime Society 2
SIGNORELLI, FRANK: Ragtime Duo. Kapp 1005
SMITH, WILLIE THE LION: The Lion. Vogue No. 56. 693-30
    Original Compositions. Commodore 30,003
    Reminiscing the Piano Greats. Dial 305 (10")
    The Legend. Grand Award 33-368
    The Lion Roars. Dot 3094
    Harlem Piano. Good Time Jazz 12035
    Grand Piano. Exclusive 501 (S)
    The Memoirs of. . .RCA LSP-6016 (S)
    Live at Blues Alley. Halcyon 104 (S)
SPEAR, SAMMY: Authentic Ragtime Music. Mercury 20116
SUTTON, RALPH: Piano Solos. Riverside 212

Backroom Piano. Verve MGV-1004
Piano Solos. Commodore 30,001
A Salute To Fats. Harmony HL 7019
Ralph Sutton Piano. Ace of Hearts 39
Ragtime U.S.A. Roulette 25232
Knocked-Out Nocturne. Project 3 PR-5040 (S)
THOMPSON, BUTCH: Plays Jelly Roll Morton Vol. 1 Center 4
  Plays Jelly Roll Morton Vol. 2. Center 9
THOMPSON, CHARLES: Golden Reunion in Ragtime. Stereoddities 1900
TICHENOR, TREBOR JAY: Mississippi Valley Ragtime. Scroll 102
They All Play Ragtime (Arpin, Ashwander, Lamb, Lundberg, Morath,
  Shea & Tichenor): Jazzology JCE 52
TURNER, RAY: Honky Tonk Piano. Capitol T-188
  Kitten on the Keys. Capitol H-306 (10")
WALLER, FATS: Classic Jazz Piano Style. RCA LPV 543
  Thomas Fats Waller. Edited Mike Montgomery. Biograph 1002Q
  Valentine Stomp. RCA LPV 525
  Fractious Fingering. RCA LPV 537
  Handful of Keys. RCA LPM 1502
  One Never Knows Do One. RCA LPM 1503
WATTERS, LU: Yerba Buena Jazz Band. Good Time Jazz LP-8 (10")
  1942 Series. GTJ 12007
  San Francisco Style Vol. 1 GTJ 12001
  San Francisco Style Vol. 2 GTJ 12002
  San Francisco Style Vol. 3 GTJ 12003
  Dixieland Jamboree. Verve MGV 1008
  Blues Over Bodega. Fantasy 5016
When Grandma Was a Teenager. Vintage Jazz Music VLP 2
WHITE, ALBERT: Your Father's Moustache #2. Barbary Coast 33008
  Your Father's Moustache Vol. 2. Fantasy 8040 (S)
WILLIAMS, QUENTIN: Ragtime Piano. Saydisc 118

INDEX

INDEX

INDEX

INDEX

INDEX